LIFE AMONG

THE SURREALISTS

LIFE AMONG THE

A Memoir by

Matthew Josephson

Illustrated with Photographs

HOLT, RINEHART AND WINSTON

New York

surRealists

To L.A.,
who played his part in all this—
out of old friendship.

*They change their sky but not their mind
who run across the sea.*

— HORACE
Epistles

CONTENTS

xi

LIFE AMONG

THE SURREALISTS

ONE

INTRODUCTORY :

A CHANGE OF SKY

As the decade of the 1920's recedes into the past, some of us who were then in our own twenties have been greatly tempted to look back with the perspective of a third of a century and recapitulate our adventures, our friendships, our follies, and our little triumphs, such as they were. It would seem I have failed to resist this temptation.

The period of the twenties has continued to hold our interest in a remarkable degree. No doubt because of the onset of age most of us think of that time as a very diverting and carefree period and so "happier" than the present. Like Stendhal who often reviewed the story of his life, "without illusions about it," in those secret writings he used to address to posterity, we are curious to know what we really were.

In retrospect, the literary generation of the 1920's seems to form a distinct epoch in history, as may be true also of the later postwar period of the 1950's. The lives of a good many of us were stamped with a common pattern of experience: we were born at about the turn of the century; we had some acquaintance with World War I, even if slight or inglorious, so that the excitement of foreign war lifted us out of the *train-train* of every-

3

day life; during our apprentice years we traveled off to Europe, either in wartime or shortly afterward, and formed some contacts with its war generation and its cultural movements. For some years many of us considered Paris our Second Country, and I confess that whenever I had occasion to leave it and return to my First Country, my native land, the fear would come to me that I would never be so happy again. We returned sooner or later, nevertheless, to adjust ourselves again to life in the United States during a cycle of unrivaled prosperity that suddenly ended in the grand climacteric of 1929.

The pleasures of reliving in recollection those moments of our past when we were young and far from home, and when the pursuit of happiness was in full cry, have inspired numerous authors of memoirs before this. I thought, however, that it might be useful, as well as pleasurable, to set forth more of "the little true facts," while the memory of them was still alive, than have been given us in other published accounts of that period. Instead of presenting only an apologia for myself in these pages, I would attempt to make a group portrait of the circle of my friends and acquaintances who were active in the literary and art movements of the 1920's. It was also part of my plan to trace the chain of ideas we pursued more or less consciously, while sharing certain common experiences. In effect, it would amount to viewing past history in the context of a particular group's life-experience—a group whose individual members, too often, alas, seemed to agree "in everything except opinions."

Doubtless there were many other and more notable coteries among the artists of the 1920's who were outside my purview, or whom I knew only as passing acquaintances. Yet their members often formed interchangeable parts with those of my own circle. Whether they originated in Chicago or Brooklyn or Cambridge, Massachusetts, the different cadres of America's gilded youth in those years all had their delegates at the high councils that sat down together in the cafés of Montparnasse. Yet I shall speak mostly of my own circle, for I am still easiest with them after four decades—we have been ragging each other for many years—though we meet nowadays after longer intervals of time, and some are dead.

In another respect my experience as one of the literary tourists of the 1920's appears to have been especially fortunate; several of my transatlantic friendships with Europeans of the avant-garde of those days have endured for more than a third of a century. Some of these persons, who were young Dadaists, Surrealists, or Abstractionists, have become figures of history; or, at any rate, part of the history of ideas in our time. Through the agency of Americans like myself, the young Europeans transmitted their advanced ideas to the United States; and at the same time we young Americans were, in some degree, carriers of new American influences and tendencies to Europe.

It happened that I was also actively associated, as an editor, with several of the "little magazines" of the 1920's that were published by Americans abroad as well as at home. They provided one of the mediums through which young talent, destined to fame, first broke into print. Thus I was often in a good position to watch this burgeoning process.

A good deal has already been written about the "brilliant twenties" by contemporary searchers and scholars. Yet, after reading only a portion of this growing literature, I have noticed, with feelings of mental distress, that it abounds in errors of fact and interpretation. Of course, perfect truth in history is an ignis fatuus. But I have been thunderstruck at coming upon a certain disgraceful story, repeated several times in printed form, about three now celebrated poets having come to "my" house "in France" and amused themselves by burning a heap of books by authors they disliked in what was alleged to be "my" fireplace, then afterward extinguishing the blaze by the vulgar procedures of Rabelais' hero, Gargantua. But it was not "my" house, and I was then in another country an ocean away.

The fact that statements have been published concerning my own activities that are three thousand miles wide of the mark has hardened my resolve to contribute my own recollections. I can see plainly that the Age of Industry in scholarship is upon us, and that fallacies are being borrowed, repeated, and compounded by the current breed of literary historians. All the more need, therefore, that some of us who "were there" retell what actually happened, before error becomes so thickly rooted that men after us will not know how to distinguish fact from fancy.

None of us can pretend to be authorized spokesmen for a whole generation. The very idea of a generation is only a convenient mental construct; one does not know finally where one's generation begins or where it ends, nor whether it was "lost" or found. However, one's memories, as subjective testimony, may furnish useful evidence about the movement of ideas in a certain time. There is no denying that young Americans, like their nation itself—whose military forces had recently crossed the Atlantic to join in the conflict of the Great Powers—were at the phase of their *Wanderjahre*. After the first of the great world wars that have distinguished this century many of them were filled with an unrest that derived both from their extreme youth and the Time-Spirit. Young people were on the move from the country or from their small towns to the big city centers, Chicago or New York; others journeyed to Europe (which many had visited in wartime), returned home, and traveled away again. In short, we looked for "a change of skies," as American artists—for example, Copley, West, and C.W. Peale —had done since the earliest days of the Republic in the hope of improving themselves by foreign travel and study. But this does not mean we were "lost."

We must dispose of the fallacy of the Lost Generation once and for all. How did this misleading nomenclature come into such wide usage? It was not we who lost the flower of our youth in World War I, but the Western Allies and the Central Powers. American land forces participated actively only in the

last four or five months of that war. I know of very few American
writers who served in it as combatants; but I know a considerable number who acted as noncombatant volunteers in the
ambulance and medical units aiding the Allies in 1917–1918,
and who were observers of the war, usually working in the rear
of the battlefront and encountering no great danger. Ernest
Hemingway's case is exceptional: he, too, was a noncombatant
who, after a few weeks' service with the Red Cross in Italy,
volunteered for front-line duty at the time of the defeat of the
Italian Army, and happened to be severely wounded. For a good
many years the story of Hemingway's having been "buried alive
for four days" as a result of a shell burst circulated about. A
friend of his had written such an account in a learned literary
review. But he himself told me that the four days of immolation
were pure myth.

Though the impact of World War I upon American destiny
was immense, it is nonsense to hold that a generation of American youth were "lost" or driven to despair as a result of that
brief war. Was the term intended to convey the idea that a
considerable number of young persons became morally lost, that
is, "lost to all virtue"? To be sure, some relaxation from social
constraints was observed during the stress of wartime, which
was nothing new in United States history. But where is there
any evidence that the young man of 1919–1929 was more
libidinous than *l'homme moyen sensuel* of other times?

The origin of the misnomer the Lost Generation is to be
traced to Ernest Hemingway's novel *The Sun Also Rises* and
its famous epigraph made up of a quotation from Miss Gertrude
Stein addressing young Mr. Hemingway in terms of bitter reproach: "You are all a lost generation!" The novel, moreover,
was widely accepted as a picture of a representative group of
sad young men and women of the postwar era, expatriated and
disenchanted, living out their days in the pothouses of France
and Spain. With the popular success of Hemingway's novel,
Miss Stein's phrase became the hallmark of a numerous body
of persons of about the same age who were making the grand

tour to Paris. The ridiculous tag hung on, it has been suggested, because the people to whom it was applied accepted it in a perverse or boastful spirit.

At the time when his novel was published in 1926, Hemingway, however, denied that he had intended to stigmatize a whole generation as being abandoned to despair, alcoholism, and moral turpitude, remarking: "Gertrude Stein's *mot* should not be taken too seriously." Miss Stein herself, in her memoirs, also stated that her much-quoted words had been uttered in a context that was very different from that which was generally attributed to them.

The actual incident was described to me some years ago by two good friends of mine who were eyewitnesses of it, one being the French painter, André Masson, and the other the American poet, Evan Shipman. They had been dining and wining rather heartily with Hemingway in Paris one evening. "*Allons chez Gertrude,*" Hemingway proposed, when they had finished; and so they went off to visit the *grande dame* of the rue de Fleurus, who was having a little gathering of her devotees that evening.

As usual the circle of admirers sat about and were hushed, while Miss Stein, in all her imposing bulk, paced back and forth slowly delivering one of her characteristic monologues—when Hemingway's party came clattering noisily into the salon, then relaxed, or rather relapsed, together upon a divan. They had arrived late, had interrupted Miss Stein, and what was more they were plainly tight. She appeared affronted, but after a moment resumed her speech, walking up and down, while fixing those three red-faced young men with her cold blue eye. Hemingway or Shipman may have ventured some observation that was displeasing to the hostess. At length, she exclaimed with feeling: "*Vous êtes tous une génération fichue!*"[1]

Miss Stein afterward related that an old automobile mechanic, who used to service her Ford car, had used the same phrase in referring to the troubles he had with young apprentice workers serving in his shop in those days. After their years of war they were ill-trained and wanting in manual skill as mechanics, and so he had damned them as a "lost generation." So Miss Stein, finding Hemingway and his friends logy with wine, had applied the same reproach to them. Out of that chance remark, made in a moment of petulance, came the monumental misnomer of the Lost Generation.

The appellation of "exiles" often given to my American contemporaries who were touring Europe in the 1920's has also seemed to me misleading and dubious. Literary historians have long expounded the theory that a marked trend toward "expatriation" set in among Americans after World War I, and that it constituted, in effect, a reversal of the historic westward flow of Europe's emigrants to America.

The prophet and leader of the new émigrés was long supposed to have been Harold Stearns, a thirty-year-old journalist who lived in Greenwich Village and occupied himself a good deal with the problems of "America and the Young Intellectual" (the title of one of his books). He also compiled a symposium, *Civilization in the United States,* published in 1922, to which thirty distinguished authors and scholars contributed chapters surveying almost every aspect of contemporary American society. Their findings were in the highest degree disconcerting and pessimistic. Our ruling classes were convicted as money-getting puritans whose standards of ethics or education were dictated only by their "business morality." Domestic life in America was reported to be ravaged by "sexual starvation." Moreover, we owned neither an art movement nor a literary life, according to Van Wyck Brooks, who prophesied that our poets were doomed to be "early blighted" and that our young novelists would find themselves "unable to grow up." Summing up this gloomy balance sheet, Stearns, as editor, asked the question: What is to be done? Nothing, he answered, except to quit the camp and take flight to Europe where one might drink wine, pursue the intellectual life, and read that amiable cynic Anatole France without fear of the police.

Having said so much, Stearns shook the dust of America from his feet and sailed for France in the summer of 1921. His departure, it has been observed, marked the beginning of a "great migration eastward into the new prairies of the mind" —at least for such Americans as could afford a steamship ticket.[2]

The only trouble with the theory of Harold Stearns as a latter-day Mahomet leading a pilgrimage of Yankees to the Left Bank of the Seine is that most of us who went there had never heard of him. His symposium, *Civilization in the United States,* was not published until the spring of 1922, months, or even years, after many of us had already left for Europe; thus we could not have known how imperative it was to go into exile until after we had been gone quite awhile.

When we came upon the author of *America and the Young Intellectual* in the cafés, he himself no longer looked young and was not very intellectual. It seemed that his interest had shifted to the horses. After a given number of *apéritifs,* he often became inarticulate on all subjects; while as an example of one who had taken his own moral sermons at the letter he proved unfortunate, publishing almost nothing for many years, though formerly he had been a man of promise and a prolific writer. Meanwhile, others who had come to Paris earlier than he, or without his counsel, such as John Dos Passos and E.E. Cummings, were at work with great zeal; or, as in the case of the young newspaperman, Ernest Hemingway, were diligently entering upon their apprenticeship as men of letters in the great "literary workshop" that was Paris. After many years of self-willed exile, Stearns went home and, in repentant spirit, wrote a book entitled *America: A Re-Appraisal* (1937). By his own admission, Stearns' argument for expatriation had broken down.

The only proper exile was Ezra Pound. He had been that before the war, ever since 1907; for years thereafter he had been urging his fellow Americans who had some taste for literature or the arts to leave their "half savage country" and come to England or France. T.S. Eliot, a native of St. Louis and graduate of Harvard, soon joined him. Toward 1912, many years before anyone ever heard of the "expatriates" of the twenties,

a very distinguished group of young American poets, who
could not find publishers in America but were hospitably received by the English, had gathered in London. It included
Pound, Eliot, John Gould Fletcher, Conrad Aiken, Hilda Doolittle, and, somewhat apart from Pound's circle, Robert Frost,
who had come to England even earlier than the others.

The example of the famous expatriate Henry James haunted
the mind of Ezra Pound. James fervently believed that for him
to have remained in America would have meant ruin for his art
and for his life. As he said in his book on Hawthorne, for a
writer, life was unthinkable without Europe's old cathedrals and
manor houses, or her aristocracy and peasantry and all their
quaint customs that made up "the elements of high civilization" absent from the texture of American life. But on the other
hand, James could no more forget his native land than the self-
exiled Turgenev; the problem of the transplanted American
held his attention constantly.

The change of scene, the stimulus of foreign travel, and study
of Europe's expertise in the arts had always proved beneficial to
Americans of talent. Yet how little geography itself helped to
solve the problems of the artist's personality. It was Henry
James's literary genius that made his emigration a success. Ezra
Pound was to exile himself three times over, first to England,
then in 1920 to France, and four years later to Italy. He had
failed to conquer literary London, failed to adjust himself to
the French—who "spoke English badly," as he complained—
and in Italy had little contact with contemporary art movements, as I was informed later by his friend Camillio Pellizzi,
once Director of the Institute of Fascist Culture. There, too,
Pound apparently put down no roots. His mind always turned
back to the United States. What is America thinking of me?
Why does she not recognize her great poets?

Almost as far back as one could remember there had always
been Gertrude Stein in Paris, where she had come to live in the
early years of this century. But aside from her interest in
making a collection of modern painters, such as Matisse, Pi-

casso, and Gris—under the inspiration of her brother Leo Stein, the art critic—she too, for long years, had a rather slight contact with the literary world of Paris. Though physically transplanted, and enjoying the ease of life in France intellectually and sensuously, Miss Stein, one felt, had never really left the U.S.A., where she was formerly even less known or read than Pound. She thought of America and wrote of America almost exclusively, devoting over nine hundred pages, for example, to her major work, *The Making of Americans*. Miss Stein's case is a very particular one and affords no clear answer to the question of expatriation.

On one occasion she wrote, in response to queries about her affiliations, that "the United States is a country the right age to have been born in and the wrong age to live in . . . a rich and well nourished home but not a place to work." It was for her "the most important country in the world—but a parent's home is never the place to work in." Then this woman, often so astute in her observations, remarked that it is a good thing for a writer looking at his own civilization to have the contrast of another culture before him. Later on, perhaps, there would be places in the United States where one could get away; and then there would be "creators who will live at home."[3]

The movement of American writers and artists to Europe after World War I, despite Mr. Pound's exhortations, was in no sense an exodus of massive proportions, though it was in many ways significant. At the end of the 1920's I came upon some records compiled for the Paris press, showing that there were about ninety Americans residing more or less permanently in France who considered writing their vocation. A few more of the same sort lived also in Italy and Germany. In numbers they represented only about one per cent of those who listed themselves in the U.S. census as professional writers. In quality and character, however, they were different from Americans who had come to Western Europe during earlier migrations.

Formerly, Americans of the wealthy rentier class, like Henry James and Gertrude Stein, often came to "finish their education"

in Europe during long sojourns. But the interesting thing about
the movement of the twenties was that many young persons
wanted to go abroad who were so poor that they scarcely had
enough to eat after they got there. In 1921, when I first arrived
in Paris, I saw numerous impoverished young American artists,
writers, and music students, who had come there at about the
same time as if with a single impulse. What was the nature of
the wanderlust that sent them upon this latter-day Children's
Crusade?

The era of world war and revolutions after 1914 brought
with it the realization that the nineteenth century had finally
come to an end. For some years previous to this, young America
had been vigorously outgrowing that Genteel Tradition, so-
called, which had ruled our literary world for many decades;
we were a spiritual colony of Victorian England then still
holding its dead hand over us. A New Poetry movement
had already announced itself in 1912, whose adepts dared to
write in free verse. Ezra Pound at the time predicted the coming of an "American Risorgimento that would make the Italian
Renaissance look like a tempest in a teapot." The young Edna
St. Vincent Millay also promised us "Renascence" in a famous
poem that was symbolic of rebirth and the bursting of the narrow values that had ruled our society. The great Armory Show
in New York in 1913 exhibited the new Postimpressionist, Cubist, and other experimental schools of painting by Europeans
and Americans, with startling effect, making a sort of water-
shed in the history of art. Other intellectual innovators were
already disseminating the teachings of Dr. Freud. Just prior
to America's entrance in the European war in 1917 many voices
were prophesying a "New Day." Most Americans had never
thought much about Europe (leaving aside the leisurely rentier
class); now, as we went to war, President Wilson called upon
his people to become citizens of the world. "We are provincials

no longer" he exclaimed at Versailles as the League of Nations was born.

Nothing appeared more certain than the prospect of a new order after the war; our universe seemed to be changing before our eyes. Yet, through the effect of the "cultural lag," as Thorstein Veblen interpreted it, the old regime and its spokesmen still hung on in our educational world, as in our literary institutions. Van Wyck Brooks, himself one of the voices calling for a New Day, was then working in the old publishing office of the Century Company in New York, "where one saw drifting in and out the gentlemenly old-fashioned authors of the 'Howells and James Age.' " These usually kindly old men of letters, he recalls, "with one voice denounced the outlandish and ill-mannered new novelists and poets" who were already appearing all about them, the Edgar Lee Masters and Amy Lowells, the Theodore Dreisers and Sherwood Andersons.[4] I, too, remember coming to the Century Company's musty old mahogany-paneled office in 1919, when I was still a college undergraduate, and finding that one had to wait an hour after lunch to see the aged editor, who regularly took his siesta at that time. The old men were sleeping, while the young writers waited impatiently in the anterooms.

TWO

FAREWELL

TO BROOKLYN

Having been born in the closing months of the last century, I can remember about fifteen years of childhood and boyhood passed in the relatively quiet and slow-moving world of the days before the war that was still, in our backwater of Brooklyn, illuminated mostly by gas, a world that seemed stable and peaceful and still appearing very much as it did in the time of President Grant. In these remote outskirts of the city, there were truck gardens near my home. Next door to our old-fashioned, wood-frame house there was an old fire station. Though forbidden by my mother to enter it, as soon as I could crawl or walk I made my way there and played happily among the glittering fire wagons that were all of brass, won the favor of the firemen, and became their mascot. On practice trips they used to take me up and place me beside them on the high seat of the engine truck, above the great draft horses, and I would go riding about the district in triumph, the proudest two-year-old in all Brooklyn.

Toward 1905, my father's idea of a Sunday's recreation was to hire a horse and carriage and take his family for a drive in the flat Long Island countryside about ten miles out. Stopping beside a sun-scorched potato field, under the shade of a poor tree, we picnicked, then returned. Those drives in summertime were uncomfortable; my parents were dressed up in too many clothes, and my father perspired freely in his Sunday suit and celluloid collar while trying to spur on our nag. The tempo of life was at the pace of that old carriage horse, about six miles an hour.

The war shook up our lives, with the effect of a prolonged moving day, and at about the same time the roads were suddenly full of automobiles. Soon people seemed to be on the go everywhere toward the centers of profitable war industry. A few years later, great bodies of soldiers moved through New York, toward training camps or ships bound for France. Not very long after that, they returned en masse, to be met by cheering crowds waving little American flags.

The internal migrations in America at the same period seem to me fully as important as the transatlantic movement. Many of my own contemporaries, quite as described in Sinclair Lewis' famous novel of that day, were "escaping" from the Main Streets of their small towns in the provinces to the big cities such as Chicago or New York. They were saying "Good-bye Wisconsin" (like young Glenway Wescott), or good-bye Ohio or Kansas, as they rode eastward to New York, where those who were of the artistic temperament often congregated, during a stage of their lives, in Greenwich Village, before going on across the ocean.

I, too, made my escape from Brooklyn to Manhattan—which we Brooklynites spoke of as "New York," as if it were a world apart—a flight amounting only to an hour's ride in a trolley car, or less than that by the new subway. It was nonetheless a decisive action by which I separated myself from my family and Brooklyn, to live at first at the big city university on Morningside Heights, then for a season or two in Greenwich Village, finishing up in Paris—quite in the pattern established by the literary intelligentsia of the time.

Since the days of my youth I have met many Brooklynites who have run away not only to Manhattan but to the ends of the earth. I must hasten to add that they usually cherish the happiest memories of their boyhood in the native borough. Not long ago I met a newspaperman in San Francisco who, after twenty years there, still held to his Brooklyn accent, saying "pernt" instead of point and "boid" for bird. I asked him how he liked life in San Francisco. He said that from the start it was so pleasant and friendly a place that "it was just like Brooklyn!" His wife fell sick and went to the hospital just as they arrived; but the neighbors came through the back yard and acted as baby-sitters for his young children, as they did in his home town.

In my boyhood, Brooklyn had not a third of the population it now holds, and was made up of a congeries of big villages varying in local character from such handsome residential quarters as Brooklyn Heights and St. Marks Avenue, with their mansions and rhododendron gardens, to the featureless new "developments" of row houses in gridiron streets, where everyone knew everybody else.

We children of the century, with one or two exceptions, all sprang from the great American middle class, and grew up in sight of an urban landscape in some bustling industrial city of the East or Middle West. Most of us attended free public schools that were democratic and crowded, and only one or two I knew of (in my own circle) had gone to one of those imitation English private schools limited, as Scott Fitzgerald said, to the sons of the rich. We all began to write things at the high-school age; and this, in almost all cases, aroused feelings of dismay, rather than satisfaction, in our parents.

We might be of mixed English, German, Irish, and French ancestry, or, as in my own case, Jewish, yet the prevailing "Protestant ethic" of middle-class America seemed to possess all our parents alike. They were anxious and mainly preoccupied with all that was material and useful in "getting ahead"—which they did not always succeed in doing, though they hoped that we would do so. By contrast, our English contemporaries were growing up in the same pre-war era, as I have read in their memoirs, in charming old country houses filled with good books and music, and with personages like George Meredith or Rudyard Kipling dropping in for tea with their parents. Under such conditions, so favorable to the care and feeding of infant poets, how could those golden boys of Sussex have failed to become veritable lords of language? But in grimy Pittsburgh, or the milltowns of Massachusetts or Ohio, or Brooklyn, there were no avuncular authors to serve as our models; and in our hard-driven elders there was little interest in the arts of leisure.

My own situation in life might have been considered more secure than most. My father, who had come to this country as a young immigrant in the early 1880's, was a successful man of business and something of a political bigwig in our locality in his later years. When our old house was converted into a business building, during one of the real-estate booms of that time, we moved to a larger home with a garden in front and a spacious back yard, on Jamaica Avenue near the line of the borough of Queens. I was much given to sports and became a valued member of a baseball team, made up mainly of Irish boys with whom I played on sand lots at an ocean beach near the city where my parents rented a summer cottage.

At the age of twelve it seems that I formed the habit of reading books at all hours of the day and night. I would hide myself in a little branch library of our neighborhood and go right through all the novels of Charles Dickens. My playmates would come looking for me, and, eventually tracking me down, would set up such a hullabaloo in the library that I would be asked to leave, and those young rascals would carry me off by main force to do my duty as a pitcher.

My father's health declined when he was in his forties. As I was the eldest son (I had two young brothers and a sister), my parents pinned their hopes on my entering the family business, a small local bank, after finishing with high school, and so becoming an arm of support for the family. When, however, I turned out to be quite different from what they would have liked me to be, showing a marked distaste for business, they were both sorely disappointed, though my father was a rather gentle soul and seldom expressed such feelings openly.

I became wedded to literature as soon as I began to attend the old Boys' High School of Brooklyn. The Brooklyn literati of fifteen or sixteen undoubtedly had some local particularities worth noting that set them apart from others of the same species. I remember one incident at the school that led to my forming a friendship with a rather odd and extremely temperamental boy. It occurred at the opening day of my second year, when instruction had not yet got under way in systematic fashion. I was using the old trick of reading a novel that I concealed under my lesson books while the teacher droned on. There was a great deal of noise and laughter in the classroom just then. Some restless boy behind me was trying to attract everyone's attention, including my own, and I was deaf to the world. I had moved on from Dickens and was now devouring *The Picture of Dorian Gray*, while the boy just back of me kept twitching about and craning his neck to see what I was reading. When the class was dismissed and we all got up to leave, he suddenly rushed at me, seized my book, and flung it on the floor, crying out: "What do *you* know about Oscar Wilde? I know more than you do," and, in theatrical fashion, in a deep manly voice, began reciting "The Ballad of Reading Gaol."

He was a rather short, stocky boy, with delicate features, a huge head that was too big for his body, and long black hair; he was dressed, with a sort of Edwardian elegance, in a coat with a velvet collar and was wearing a Windsor tie. I protested angrily at his rudeness; at once we were scuffling, rolling about on the floor, banging each other's faces against the wrought-iron legs of desks and benches. Then we got up together, brushed ourselves off, and in chivalrous fashion he offered me his hand, earnestly inviting me to come to his home for tea and cakes. I went along and we talked in the friendliest fashion. He told me his name was Clarence Newman, and that this, as well as his dress, was the cause of many fights with the other boys.

After his mother had served tea and left us to ourselves, Clarence declared in a heavy stage whisper that he was a "neuropath" of deeply melancholy cast, and was unable to sleep at night owing to the tormenting awareness of what he pretended was his precocious sexual development. At that early age, he confessed, he had made visits to "paid harlots," as he phrased it, in the company of an older relative who thought such indulgence might dispel Clarence's insomnia. But on leaving such women, he was often assailed by thoughts of committing suicide, and assured me that he had not long to live in this world.

I was both fascinated and deeply concerned for this romantic prodigy, who at an early age knew so much evil and sorrow. Clarence assured me that he had no friends, that no one understood him, and that he needed me as his confidant. He was now as demonstratively affectionate as he had been combative at our first meeting. I realized that I had lived hitherto an absurdly normal existence among average people. Never had I known anyone who was given to such towering passions, or such mercurial changes of mood, or with such capacity to vocalize his emotions. Thanks to Clarence life took on an added interest, for I enjoyed sharing his mental storms and "tragic" moods and tried to give him help and counsel.

Books were what first drew us together—books of an esoteric type—in a sort of freemasonry against the Philistines of our families and our school. At first I produced such standard classics as I had discovered for myself: my volumes of Keats, Tennyson, and Browning. But Clarence introduced me to Sigmund Freud's *The Interpretation of Dreams,* which had just appeared in English in 1915. We digested Freud as well as we could at age sixteen, then went off to analyze the dreams of two nice girls Clarence had recently met. We would invite them to recite their dreams to us, and, pretending to be scientific in method and vocabulary, proceeded to interpret those dreams in a sense we hoped would be advantageous to ourselves.

The girls were sisters who were the daughters of a doctor in the neighborhood, the elder one being about nineteen and much too old for us. As for the younger one, Eleanor, Clarence "analyzed" her indefatigably until he ended by falling head over heels in love with her. After that he would spend almost every evening with his girl, but would often manage to come to my house at some late hour on his way home, throw a pebble against my window, enter my room secretly, and begin verbalizing before me about every step in his love drama with Eleanor.

Such was passionate love, I thought to myself, wondering if I, too, would one day enjoy the same romantic experience. Eleanor struck me as a girl of good sense and character, handsome enough, but to my taste a little on the stout side. A slight strabismus of one eye made it hard to know whom she was looking at; yet, as is often the case with slightly cross-eyed women, the defect really added to her beauty. And she had a voice like an angel's. To my friend she was the reincarnation of Tolstoi's Anna Karenina.

Late one night Clarence came to my room in the usual secretive way, via the back door to my house, looking pale and disheveled. A crisis had arisen in his affairs of whose nature he gave only vague hints. But it seemed that Eleanor wanted to see me alone, and he insisted that I go to her that very evening while he waited in my room for my return. From something Clarence said, I had the thought that he *might* possibly kill himself. I believed everything he told me then with deadly seriousness. (Later, when his Byronic posturing and his tall tales made him a byword in Greenwich Village and Montparnasse, I, like others, tended to discount his statements.)

When I had last seen Eleanor with Clarence it had been a merry occasion; the three of us had gone to the back room of a saloon and had managed, despite our youth, to have liquor served us, so that I became drunk for the first time on two Manhattan cocktails and grew cheerfully loquacious, as Eleanor remarked. Now we were alone together; I felt much involved in Clarence's storms, and my mood was grave.

We went out for a walk in a park nearby. Eleanor now confided to me that she and Clarence had quarreled bitterly;

his unstable and "neurotic" personality made him cruel and unjust to her, and she felt she had had quite enough. I defended Clarence with ardor, while she held to her own views, and our talk dragged indecisively. Some expression she let slip at one moment made me wonder if she had in mind a successor for Clarence; I felt much disturbed and withdrew my arm which she had been holding. On a sudden whim I directed our steps toward a cemetery that adjoined the park.

Why the cemetery? she asked. Because it was dark, I explained; it suited our mood. We took one of the paths through the cemetery and sat down on a tombstone in the deep dark, at a polite distance from each other. It was a dreary place to go with such a nice girl. During our halting conversation she made some shy allusions to her change of heart and her growing interest in myself. I became much alarmed at her hints, thinking of the terrible scenes there would be with Clarence if I responded to her overtures. The worst of it was that he would never stop talking at me about every angle of this mixed-up situation.

Only in later years did I realize that this was my first confrontation with one of those New Women (whom I had then only begun to read about in Bernard Shaw). The time would come afterward when I enjoyed having women make proposals to me; but at sixteen I was graceless and tiresome in repelling Eleanor's modest advances, and recalling her to her duty to "save" Clarence. I thought I spoke movingly on the subject of the poor fellow. But Eleanor was rightly vexed, stood up from our stone couch, and said: "But this is getting to be very stupid, and it is cold here."

After I had accompanied her home, and returned to my room, it was very late. Hearing my steps, Clarence jumped out from behind the door, just as I entered, and confronted me with a naked knife he had drawn from his pocket. His expression was a frozen, tragic smile. I didn't like it at all. Was he going to kill *me*, I wondered?

I stationed myself at the opposite end of the room and exclaimed: "Drop that knife!"

Clarence gestured with the knife toward his heart and said:
"This was meant for me, if you had taken up her proposal."

I didn't care what the thing was meant for, but the knife
business made me nervous. In reality it was a dull old hunting
knife which had served as a wall decoration in his home. Clarence was being corny, and using a great deal of overemphasis;
but I did not understand that until later.

I said I was sure his Eleanor would return to him; he shed
a few easy tears, gave me an expression of deep gratitude, and
turned his knife over to me. It went through my mind then, and
afterward, that there was something insincere in his attitude at
the moment, that he had really wanted me to fall in love with
his girl, and then there would have been jealous storms enough
to keep him going in perpetual excitement.

As I had foreseen, they were reconciled and, a year or two
later when they were students of about nineteen, were married,
making it almost a child marriage—which did not last beyond
two or three years. After he had simmered down and become a
competent newspaperman, I found Clarence had turned into a
middle-of-the-road sort of fellow and a solid citizen, quite unlike the half-tragic, half-frantic boy who used to pretend that
he was a doomed victim of what he called "dementia praecox."

I have given these random reminiscences of Clarence and
Eleanor to suggest something of that special atmosphere of
storm and stress in which we enfants terribles of Brooklyn lived
for a season or two. Our heads were filled with bad poetry and
gloomy Russian novels, such as Dostoevski's, whose sickly creatures we were probably trying to impersonate—while our parents knew nothing or could make nothing of all this.

The Boys' High, which then occupied a rambling brick building dating from the Civil War era, was a famous "grind factory"
in those days. Avoiding the groups that devoted themselves to
sports or to political debating, I confined myself to writing, and
eventually won a prize of a $2.50 fountain pen for a short story

published in the school magazine. As one of the editors of that publication I became, in my senior year, a sort of literary dictator of the high school. Many years later Aaron Copland, the composer, told me that when he happened to submit some poems to me, I treated them to such ferocious criticism that he promptly gave up all hope of becoming a writer and turned to music instead, with such effect that, by 1928, when he recalled the incident to me, he had achieved an international reputation. I remembered him vaguely as a timid, owlish-looking little boy. "And so I owe it to you, to some extent, that I became a musician," Copland said banteringly. I remarked: "If what you say is correct, then I worked far better than I knew!"

I have not much to say for my character as an "artist" of sixteen. In my immensely awkward age it was said that I gave the impression of being toplofty. I had numerous friends, and yet felt much alone. I was learning things by myself; neither my teachers nor my parents could be of help to me, I believed. At home I was intolerant enough on some occasions to blurt out that the family conversation at table *bored* me, and that I was happiest when alone in my room, where I used to shut myself off even from my younger brothers and my sister, though they were amiable enough.

There were often numerous relatives making up big family parties at our house, especially on high holidays, as was the custom among the Jews. They were as a rule small tradespeople. I would take no part in their talk, which was about the business they necessarily pursued, but would sit in silence, as remote as possible, reciting under my breath Shakespeare's sonnets or other poems I had committed to memory.

Perhaps we literary novices of that time lived too much in our books, as compared with the youth of the 1940's and 1950's. But when we looked up from those books, we saw no enchanted woods or lakes, no crenelated castles such as we read of in our Victorian poets, but only the dreary urban landscape of the Brooklyns of this world, and the Pittsburghs and Clevelands, with their gridiron streets and their new-made slums. There were

a few among us who would later make a great deal of the urban
American landscape when they came to write about it, but at
that stage I wished myself in imagination as far away as possible
from the Brooklyn scene.

Part of my discomfort during this phase of adolescence derived from the fact that I was working as a bank teller during
the summer, and thus earning a bit of the money needed for my
schooling. But I disliked doing my duty by repeating the same
gestures all day long *in my cage.* At the end of the day I would
lie down on the floor of my room, feeling all washed up, unable
to think or to read anything, and would sometimes weep with
vexation. I associated my condition of "slavery," as I called it,
with the world of business, and small business at that, and with
life in my native Brooklyn; and I believe I began to hate Brooklyn. The place was forever bound up with memories of my time
of painful growth, self-doubt, and wild hope, and all the commonplace frictions of every day with my well-intentioned family.
Yet there were trees in Brooklyn, and charming old quarters I
loved to walk in, which were replicas of parts of Victorian London, as I found later. I was also very fond of the great beer
garden at Trommer's Brewery on Bushwick Avenue, near our
home, where my father used to take me sometimes on summer
evenings, and where a brass band played under the little electric-
ally illuminated trees while I sipped a lemonade. A good many
of my compatriots, such as Heywood Broun and Douglas Moore,
the composer (whom I knew only long afterward), have spoken
of their boyhood years in Brooklyn with true nostalgia. But
their reminiscences are usually qualified by the added observation that Brooklyn was "a good place to get away from," as so
many say of other towns where they were born and raised.

It was not Brooklyn that I hated; it was rather the way of
life that Brooklyn represented for me. There were my parents
saying repeatedly: "Poetry? But how *will* you ever earn your
living?" In reality, my father, who certainly thought me an odd
one, was a sensitive man and showed far more tolerance toward

me than I possessed for him. "Oh, he will get over his dreams in time; they all do," he would say good-humoredly.

Stendhal, in his memoirs, has related that from his boyhood on he "hated" Grenoble—though it boasts one of the most beautiful sites in Europe—because it was associated for him with the severe Jesuit priests, who were his mentors, and his father, who disciplined him harshly. I had no such reason for disapproving of my father. In any case it was not he, but my very possessive mother who, after business hours, was the figure of authority in our family. In truth, I felt a deep affection for my father, as did many hundreds of persons who knew him, for he was a well-loved figure in the Jewish community of Brooklyn, and something of a local philanthropist to whom everyone came running when in trouble. But I was resolved, nevertheless, upon "beginning to live my own life"—by escaping from Brooklyn.

Occasional glimpses of Manhattan, with its anonymous crowds, its fashionable shops, and ornate carriages, revealed a style of life that was as alluring as it at first seemed frightening. Its intensely metropolitan character and electrifying tempo seemed to drain the neighboring borough of all attraction, making it by comparison utterly provincial, "the dormitory" of Greater New York.

My parents had the means to send me to college; we quickly decided upon Columbia College, which then enjoyed much prestige. There were some recriminations between us when I stubbornly refused to be a day student commuting to my classes from farthest Brooklyn and insisted upon a small additional allowance that would permit me to live, even though penuriously, at the college. In the end they yielded. They were troubled at the idea of my living on my own, and I was filled with joy at the very idea.

THREE

OUR COSMOPOLITAN

UNIVERSITY

I had formed the highest anticipations about Columbia College and my new life there. Actually it contributed only a modest increment to my store of learning; the real profits were intangible and extracurricular.

Even in 1916 Columbia University suffered from the Curse of Bigness. For years, President Nicholas Murray Butler had been trying to make the place over as an imitation of one of the great German universities which he admired. His other prime object was to turn it into a bulwark of social and religious conservatism, in spite of godless and cosmopolitan New York and its melting pot of racial groups. The College of Liberal Arts in Hamilton Hall, which I attended, seemed a small body lost in the stomach of our academic leviathan. On the other hand, thanks to the new elective system, one could, after the prescribed courses of the freshman year, branch out into all sorts of graduate studies or attend lectures on almost everything under the sun. In such a big place one might even find a few people who cared passionately for their subjects and adored teaching them. And if, during a few years of the academic scramble, you came upon three or four such vital personalities as Charles A. Beard,

27

28 LIFE AMONG THE SURREALISTS

on government, and Franz Boas, on anthropology, or some of
the brilliant scientists of the School of Mines faculty, then you
might absorb something of their method and spirit and receive
at least the fragments of an education.

It was its good fortune that this university in the midst of
New York was a true product of cosmopolis, in spite of Dr.
Butler, and nothing like your "country-club" type of college.
One could choose one's acquaintances from a very broad spectrum of human types; there was a young music student from
Peoria, Illinois, in the room next to mine who introduced me to
Bach and Wagner; and down the hall a native of Peking who
translated Chinese poetry of the T'ang Dynasty for me; and
at the co-educational School of Journalism across the campus a
whole band of Flaming Youths. One of these, H.R. Knickerbocker, son of a Texas minister, and later a famous newspaper
correspondent, went to a ball in Greenwich Village armed with
a revolver; as the party seemed dull he fired a shot at the ceiling and was arrested, but released soon afterward. This was in
part due to the political influence of my father, who was on a
friendly footing with the reigning Mayor of New York, Mr.
John F. Hylan, a Brooklyn neighbor of ours.

From my penthouse room atop Livingston Hall I had a commanding view of upper Manhattan and its two rivers. I could
take off after classes and wander through the city, doing second-
hand bookstores and sometimes theaters, usually choosing fifty-
cent seats among the gallery gods. I had two girl friends at the
University, but on our walks could not even afford to buy them
a cup of tea; I was poor and sometimes hungry, but a free man.

In 1916 and 1917, on the eve of war, the atmosphere of
Columbia was electric with dissent. Among a lively minority of
the students there was always a babel of talk going on about
everything, from the war in Europe or the Tom Mooney case in
California to the pragmatic philosophy of John Dewey. The
faculty was especially strong then in the branch of social
sciences, with a vigorous group of nonconformists such as
Dewey, James Harvey Robinson, and Charles A. Beard opposing

its prevailing conservatism. Thus the discussion of human affairs was pursued with a zest and a freedom unsurpassed at any of the old Eastern colleges.

In my own case, and that of a few literary friends I soon acquired at the College, the ikon-breaking mood showed itself mainly in artistic form. We were calling not only for *vers libre*, but for as many other liberties as we could conceive of. In the literary field, however, the University then was very strong for tradition.

I had recently heard Miss Amy Lowell lecture on the New Poetry, and after her talk introduced myself and addressed some questions to her. We corresponded thereafter, for she was unfailingly generous in helping young poets of every sort. But when I undertook to champion Miss Lowell's ideas at the College, I was ridiculed and assured that she knew nothing of poetry. Columbia may have been a center of literary learning, but evidently news of the "American Risorgimento" had scarcely penetrated its campus.

I have since heard that at some public occasion at Harvard in 1915, E.E. Cummings, then a college senior, ventured to read a paper on the new art of the Cubists and the literature of Miss Gertrude Stein; it was received by his academic audience with the silence of embarrassment. However, a year later, E.E. Cummings and S. Foster Damon founded the Harvard Poetry Society, which seems to have been in advance of anything we had at Columbia just then. There, we were still supposed to pay tribute to the "Anglo-American" past. The literary lion of this campus was still old George Edward Woodberry, whose Tennysonian lyrics used to grace the pages of our family magazines, and who, like his friends, W.D. Howells and Robert Underwood Johnson, was the very embodiment of the Genteel Tradition. Woodberry had retired a few years before as Chairman of the English Department, but his influence was still reflected in the teaching of his younger associates, such as John Erskine.

We had professors of American literature, for example, who had discovered nothing as yet of Herman Melville or Emily

Dickinson. I also remember hearing Henry James much disparaged—in terms that were then commonly used—as one who could not write novels as interestingly as his brother William wrote philosophy. In studying the classics of English literature under certain dull-witted scholars, I sometimes heard the Elizabethan and Restoration poets condemned, in the neo-Victorian vocabulary of the period, as "coarse" or "immoral." That would be all I needed to direct my attention to Donne or Congreve, whom I read with the joy of first discovery.

Soon, a few of us who pretended to be literary rebels came into collision with the legatees of the old regime. I remember attending for the first time, toward November, 1916, a meeting of the Columbia College literary society quaintly called—and well named—The Boar's Head, and presided over by Professor John Erskine, an accomplished lecturer who then wrote poetry profusely, if not well. There were a dozen very proper and, I daresay, very soulful young men present, who read their poems one by one, then had these subjected to some critical discussion in rather polite terms. Those students were going to become teachers, journalists, advertising agents, and, in one or two instances, Hollywood playwrights—in other words they were really down-to-earth fellows. I don't know where they got their old tags about Grecian nymphs and mythical heroes or scraps of moonlight and fading roses and other such sentimental properties, with which they burdened their poor lines. At length, a short, thin, bespectacled youth of pale and intellectual appearance, and a shock of black hair, spoke forth in very different voice from the others; he was a young *révolté*, reading harsh unrhymed verses that described a dream carrying overtones of repressed and melancholy sexual desire!

John Erskine at once rounded upon the poet, declaring himself firmly opposed to experiments in free verse, and to a "realistic" treatment of subjects he characterized as "ugly." In the words of Matthew Arnold, he urged that we "see life steadily and see it whole." I ventured to come to the defense of the luckless poet, arguing that, in the light of Freud's teachings, we moderns could no longer write of love or sex in the terms of Elizabeth Barrett Browning. Whereupon Erskine, in great wrath, bore down upon me, shouting that Freud was but a charlatan who perverted young minds with his unwholesome theories about the common ordinary progenitive functions. Several years later Erskine was to reverse himself and write some rather risqué novels, such as *The Private Life of Helen of Troy*. But for the present, he used all his artillery to crush out the freshman rebels at his literary tea party. As our meeting broke up, the small young man who had brought down so much moral censure upon his head gave me thanks for coming to his defense and introduced himself as Kenneth Burke, a native of Pittsburgh. The future literary critic and psychologist of language had then barely turned nineteen. I commiserated with him as we crossed the campus in the dark, and proposed that we have an ice-cream soda together at the drug store on Broadway and 116th.

The young man turned upon me, grinned with all his teeth, and said sardonically and with a pronounced drawl: "Ice-cream soda! No, not ice-cream soda; but I'll have a *beer* with you."

I felt embarrassed to the point of chagrin, and wished to heaven that I had never breathed a word about ice cream to this young rakehell. How, indeed, could we be modern poets if we nourished ourselves on such pap? He had me there. Though I was all of seventeen and a half in age, I had never hitherto enjoyed the taste or smell of beer; but now readily agreed to go off to the Red Lion, a café just outside the college bounds, and gulp down some beer while we talked of the Russian novel, the decadents of the 1890's, the poetry of Paul Verlaine—and of going to Paris some day.

In our rebellion against Victorian traditions we teen-agers enjoyed posing as frightful cynics and even as decadents, little though we knew about the world. We pretended to be interested chiefly in the abnormal, the morbid, and the neurotic; even I aped the attitude of extreme world-weariness assumed by other literary adolescents, such as Kenneth Burke—sworn foe of ice-cream parlors—who became henceforth one of my most esteemed cronies. He was a veritable *Dichter*, a spark, a man of wit; though four or five inches shorter than I, he possessed the towering advantage of greater age (by a year or so) and a voice like a barrel organ, in which he would boom out his aphorisms, the aggressiveness of his tone evidently compensating for his stature.

"K.B., a young man of sixty-five inches and sixty-five hundred dreams of empire"—thus I addressed him in a letter of 1917. We both felt ourselves "outsiders" among the pack of collegiate Philistines all around us; we were adolescent egotists, now exalted by feelings of snobbish pride, now cast down by self-doubt, and pining to see our bad verses in print. But we helped each other.

The next time I encountered a man of letters in embryo I was all ready for him, and there was no more nonsense about ice cream. He was a handsome youth who, while seated next to me in the University library, kept peering over my shoulder trying to read the book that was in my hands, a passably diabolical novel, *A Rebours*, by J.K. Huysmans. He was by name William Slater Brown; came from Webster, Massachusetts; and attended the School of Journalism at Columbia. At once I proposed that we go off to the Red Lion, which I had already visited with Burke, and drink some beer together, or whisky, or a cocktail for all I cared. I felt myself absolutely reckless, but this time I hoped to make a decent impression from the start.

Our meeting must have taken place sometime at the beginning of 1919. We vied with each other—we too—in reciting passages from Verlaine. Brown possessed not only a fine memory for poetry, but an excellent French accent, for he had recently spent almost a year in France as a volunteer member of the Norton-Harjes Ambulance Corps, which furnished medical aid for the Allied armies. I found all that he had to tell me of wartime France of enormous interest. After we had known each other for some time, Brown confided to me the dreadful story of his having been arrested and thrown into a concentration camp by intelligence agents of the French Army, because of his extreme indiscretion in writing letters home frankly describing conditions at the front. Together with Brown, his fellow-volunteer, E.E. Cummings, had also been arrested and imprisoned, solely because he was Brown's close buddy. The story of their imprisonment under terrible conditions during long months, as a consequence of which Slater Brown almost died of scurvy before they were freed, was to provide the material for Cummings' eloquent memoir of their prison camp, *The Enormous Room*, written several years afterward and published in 1922. Brown is the young American named "B" in Cummings' narration.

Brown had much sweetness of manner and a quite whimsical humor, expressed in playful verses he used to write in the style of Edward Lear's *Book of Nonsense*. But for a year or so after his return from France, I felt an undercurrent of melancholy in him that was perhaps an after-effect of his sufferings in military prison.

Another of my acquaintances of this period, who served as a volunteer ambulance driver (later also in the French transport service), was Malcolm Cowley. He, too, was from Pittsburgh, and an old schoolmate of Kenneth Burke, who brought him one day in the spring of 1917 to my dormitory room at Columbia. Cowley was a student at Harvard, but was en route to France. He was then not much more than eighteen, ruddy and chubby-faced, and looked like a big overgrown country boy. In fact, he had spent many summers at a farm his parents owned in western Pennsylvania. But within this awkward, rustic-looking youth with the broad smile, there was a keen student of poetry who wrote with grace and clarity when he put pen to paper.

He had much to tell us when he returned in the early autumn, wearing the uniform of the French transport service. Life behind the front had been sometimes arduous, but hardly dangerous, he related. On days of leave in Paris he had improved his French with the help of some little *poules* he met, who corrected his accent when he read Baudelaire to them. Hearing him, we were all the more highly resolved to get to France, war or peace.

At about the same period, quite by chance, I first encountered Hart Crane, then about nineteen, who had come to New York from Cleveland. We were already submitting our first manuscripts of poems and prose to editors of literary magazines, and accumulating rejection slips. It was thus that I happened to set off one afternoon to visit the office of *The Little Review* at 24 West 16th Street, which was also the home of its editor, Margaret C. Anderson; I carried a manuscript in my pocket, of course. To my disappointment, no one answered the bell; the editors were out and they had no secretary. Then, at last, the door latch was pressed open and someone called to me from upstairs that Miss Anderson was out of town, adding that if I had a message or wished to leave something for her, would I come up and give it to him. A stocky young man with a big round head, brown hair, and large blue eyes soon appeared and, in very breezy fashion, invited me to come in and visit with him. Such was Hart Crane, who then occupied a furnished room above the publishing office of *The Little Review* and often, out of loneliness or restlessness, intercepted its visitors. My first, incorrect, notion that he had some official connection with Miss Anderson's already esteemed magazine was soon removed. He had been pressing his manuscripts upon the editor for some time, though in vain; then he had moved into the vacant room above her in order to urge his cause more effectively.

He impressed me as a most friendly and hospitable young fellow. Soon we had each whipped poems out of our pockets and were reading them to each other. My reaction to his earliest verses was tartly unfavorable: they were "old-fashioned" or "Swinburnian," I declared, and what could be worse? In my youthful arrogance I even recommended that he throw them away and do something "modern." Crane was rather jarred, but accepted my strictures in good spirit; we remained friendly thereafter, meeting for lunch or supper every two or three weeks during 1919. After he returned to his home in Cleveland at the end of that year, we corresponded frequently.

I am giving here the roster of my literary friends whom I met toward 1919 and with whom I was intimately connected throughout the 1920's; it included principally Kenneth Burke, Malcolm Cowley, Slater Brown, and Hart Crane; two or three years later, these were joined by Robert M. Coates, John Brooks Wheelwright, and Allen Tate. We rotated in the same orbit because our great single-minded preoccupation was working with words. ("What am I but a *word man?*" Burke used to say, and surely he was that.) Born within the closing months or years of the last century, coming from different parts of the country— New England, Pennsylvania, Ohio, and Brooklyn (in my own case)—and constituting quite a mixture of different racial strains, we formed, as I realized in later years, a sort of cross section of the literary generation that came of age in the 1920's.

We were youthful but not carefree; our anxieties dogged us. Whereas a Scott Fitzgerald tried to shine among the crowd at Princeton, accepting their values unquestioningly, we, in our small isolated circle at Columbia, shut our ears to the hurrahs of student social life. We pretended to be too "old" for the jollifications of the freshmen and sophomores, and acted as if we were Outsiders. Kenneth Burke and I together used to haunt the swimming pool at University Hall, which had a dome of blue-tinted glass and was by all odds the most beautiful place in all the University. We would swim there or walk back and forth at the water's edge, conversing interminably in the manner of peripatetic philosophers. "Here, at any rate, we are as Romans," Burke used to say. But we were very small Romans, as he well knew; he was but giving rein to the spirit of paradox always strong in him.

Where would we go with our poetry? That was the question which our families constantly pressed upon us.

In my youth those old-fashioned pioneering capitalists, Tom

Edison and Henry Ford, who provided the nationally accepted image of the self-made American, used to ridicule higher education. Our bourgeoisie were an energetic breed; the richest among them would drive their sons to begin work at the bottom of the ladder in a factory, and no nonsense about learning or art or the pleasures of leisure life which engrossed rich Europeans. Hart Crane's father, for example, was a successful man of business who would have liked his son to become a manufacturer of chocolate candy like himself. He was no doubt horror-stricken at discovering that Hart, when already at high-school age, occasionally played truant and stayed in bed all day reading books and scribbling poetry. Malcolm Cowley's father was a doctor in a working-class district of Pittsburgh, an excellent and generous man who never collected enough fees from his impoverished patients. Malcolm's mother, as I heard, sometimes reproached her son for wasting his time with poetry, and held up to him the example of a cousin of his who, after graduating from high school, turned at once into a prosperous jewelry salesman. These were much the same terms my own mother used in considering a choice of possible careers for me, though in my case I was expected to settle myself into the teller's cage of a bank.

Kenneth Burke was the most brilliant of students; his prose and verse surely made him one of the glories of Peabody High School in Pittsburgh. As was usual in such cases, his parents were both proud and disconcerted. After high school, however, Kenneth stayed out a year, working in a bank. His father decidedly wanted him to "go up" by getting down to business. He then attended Ohio State University for one semester, but transferred to Columbia College when his parents moved to New Jersey. Gentle and affectionate as Kenneth's parents were, I gathered that, by hints and sighs, they again prevailed upon him to leave off the costly business of higher education. While still in his sophomore year, Kenneth arrived at the resolution to quit the University, though he had prospects of being appointed to its faculty if he had stayed. Making a virtue of necessity, he declared that he had spared himself the dire fate of a college-teacher's life, which might have been ruinous for the budding writer in him. It was only after a long detour, in his middle years, that he was to return to the university world which he was so fitted to ornament.

Among my friends, only Slater Brown enjoyed what was then a liberal income for a young man, about $1,500 a year, which he received while attending college. However, as he was a young blade who always spent his monthly remittances in the first week, he usually had the appearance of being just as poor as the rest of us.

American youths are supposed to lead "cloistered lives" during the years of school and college, under the economic protection of their parents. We, too, were thus protected; but our being passionate amateurs of literature when nobody asked us to be that created some problems. Hart Crane, under his surface joviality, was unhappier in his relations with his family than any of us, because of the torment he suffered during a period of conflict and separation between his parents, that was soon to end in their divorce. As he took his mother's side with great passion, he became completely alienated from his father, of whom he spoke in my presence with hysterical hatred as "a wolf of a man." The storms going on in the Crane family caused all thought of preparing Hart for college to be put aside. His father, in any case, cared nothing about that—though the father's principal fault may have been his failure to understand the difficult personality of his talented son. When I first saw Hart he was trying to win his bread by selling hideous colored lithographs that his father's firm distributed. Returning to Ohio in the latter part of 1919, and resolving to be completely independent of the elder Crane, he found work as a factory hand in one of the rubber-tire plants of Akron, an arduous labor that left him too exhausted to write anything.

At that time I could not discern how tormented a creature Hart was. I had only vague notions of the problems besetting the Oscar Wildes of this world, notions taken only from books. Hart

was most effusive in showing affection for his friends, for he
hungered for their love. Outwardly there was nothing odd or
effeminate in his manner; when he was being merry, he had the
air of a stout "bully boy," which is what we used to call him.
Moreover, toward 1919, he had not yet come to a final resolution about what his sex life was to be; when he did, not long
afterward, he showed, as I now realize, much innate courage.
And then to cap everything, Hart, vengeful toward his father,
was determined at all costs to make himself the Great American
Poet, which was also not easy.

We may have been the "happy few," but we felt ourselves
very few indeed, and the enemies of poetry many and strong
all about us. Our sense of isolation in our America was reflected
not only in the disconsolate letters which the literary novice,
Hart Crane, often wrote me from Ohio, but also in those of a
man like Sherwood Anderson, already winning renown as a
novelist by 1919. It happened that Hart had met Anderson in
Cleveland at this period, and gained the sympathetic interest of
the older writer. If Hart made lament in his letters at finding
himself alone in a grim factory town like Akron, starved for
good talk or books, then Anderson did no less, for he wrote
Hart rather touchingly that December: "One hungers for
brothers—you in Akron, another man in California, and a fellow
like Fred Booth shivering in some cold room in New York. The
land is indeed vast."[1]

At the time I entered college, the country had been through
a whole decade or more of reform politics, beginning with the
presidency of Theodore Roosevelt and continuing through Wilson's first term. When we came to the brink of war with Germany in 1917, controversy raged among the illuminati of Columbia, as was the custom then. There were meetings in support of
the "Plattsburg Movement" for voluntary military training and
Preparedness, countered by rallies of those who favored keeping out of the war. I remember hearing Randolph Bourne, a

hunchback with burning eyes, speak as a convinced pacifist. One of my instructors, Leon Fraser, like Bourne a Columbia graduate, also spoke against Preparedness and in favor of neutrality. A few weeks later, in April, 1917, just after war had been declared, Fraser, who was giving a course in Politics, was abruptly suspended from the faculty by order of the Board of Trustees. This was done over the protests of the departmental faculty committee, of which Charles A. Beard was chairman. Beard, in fact, favored our entrance into the war against Germany, but in a number of forthright public statements assailed Butler and the trustees for suppressing freedom of speech in the University when the country was entering upon a "crusade" for world freedom. When he found that his petitions in behalf of his assistant, Fraser, were vain, Beard resigned from the faculty in protest.

By the autumn of 1917, the war had laid a blight on the college; some of the ablest members of the faculty departed or entered some war service, while the students waited restlessly to be drafted or begin training in the R.O.T.C. After June, 1918, the college was shut down; while waiting to be drafted, I went off to work in a shipyard on an island in Newark Bay. (I had been rejected for Reserve Officers' Training on the ground of defective hearing, though the defect was then slight.) For the next six months or so I lived in a furnished room in Greenwich Village, commuting each day to the shipyard. That season Greenwich Village was my "university."

FOUR

THE

"VILLAGE"

Although I was born within ten miles of the Washington Arch I knew nothing of Greenwich Village until the autumn of 1917, when Kenneth Burke took me there to visit his friends from Pittsburgh, James and Susan Light, then living at 86 Greenwich Avenue. These enterprising young persons had recently been undergraduates at Ohio State University where they had published a few issues of a little magazine called *The Sansculotte,* dedicated to "literature for its own sake." At the time when war was declared against Germany, however, they had left college and come to New York. Their home was a rambling seven-room apartment in an old triangular tenement, long ago demolished and replaced by a large motion-picture theater. On the outer wall of the theater there is a bronze plaque stating that Georges Clemenceau, the premier of France during World War I, had lived on this site when he fled to America as a political refugee after the revolution of 1871. Those of us who used to frequent 86 Greenwich, more than forty years ago, have long referred to the place as "Clemenceau Cottage."

Jim Light—tall, very blond, and soft-spoken—was a versatile youth who had tried his hand at painting as well as writing, and

40

was soon occupied in acting and directing plays at the Province-town Players, which had recently been founded by George Cram Cook. Sue, a vivacious and comely young woman, earned her living as an editor of a magazine of light fiction. It was still somewhat unusual then for a young married woman to go to work at a business office; and it was also novel for her to wear her hair in a Dutch bob, as it seemed to me, for I had seen no short-haired women in Brooklyn.

As the Lights had more space than they needed, they rented out three or four of their rooms to friends at cost, which was very little. Djuna Barnes, a tall, handsome poet, then in her late twenties, occupied one room; the much younger Berenice Abbott, who came from Ohio and was then an art student, but later became a most expert photographer, occupied another; down the hall was the room of Charles Ellis, who painted in the day-time and acted at the Provincetown Players at night; and in still another and smaller room, Kenneth Burke, who had quit college, was lodged during the winter and spring of 1918. "I've burned my bridges," he said at the time. Having borrowed a small sum from his father in lieu of college tuition, he lived on iron rations of oatmeal and milk twice a day and worked at stories and essays which he was very eager to publish before his funds gave out.

This group usually kept up a lively chatter and in decidedly informal manner. They were often joined by other kindred souls. Among those I remember were Dorothy Day, a news-paper reporter and militant suffragette, who lived in an apart-ment downstairs; Peggy Johns, wife of the poet Orrick Johns, but recently divorced, who was a neighbor; Floyd Dell, one of the editors of *The Masses*, a weekly devoted to socialism and literature; and Eugene O'Neill, a shy and silent man with a tense dark face, who became very taciturn when he had been drinking. There were sometimes so many who visited the place that it resembled a village gristmill, where persons who were by no means peasants came together.

As an artists' quarter and center of Bohemianism, Greenwich

Village was of quite recent growth. Some of the artists of the "Ash Can School," such as John Sloan, William Glackens, and George Bellows, had first settled in the region of Washington Square a few years before 1914. The former resort of New York society by then was full of dilapidated mansions converted into cheap rooming houses, where the artists could find space and light at low rent. Later a few writers such as Theodore Dreiser and Hutchins Hapgood came to live in the neighborhood. Soon there were two or three little basement restaurants serving wine, such as Polly's; there some of the painters and writers foregathered in the evening and tried to reconstitute the atmosphere of the old artists' quarter of Paris, in which some of them had lived as students.

Toward 1917–1918 the community probably boasted of a dozen such coteries as I found at the Lights' in Clemenceau Cottage. There was one associated with Max Eastman, made up of writers and illustrators for *The Masses*, of which he was editor; another centered about George Cram Cook and his wife, Susan Glaspell, the playwright; there was a radical group of I.W.W. adherents who gathered at Mary Heaton Vorse's on West Tenth; and there were also wealthy Bohemians, such as Gertrude Vanderbilt Whitney, who did sculpture of sorts, and Mabel Dodge, who held soirees at her Fifth Avenue mansion. A good many of the women writers in the neighborhood, such as Inez Haynes Milholland and Katharine Anthony, were militant suffragettes, and this helped give the "Village" its special repute at the time as a stronghold of feminism.

Here, at any rate, America's artistic "renaissance" was in full progress. At 86 Greenwich Avenue the Little Theater movement bloomed; Eugene O'Neill's first one-act plays were being staged, and everyone's hopes were pinned on him. The young artists were imitating Cézanne and also the Cubists—whose works we saw for the first time with amazement. Near Washington Square there were two or three small art galleries of the advanced type, one being directed by the pioneering Robert Coady, where I had my first sight of African masks and wood carvings full of magic.

At Albert Boni's bookstore on Eighth Street we could buy the thin volumes of the experimental poets who called themselves Imagists, and copies of *The Little Review* with its installments of James Joyce's *Ulysses*. Some of the issues of that magazine, which were denied mailing privileges by the Post Office Department, were eagerly snatched up and passed from hand to hand, for we were highly excited at first reading the new Irish master.

My exposure to life in Greenwich Village, at age seventeen to nineteen, in some respects had a revolutionizing effect on my education. All sorts of novel impressions and paradoxical ideas came into my head at the same time and kept me at first in a state of pleasant bewilderment. But my memories of the Greenwich Village community at the time of World War I do not conform with those of others, who have pictured it as a continual carnival of amiably promiscuous young men and women. It was really nothing so carefree or careless as all that. There were, to be sure, some cheerful drinking parties on Saturday nights, and at regular intervals those costume balls at Webster Hall for the benefit of noncommercial groups, such as the Independent Artists or *The Masses,* which enjoyed a certain fame for a while. These were usually well advertised in advance, so that a strong contingent from Park Avenue would turn up to dance till dawn with the "Village" artists and their girl friends or models. Such affairs, distinguished by extravagant costumes or lack of costumes, were no more scandalous than those held uptown at the old Waldorf at the same period.

The real social life here, however, was very different from what one might have expected. Most of the "Villagers" were people who had rebelled against their middle-class background and family and "escaped" from their home towns, large or small, to New York, then found their way to the quarter south of Fourteenth Street. Many of them were single women, the New Women, college-educated or of the flapper type, and usually came from the hinterland that is west of the Hudson River. But having taken up arms against the Philistines of their native Main Streets, having escaped and then congregated in Greenwich Village with persons much like themselves, they proceeded to set up some clearly defined moral conventions of their own, and cleaved to them.

The New Women, ardent feminists that they were, seemed to me key figures in the "Village" circles of those Wilsonian days. I remember many of them as big-bodied and dressed in masculine clothes; sometimes, at social gatherings, they affected "exotic" costumes of loosely flowing and shapeless robes; generally they cut their hair short, used neither rouge nor powder, and smoked cigarettes constantly, which was something new to me.

At lunch with one of those self-reliant women in Polly's restaurant, where one ate well for thirty-five cents, it happened that out of old-fashioned notions of gallantry I picked up both our restaurant checks, only to have my hand slapped down. The lady firmly took her check from me and reminded me that the New Woman "paid her own way."

The same code held for the neighborhood bars, such as the Working Girls Home, which was the back room of O'Connor's Café at the triangle of Christopher Street, Greenwich, and Sixth Avenues, where our checks for beer and stout were scrupulously divided among male and female clients. Here, also, the girls with the Dutch bobs observed the rule of the Dutch treat.

One might not have perceived at first glance that young women like Dorothy Day, who downed drink for drink with the men at the Working Girl's Home felt they had a serious mission in life. That became clear enough later on, in the account Miss Day wrote, in a spirit of sincere repentance, of the stages of her conversion to the Roman Catholic faith. But back in the autumn of 1917, Dorothy Day went to Washington with her friend, Peggy Johns, and, with a whole band representing the National Woman's Party, picketed the White House. They were arrested, sentenced, and imprisoned for several weeks in a Federal jail, where they went on a hunger strike and suffered most brutal treatment. I happened to meet them with a group of their friends as they returned to New York, and remember how they talked of their experience as if it had been a lark.

The American woman had long been placed on a pedestal by man, for her own protection and for the sake of the family (as I have often seen it explained). All this is supposed to have started when we were a frontier society and somewhat short of females. But now the American woman wanted to climb down from her pedestal and take her chances as an equal with man in the wars of politics, business, art, and love.

There was a good deal of light talk going on about free love and philandering, around the time that several of us who were still of undergraduate age turned up in Greenwich Village. After Kenneth Burke moved from Clemenceau Cottage I rented his small room for a while; Malcolm Cowley also turned up at intervals in that stronghold of Bohemianism, between periods of war service. And there were other eager youths like us who, doubtless, would have liked nothing better than to choose *une maîtresse convenable* from among the eligible women artists or poets or their sisters; one who could pay her own way. It would seem that delectable opportunities invited us on every hand. But it was not quite as simple as that.

At this period there was also much solemn discussion of the need for overturning all our established ideas about sex, love, and marriage in *The Masses,* where Floyd Dell tried to popularize the teachings of Sigmund Freud. In short, Dell advocated the fullest sexual liberty and the relaxation of the marriage bond as a great cure-all (certainly a gross simplification of Freud's ideas). Joseph L. Freeman, one of my acquaintances of that period, has written that on first meeting Floyd Dell, he received the advice that he get himself at once to a psychoanalyst and have his complexes unraveled; only thus would he rid himself of his secret fears and taboos, discover the hidden pattern of his life, and qualify himself as a literary "genius." (In later years, however, Dell greatly modified his views and became a champion of the marriage institution.)[1]

Among our circles of the emancipated, there was endless talk of being, above all, "free" or "expressing oneself freely." According to the accepted code, people must be "let alone" no matter how censurable their conduct; that is, they must be allowed immunity from criticism based on "middle class" moral standards. Thus X must be free to leave his girl friend Y and seek inspiration elsewhere, while she must be equally free to go and do likewise, whatever inconveniences resulted therefrom. Moreover, all such domestic rearrangements were supposed to be open to full and frank discussion by everybody concerned and his or her friends—not in secret or hypocritically—which gave large scope to gossip.

Under this new social code there were losses as well as profits. One of my friends, for example, soon after his escape from the provinces to the "Village," had the good fortune to win the favor of a beautiful young woman who had recently come to New York to play in one of the little theaters. For two days my friend was in transports, knew himself in love for the first time, and talked of nothing else; but on the third day his inamorata went off to another's bed. My friend could make no protest, no appeal to any legal or moral authority, and was all broken up by his unhappy experience. In rebound from despair, he threw himself into the arms of the first woman he met—and married her.

Another young friend of mine, however, carried on his pursuit of happiness in a more methodical spirit. He would go off on Saturday nights to the dances of the Rand School nearby, which were frequented by "Village" girls of Socialist leanings. "I would ask some girl there to dance with me," he confided, "and then bring the conversation around to the subject of Freud's teachings, warning her about the evil effects of sexual repression and offering to interpret her dreams. Sometimes it didn't work, but often they would come to my room."

Thus, under the regime of freedom, woman was allowed an active rather than a passive role in choosing her partner. She need not wait to be called, but called to the man herself—often with an eye to her social and artistic advantage. Now the difficulty for us younger chaps was that, as literary apprentices, we were, if not mute, inglorious, unprinted, unsung. The poetical and aesthetical females in these circles were often older than we, and seemed frightfully knowing. They would look past us at the males who had already won their spurs as writers or theater directors or editors, those who were Somebodies in the Greenwich Village hierarchy. After all, the stickiest problem for an aspiring woman poet was breaking into print. Gradually the suspicion was formed in my mind that certain of these young women, with a view to seeing their works published or staged, offered more than the charms of mere literature to the men they singled out for their attentions. Indeed, I knew of one quite middle-aged character, an editor of an important journal of opinion, who regularly captured the prettiest of the young literary women, as soon as they arrived in New York by the train from Indiana or California with manuscripts in their valises. Poor subalterns that we were, we younger men came to believe that editors had all the luck. All the keener was our impatience to be published, to arrive, even perhaps to be editors someday!

Finding a respectable mistress with a college degree, who would pay for her own meals, seemed less simple the more one studied the question. The New Woman was bent on exercising her moral independence as well as her economic virtue. This phenomenon was well illustrated by a striking phrase in a speech of Emma Goldman, the famous champion of women's freedom as well as anarchism: "Women need not always keep their mouths shut and their wombs open!"

In his book, *A Victorian in the Modern World* (1939), Hutchins Hapgood, for long years a pillar of Bohemian society in this quarter, expressed his conclusions on the subject with much wisdom. I happened to meet Hapgood during a winter's vacation in Florida, long after he had retired from the pursuit of extramarital happiness, in which he was supposed to have shown eminence. He was by then almost seventy, still drank his four martinis before dinner, but even so was a handsome figure of a man, despite his big bay window. Since he was trying to reduce his girth, he used to exercise on the beach by standing on his head or walking on his hands while he discoursed with me. "To sum it all up," he exclaimed one day, wheezing because of his upside-down posture, "I have had a *wonderful wasted* life with women and drink."

Love in Greenwich Village, he contended, was very different from what the uninitiated supposed it to be. It was not a frivolous, but a very serious business. In Europe's Latin Quarters, which Hutch had observed carefully in the 1890's, a young man might easily find a pretty working girl who would consent to be his "sweet submissive little creature," and make no demands upon him; he could take her or leave her. Whereas in Greenwich Village, American women living on terms of free love with their men were often very "strong-willed," Hutch had found; they would demand for themselves what men had formerly held to be their own historic rights or privileges; indeed, they were always fighting to be "more equal" than their men, according to him. As a consequence, the men suffered a good deal at the hands of the new, masterful type of woman, the feminist who insisted upon all her rights.

It might be that Hutch Hapgood's conclusions were influenced by his own disposition to fall into the hands of strong-minded females. But just the same life in our outpost of modernism and Bohemianism seemed to me neither simpler nor easier than under the older conventions. Who could say that love was ever free? In fact the terms "free" and "love" are logical contradictions. Else why did that unwedded couple in the furnished room next to mine in Patchin Place in 1918—the woman being a gifted writer, the man an intelligent and amiable character— beat each other up during the night so that they used to appear in the morning with a black eye or other contusions?

How often what was intended to be a casual affair turned into a compromise between life and youth's dream of love. "Some drizzly morning late in April you woke up to find yourself married, . . ." one of my companions has written of the milieu we both frequented.[2] Married? There was nothing modern and free about marriage, yet many early marriages I knew of were contracted in the "Village." Occasionally, it might be the unexpected auguries of child-bearing that led people to the altar or City Hall. More often than not, as I observed, the sort of young fellow who was ridden by his ambitions or anxieties about his writing or painting proved to be uxorious, needing the constant solace of some maternal female and frequently a woman older then himself; the early marriage often proved to be enduring, though people spoke of the institution lightly and divorce was in high fashion. After all, the calculating Don Juans of this world, who "collect" their successes with women as tennis players collect their silver cups, must give much time and effort to their sport and keep their minds free of all other cares; they must remember to bring gifts of flowers or perfume at the right time, and must have the means to buy them.

One of our fledgling writers, the pink-cheeked, twenty-year-old Malcolm Cowley, at the end of the war fell in love with Peggy Johns, who was several years older than he, and they were married. In her younger days the amusing Peggy was very pretty. Malcolm, as it happened, had very tidy personal habits bred in him by his (partly) Pennsylvania-Dutch forebears. Peggy, however, liked to live in a charming disorder. If they were forced to borrow ten dollars in order to eat, she might spend most of it on flowers. She also loved to keep all-night poker games going in the kitchen of their cold-water flat, which was also its living room. On occasion, I would come in to see Malcolm in the evening and find his home in complete disarray, a noisy game of cards in progress, and soiled dishes, empty wine bottles, and also flowers everywhere about. But in a corner of the kitchen, Malcolm had set up a small table with a portable typewriter and his papers and books. Here everything was beautifully neat and clean, so that his little writing corner was in marked contrast with the rest of the place. At times, he would go to his corner and set to work doggedly—for he had great resolution—while the poker game raged around him all night. In the end, however, literature prevailed over poker and wine; he and Peggy were divorced, and he married a younger woman who, besides having other virtues, kept his household in beautiful order.

As for myself, I must confess that life and experience among the New Women of Greenwich Village—when I was eighteen to nineteen—did not really come up to the high hopes I had entertained in this direction. I admired the latter-day bluestockings for their high principles, but my own mooncalf ideal of womanhood was of something more *mignonne* than they generally were. In a letter to a friend, written in 1918, evidently in a mood of irritation, I said: "I am overwhelmed with disgust for 'intellectual women.' . . . You would be amazed at the mean gossip and the chatter of personalities circulating all about." An unending chorus of gossip always accompanied the more or less spectacular "affairs" of the moment. It seemed to me that such love affairs were conducted in a goldfish bowl, so that all who passed through this Bohemian aquarium could enjoy the spectacle. I understand that the Beat Generation, who have appeared among us since World War II, like the Bohemians of the earlier war period, are also much given to histrionics and enjoy putting their bouts of jazz, sex, or marijuana on view. I wonder if they, too, will in time develop a set of distinct moral conventions such as characterized the "Village" coteries of forty years ago.

The highly articulate group at Clemenceau Cottage, which included some of the most personable of the New Women, impressed a collegian still younger than they as being not only brilliant in conversation—they were always getting off stunning paradoxes—but also as immensely "sophisticated." That, indeed, was one of their key words, and was related to a whole series of social and artistic taboos recurring in the pattern of their talk. All that was judged "conventional" and "bourgeois" in social behavior fell under their contempt; similarly, in artistic matters, they upheld the realistic, and therefore truthful, style, as against the "sentimental," which was associated with bourgeois weakness. The current of opinion here certainly affected those of us who were then young and plastic.

"Above all we must never be *sentimental,* must shrink from all manifestations of sentimentality," I wrote to Kenneth Burke in 1917. I had certainly committed many sins of that category before coming to this high resolve.

Kenneth, Malcolm, and I at about this period also formed what we called our Anti-Logrolling Society, a challenge to the vices of puffing and mutual admiration already manifested in the small literary world of New York. We sometimes engaged in rather collegiate competitions with each other: to write a sonnet within a time limit of twenty minutes or forty minutes upon a common theme—such as "A Sunset" or "A Rose"— which, in our ironic humor, we made as banal or mock-sentimental as possible. After working against the clock, we would stop and read aloud what we had produced. Thereupon we were in honor bound to begin our critical comments upon each other's verses, by emphasizing what was worst in them or pointing out all that might be held to be vulgar or trite or "adjectival."

Burke, a master of this vinegarish sort of criticism, would say: "Well, of all the stinkin' rotten lines . . . !" Malcolm would prove to be the most resourceful in writing occasional or light verses on a selected subject. When, perchance, something good or amusing turned up, we would admit as much with evident reluctance. But more usually we were just a trio of loving little friends, who never failed to say their worst for one another. The habit continued for long years, and "soft" people who overheard us, knowing nothing of our masonic rules, could not understand that we were only being helpful to each other in the Anti-Logrolling spirit.

One evening at Clemenceau Cottage all the bantering and the buzzing over paradoxes stopped, when one of the habitués came in with a small auburn-haired young woman of about twenty-six.

She had a tiny uptilted nose and a rare smile; though not uncommonly pretty, she was very graceful, spoke softly, and seemed to be walking on air. She was Edna St. Vincent Millay, one of the authentic new voices in American poetry, whose poem, "Renascence," had won eminence for her some years before and made her a charming sibyl of the new era. At the time her play, *Aria da Capo,* in which she was to take the leading part, was being rehearsed by the Provincetown Players under the direction of Jim Light.

Edna Millay, the little pixy from Rockland, Maine, and Vassar College, easily created an air of enchantment about herself that everyone wanted to believe in. We hovered over her, hung over her words, spoiled her a little; these people whose humor sometimes grew malicious now spoke gently. After she was gone, we discussed her with intense interest. There were already two slim volumes of her poems on hand. Some of us who also wrote poetry, but in the mode of the Ezra Pounds, asked if there were not still a bit of nineteenth-century cant about Nature and Life in her work; but the others indignantly shouted us down as if we were blasphemers. They pointed to numerous passages of direct and forceful statement that reflected Miss Millay's distinct personality and had no verbalizing for rhyme's sake. These expressions of her high spirits and courage for life had great appeal for the feminists throughout the twenties. Young ladies would come down from Radcliffe or Vassar College to make their careers in New York, spurred on by lines such as: "Oh world, I cannot hold thee close enough——." They would talk bravely of burning their candles at both ends—and ride out on the ferry boat to Staten Island with a boy friend.

Of her enjoyment of the pleasures of love Edna Millay certainly wrote with an explicitness seldom known among women writers, perhaps since Sappho; she also gave frank evidence of her will to be *inconstant.* It was all very well for a man to be inconstant in the old days, but for a young woman to declare that the attraction she had felt for some member of the male sex was only passing and

. . . insufficient reason
For conversation when we meet again.

was something that rankled in a real man's bosom. And she went on to say:

What lips my lips have kissed, and where, and why,
I have forgotten, and what arms have lain
Under my head till morning . . .

Some of the gallant stags in our literary circle were, no doubt, piqued by the challenging character of such statements. Recently I questioned one of Miss Millay's old friends, Susan Light (now Mrs. Susan Jenkins), on this point. Did not some of those fellows feel some curiosity about Edna's ability to *forget* their manly charms, I asked? "Oh, they just wouldn't *believe* her," was the reply.

To my regret, I did not see much of Miss Millay until several years later, when she was in Paris. There she was not really in her element, as she was on a Staten Island ferry or the coast of Maine; there were no ocean waves, nor wild cliffs, nor seagulls to circle round her charming head. But one can never forget her inspiring effect, as a sort of American George Sand, on the morale of the girls of the twenties.

Before our entrance into the war, the issue of American intervention was debated as passionately in Greenwich Village as on the Columbia campus. Some opposed the war on individualistic grounds, while others wanted to take some collective action; but among the circle of people I knew, who came from many different parts of the country, the war was unwanted. After war was actually declared, some talked of doing something to oppose the war effort. The more impetuous ones were determined to refuse military service, and either go to prison as conscientious objectors or flee the country. While my friends and I usually felt most deeply attracted to the cultural traditions of France, the "nation of glory," we were skeptical when reading

Allied propaganda about the alleged war atrocities against civilians committed by the countrymen of Goethe and Beethoven.

My ever-daring young friend, Clarence Newman, meanwhile, had moved on to Greenwich Village, where he soon became absorbed in radical politics. The American Socialist Party, which had won the support of a million voters in the last election, by 1917 became seriously divided over the war issue, one faction being determined, as patriots, to stand by the war government, while the other held a separate convention and declared for opposing the war effort at all costs. Clarence, full of derring-do as he was then, interested himself in the anti-war Socialists, and directed our attention to an organization called the "Guillotine Club" which was meeting in Greenwich Village and planned to oppose the war actively. I should have been on my guard against any enterprise promoted by my incredible, ineffable friend Clarence; yet out of mixed feelings of curiosity and hope I went along to the Guillotine Club.

We sat on the floor with two dozen other rather solemn young men and women of Greenwich Village and listened to tedious speeches about "what is to be done"; we contributed our few pennies and promised to attend the next meeting, to be held the following week at an East Side restaurant.

The group of Socialists and pacifists realized that once the Federal government assumed full wartime powers and decided upon repressive measures against dissidents, severe penalties might be visited upon such groups as the Guillotine Club. Their executive committee, therefore, voted to become a secret organization and go underground. At eighteen I was so unfamiliar with the customs of secret conspiracies that I addressed a post card through the mails making a rendezvous with one of my friends for our next meeting: "Wednesday, July 24, 1917— Guillotine Club, right in the Village, same time and place as Sunday. Perhaps we can do something there?"

At this second meeting the members were to vote on the proposal of the leaders that we prepare for a dangerous struggle and the risk of imprisonment by accepting henceforth an autocratic discipline imposed from above. Kenneth and I, however, counted on putting up a fight against such undemocratic procedures and hoped for a chance to debate the issue. I was under the impression that Clarence was in full agreement with us and would stand by us.

When we arrived at the meeting place we were stopped at the door and denied entrance to the hall by a man who sounded as if he were one of the I.W.W. element in the group. He informed us that before being allowed to take part in the meeting we would have to undergo a private interrogation. On being questioned by this person, in an anteroom, as to whether we were willing to carry out orders from our leaders that might involve danger for ourselves, and perhaps for others as well, both of us in all honesty gave the same negative reply. We were not ready to obey orders by persons unknown to us, nor were we prepared in our minds to join in any actions going beyond the law. Thereupon we were coolly dismissed. Both of us no doubt looked rather young and brittle for such work, yet both of us felt somehow disappointed or frustrated. As would-be revolutionists we had failed to pass our first test.

We waited for Clarence, also undergoing inquisition. To our surprise, he came out glowing with joy and pride, exclaiming in triumphant tones: "I'm going along with them! I've been accepted by the executive committee. Good-bye!" Under the excitement of the moment our theatrical young friend had changed his mind, we realized. He must have given them a red-hot sales talk too, and they had been taken in by him. We laughed incredulously, wondering aloud what sort of underground organization the Guillotine Club would be with such a man as Clarence in its ranks, one who would call attention to himself at all costs. But a week later he was back in our fold, done with the Guillotine, which soon gave up the ghost.

During the first year of America's participation in the war, when very few of our ground soldiers had gone into action over-

seas, many college students, and especially the literary men
among them, volunteered for service in the Ambulance Corps
in France or with Red Cross units in Italy. Malcolm Cowley was
one of the Harvard contingent, which included, among others,
John Dos Passos, E.E. Cummings, Robert Hillyer, and the
young composer, Roger Sessions. Among the Columbia men who
volunteered for the Ambulance Corps there were Louis Brom-
field and my classmate, Slater Brown.

A good many of these "literary volunteers," as Dos Passos
called them, went for the excitement of the thing, and in order
to enjoy a front seat at the greatest and bloodiest show in history. Hemingway's idea was, as he remarked later: "What a
great advantage an experience of war would be to a writer." A
number of the volunteers, however, were at heart pacifists, with
no wish to engage in deadly combat, but the desire to perform
a humane service. Slater Brown, for example, at age sixteen had
been a member of a little sect of Christian Socialists, and used to
pass out leaflets in the street calling people to the Church of
the Social Revolution, presided over by the Reverend Bouck
White, a radical orator and writer.

John Dos Passos was also a fervent Socialist who lived in
the hope that the French and German soldiers, like the Russians, would both rise against their officers and put an end to
the mass slaughter. Like Brown, Dos Passos saw something of
the widespread, but unreported, mutiny going on in the French
Army in 1917, and incurred the suspicion of French intelligence
officers by mentioning such facts in letters he wrote home—
though his terms were more guarded than the unlucky Brown's.
But one day Dos Passos was abruptly dismissed from the American Ambulance Corps, though there were no charges against
him; he then managed to transfer his services to the Red Cross
in Italy. Because they were not under the rigid discipline of
the American Army, the ambulance men were able to see a
good deal more of life in wartime Europe than the soldiers, and
on their return told us much that fired our interest in going to
Europe.

Those who remained at home waited restlessly to be drafted, as the war took a grave turn for the Allies in the spring of 1918. Some of us filled temporary jobs in war industries, as I did, when serving as a time clerk along the ways of a shipyard, one of the great "war babies" of the period. We were "beating the Huns" by turning out steel cargo vessels in a mad uproar and with a haste and waste even I could judge.

Our war industries were booming as never before by the second summer of the war, prices were rising, and everyone felt prosperous for the moment. New York was full of martial spirit; there were uniforms everywhere, and thunderous military parades almost every day. But the undertone of anxiety about the future was also there.

At the end of October, when the government began to conscript the nineteen-year-olds, I was called up for Army service by an order signed by my father, who was chairman of my local draft board in Brooklyn. Like most of my friends, I did not "believe" in the war, but wanted to see something of it. However, the false or premature announcement of the Armistice coming soon afterward, on November 7th, an occasion celebrated by a tremendous mass demonstration of joy on the part of civilians, soldiers, and sailors in New York, gave notice that I would not put on a uniform.

Early that afternoon I left my work, made my way to the center of the city, and wandered among the intoxicated crowds in the neighborhood of Madison Square and then lower Fifth Avenue, where thousands of men and women were dancing to ragtime music on the café tables. During the evening I was at the Brevoort hotel with a friend, and had occasion to go downstairs to its lavatory. My memory of the Armistice celebration is always associated with the image of a young man in evening dress lying stretched out on the floor, unconscious, and with a long stain of blood that had dripped from his mouth upon his shirt front, while a line of men regularly and with indifference stepped over his body to approach the urinals. Bending over him, I saw that he was breathing regularly but smelled like a distillery. I informed the manager about the man who was down and out, was assured that he would be looked after, and went on my way.

FIVE

A WALK IN

THE GREAT SWAMP

It was exasperating to go back to our school desks at the beginning of 1919, after the dislocations of wartime. Many of us twenty-year-olds had to finish the interrupted business of gathering in our college degrees. If this seemed vexatious for me, it must have been harder for the student next to me, who had recently been decorated on the battlefield; or for Slater Brown, with the memory of six months in the hell of a French prison camp. We were trying to concentrate our attention upon the weighty matter of Philosophy 61, the famous "History of Philosophy" course for upper-class students given by F.J.E. Woodbridge, a lecturer in the "grand" nineteenth-century style.

For my own part, I managed to hasten things by taking as many courses as I dared, including night sessions, and so completed my requirements in one more year instead of two. A French friend, who lectured at American universities, remarked to me: "You drag out your college period too long; your senior students always seem terribly bored in the last year."

1919 is generally characterized by our historians as a year of intense political reaction, a time of widespread disappointment over the terms of peace, followed by the spectacular decline of Woodrow Wilson's powers, physical and mental. The prevailing mood of political pessimism spread to our campus. What could one do with a university president who never laughed, and who expelled a student for lampooning him in *The Jester,* Columbia's magazine of collegiate humor? The tone of the college seemed to me (then full of the impatience of my age) to have become noticeably Pecksniffian. The brood of young hotheads at the School of Journalism were quelled; and in the other schools the students settled down to the prosaic business of preparing to be doctors, lawyers, teachers. We, who liked to consider ourselves young poetical and aesthetical rebels, assumed a pose that was more ironical and world-weary than ever, and, to the exclusion of almost everything else, gave ourselves to the pleasures of pure literature.

Around this time one of the young English instructors, Raymond Weaver, was denounced by one of his pupils before President Butler for having spoken in class with extreme enthusiasm of the writings of Oscar Wilde. The threat of expulsion hung over Weaver. I circulated a petition in his behalf that was signed by a number of senior students and printed in the college daily. Afterward, Weaver with tears in his eyes thanked me, saying that we had helped save his job for him. Several years later he published the first biography of Herman Melville, a work of original scholarship that directly contributed to the revival of the forgotten American master.

The group of young literary men whom I had come to know at Columbia or in the "Village" had been somewhat dispersed during the war, but we corresponded regularly and occasionally came together to read each other's manuscripts and continue our traffic in ideas.

The Imagist movement in poetry had engrossed us during recent years. According to Ezra Pound's interpretation of its theory, ideas were to be represented in the form of images, which meant that these served, in effect, as symbols. Though Imagism began as a literary movement of English and American poets centered in London toward 1912, its aesthetic seemed to derive from the prewar school of Symbolism in France. Pound's critical exposition was often fuzzy, though his intuitive taste was keen; my friends and I admired his early volumes of lyrics, *Personae* and *Lustra*, for their terse, stripped-down, neo-classical language, which made Ezra Pound unique among poets writing in English—our great "decadent" as we called him then.

Amy Lowell was much in the public eye at this time, for she went about lecturing and, indeed, crusading strenuously for poetry, for free verse and for Imagism, so that her name became a byword and it was fashionable to make fun of her. John Brooks Wheelwright, then a Harvard undergraduate, once characterized her as "the Biggest Traveling One-Man Show Since Buffalo Bill." On meeting her again, when she came to lecture in New York in 1919, I was invited to call on her the next day at her hotel. She was truly a mountain of a woman, her great bulk topped by a small head with very bright blue eyes, and she affected cigars. On leaving, I accompanied her to her horse-drawn cab, which literally trembled and groaned as all her two hundred and forty pounds were crammed into it, entirely filling the interior.

In 1917 she had kindly given her blessings to the verses I wrote, saying that some of them were already "good enough to print." She was also instrumental in having one of them published in *Poetry*. But two years later, the style and tone of my pieces had undergone a considerable change and brought from her a letter of severe criticism:

I am afraid I must tell you that I do not think they are as good as your earlier ones. I do not like the note in them. It has a sort of 1890 decadence in it which seems to me out of date and rather feeble. . . . You are evidently going through a period of imitation. I imagine you will do better work when this moment is passed.

Miss Lowell spoke justly; many of us when young go through a phase (more or less instructive) of imitation; her allusion to my note of "decadence" reflects the sort of giddiness that seized us in youth. I was really on the threshold of life, with little experience of it, yet claiming vices I never had, lusting for the fleshpots which I pretended to renounce before having enjoyed them, and writing in a tone of "despair" borrowed, no doubt, from Baudelaire or the Mallarmé who lamented:

La chair est triste, hélas, et j'ai lu tout les livres.

Our affectations were a shared contagion; I was not the only one to show the symptoms. In replying to a melancholy, world-rejecting letter of Kenneth Burke's, in March, 1919, I wrote:

I am very bored with the world . . . feel an exalted boredom. I pay my respects to different ladies and I am not in love.
There is B. He too is bored. He is even more successful at it than I.

I would be sitting at the dormer window of my penthouse room at Columbia, before its fine view, drinking cheap sherry with a friend while we read aloud the Imagist poets and in particular T.S. Eliot. A passage in *The Letters of Hart Crane* relates (as of December 13, 1919):

[Josephson] says he has had a falling out with Amy Lowell, but a falling in with T.S. Eliot by way of compensation. His letters . . . buck me up a good deal.

It was Miss Lowell who had told me of the young American named T.S. Eliot, then working in a bank in London, who seemed to be a poet of promise. I was able to obtain a copy of *The Love Song of J. Alfred Prufrock*, in the London, 1918, edition, and found the low-keyed verses of Eliot haunting and jaded enough to suit my tastes of that season. I wrote Eliot of my enthusiasm for his poems, telling him also of my intention to go to Europe in the following year and live in France. Eliot replied courteously, declaring that my letter had been heartening for him. He sounded like a lonely soul with few readers. Although he had formerly been rather Francophile and had lived and studied in Paris, he now said that he much preferred to reside in England. It would be to my advantage, he advised, to fix myself in London where I could maintain contact with the

pure English language. When I came there, he added, he and
Ezra Pound would be happy to receive me. In those days Eliot
was apparently very much under the wing of Pound, who ruled
over the circle of Imagist poets in London like a king in exile.
However, sharing the mood of my friends who had been over-
seas during the war, I felt indifferent to England and was all
for France.

Pound himself angrily departed from England in 1920. I
have been told that his loud and provocative utterances on Art
and Sex—in the manner of the American cracker-box philosopher he always was—made him unpopular in London literary
circles, which were much given to light, inconsequential talk. It
was Eliot, the boy from St. Louis, Missouri, who adopted the
unemphatic manners of the English and who was destined to win
the great social success in literary London that eluded Ezra
Pound.

Although I pretended to be an indifferent student, I was
really engaged in prolonged readings of the Elizabethan and
Tudor writers of England, and came under their spell. A passage
in a letter from Hart Crane, whose university at the time was
a rubber factory in Ohio, recalls our earnest communications
on the Tudor Age:

Josephson sends me a list of names for reading that you might be
interested in. Marlowe is one of his favorites, John Webster, and
Donne; the last is a wonder speaking from my own experience.

The sonorous language, the verbal conceits of the Eliza-
bethans were infectious for Hart; his poems dating from the
autumn of 1919 show a marked change from the conventional
style of his earlier work. On sending one of the new poems to
Sherwood Anderson, Hart found to his disappointment that the
author of *Winesburg, Ohio* "could not understand" it, and
seemed, as Hart wrote, to have no ear for poetry. On the other
hand, he was gratified because I considered the most recent of
his poems ("My Grandmother's Love Letters") the best thing
he had written to date. Previously he had found me very "par-

ticular" and "difficult" about his work, he remarked, and went on to describe the sort of sharp young brassbounder I pretended to be:

He [Anderson] and Josephson are opposite poles. J. [Josephson] classic, hard and glossy—Anderson, crowd-bound, with a smell of the sod about him, uncouth. Somewhere between them is Hart Crane with a kind of wistful indetermination, still much puzzled.[1]

Veering from the Tudor Age to the nineteenth-century French, without faltering in our stride—I found later that Malcolm Cowley and Allen Tate were each pursuing the same line of march in Cambridge, Massachusetts, and Nashville, Tennessee —we came face to face with the problem of literary form and the possible creation of a "pure" poetry for the modern age. At the time, Ezra Pound earnestly called our attention to the "modern French," from Baudelaire to Mallarmé, who provided us with specimens of pure poetry.

"I feel that we don't read writers for their ideas any more, it is only their style that commands our attention," I had written to Kenneth Burke as early as 1917. It was an extreme statement, but it reflected our overwhelming concern, and especially Kenneth's preoccupation, with craftsmanship and the theory of literary form. Even then the question of how we were to use language interested Burke above all things; in the end the theoretical critic and psychologist of language outweighed the poet and storyteller in him. He fairly bubbled with ideas for renovating the technique and form of literature. Often and again he would come to my room, throw his hat into a corner, and exclaim: "I've got a new theory, by God!" When he had left, as I remarked then, "my mind would be buzzing and talking to itself for hours afterward." But when I had not seen him for some time, I would write: "Please send me a theory to play with."

I remember one evening with a group at the "Hell-Hole" in the "Village," when Kenneth was talking brilliantly about criticism—but everybody else was shouting drunkenly at the

same time—and several persons cried that they could not understand what Burke was saying and would not listen to him anyway. He arose and said: "Very well, then I will give my lecture
on Robert Louis Stevenson in the corner for myself." And he
went to a corner of the café, turned his face away from the rest
of us, and talked to himself, moving his lips rapidly like an old
priest saying his prayers.

We were then reading the current French literary periodicals,
such as the *Mercure de France* and the *Nouvelle Revue Française*, and could follow the quarrels of the modern schools over
literary form: there were the Cubists championed by Guillaume
Apollinaire, the Unanimists typified by Jules Romains, and a
diversity of other movements that gave the effect of a great
intellectual ferment in Paris. Paris, in fact, seemed to have accumulated the experience of generations of conscious craftsmen.
The spirit of Gustave Flaubert was still alive in people there, as
it was in his spirited correspondence; he had been a martyr to
his chosen art. Where in all America could we find a man who
would torment himself for months on end in his hunt for the
"exact word"? Nowadays his quest seems a little absurd; but
the young Americans who were enjoying their first exposure to
French method and tradition piously placed Flaubert in their
calendar of true literary saints. In Chicago, Ernest Hemingway,
then a young newspaper reporter, after reading Flaubert with
close attention, resolved to go to Paris because the tradition of
literary craftsmanship had become so deeply rooted in that great
literary center. Few of the young men cared any longer about
our Anglo-American past.

During the period of letdown at the end of the war, when
the rulers of our society seemed to have turned stupidly conservative again, some of us (who were more or less consciously
disenchanted with political reform) seemed to take all the greater
delight in the effort to master the techniques of our chosen art
medium and demonstrate this in a new way. We were ready to
forget everything else. If enough of us functioned well, making

better poems or better paintings, might we not contribute something, at least, to our civilization?

Many of us also felt the urge to travel abroad in order to continue our studies and learn what we could of the perfection the great contemporary Europeans had achieved in the arts. From his post of exile Ezra Pound addressed his fellow writers in America as "Oh helpless few, oh remnant enslaved," while exhorting them to join him.

But we knew, of course, that art would be long. I had recently met a famous composer and concert pianist, and learned from him that he practiced his piano exercises twelve hours a day. "Will we not need to slave as much as that musician for years on end, in order to perfect our art?" I wrote to Kenneth.

Most of us, however, had no prospects, no "situation in life," nor influential families nor friends to aid us. We would need time for our apprenticeship and our experiments, not to speak of money to live on, as well as to journey abroad. There was the gap before us, as wide as the ocean. How in the world would we bridge it?

A blond giant named Jim Butler, who had wandered back from the wars to visit my friends in Greenwich Village, offered one answer to our problem. Though born in Ohio, Jim was actually half-French, his mother having been the foster-daughter of the painter Claude Monet; his American father had been an artist who lived in France most of his life. Jim had spent some years roaming afoot, not only in France, but recently in the eastern part of the United States, subsisting by hunting and fishing; he was not only a Back-to-Naturist in the mold of Jean Jacques Rousseau, but a skilled sportsman. Moreover, he had lately established something like squatter's rights to a small abandoned cottage beside a river in western New York, and obtained an option to buy it for some trifling sum like two hundred dollars. He described the place as a sort of earthly paradise, abounding in game and trout. As he was returning to

France for the present, he invited any of us who cared to do so to live in his cottage free of rent.

In short, Jim was all for returning to Nature: let the artists be Noble Savages (for he, too, was a painter) by learning to live without money, which Jim, part French-Norman, knew well how to do. When visiting us in the city, he would roll up in a blanket and sleep on the floor; with sums others used in a month, he could hold out for a year, living on some staple groceries and game he caught, while he painted batiks.

My friend Kenneth was ravished by the whole idea. Those of us who had finished our schooling were now working at distasteful jobs, easily obtained and as easily dropped or exchanged for others, while we kept postponing the writing of that book or novel we had planned. The cost of living had virtually doubled, thanks to wartime inflation, while our earnings had lagged. Kenneth had accustomed himself to a diet of the strictest economy, though he was motivated in part by an honorable resolve to save pennies for the pleasures of beer in the evening with friends. Moreover, he had recently been married to one of those self-sustaining college women who had come directly from the provinces to Greenwich Village. Lillian was a tall girl from the Great Smoky Mountains of North Carolina, who as it happened was a trained mathematician. With their capital of one hundred dollars they could leave the city and live for months at Jim Butler's forest cottage, near Candor, New York, four hundred miles upstate. Thus they could hold out until cold weather came, time enough to write a whole book. In the early spring of 1919 they packed up and left town.

I came to visit with them for a week in June and promptly fell in love with country life myself. We lived on grits, hominy, dried peas, and dried codfish, our meals being sometimes embellished with a little game we caught. We had no gun and couldn't afford one, but one day we smoked out a woodchuck and Burke slew him with an axe, so that Lillian was able to dish up a stew. On another occasion we made a rather crude job of trapping and butchering a big river turtle, which we consumed

in the form of a soup. We were all city slickers and not in Jim
Butler's class; he was known to catch squirrels and trout, too,
with his hands.

It was most refreshing to sleep soundly and awaken early in
the depths of the country, then to be able to set to writing or
reading with a concentration seldom possible in the city. Our
subsistence economy, calculated by Lillian at fifty cents per
diem, gave me a sense of liberation from the drudgery of the
world.

The idea of gaining time by going to live in some country
retreat—the time so vitally needed by the apprentice writer—
was so appealing to me that I repeated the experiment two years
later for the period of an entire summer. On this occasion I
joined the Burkes in a remote locality of northern Maine, rent-
ing a house for five dollars a month. The place offered almost
no social resources for our amusement. But this time I came
provided with a wife.

As if in a concerted movement of reaction against *la vie de
bohème*, a number of my impecunious young literary friends
had recently leaped into marriage, some of them with older
women. However, my own early marriage, at twenty-one, was with
one younger than myself, who had recently been studying journalism at Columbia; she was under twenty, unbobbed, small, and
mignonne, but had much courage—courage to leave her job as a
newspaper reporter on a New York daily and come with me to the
woods of Maine, so that I might write poetry; and soon afterward to go to France with me when we had very little money with
which to live there.

When we were married in the City Hall in New York, by a
perfunctory clerk with a great red bulbous nose, she wore, as I
remember, a large blue hat whose brim seemed almost a yard
wide, so that I could only look into her eyes by bending down.
That wide-brimmed hat, the color of her eyes, made her seem very
different from the "Village" bluestockings I had known, as she
was indeed—though she certainly took her stand with the New
Women and even bobbed her long corn-colored hair shortly

after we were married. What did we know of marriage? Perhaps six months, a year would be enough, we said. But the next year in Paris, when one of my friends, with some knowledge of the world, saw the laughing little person I had married, he prophesied correctly: "You are going to be married for a long time. It is not only that your wife has charm; she has the very happy temperament."

After finishing with college, I had drifted from one innocuous job to another; at the time of my marriage I was at work in the sumptuous office of a great foreign trading concern, a satellite of Standard Oil, editing and writing their market reports for a beginner's salary that was less than my secretary's. After that I shifted to the job of a newspaper reporter in Newark, New Jersey. The old-timers on the staff of the Newark *Morning Ledger* had suddenly been fired by a new management and replaced by a band of green collegians, with my friend, Hubert (Red) Knickerbocker, in charge as acting city editor, the very same young fellow who had been arrested for firing off a revolver during a "Village" ball. In each case my employers assured me that my future would be bright, if I kept at my work steadfastly; but they gave no guarantees against tedium vitae, and I never stayed anywhere more than six months.

I was trying to live by my wits, working in 1921 in the treadmill of a commercial publishing office in New York, sometimes stealing the boss's time by doing writing of my own, and beginning to publish a few small things; yet I knew I was getting nowhere. After talking things over with my young wife I came to the resolution that I must somehow win a year or two of freedom and give all my time to writing. We agreed that we must both quit our jobs and make a break for it, and sooner rather than later. We considered the alternatives of living cheaply in the country or going to Paris. In the end we decided to try both, spending the summer in Maine and leaving for France in the early autumn.

I was jubilant as we left New York that summer and sailed for Maine on one of the old coastal steamers; I was escaping from that allegorical button-molding machine with which Death in Ibsen's drama threatens to mold Peer Gynt into such a button as all the others, a fate which that wayward elf always manages to evade. After changing at Bangor to a narrow-gauge train, we climbed the Appalachian foothills up to the village of Monson, once a busy quarrying center, now almost a ghost town. There Kenneth and Lily met and conducted us to our home for the summer, a half-mile from their own; it was a tumble-down cottage in an old apple orchard overlooking a marvelous blue lake surrounded by pine woods. The roof leaked, the bed was made of corn shucks, the stove was broken, and there were only packing boxes for chairs. The local people assured us that in paying five dollars a month for rent we were overpaying by that much. But we were happier than we had yet been anywhere else, and I was free to write whatever I pleased.

The great sky of Maine was pure and brilliant in the daytime; the nights were dark-dark; there was only a single oil lamp in our house, and for reading matter only the books we had brought with us. One hardly ever saw a newspaper in this secluded place. But the woods and lakes all about resounded with the "shop talk" Kenneth and I carried on perpetually, for it was our principal divertissement. We were forever taking the pulse of the literary movements of our time. After Imagism what would come next? We must experiment or die. We evolved plans for stories without plots that assumed the form of sonatas, or novels having the structure of symphonies, or poems without words.

I had recent books by members of the French avant-garde; also copies of the *Nouvelle Revue Française,* which published the new master, Marcel Proust; and *Littérature,* the organ of the Paris Dadaists. We considered the opposing claims of the new schools. There was, for example, Guillaume Apollinaire, expounding his visions of a "new truth" and a "new laughter" exemplified in his poetry, in which he used the devices of "visual lyricism" as he called them; that is to say he broke up solid lines

of verse in the manner of an advertising layout (an old trick
used later by Cummings). The young postwar group in *Littérature* espoused "Dada" as their absurd deity; we did not yet understand them, but saw their movement as a derivation of Apollinaire's. Burke was now more interested in the classical philosophers of aesthetics than in the French modernists. However, I was
intrigued by the French innovations, and undertook some experiments in "Cubist" poetry. A passage from one of these
gives suggestions of images borrowed from the new painting:

> In the whole valley there was but one light,
> a lamp in a farmhouse shooting through four windows . . .
> the small still light which from the four windows
> past fronting trees stabbed long yellow lines
> toward the four corners of the valley, where they lay
> demolished at the feet of the hills. . . .

In Maine we were too far away from everything and thrown
upon each other's society so exclusively that it made severe demands on our temperaments. We shared a rowboat in which we
carried provisions from the general store two miles down the
lake. On one occasion, while rowing back from the village, the
Anti-Logrolling spirit in us rose so high, our "dialectics" became so furious, that we almost sank our boat and all its cargo
of groceries. But after having eaten each other up for awhile,
Kenneth and I usually became affectionate again.

Under Lillian Burke's tutelage, my wife and I lived tolerably
on a budget of seven dollars a week. We used our orchard to
furnish us with applesauce for breakfast, fried apples for lunch,
and apple pie for supper, until we could not bear to look at an
apple again. Bored by our lean diet, we allowed ourselves some
extravagances for our Sunday breakfast, which added another
dollar to the cost of living. When Kenneth and his wife, on
being invited to breakfast on a Sunday, discovered that we took
bacon and eggs, even cream with our coffee, and spent eight
dollars a week, he exploded in wrath, crying: "Traitors! You
are cheating. This is scandalous!" True enough, we had violated

the doctrine of Henry Thoreau and Jim Butler, observance of which would allow us more freedom for creative work.

In Maine I had become thoroughly at home in the country, and, though city bred, learned to relish even its solitude. My eyes were opened thereafter to the variety and subtle movements of natural things, and I would always miss the sense of physical well-being enjoyed in the country when city-pent too long.

Several months before the visit to Maine, while I was gathering material for feature articles for the Newark *Ledger*, I had come upon Dr. William Carlos Williams, who was practicing medicine in the suburban town of Rutherford, New Jersey. He made an excellent subject for a Sunday article on a country doctor who had the odd habit of writing poetry while waiting for the delivery of babies.

In those days there seems to have been, in the region of New York, no focal place, no café, for that matter, where one might meet and converse with such persons as Williams, whom I had already singled out as one of the most appealing of our contemporary poets. As I wrote to Kenneth Burke (in November, 1920):

One of the brightest spots in my . . . life was [meeting] William Carlos Williams. He lives in Rutherford, about ten miles from Newark, and is a successful physician.

I liked him a good deal. He is very simple, unaffected, boyish. A bit Spanish too; especially notable are his faun's ears, small, triangular, the most uncanny ears you ever saw. He is very much alive, and is publishing a little magazine of his own named *Contact*.

I intend to make pilgrimages to Rutherford every now and then for the good of my soul.

A few weeks later I wrote Kenneth that I had arranged for us to spend a Sunday walking with Williams in the New Jersey countryside.

He was then thirty-five, but seemed much younger. Since his early youth—at the University of Pennsylvania, where he had

come to know Ezra Pound—he had been turning out poetry in
bales. At an early stage, however, he had taken a vow that he
would never seek to earn money by his pen, but, avoiding the
low shifts of the commercial writer, would live by some other
calling. Thus he had become a doctor, and a good doctor. His
verse was a very simply cadenced *vers libre*, but his language
was direct, stripped of rhetoric, and had the echo of true American speech. If his work was uneven it was because he frequently
wrote in haste, often during the small hours of the night while
attending a patient, and suffered many interruptions. In adapt-
ing himself to these conditions he had formed the habit of expressing himself quickly, with the automatism of his reflex actions. As he related afterward in his autobiography:

I decided I would write something every day without missing one
day for a year. I'd write nothing planned, but take up a pencil, put
the paper before me, and write anything that came into my head.
Be it nine in the evening or three in the morning . . . I'd write it
down. Not a word was to be changed, but I did tear up some of the
stuff.

His method was very close to the automatic writing and drawing of the Surrealist writers and painters, whom he may have
anticipated.

At all events, Doc Williams, in 1920 as in 1960, was the embodiment of what we used to call, with pride, "the amateur
spirit." Today our commercial-minded writers train themselves
to write a corporate prose that is "processed" in Madison Avenue skyscrapers and distributed by mass publications. To Doc
Williams writing was not a trade, but part of his very life; it
was done on the spur of the moment that was snatched from his
long, hard working day.

Above all he desired to "contact" nature and life as swiftly
and as directly as possible, without much rationalizing or ana-
lyzing, and to give evidence of such contact in racy native
speech. Thus he outlined his fairly simple *ars poetica* for us
during our long walk together that January afternoon in 1921.

It had not been easy for Williams to be free of his patients, even on a Sunday; Burke and I had looked forward eargerly to this occasion. However, there was a fourth person on hand, one Robert McAlmon, a fair-haired youth cf about our age, with handsome features and "hard blue eyes" (in Williams' description). A Middle-Westerner, McAlmon had recently roamed across the whole country, working his way by serving as a dishwasher, a sailor on Great Lakes steamers, and, more lately, as an artists' model who posed, as he boasted, before mixed art classes in New York. He was also a poetic disciple of Williams; some verses he had published recently in *Poetry* were obvious imitations of the Doctor's writing, though with nothing of Williams' compactness of language.

McAlmon affected the airs of a young man of enormously greater experience than two such bookish fellows as Burke and I; and we, on our side, did not kindle to him. He told us, for example, in jocular fashion, of how he had happened to meet the well-known artist, Marsden Hartley, at an art school where he had been posing for a dollar an hour; and how affectionately that gifted but unhappy man had received him on one of his first days in New York. Hartley had shown him the sights of the city from a trolley car; then, as if under a sudden, overpowering impulse, had seized McAlmon's hand and covered it with kisses. " 'Ah, so New York is *like that!*' I said to myself," McAlmon related with his Western drawl.

Toward sunset we halted at a tavern in Newark where we were served bootleg beer, which Williams studiously avoided. The small-town Doctor became ebullient, however, talking with gusto, his laughter sometimes ringing out like that of a small boy. He told us many stories of his medical work among the plain people of Rutherford and Paterson, who were to figure later in his saga, *Paterson*.

On the surface he seemed a solid citizen, well harnessed to his duties as small-town doctor and paterfamilias. But beneath the skin there was a wistful, troubled rebel in him who often gazed longingly across the great swamp, which Rutherford neighbors, and beyond the Hudson River, to the distant lights of Manhattan. At intervals, he would slip away to Greenwich Village, see Miss Margaret Anderson of *The Little Review,* and sup with her group of choice spirits who paid homage to free art, free verse, and illicit wine. Often, Dr. Williams would be the only one who had the price of the food and wine. The dual personality of the man came out in the course of an hilarious account he gave of a burlesque affair he had with a certain Baroness Elsa von Freytag von Loringhoven.

I myself had sometimes glimpsed that strange lady with the two particules in her name, walking about Washington Square in the most startling of costumes. She was said to be the widow of a German nobleman who had lived for a time in New York. She wrote poetry in a mixed German-English, and also made Dadaist artifacts in imitation of Marcel Duchamp, as well as sculptured reliefs that had bits of colored rubbish and tinfoil in them and looked, according to Williams, like "chicken guts." Being a woman of lean masculine figure and with a gaunt ravaged face, she was sometimes in demand as a model for artists painting in the futurist or expressionist style. She also decorated her own person in a mechanistic style of her own device, shaving her head and painting it purple; wearing an inverted coal scuttle for a hat, a vegetable grater as a brooch, long ice-cream spoons for earrings, and metal teaballs attached to her pendulant breasts. Thus adorned and clad in an old fur coat, or simply a Mexican blanket, and very little underneath, she would saunter forth to serve as one of the truly curious sights of the "Village" forty years ago.

Williams had had the folly to express some interest in the Baroness Elsa's artifacts and even in her curious Germanic or pigeon-English poems (which were not without merit). She, in turn, wrote him that she admired his poetry above all others, enclosing a photograph of herself in the nude, as was her custom. She also urgently invited him to call on her. When he came and saw what a woman he had there, he managed to escape from her clutches and rushed home to New Jersey as fast as he could go.

She pursued him, however, coming to Rutherford at night, and, by the trick of having someone call him out to treat a supposedly sick person down the road, caught him in the dark, on his lawn, as he was getting into his car.

"Villiam Carlos Villiams," she cried hoarsely, "*I vant you!*" When the handsome doctor refused to yield to her entreaties, she hauled off and hit him a blow in the neck that he remembered for a long time. A policeman happened to walk by; with his aid, the Baroness was persuaded to return to New York.

But he was not done with her, for she came once again. This time he was ready, having practiced boxing with a punching bag in his cellar. Before she could attack him physically, as was her pleasant habit, he drove a stiff punch to her jaw; calling the police, he had her arrested, while she shouted: "What are you in this town? Napoleon?" On her promise to molest Williams no further, she was released and sent back across the Hudson. Later, with some money Williams sent her, she left for France; there she is reported to have died in a cheap hotel room where the gas jet was turned on, whether by herself or someone else was never known.

Williams' account of the Baroness had provided the high point of our ten-mile walk along the meadows on that gray Sunday of early winter. It turned out that Robert McAlmon, too, had an extraordinary tale to tell us, before we left, of a sudden miraculous change in his fortunes: within a few days he was to marry an English heiress he had recently met in New York, a Miss Winifred Ellerman (of the famous shipping family of that name), who afterward published poetry and prose under the pen name of "Bryher."

Later I learned that upon marrying, by the terms of an existing will, Miss Ellerman, who had been at odds with her family, came into possession of an independent fortune. Immediately after their wedding the pair were separated, as if by prearrangement, Mrs. McAlmon going to England with a woman friend,

while Robert went to Paris where he lived thereafter on the comfortable annuity—the "McAlimony" some jesters called it—
provided by his wife's estate.

In any case, McAlmon talked grandly, like a man who had
come into an inheritance, of publishing Williams' magazine,
Contact, formerly mimeographed, in a beautiful printed format,
and establishing a press for the advanced writers who were rejected by commercial publishers. McAlmon did found the Contacts Editions Press in Paris a year or two later, and performed
an excellent service in printing books by Williams, Gertrude
Stein, and the first stories and poems of Ernest Hemingway. He
also published a volume of his own collected tales. One of these
bore the title "The Hasty Bunch"; and James Joyce suggested
that this be used as title for the whole volume, since the phrase
"very aptly characterized" McAlmon's writings.

Toward the end of that walk in New Jersey, our talk sputtered
slowly along; it became a laggard fire of green wood that kept
going out. Williams was all charm; both Kenneth and I remained
on a very friendly footing with him all our lives. But McAlmon
assumed an anti-intellectual pose toward Burke, the man of
many aesthetic theories; he also seemed to regard me as if I
belonged to an equally reprehensible species of egghead.

We had grown weary of tramping for hours amid the dun
winter scenery and pungent stench of the Great Swamp of New
Jersey, and Burke and I had the feeling that "contact" between
our two parties in this meeting was beginning to fade off. We
had been walking through mean streets of the industrial suburbs, past dilapidated factories and warehouses, grimy railway
yards, coal bunkers, and mountains of rubble and tin cans; in
short, one of the ugliest and most blighted areas in all America,
which Ludwig Bemelmans somewhat later, in his book *My War
with the United States,* so aptly called the place of "Beautiful
Dreck"—we had all the panorama of American junk that is to
be seen on the outskirts of all our great cities. Alas, there was
no Regent's Park, no Serpentine, no palace-lined Tuileries Gar-

dens in which poets might take their Sunday walks, but only this Great Swamp of New Jersey.

It was high time for us to be off on our travels. American society had sunk so low that the machine politician, Warren G. Harding of Ohio, had just been elected to the presidency. "If Harding is elected," I had said to my wife, "we must leave the country." Several months after his inauguration we were on our way; when we returned, two years later, Harding was dead.

SIX

"MY SECOND COUNTRY":

PARIS IN 1921–1923

Our old French Line tub, the S.S. *Roussillon,* backed slowly out
of its berth into the Hudson River, with all its bunting flying
and its siren blowing, making a brave fiesta of our departure.
We took the long southerly course, touching Spain en route to
Le Havre, rolling gently in the blue Gulf Stream, while the sun
shone and the sea laughed at us all day long. There were few
tourists on board, but everyone was very gay over the new-found
table wine. With some of these tourists we formed close friendships, as one does during a long sea voyage, pledging each
other affection for life, then seeing our shipboard friends no
more after debarkation.

It was night when our boat train reached Paris, and we drove
across town to our cheap hotel in Montparnasse in one of those
1914 model taxis that had fought the first Battle of the Marne.
Passing the Place de la Concorde we did a half-circle around it,
marveling at its magnificent fountains in full play and at the
thousands of lights reflected in the river. In those days, New
York, by comparison, seemed dimly illuminated.

"Look at the lights, the lights of Paris!" my wife exclaimed,
and she burst into tears, as she often would when she heard
music.

"C'est Paris, la Ville Lumière!" the driver said to us sententiously.

Dropping our bags at the hotel, we rushed out to see the town. Turning the first corner into the Boulevard Montparnasse, we saw Clarence Newman sauntering down the street and looking very much at home here, for he had arrived a few months earlier. After a brief exchange we left him and entered an adjacent café. Newman would have told us all about Paris in his own vocabulary, but for this hour we wanted to receive our first impressions as our own.

For days we walked everywhere as goggling "rubbernecks," using our eyes but no Baedeker, and "doing" the entire city. We loved the core of ancient Paris along the River Seine; also the spacious Second Empire Paris, whose broad tree-lined avenues radiated from the heart of the antique city, and, following the plan of Baron Haussmann, encompassed broad plazas and public gardens and vistas of public buildings, a scene that invited one to walk or remain out of doors a good part of the day in that soft air and light. E.E. Cummings, who was in Paris at the time, afterward said very perceptively that it was a city that seemed above all human and designed for living; it gave one the sense of a "marriage of material with immaterial things" and was "a human coherence" in architectural form.

At the farther end of the Boulevard Montparnasse, I found the old Café de la Closerie des Lilas adjoining the Luxembourg Gardens, with its battalions of clipped trees drawn up in military ranks, its flower beds, and its great pearl gray sky which I came to love even on days of autumn rain. I would take books and paper with me and work at the terrace of the Closerie des Lilas, where one had almost the feeling of being in the country. With its old marble and wrought-iron tables and green-shaded lamps, the interior of the Closerie was then something out of the days of Paul Verlaine. I knew that it was the haunt of the Symbolist poets, some of whom, aged men in sober black, with wide-brimmed hats, like Paul Fort, the so-called "Prince of Poets," still appeared there to give readings of their poetry on occasion in the long, dim-lit room upstairs. I also used to read in the Luxembourg Gardens, where I was surrounded by a whole cheerful population of statues of the queens of France in medieval dress; and sometimes I would move to the quais by the river for my afternoons.

We came soon enough to the famous carrefour Vavin, the site of the several cafés mainly patronized by the Americans residing in the Montparnasse Quarter. The Dôme was at one side of the boulevard across the street from the Rotonde. These cafés were formerly the rendezvous of the Cubist painters—Picasso, Braque, Delaunay, and company—but most of the famous artists had by then moved across the river to the Montmartre. One saw these great men occasionally at the Rotonde and Dôme, however, on Sunday afternoons, when they were not working. The lesser artists of every nationality and color still lived in the old artists' quarter.

What was astonishing was the number of Americans here, scores of them who seemed to have been transplanted from Greenwich Village, and some already known to me. I could easily reconstruct their itinerary: Kansas City—New York—Paris; or the point of departure might have been Columbus, Ohio, or Brooklyn. And after journeying all the way to France they met each other!

In a letter of November 4, 1921, to a friend in New York, I wrote:

The cafés at the corner of the Boulevards Montparnasse and Raspail are *thick* with Americans. They cling to each other so closely that one tends to forget all the French one has learned in the United States.

After two weeks or so of adaptation, I found even the air of Paris stimulating. I began to write and meet people. The cheapness of living makes a man feel freer than elsewhere. And then the perfect ferment of activity all about you is stimulating in itself. . . . Paris seems the best place to starve in. . . . I suddenly got the conviction that I would stay in Paris a long time . . . .

If those people stuck to each other like postage stamps in the "American cafés," it was because many of them fell into straits, and, like Bohemians in Paris since time immemorial, relied on their compatriots to pull them through.

The French currency was then fairly stable at thirteen or fourteen francs to the dollar (against the prewar parity of five to one); inflation was reflected in the postwar rise of all prices, which made it hard for wage-earners to make ends meet. But compared with the cost of living in postwar America, everything here seemed about fifty per cent lower. Life had always been relatively cheap in France, with its abundance of home-grown food. We could enjoy a simple evening meal for as little as three or four francs, and a light lunch at a *crémerie*, topped off with magnificent cheese and wild strawberries, for half that sum. The good French bread alone was enough to sustain one. To be sure, I would earn much less than at home, and that only if I managed to sell things for publication in the United States. After paying our passage, we had a reserve capital of only three hundred dollars left, which dwindled steadily.

It was not long before my wife and I were in the same impecunious condition as most of our young compatriots. In the damp ground-floor apartment I had rented for the winter, I would waken at 8:00 A.M., the time the little blue-and-red uniformed letter carrier arrived, praying that a check for fifteen or twenty dollars might appear in the morning mail. Hurriedly, in bare feet, I would run across those cold, uncarpeted rooms to see what had been slipped under the door; but, oftener than not, finding nothing, would hasten back to bed to keep warm for a while. On some days we were reduced to taking only a late breakfast of café au lait with a spear of bread, which had to suffice until our evening meal. We rarely had to forego wine, since an excellent Anjou was to be had for nine cents the liter, drawn from a barrel in one of the basement shops bearing the sign BOIS CHARBON VINS.

Many of the Americans in Montparnasse often shared our feeling that the wolf was at the door. Some of them told me that they could hang on through the winter by moving into a small hotel and pledging their wardrobe trunk with the proprietor while running up a bill. In the spring, when the tourists arrived, there was always the chance of a job at one of the American or English newspaper bureaus or business offices.

At the Dôme, Harold Stearns remained the figure of the Eternal Exile, grown shabby, drinking steadily, and becoming more taciturn the more he drank. Often the *soucoupes* (those saucers with the price of one's drink labeled on them) piled up like a little hill, while poor Harold waited for some friend with money in purse to salvage him.

There were even two or three of my fellow tenants of Clemenceau Cottage, Greenwich Avenue, in Montparnasse at the time; Djuna Barnes worked at her own noncommercial writing, while depending on the proceeds of a few occasional articles sold to popular American magazines. At one period, I was told, she lived on as little as fifty dollars a month given her by a rich American woman. There was also Berenice Abbott, that formerly awkward young girl from Ohio, now very much a woman of the world in Paris. She was working as the assistant of Man Ray, the brilliant American photographer and painter (who removed himself to Paris in 1921). Berenice herself was to become, in time, one of the finest of modern photographers; but in the days of her apprenticeship, she earned barely enough to keep body and soul together.

Among the Americans at the Dôme, one who was very congenial to me was a tall redheaded youth of rather shy manner named Robert M. Coates. He had gone to Yale, served in the Navy Air Corps toward the end of the war, and worked a bit at a newspaper office; but had come to Paris with determination, although too little money, to take up writing in earnest.

In addition to the writers, there was quite a band of young American artists in residence. Among those I met in the winter of 1921 to 1922 were Niles Spencer, Julian Levi, Hilaire Hiler, and Wynn Holcombe, all of them living on small remittances from their families, except for Spencer, who had some private means. The artists worked through the day at their studios or schools, but at the stroke of five usually appeared at the Dôme. In Paris, Niles Spencer embraced the Cubist style for good and all. Thirty years later this accomplished painter used to say, "I'm just an old Cubist dating from the early twenties." He had come with his wife, Betty Lockett Spencer, an imposing and forthright example of the New Woman. At the month's end, when some of the members of this group of American art students had used up their remittances, they often turned up at the Spencers for dinner; or they would wait in the Dôme for other friends to take them out. Toward 1923, Hiler, a stout red-faced youth with sad eyes and drooping mustaches, in association with the small, peppery Holcombe, tried to run a little night club called "The Jockey," which they decorated themselves, and where they played American jazz.

In the off-season, during the chilly winters in Paris, the supposedly numerous colony of American "exiles" in Montparnasse numbered only a couple of hundred, as I recall. This estimate would include a considerable, though unknown, proportion of dilettantes or camp followers of the arts. Of these, only about one in ten enjoyed a private income permitting him to live in security. I can vouch for it that most of the Americans in Paris were rather hard up a good deal of the time, as my wife and I often were.

Therefore, I am not amused when I read overblown accounts of the Roaring Twenties in Paris, as set forth by scholars who are too young to have been on the scene; and feel that some corrections of these literary histories are in order. Even so estimable a writer as Professor Richard Blackmur of Princeton University has published some tish-tosh about the American "expatriates of the arts and the bars," who lived for years in Europe as "parasites" upon society. And another commentator has pictured the American residents in Paris as "intoxicated with their postwar freedom from moral and practical obligations and . . . as wonderfully irresponsible as they were futile."[1] Others, still, have represented us as abandoning ourselves on all-night drinking bouts or to carnivals of lechery with the Parisian *cocottes,* thanks to the favorable dollar exchange. But the truth is that most of us had few dollars to exchange.

To be sure, we had not come to Paris to behave like Epworth Leaguers. The young American artists in Montparnasse gradually assumed the dress and manners of the Bohemian crowd there. The cafés in the old artists' quarter were, in truth, international gathering places, full of Polish, Russian, Hungarian, Scandinavian, and even Japanese artists. These affected French workingmen's blouses or suits of cotton velveteen; and the Americans often imitated them, some wearing also broad-brimmed black hats and allowing their mustaches to grow luxuriantly. They also aped the rather free manners of the Montparnasse cafés, which derived of course from the demimonde rather than from proper French society—foreigners really had little contact with bourgeois French families, which observe the most rigid conventions in the world.

In the cafés the talk of the American habitués often assumed the amusingly matter-of-fact tone of the quarter's old denizens on the subjects of life and sex, or their girl friends, or of the little concubines they sometimes took up with. In the simplified American view, as expressed by the poet Cummings, France and Paris "meant freedom"; and the French, like other Europeans, were "non-puritans." Traditionally, the police of Paris tolerated every freedom except breach of the peace or crimes against property. In the early 1920's, most of the American residents who were working writers or painters committed no excesses unusual for their age or unattached situation, and a good many were "attached." There was a great deal of talk and gossip in the cafés about the American and other local personalities, and their indiscretions or their philanderings; but there was also much tedium in such talk. What if that nice middle-aged woman from Boston had caught the v.d. from her young Polish sculptor, whom she had been kindly supporting? Was it so very funny? Surely nothing can be more boring than hearing the accounts of *other* people's fornications.

A few Byronic figures loomed among us; they owned private incomes and showed no great urge or haste to fill many volumes with their written words. Laurence Vail was such a one, who wrote and also painted a little, but more often and more seriously seemed bent on painting the Left Bank of the River Seine red. The son of well-to-do American parents who lived long years in France, Laurence was a native-born Parisian, had been educated in both English and French schools, and, as a consequence, spoke with a mixed French and British accent. With his long mane of yellow hair always uncovered, his red or pink shirts, his trousers of blue sailcloth, he made an eye-filling figure in the quarter. Moreover, he was young, handsome, and for all his wild talk, a prince of a fellow; whenever he came riding in, usually with a flock of charming women in his train, he would set all the cafés of Montparnasse agog.

Laurence literally "knew everyone"; and even if he didn't, would buy him a drink. His vivacious sister, Clotilde, who resembled Laurence in appearance as in his high spirits, would usually be one of his café-crawling party, a band of Dionysiacs gathering followers at one bar after another. It is not surprising that Laurence's first wife, Peggy Guggenheim, whom he married in the spring of 1922, called him the "King of Bohemia."

At some point in the evening, Robert McAlmon, now, thanks to his marriage, a man of fortune also, would turn up to join the Vails. In the small hours of the morning, when they could hold no more firewater, they would sometimes repair to an all-night bistro near the Montparnasse Station for onion soup. Having eaten, the extravagant Vail and McAlmon would wind up the party by hurling their beer glasses at the mirrors along the wall, pay for the destruction, and be kicked out into the street.

A good deal of the life in the quarter was passed in the café, or at its terrace, as in a street scene. There were those who came to relax at the end of the day's work, and others whom the industrious literary apprentice, Ernest Hemingway, described as never waiting until five o'clock to begin their labors at the cafés. In America, most men took a quick gulp at a bar, then returned to office or home to bear their cross alone. But here, they adopted the leisurely habits of the Europeans to whom the café is not only another home, but also a neutral ground for an informal social life with café acquaintances or approachable strangers— in fact, a window opening upon the world. Warmed by coffee or alcohol, many forget their anxieties and assume a character different from that of every day among familiars, and often wholly imaginary. Before an audience that is always changing, including flower girls, Arab pedlars, and newspaper vendors, they become inspired to much taller talk than they would normally indulge in, passing themselves off as much bigger artists or men of affairs than they have ever been. How many amorous conquests I have heard tell of by the Hercules of the café table! And such tales of travel and high adventure in exotic regions the narrator had never visited. (And while he talks on perhaps That Woman will turn up again tonight?) Truly, in the café "all life is a stage," that is to say, a substitute for life, a wishful fantasy, a mirage. Not for anything would I have missed some of the great phoneys I have met in Paris cafés, whose talk was all the more diverting and challenging to the imagination because of its patent falsity.

However, the published accounts of Paris in the 1920's, which have tended to describe my American confreres as conducting conversations on mainly literary, aesthetic, and esoteric subjects, appear to me quite misleading. One such relates that they "mingled freely with their French contemporaries, . . . Their talk over the marble-topped tables of the Dôme and the Rotonde was a continual and bizarre excitement over the gods of the Dadaist movement."[2] In truth, few of the American habitués of Montparnasse absorbed any French literary influence, for the reason that French writers of note seldom came to those places. Their favorite rendezvous were on the Right Bank or in the St. Germain Quarter. (On one occasion, in 1922, I did happen to see Jean Giraudoux curiously observing, through his horn-rimmed spectacles, the antics of the "American barbarians" in the Rotonde.) All but a few of the Americans, like Harold Stearns, had very little to do with the representatives of that French civilization, which they pretended to admire as superior to the American variety.

Robert McAlmon has related that Djuna Barnes one day expressed disappointment at the limited form of social life in these parts. "I came to Europe to get culture," she declared. "Is this culture I'm getting?" If it amounted to no more than this idle talk, "then I might as well go back to Greenwich Village and rot there. Give me another Amer Picon." To which McAlmon replied that "It's nicer to go to hell in Paris."[3] Miss Barnes, however, stayed on for a good many years and managed to complete some highly original work, including *Nightwood*, a tour de force done in Tudor English, antique in flavor but showing not the slightest vestige of French influence.

"It occurs to me that seldom were French writers or painters in our group," McAlmon goes on to say.

In 1924, William Carlos Williams visited Paris and asked McAlmon to present him to some of the young French poets of the modern school. McAlmon said he didn't know any of them, and understood they had no talent anyway. Williams seemed surprised that, after three years' residence in Paris, McAlmon knew none of the avant-garde French. "I suppose Williams felt I let him down," McAlmon remarks rather lamely.

As for Ezra Pound, for more than ten years he had been exhorting Americans with a taste for the arts and for personal freedom to join him in his European exile; but now that they had come in great numbers he avoided most of them, declaring that the new generation of American "pilgrims" gave him the horrors.

I used to see the ungainly, red-bearded Pound occasionally marching down the Boulevard St. Michel, keeping himself about a mile away from the "American cafés"; he was then about thirty-seven, wore lemon-colored plus-fours, a velvet coat, a Windsor necktie, and sported a yellow cane. A few young Americans came to have tea with him, and he continued to be hospitable and to give excellent counsel to those he considered talented.

Although T.S. Eliot had written me two years before, inviting me to see Ezra Pound as well as himself when I came to Europe, I did not call on Pound, as some of my acquaintances did. He had played a leading part in the "American Renaissance," but his recent utterances seemed to me devoid of interest at the time I first came to Paris and, no doubt inspired by the change of skies, felt myself stirred by new ideas and new friendships. Pound even then seemed to be living in a world of his own illusions, formed by the books he was reading in Provençal, Italian, or Chinese; the *Cantos* themselves were in part a pastiche of his bookish borrowings, and divorced from the realities of this world.

Ernest Hemingway had arrived in Paris in the late autumn of 1921, armed with letters of introduction from Sherwood Anderson to Miss Sylvia Beach, proprietor of the Shakespeare bookshop in Paris, and to Miss Gertrude Stein. The letters described Hemingway as a sober young fellow, who, unlike other Americans abroad, would not be given to heavy drinking sprees. He came with his first wife, Hadley; in 1923 a son was born to them during a visit to Canada. Hemingway had made arrangements to do articles as a roving European correspondent for the Toronto *Star*. It is my impression that he liked to get to his work early in the morning, and also kept in good physical shape by exercise, such as boxing, which made him different from the other literary tourists. Up to this time he had never published anything save newspaper articles. However, in looking up an old copy of *The Double-Dealer* (New Orleans) for May, 1922—an excellent little magazine of the period, to which I contributed—I found what may have been Hemingway's first published literary exercise, a little fable entitled "A Divine Gesture," written in imitation of Anatole France's ironic sketches. The editors described Hemingway as "a young American living in Paris who enjoys the favor of Ezra Pound."

Lewis Galantière, a Chicagoan of literary tastes, who held a commercial job in Paris in the 1920's, has told me that when Hemingway first came to see Pound he felt all the irritation

which that egocentric gentleman often inspired in others without even trying to do so; and Hemingway proceeded to write
an obscene lampoon of Pound, which Galantière begged him
not to publish, holding it was unprintable. A few weeks later,
however, Hemingway submitted to Pound the manuscript of a
short story, which caused the poet to speak with great warmth
of his promise. Thereupon Hemingway reported to Galantière
that they "were now getting along fine." He explained: "I'm
teaching Pound how to box, and he's helping me with my writing." Nevertheless, in 1924 Hemingway did publish some profane verses about Pound that appeared in English in the German review *Der Querschnitt:*[4]

> They say Ezra is the s——t . . .

runs one of its lines; and there is also the obscene suggestion
that a "monument" be built in honor of Pound out of wind.

My whimsical college classmate, Slater Brown, turned up in
Paris, and made an excellent companion for my afternoon
walks. During the preceding summer (1921), he had spent
several months at the Cummings' summer home in Chocorua,
New Hampshire, where Cummings, in a prolonged session of
writing, completed *The Enormous Room,* the story of their
prison-camp experience, while Slater Brown remained at his
side, prompting his memory. In the autumn of 1921, Cummings
and Brown, having come to Paris, went off an a bicycle trip of
two thousand miles, to Naples and back, often sleeping in the
open by the roadside, and stopping at many points on the way,
especially Rome, where Cummings said he spent whole days
lying on the floor of the Sistine Chapel, gaping at Michelangelo's
murals.

I had first met Cummings in 1920 in his big dusty studio on
Fourteenth Street, New York, which he shared with Brown and
a young artist from Boston named Edward Nagle. Cummings'
very eccentric friend, Joe Gould, a decayed gentleman from

Maine and Harvard, who had been an inhabitant of New York's Skid Row for many years, was also on hand at the time. He was a bewhiskered dwarf in oversized, cast-off clothing, who kept writing his multiple-volumed, ever unfinished *History of the Modern World*, made up principally of anecdotes of all the persons he met in his daily rounds. In effect, Gould served as Cummings' court jester.

The poet's relations with Gould show a curious side of his nature. He would begin, in boyish spirits, to make fun of Gould; but as his sallies became ever wilder and sharper, the farce would become a little cruel. Gould, who evidently enjoyed being thus tormented, would improvise some very funny stories himself, plus a profane couplet or limerick at the expense of some eminent public figure like President Wilson or Professor Josiah Royce, under whom he had studied. Whereupon Cummings and the others would give Joe a little spare change, for he lived by panhandling in the "Village" bars, where he was esteemed as a famous buffoon. If one of his friends happened to be affluent and gave him a lump sum, five or ten dollars, then Joe would draw himself up to his full four feet ten inches and say in his precise, dignified, and nasal tone: "Well now, my dear fellow, that lets you off for awhile!"

At first, Cummings lived in a crummy hotel in the labyrinth of narrow winding streets that make up the old Latin Quarter. Later, he moved to a furnished room in Montmartre where, for economy's sake, he used to cook his lunch over an alcohol burner. There he painted his pictures and wrote his "millions of poems"; for he was in very happy mood to find himself in Paris ("heaven on earth" to him) and among its cheerful "impuritans." He was also in love, just then, with a very attractive young woman who sometimes came all the way from New York to visit him. Moreover, his poems were at last beginning to be published; for his Harvard friends, Scofield Thayer and James S. Watson, Jr., had recently reorganized the monthly *The Dial* as an imposing literary review which printed Cummings in quantity. *The Dial* purported to be the *Revue des Deux Mondes* of America; but some wag called it "a sort of postgraduate version of the *Harvard Literary Monthly*."

Cummings' *The Enormous Room* appeared in the spring of 1922 and enjoyed a great success of esteem, but its sales at first were modest. His earnings from writing were still minute, and he depended in great measure on small remittances from his parents.

He was nothing if not vivacious in those days; and, in fact, was a man of irrepressible wit and a great mimic as well. His pale blue eyes, which Edmund Wilson once described as "narrow and self-regarding," used to take on a wicked light as with breakneck speed, he delivered himself of his monologues that ranged from absurd variations on President Harding's clichés or the one-hundred-per-cent-American orations of Chicago's "Big Bill" Thompson, to parodies of the saccharine verses of Witter Bynner and Harold Vinal.

At twenty-eight Cummings was tall, bony, and long-legged, with a mop of blond hair. Sometimes his expression was a little mocking and hard; he would throw back his head and jut his jaw when in his "challenging" mood. But often he wore a fine broad smile, and his sudden laughter was infectious; he seemed then just a light-hearted minister's son in Paris. By contrast, Slater Brown, his constant companion of those days, was of medium height, very personable, and also had very sweet and disarming manners—which were somewhat deceptive inasmuch as he had, in his own way, considerable temperament and a sly wit that usually found expression in a tone of underemphasis.

In contrast with his power of language, Cummings' range of intellectual interests seemed limited, consisting in two or three ruling ideas: Cummings must be "alive"; he must live in "freedom" and in full reaction against the typically Protestant-American training he had received—that is, as a non-puritan. He loved his parents tenderly, and wrote warm testimonials to them after their death; they, in turn, were most devoted and generous to him. What is more, they were cultivated enough to tolerate what others might have considered "idleness" in their son—which was, of course, nothing of the sort, but a prolific outpouring of poems and drawings, produced with such speed that his slower-moving friends often felt confounded watching him function. Nevertheless, though the Reverend Mr. Cummings admired and aided his son, there were often rather heated arguments between them, because e.e. was certainly in full rebellion against the family values and especially his father's puritan-Unitarian authority.

It is a curious fact also that the older Cummings was for years the head of the Watch and Ward Society of Boston, thus an ally of Anthony Comstock and his censorious league, helping to police the morals of the people of Boston against indecent theater shows, movies, and books. I have often wondered what the Reverend Mr. Cummings must have felt on reading his son's epopees, joyous and unconfined, on the pleasures of the flesh, or his rude drawings of burlesque queens.

Cummings first escaped from Boston to New York, where he discovered Second Avenue, Minsky's Burlesque Theatre, and the Cafe Royale at Twelfth Street (now demolished). This was the rendezvous of Jewish journalists, chess players, and actors of the Yiddish language theater. In those days he was quite fond of his East Side circle—a world so exotic to him after Unitarian Cambridge—and especially of the Jewish poet, Machum Yud, who once called Cummings "an allrightnik." Cummings asked: "What does that mean?" And Yud replied: "Oh it means Cummings, he is too much allright." There was also an actress of the Jewish theater whom Cummings cultivated for a time, though, to his disappointment, nothing came of it.

Up to the age of twenty-two or twenty-three Cummings had been writing rhymed lyrical poems in highly regular meters and with the rhetoric of Swinburne. Around 1917 one of his Harvard friends, the very knowledgeable Foster Damon, urged him to stop being romantic and "go modern" by writing *vers libre,* showing him specimens of the new French poets and their experiments in a rebellious typography (as instanced by Apollinaire's *Calligrammes*). Cummings then reversed himself, and

began to use a most lawless orthography, running words together, dropping the majuscule, and breaking the solid lines of
his verses into flying typographical fragments. The undertone
of romantic sentiment was often in evidence, nonetheless.

In Paris, avoiding the well-worn path of the American café-
goers, Cummings found his favorite byways in Montmartre, with
its music-hall shows of nude women thickly covered with pink
powder and standing as if in a trance, though the places were ill-
heated in winter. Or he would go out to the working-class
quarter of the Place de la République, with its street singers and
popular fairs; or to the Cirque d'Hiver and its clowns; or even
the Luxembourg Gardens with its ponds, children, colored balloons, toy boats, and merry-go-round—all of which went pell-mell
into his lyrical-impressionist poetry.

Both Cummings and Brown then had a youthful disposition
to untidiness about their dress and their rooms, which (so Cummings relates in *The Enormous Room*) got them into difficulties
with their officers in the Ambulance Corps. Occasionally, however, one of Cummings' or Brown's respectable female relatives
would arrive from Boston to tour Paris. Then the two would
rush off to a public bath, wash and shave themselves, and show
the old ladies from Boston the most elevating sights in town, including the Jardin des Plantes and the Cluny Museum. That
done, they would go back with relief to their unshaven and
grimy ways and their prowls in all the back alleys of the city,
which contained for Cummings all that was "alive" and "human."

On a number of occasions Cummings joined my wife and me
for a drink and supper in some bistro of Montparnasse. He
would come loping along the street toward us, wearing tennis
sneakers, a worn shirt, and seedy jacket, arriving breathless
with excitement over something new and strange he had seen. It
might have been an Algerian rugseller he had engaged in conversation, or something he had sketched at the circus. On one of
our first meetings in Paris he told us a story that, presumably,
reflected on his own sometimes unprepossessing appearance.

"I was at Harry's New York Bar, near the Opéra, and a Harvard man drew up alongside and said to me: "What do you do?' 'Poetry,' I answered. He looked at me, unbelieving, and said: 'Hell, we got a poet, a Harvard man, who's greater than Kipling, writes the most wonderful poetry.' "

"What's his name?" asked Cummings.

"E.E. Cummings," the man said challengingly.

"Do you know him?" the poet asked.

"Hell, yes; very charming guy, short, pale, dark," the man went on.

"Never heard of him. He must be lousy," Cummings said.

It is my recollection that Cummings fell into difficulties with the police of Paris on at least one occasion, which I place in the early winter of 1922. Slater Brown would come in and drily, with impassive countenance, report such bits of astonishing news about his friend.

"Cummings"—one never called him Edward or Estlin— "Cummings was arrested by the police last night and then released." But why was he arrested? we asked in concern. "Oh, he always rides around on his bicycle wearing rubber sneaks and the police thought he was a suspicious character. You know, the second-story men in Paris wear rubber shoes so you can't hear them when they come in through the window."

"Well," I said laughing, "it's true, Cummings sometimes does look a bit like a 'suspicious character.' "

Brown, in fact, avoided giving us the true reason for Cummings' arrest, which I learned later. He had had the whim to pass water at a dark corner of the boulevards on the Champs Elysées, just as some policemen came riding by. At the police station, after showing his American passport and protesting *"qu'il n'a jamais eu l'intention de pisser sur Paris,"* but loved her with all his heart, he was released with a reprimand. Perhaps his unhappy wartime experience had affected Cummings so that he always became a little furtive when he was in the presence of police or of Army officers, whom he detested.

For our apéritif we usually drank vermouth. But on one

afternoon, Cummings and I ordered some Calvados and my wife, though unaccustomed to strong liquors, also ordered it. Cummings exclaimed to her: "Heavens, you're not going to drink *that!*" He had been merry enough and full of capers up to now, but suddenly assumed a tragic expression and began to tell us perfect horror stories of how the French-Norman peasants made this apple brandy out of putrescent fruit that had turned to green slime, mixed with every sort of *immondices* in filthy or rotten barrels. My very impressionable young wife listened wide-eyed, then began to feel faint, and turned green in the face herself. Seeing the effect of his words, the knavish Cummings continued his tirade, piling on ever fresh horrors, until I stopped him and led my fainting wife out into the winter air and then homeward.

He was forever trying to pull one's leg; one had to be on guard against his heartless mischief. His sallies at the expense of some of his friends or acquaintances were sometimes so destructive, that on one occasion in New York I saw Hart Crane, who was being victimized, burst into tears.

On the other hand, Cummings could be very handsome in his relations with people, when he chose to be so. As I was then much given to argument, and he was very contra-suggestive himself, our conversations became a tug of war, whether on the merits of Michelangelo or the literary methods of James Joyce. But when I called on Cummings to contribute some of his poems without payment to one of the little magazines I was editing in Europe at the time, he responded generously, making repeated contributions of some of his most amusing pieces.

Though he was thoroughly at home in Paris, and learned to speak French fluently, I am not aware of his having made contact with any contemporary French writers until I introduced him to some of the younger people with whom I had become acquainted. By contrast, his friend, John Dos Passos, who was also in Paris at the time, showed more intellectual curiosity, and followed the work of the new literary schools with intense interest, particularly that of Jules Romains and Blaise Cendrars, whose influence is reflected in his early writings.

To complete my (partial) roll of young Americans who, though transplanted to French soil, were neither idlers nor wasters, there was my old companion of Clemenceau Cottage in Greenwich Village, Malcolm Cowley, established, thanks to a fellowship he had won, at the University of Montpellier, four hundred miles south of Paris. He was studying classical French literature and writing a monograph on Racine; but he complained of the boredom of university life in the provinces, where he was out of touch with the intellectual ferment of Paris.

By eating at a pension near the Sorbonne for a whole month, among chattering French and foreign students, we economized and also learned to speak the language. Lessons in conversation given us by the daughter of the *patronne* improved our diction; while some lectures I attended at the Sorbonne whetted my interest in establishing contact with the living literature of France hitherto known only in printed form.

I had undertaken to write some articles for *The Double-Dealer* which would come under the category of "Paris Letters." My first subject was a study of Jules Romains, whom I desired to know more about. His novel *La Mort de quelqu'un*, translated into English in 1914 as *The Death of a Nobody*, thanks to its technical innovations had aroused intense interest in the literary world. It was a novel without a plot; its hero dies on page one, and the repercussions of his death upon an anonymous group of persons, merely encountered by the hero, become the subject of the pages that follow. Romains had established himself as the head of a new school of writers calling themselves "Unanimists," whose novels gave expression to a sort of urban pantheism, and pictured crowds of unknowns rather than individuals treated in detail or analyzed.

The surface effect of such writing was curious, if dull. One felt that in Romains' art the machinery, the formulae prescribed by his theories were too obtrusive; it was like a geometrician writing fiction. Nevertheless, James Joyce was said to have been influenced by Romains in conceiving his *Ulysses* as a panorama of Dublin; while Dos Passos used a similar method, though more interestingly than Romains himself, in *Manhattan Transfer* (1925) and in his later novels of the *U.S.A.* trilogy. Kenneth Burke had also found the "Unanimist" scheme intriguing, and managed to complete an example of the plotless novel in his *Towards a Better Life*.

More lately, the Paris press had reported that M. Romains was about to open a school for poets at the Théâtre du Vieux-Colombier. The newspaper wits cried scandal, one of them saying:

> Shades of Victor Hugo! The Muse will no longer visit the pale young man in a tiny attic room without first inquiring of the concierge whether he is versed in all the media and bears an authentic license . . .

After arranging for an interview, I came to the Vieux Colombier and, on an upper floor of the building, found Jules Romains, a dry little man, with a fine brow and a long, intelligent nose. I queried him as to what he hoped to achieve by forming a *school* for poets. He replied in rather reasonable and qualified terms. There was a "literary war" raging in France between the exponents of tradition and the advocates of experiment, between the extremists of conservatism and the literary "anarchists." The very businesslike Romains intended to seek the golden mean. Young people would come and work together under men of experience, "trying to develop definite laws of technique, as had been done in other great ages." In the favoring atmosphere of such a school, the student-poets would carry on research in the critical knowledge of poetry—as novices of painting worked in an atelier under the eye of a master—and this would be conducive to sound creative work.

"But what if no men of genius come to your school?" I asked.

"That does seem to be a problem," Romains said with a trace of anxiety in his manner. "But surely every age has its quota of talent."

M. Romains was decidedly a man of theories. My attitude remained politely skeptical; I do not believe that anything much came of his School for Poets, whose diploma, in my opinion, guaranteed nothing. But on the practical level, M. Romains was a pioneer who started in business too early for his time. Today, America has a dozen "writers' summer conferences" and many more university courses in "creative literature" for apprentice writers, which in most cases are given by people who are not doing much in the way of creative literature themselves.

I decided that I would wait and investigate further the embattled literary schools of Paris. What seemed so amusing was that each of them had its *chef d'école,* its special rules, its center at some favorite café; and if you were seen crossing the street to enter the café belonging to an opposing artistic camp you were practically a dead man.

A letter from Hart Crane, received in early November, 1921, told me of a friend of his named Gorham B. Munson, domiciled in Paris, whom he wanted me to know. As I remember it, a letter from Munson followed, and I invited him to call at my room, then in the Boulevard du Port Royal. He was a pale, blond, already balding young man of about twenty-six, with impressive waxed and pointed mustaches, also a minister's son who, after some years of teaching, had come to Paris to write. His manner was propitiating, though a little nervous; for Hart Crane had written him that I was a formidable character, "the most *acute* critic of poetry."[5] We had a friendly talk; at his request, I showed him some poems I had written, and he remarked: "Although I know very little about poetry, I feel that these are superlatively good."

In reminiscences published in 1932, after he had "drastically revised" his opinion of me, Munson said of our first meeting:

. . . I formed the impression that [Josephson] was of aristocratic bearing and most exacting tastes. I looked forward to seeing this brilliant personage. . . . I was, thanks to Crane's opinion . . . prepared to be bowled over.

I met a rather stiff young man, narrow in his interests, brittle in his thinking, and at moments charmingly pompous in speech. A certain pathos in his character was appealing. I looked at his verse. It impressed me, without, I may say, taking my breath away.

At the lodgings we took in December, 1921, a cheap ill-furnished studio apartment at seven rue Compagne Première, our next-door neighbors were two Americans, Arthur Moss and Florence Gilliam Moss. They had formerly published one of the little magazines of Greenwich Village called *The Quill*, and were now starting a magazine of similar type in Paris, to be printed in English, which they named *Gargoyle*. Moss very hospitably invited me to contribute to *Gargoyle*, the first of the transatlantic reviews, which ran to light gossipy articles about the theater and art world. To its credit, it also published occasionally a number of distinguished poets, among them Hilda Doolittle and Hart Crane.

Munson had also contributed to this review, and one day discussed with me the possibility of improving its quality. I urged that we needed something better, a magazine in which new writers of talent, bound together by a common outlook on art and life and who were interested in new literary experiment rather than in repeating old patterns, could exhibit their work. Coincidentally, in the autumn of 1921, Malcolm Cowley had published an essay in the book section of the New York *Evening Post*, entitled "The Youngest Generation." A postwar generation, he said, was growing up, whose members, though little known to the public, possessed talent, had some wartime experiences in common, and were diverging from the main stream of American letters. They felt more deeply interested in the problems of literary form, in craftsmanship, and in the classical modes of literature than the writers of the preceding generation; instead of trying to imitate English authors, as did so many of their elders, they were attracted to the great models of French literature, such as Flaubert, Baudelaire, and Huysmans. Cowley went on to predict that they might someday form a new "school"; what they needed, he said, was a literary organ of their own. He concluded by naming a few members of the Youngest Generation: Kenneth Burke, Cummings, Dos Passos, Foster Damon, and Slater Brown.

Munson, on reading Cowley's article, was fired by the idea of publishing just such a magazine for the new generation. He told me that he still had a good part of the sum of one thousand dollars with which he and his wife, Liza, had come to Europe, and thought of using it to print the new writers. There were other American literary periodicals; but *Poetry,* thanks to its guiding genius, Miss Harriet Monroe, still favored the neo-Victorian style in poetry; *The Dial* was more forward-looking, but gave preference to old authors of international renown, such as Anatole France and Arthur Schnitzler. I remarked that I happened to know the young men mentioned in Cowley's article, and promised that if Munson undertook to issue such a magazine I would solicit their support for it.

In January, 1922, I made a journey to Berlin and stayed there a week, seeking material for magazine and newspaper articles I was writing on financial subjects. Germany was just then entering upon the spiral of money inflation deliberately created by the Weimar Republic as a form of passive resistance to the exorbitant demands of the Allies for reparations payments. When the German currency unit, formerly worth four to the dollar, swiftly shrank to a tiny fraction of its old parity, to eighty or ninety marks to the dollar, the whole German social system seemed to go insane; prices changed every day and no one knew whether he was, economically speaking, alive or dead. Berlin, the capital of a defeated and hungry people, seethed with revolt and counterrevolt, and, in its desperate mood, seemed fascinating to me. (I would return there for a longer stay later that year.) I found that in terms of "hard" dollars, life there was cheap indeed: I was able to live in a good hotel for a week and do the theaters and night clubs with American friends for something like ten dollars. When I returned to Paris and informed Munson that I thought he could print five hundred copies of a small magazine in Central Europe for about twenty dollars, he said he would definitely go ahead. In this enterprise we were to be partners for a brief season.

Out of curiosity about all the wars of art going on in Paris, I attended concerts of new music by Erik Satie and the group called *Les Six,* being greatly amused by the tonal humor of Satie, and almost frightened out of my wits by the violence of Honegger's *Pacific 231.* I also visited the modern art galleries then showing Cubist canvases almost exclusively; and went to the theater to see the literary burlesques of Jean Cocteau, including *Le Bœuf sur le toit,* in which the players spoke their lines through Futurist masks, and *Les Mariés de la Tour Eiffel,* the settings and costumes for both works being done by the new artists of the School of Paris. Cocteau, that Child of the Century sometimes associated with the Dadaists, but now divorced from them, was one of the reigning idols of *les jeunes;* but his affectations of Baudelairean dandyism seemed to me forced, as his fantasies, his paradoxes, and his style generally also seemed contrived.

One evening in the late autumn, at the Rotonde, which was very quiet because the superfluity of tourists had departed, Gorham Munson introduced me to Man Ray, who was associated with the Dadaists, and his table companion, Tristan Tzara, one of the founders of that movement. Tzara was a pale, dark-haired, gray-eyed little man, who wore a monocle; his very intelligent and animated face might have resembled that of Leon Trotsky or James Joyce, if each had shaved off his beard.

I had read how Tzara and Dadaism, first appearing in combination in Zürich in 1916, had come and conquered Paris
four years later, and since then had carried on a scandalous
sort of propaganda aimed at overthrowing all our conventional
notions of things. I therefore pressed Tzara with questions,
too eagerly and naïvely, no doubt. Was Dada like Cubism or Futurism? I asked. No, Tzara replied, with a characteristically sardonic smile; it was opposed to those schools, was against all
"isms"; in fact, "Dada is not anything, and it is everything."
He continued in this mystifying tone; and, as in our discussion
I touched on certain names, certain authors I was interested
in, such as Gide or Romains, he gave me a demonstration of
the vocabulary of vituperation that belonged to the Dada style:
"How can you read such rubbish? Romains is a cretin!" Gide
also was *"de la littérature"* (a damning word), and Dada was
against literature as well as all culture. The novel was dead;
Tzara himself only read a little poetry, "out of weakness," for
he did not admit to being consistent in his views. If I had come
to Paris to improve myself, he counseled, "Read Littré, the big
Littré dictionary. There is an admirable work of the highest
art. I keep it at my bedside; begin reading at Z and go backward."

Was the technique of Dada poetry based on the principle of
free association of thought, or of dissociation? It was all very
simple, he said, and he demonstrated: taking up a newspaper,
he tore an article in it to tiny bits, then threw them in a heap
into his hat. "I cut out separate words, usually with a pair of
scissors, mix them all up in my hat, then take them out in any
order, and presto, there is my poem!" he said.

I thought he was pulling my leg, and for a moment felt an-
noyed, but then laughed, and went off with Munson, translating
our talk which had been carried on in rapid French. The great
panjandrum of international Dadaism, I explained, had negated
and contradicted everything I said and answered my questions in riddles. I determined, however, to find out more about
the French variety of Dadaism.

The little monocled Tzara was quite a wag, and often equal to some outrageous *boutade*, either improvised or carefully rehearsed, as is often the case with men of wit. Our next meeting occurred at an extremely odd costume ball we happened to attend during the winter carnival season in Paris. I had heard some talk in the Café Dôme one afternoon about the notorious Magic City Ball to be held that very night at the amusement center called Luna Park. It sounded as if it were to be a sort of Roman bacchanalia of all the art students and Bohemians and all the queers and freaks of Montparnasse and Montmartre, judging from what the Americans in the café were saying. The notables and the madcaps of Paris would be there, prancing about in the weirdest of costumes. My wife and I were naturally very keen to observe such a massive orgy, but our hearts sank when we learned that entry would cost us twenty-five francs (two dollars) apiece, for we were now thoroughly flat.

At our table sat Cuthbert Wright, a poet who had contributed to the anthology *Eight Harvard Poets*, and whom we knew only slightly; he was a man who often wore a sad or sullen expression and drank a good deal. Noticing how unhappy we looked, Wright suddenly came forward and generously offered to lend me the money needed for the tickets.

The ball, in truth, exceeded our wildest imaginings. Between three and four thousand costumed guests were there, the men dressed as women and the women as men, so that none could judge which sex he was dancing with. They were by no means all deviants; but some among the contingent of homosexuals exhibited such extreme forms of coquetry that they made the daringly costumed women seem, by comparison, almost dowdy.

Suddenly we saw Tristan Tzara go by, his face all painted and powdered, masquerading as a Roman matron. He looked unbelievable, the very wreck of a female creature.

He came up to us, and said: "Ah, I know what you are thinking about me," giving his rapid and nervous laugh. "But you are quite wrong. No one knows the secret of Tristan Tzara's sex! There are some who say I am a homosexual; and others who say I am impotent. But the truth is that I am a virgin!''

In point of fact, he had a very attractive American girl from Philadelphia as his *petite amie* at the time and was kept busy warding off some of his friends, who were trying to steal her.

Some time passed and the sickness of my pocketbook was not easily cured. "Paris is a good place to starve in," I had said in a letter at the time, adding: "It's not a disgrace to be poor in Paris." But another note to one of my friends in New York, dated February 20, 1922, carries accents of alarm:

I am writing you at one of my darkest moments. My resources have dwindled from several thousand to 50 francs, while I wait for . . . more funds. Money is owing me for stories, essays, poems, financial articles, and nothing has come for six weeks. . . .

The day after the Magic City Ball, I took my wife's plain gold wedding ring to the Mont-de-Piété, the dreary municipal hock shop of Paris, where, after waiting for hours and filling out many forms, I received for it only ten francs, about ninety cents. We had an appointment for tea at our apartment with Gorham Munson and his wife; my wife blithely exchanged the ten francs we had left for teacakes and cookies. Munson was on the point of leaving Paris and brought a couple of bottles of champagne to celebrate the event. After the Munsons had left, we were both empty, save for the *petits fours* we had consumed; but, being filled with good wine, fell fast asleep at an early hour, without bothering about supper. The next morning there was a letter under the door with a check for twenty dollars from *The Double-Dealer*, which sufficed us for another week.

I had written to my father for a loan, but did not know that he had fallen seriously ill at the time; when he did send me a bank draft by cable, its delivery was delayed for several weeks.

On one of those hungry days, I walked alone as far as Montmartre and there used some of my last coins to visit the Cirque

Médrano and see its famous clowns, hoping they would distract my mind from my dilemma. As I came out, it was night and snow was falling, a very soft snow that soon melted. All along my line of march, from the circus down the boulevard, there were streetgirls waiting to solicit each single man. A girl fell into step with me and pleaded most earnestly that I come with her. She was plainly dressed and, to my surprise, looked extraordinarily young and pretty, about sixteen or less, I would have judged, and hardly like a professional. She had great dark eyes on whose long lashes the snowflakes clustered momently, as we walked along together. I told her that I had no money, and saw that she was crying. There were only five francs left in my pocket; I offered them to her, saying: "I am sorry, I cannot go with you, but this may help you." The girl looked up at me with an expression of indignation, spurned the money, and rushed away.

In those days there were prostitutes covering their beat at every street corner on the main avenues. They would be stamping their feet all winter by the same street lamp, as I came home every night, many of them looking like stout servant maids from the provinces, their faces ruddy with the cold. I got to know some of them by sight. They would hail me and I would reply with a cheery greeting, wishing them luck, as I hurried by. The Frenchmen assured me that they cared nothing about these women; they were "for foreigners"; but the Americans in Paris generally managed very well without them.

At about this time a note reached me from Harold A. Loeb, editor and publisher of *Broom,* saying he had just arrived in Paris and would like me to dine with him. He and Alfred Kreymborg had recently launched their very imposing-looking "International Magazine of Arts and Letters," which began publication in Rome, in November, 1921. *Broom* had recently accepted four poems of mine and an article under the heading of "Paris Letter." Harold Loeb, inwardly a very romantic soul, outwardly with the appearance of a prosperous American doctor or businessman, conducted us to one of the good restaurants of our quarter, where, being fierce with hunger, we ate like wolves, cheered up, and eagerly discussed plans for my contributing more articles from Paris. I was also engaged to do translations of the avant-garde French and German writers. Though these assignments were offered at rates low even for those times, they helped pull us through a bad period.

Meanwhile, I had been hunting relentlessly for a job on one of the small English-language newspapers. At last I received word from a café acquaintance, Norman Matson, that he was leaving for London and would arrange to turn over to me the position he had held as a reporter for an English racing sheet called *The Paris Telegram*. I was to meet him at a café in the evening to receive my instructions; he was late, and I became so edgy that, although I said nothing, I fairly seethed with anger when he arrived, as he could see by my expression. Twenty years later, when I had a chance meeting with him again at a beach on Cape Cod, he recalled the incident clearly, saying: "You looked so hungry and fierce that I was sure you would cut my throat if I did not fix that job for you."

I was soon busy for part of the day translating clippings from the French newspapers to help fill up our poor sheet, which depended for its small public on the tourists' interest in the afternoon racing reports. Now earning what amounted almost to "an American salary," and something over that by the sale of articles and stories, I felt uncommonly affluent. If Paris was a good place in which to starve, it seemed now, with money jingling in my pocket, the most miraculous city on earth.

SEVEN

THE

DADAISTS

> We spit on humanity. . . . Dada is the abolition of
> all logic. . . . There is a great negative work of de-
> struction to be done. We must sweep everything
> away and sweep clean.
> —TRISTAN TZARA

On the occasion of my first meeting with Man Ray, he had invited me to attend a forthcoming exhibition of his paintings
and photographs, promising that I would have an opportunity
to meet with some members of the Dada movement and learn
what it was all about.

The vernissage at the gallery-bookshop called La Librairie Six
was a most engaging sort of Dada soiree. Man Ray's machine-
objects and so-called "Rayograms" were displayed along the
walls; the Rayograms were made through contact of diverse
simple objects, such as domestic utensils, combs, and the like,
against a light-sensitive sheet. One oil painting called "Cadeau,"
shown at this first exhibition of Man Ray's work in Paris, was a
picture of a pressing iron to whose ordinarily smooth bottom a
row of steel spikes was affixed that looked as if it was guaranteed
to tear apart anything it touched—a symbol of fearful destruc-
tiveness.

The significance of Man Ray's show, which I did not fully
appreciate at the time, was that it represented a union of distinctively American artistic innovations with French tendencies.
Man Ray was a native of Philadelphia who had been strongly
influenced by seeing the Armory Show in New York in 1913,
when he was in his early twenties. Then he had joined forces
with the French artists, Marcel Duchamp and Francis Picabia,
who were in New York in 1915, and were creating machine-
objects à la fantaisie, or pictures of them, in response to the
Machine Age and its "primitive" artifacts to be seen everywhere in America. Their mechanistic objects and "ready-mades"
were really provocative "actions" on their part, and constituted
a (pre-Dada) rebellion against all the art schools and conventional ideas of art at the time. Photographs of their work, and
Man Ray's also, had appeared in Alfred Stieglitz's reviews,
Camera Work and 291, as early as 1915 and 1916. Thus, part
of the inspiration for Dada "anti-art" was furnished by Duchamp,
Picabia, and Man Ray, and derived from the U.S.A.

For this occasion the ceiling of La Librairie Six was festooned
with brightly colored toy balloons, which were hung together so
closely that one had to brush them aside to see the pictures.
The place was filled with young people in their twenties, very
bourgeois in appearance and dress, but full of laughter at one
another's sallies and capers. Without alcohol they nevertheless
seemed intoxicated. Evidently they did not make the mistake of
taking Art seriously—with a capital A. At a given signal, several
of the young men in the crowd applied their lighted cigarettes
to the ends of strings attached to the balloons overhead and all
of them went popping off, while the crowd of about fifty persons
became as merry as if it were Bastille Day.

I happened to introduce myself as an American visitor to one
of the persons near me, a tall slender young man of charming
manners and very delicate physiognomy, who gave his name as
Louis Aragon. I had already read his work with admiration in
copies of La Nouvelle Revue Française while in Maine the preceding summer, and told him as much. Very obligingly he gave

me a rendezvous for the following day. Aragon was then one of the leading figures in the French Dada movement and co-editor, with André Breton and Philippe Soupault, of the review defiantly called *Littérature*. I met both of Aragon's colleagues and also the poet Paul Éluard on the occasion of Man Ray's show.

My talk with Aragon, the next afternoon, took place in one of the doctors' offices of an old hospital out near the Porte de Vincennes, where Aragon was then completing his medical internship. He had evidently arranged not to be called to his hospital duties, for he talked—nay discoursed—at me for something like four hours. I had heard a good deal in Paris of the antics of the Dadas, who were often rated as just another of the new art cults, designed to give the bourgeois a few shudders, and I had been disposed to take them only half-seriously. I was not prepared to find in Aragon a man of extraordinary eloquence, who took fire as he spoke, and sounded like something out of the pages of Chateaubriand. (Aragon now would not approve of this analogy, but he was then only twenty-four.) He had an antique Latin head and a Roman nose, for he was of Provençal origin; often during his talk, when aroused and giving emphasis to his statements, he made the characteristic challenging gesture of throwing his head back, his nose and chin high in the air. His dress was rather sober; he was always clad in black or navy blue. But there were touches of dandyism in his appearance then, such as his black string or bow neckties, and a thin mustache he sported.

The story he told, however, of the wartime experiences of himself and his comrades, and of their return to civil life, had nothing of affectation in it. We Americans knew the cold statistics of the war in Europe, indicating that some twenty or more millions were casualties; but we could not calculate its unexpected human consequences. The greater part of Aragon's generation had been killed or maimed; those who survived, at the coming of peace, had been left not merely with the sense of being "lost," but with the consciousness that they must drive for an all-out revolt against the civilization that had brought forth this long orgy of destruction.

While still in his teens, Aragon had served in the war as a medical officer, and had been decorated for heroic action at the front—as he would be decorated again for combat action with a tank division in World War II. His friend, Paul Éluard, had been gassed; Philippe Soupault had also been invalided out of the Army; while André Breton, as a medical student, had worked in the bedlam of hospitals for shell-shocked and crazed soldiers. Meeting together at the end of the war, these young men of letters found that they had in common an overwhelming sense of revulsion against the "culture" of their country and their time. Their early writings were already imbued with the mood of scorn (le mépris) toward a society whose traditions of family, religion, and patriotism seemed nothing more than a façade. Thus, they were led in time to embrace Dadaism, a movement of intellectual revolt born of the great war.

It was, in truth, an international phenomenon: initiated in 1916 by Tzara and a group of pacifists, it was taken up in Germany with great enthusiasm in 1918, and then caught on in France. I had had no idea of the large scope and social significance of this cult.

"Dada was shock-treatment for a crazed humanity," one of its German devotees declared. Another of its early advocates, Hugo Ball, who was associated with Tzara, declared that Dada opposed "bourgeois logic" as the author of modern war and chaos:

Dada is a great clownery. Since the age aims at the destruction of all that is noblest and best in life, the Dadaist courts the absurd, loves every kind of disguise, game or deception. The Dadaist fights against the agony of the times and the intoxication of death.

Launched under the stress of wartime by young men who were principally drawn from the middle class, the Dadaist movement at first had the character of a "cultural revolution." (In Germany, however, it was associated for a brief period with the Left in politics.) As a rule, the postwar generation was unpolitical up to the late twenties, much as the Beat Generation in America and the Angry Young Men in England have been largely unpolitical.

According to Aragon, the word "dada" was supposed to mean exactly nothing. Tzara was said to have found the name for the new cult by opening a big dictionary at random.

Reading over Tzara's wartime manifestoes, I found him proclaiming, in 1916 to 1918, the coming of a new and barbarous "order."

On the one hand we have a tottering world, wedded to the Glockenspiel of Hell; on the other the new men, rough, hard-riding. . . .

I say unto ye there are no beginnings, and we are not afraid, are not sentimental; we are a furious wind, ripping through the wet linen of clouds and men's prayers, preparing the grand spectacle of disaster, fire, decomposition.

Dada is our intensity. . . . Dada is life without carpet-slippers. . . . We spit on humanity. . . . Dada is the abolition of logic—abolition of memory.

Let each man proclaim: there is a great negative work of destruction to be accomplished. We must sweep everything away and sweep clean. . . .

At the "concerts" of the Cabaret Voltaire in Zürich, Tzara and his confreres hung up the paintings of Cubist and Futurist painters, and exhibited African sculptures because of the shock value such works then possessed. The artists who made them were supposed to be undermining our old culture. Then Tzara and his mates sang and danced all about like bears or waddled around in gunny sacks before a public that was constantly astounded by their antics, whom they abused and insulted as "stinking bourgeois," and who came back for more of the same treatment and even paid for it. A crude jazz music, the ringing of bells, and the thumping of tom-toms accompanied the chants of the Dadaists:

Boomboom, boomboom, boomboom,
Ideal, ideal, ideal—

At the end of 1919 the French literary group had invited Tristan Tzara to come to Paris, and with their aid organize similar demonstrations there.

Aragon pointed out to me that long before the advent of Dadaism, in fact a century before, the French had boasted of a literature of alienation of their own. It was exemplified by the writings of Stendhal, that strayed reveler of French Revolution days, who lived on during the years of the Bourbon restoration; and by *Les Illuminations* of Rimbaud, who renounced literature in his youth and left Europe to live as a trader in darkest Africa, where he contracted the disease that killed him early in life. And after Rimbaud, there had been the fantastic poet, Bohemian, and sportsman, Alfred Jarry, author of *Ubu Roi;* and Guillaume Apollinaire, poet of the "new laughter," the prophet of *surréalisme,* whom the postwar generation had already installed in its unofficial Pantheon. All these authors, little known to the English-speaking world in 1921, as well as the early Dada manifestoes, Aragon gave me to read.

It was as if he had opened a door for me, leading to a whole new zone of art and all its rebellious works. During a number of weeks in the winter of 1921–1922 he used to come to my apartment almost every morning, en route to his hospital, laden with books which he either lent or gave me, books that would serve to orient one toward the true unfaith. Among these were *Le Rouge et le Noir* by Stendhal, presenting the rebellious figure of Julien Sorel; a work long forgotten, that had only enjoyed a revival in France a few years before the war, and was not yet available in English translation. The young French were also reviving the obscure, short-lived Isidore Ducasse, who wrote the hallucinatory *Les Chants de Maldoror* under the pseudonym of the "Comte de Lautréamont." Lautréamont also was a true precursor of the modern cultural insurrectos.

Thus, I had my reading program laid out for me by the charming and generous young Aragon, who knew how to cast a spell of enchantment over us, for he always gave himself without reserve in his friendships. We were very poor young

Americans and often hungry, and knew almost nobody in Paris. Louis entertained us and introduced us to the whole circle of his friends, who were quite a lively band. Best of all, he would come in brimming with new ideas each morning, keeping my mind in a continual whirl, and leaving me dumfounded, at times, by the paradoxes I discovered in his personality.

He would pace back and forth across our living room, pivot when he came to the wall, then round upon me, talking in clipped phrases and with great animation. There was really much sweetness in his manner and in his expression; as his friend André Breton said, "Aragon had always the desire to please."

He had already known a precocious literary success; the leading avant-garde reviews in France had published Aragon's early poems, like those of Soupault and Breton, during the war; the *Nouvelle Revue Française* had also issued his first novel, *Anicet* (1921), which André Gide had declared showed the marks of young genius. But here Aragon was (like Tzara), assuring me that poetry was "dead"; the novel was "dead"; and he, Aragon, was resolved to abandon literature, as Rimbaud had abandoned it long ago, when he fled from "Europe and its old ramparts" to Abyssinia. I was quite consternated to learn from Aragon that he and his friends had no wish to enjoy literary careers of the traditional kind, such as were hospitably offered them by their elders. On the contrary, they proposed to devote their time to waging war upon society, as agitators and propagandists—for Dadaism! Their "literature" was to be *action,* action designed to subvert men's minds by laughter and ridicule, by generating a mood of disgust everywhere. In short, he was burning his bridges by quarreling with the older men of letters, such as "old auntie Gide." What was their "modern" review, the *Nouvelle Revue Française,* Aragon said, but a scheme for "making a business out of literature for snobs."

He would devote himself, then, to writing manifestoes, and to organizing public demonstrations. As he went on, I realized that he was outlining plans that he and his friends entertained for

becoming the terrorists of art and culture. For all his gentle
aspect, Aragon sounded then like an anarchist, a nihilist, nothing
less! *"Maman, maman, le monsieur est anarchiste!"* was a humorous aside in one of his own manifestoes of the time, as if
underscoring the antithesis between the sweetness of his personality and the bloody things he would be saying. *"Le Scandale
pour le Scandale"* was the alarming title of another of his dis-
courses in the review *Littérature.* Referring to Aragon's and
his own activities at this period Soupault wrote afterward: "We
simply wanted to create scandals—why should I not admit, in
the end, that we loved scandal with passion. Anyway, it was a
reason for existence. (And how many are there?) Perhaps the
time we chose was unfortunate; but we were not looking for
success. We wanted only to create sensations. And that gave us
a rare joy. But the public also behaved scandalously. It tried to
understand us, in vain. What madness!"

I had been congratulating myself upon having discovered a
young man of prodigious talent, a veritable lord of language,
who "fairly lived literature," as I wrote my friends in New York.
But to my sorrow it seemed that he intended to give up writing
entirely.

"We still write a little," Aragon said to me, "as a means of
seeking out people, a way of attracting persons like yourself." I
was touched at this remark, but felt sad, nevertheless, at the
thought that he might fail to become what he gave such clear
promise of being—one of France's great singers. (In the end,
however, he fooled us all, for he became just that; the National
Poet of World War II and the Resistance, whose songs were on
everyone's lips. Could the non-writing pose of 1921 have been
"mere literature"?)

In our rambles about Paris, Aragon showed enough nervous
energy to wear me down, walking from Montparnasse to Montmartre and back across all Paris, a whole night long, while he
told me fabulous stories, one after another. They were often
the chapters of his future novels, which he could improvise in
talk precisely as they were written afterward. He also seemed

to know every house, every stone in Paris, and had the tallest tales to tell of each site we came upon, for he remembered the plots of thousands of novels he had read long ago. Nor did he ever seem to need sleep: *"Je cherche toujours la fatigue,"* he would say.

Sometimes I felt anxiety for Aragon's safety. Would not this delightful companion, who talked so freely of overturning our modern society, be taken from us one day and lodged in the prison of the Santé? On the other hand, I also felt the excitement of danger as I found myself being drawn into the absurd and scandalous enterprises of the Dadaists, as their American recruit. There were risks in this business, but there were special satisfactions too. At least we writers would leave our sedentary lives in our studies, cafés, or the parlors where we used to read our poems to old ladies, and go forth into the streets to confront the public and strike great blows at its stupid face.

I also feared that I myself might possibly be courting arrest. Or perhaps, what was worse, public ridicule. But, on the other hand, it was reassuring to observe that our demonstrations were largely verbal; our bombs were only words.

Paris, moreover, was traditionally tolerant of the most extravagant of cults, since Hugo's Romantics of 1829, provided they continued to be amusing; and the Dadaists were original enough in their methods of insulting the public. Much was owing to Tzara for having adopted this ancient device of circus clowns.

As I met the several apostles of Dadaism one by one, I penetrated further into the arcana of their system of unbelief. André Breton, by the autumn of 1921, was outstanding among them; by virtue of his cold intelligence and crushing power in argument, he had gradually assumed command of the Dadaist cenacle in Paris, and was their tacitly acknowledged "pope," or "archimandrite." Usually, he would be seated at the head of the table at their chosen café, Cintra's, a dim tavern situated on the Right Bank of Paris in an arcade between some old buildings (now

demolished) back of the Opéra. In full daylight it was always
dark at Cintra's, whose non-literary guests had a somewhat furtive and even sinister air.

At twenty-five, Breton made an imposing *chef d'école*. He had
a huge head, like one of the old Jacobin leaders, a mass of wavy
brown hair, pale blue eyes, regular—though heavy—features,
and jaws of granite. Like the men of 1793, he had in him a
combination of fanatical idealism and ruthlessness. Whereas
his closest friends, Aragon and Philippe Soupault, were spontaneous in manner, he was deliberate, speaking in long periods
like an old-style orator and in a voice of deep and musical
timbre. More the scholar than the other men, he had absorbed
much from the iconoclastic writings of Nietzsche, and from
Nietzsche's disciples in France such as Maurice Barrès in his
early phase when he wrote *L'Ennemi des Lois*. Breton's medical
experience in the treatment of mad soldiers had also turned his
interests toward psychiatry. The relationship between the illusions of mad persons and the creative processes of art absorbed
him for years. At periods he even dabbled in mesmerism, and
played the medium and the psychoanalyst for his friends.

André Breton divided the world into fools and angels. A
person unknown to him might be received at first with the most
exquisite courtesy; Breton would listen to him attentively, using
terms of such elaborate politeness that to some observers his
good manners seemed to serve mainly as an armor of defense
and were, on occasion, disconcerting rather than pleasing. Then
in an instant his blue eye might blaze with anger at some idea
he disliked, his heavy brows turn scowling, and he would proceed with measured words to tear the man before him apart, as
if he enjoyed eating him up bit by bit. Though his air of pride
and solemnity sometimes made him appear absurd, this complex young man could be very seductive in his friendships, and
often used a delightfully paternal manner with his younger
disciples, who sat at his feet submissively, but were also the
recipients of his generous aid.

As a student in Paris Breton had frequented the circles of

the Symbolist poets, and had begun to publish some of his verses at sixteen, verses that were those of a self-conscious aesthete, in the manner of Mallarmé. They had gained him the friendly attention of Paul Valéry, who was then living in self-willed obscurity. Valéry was another great poet who had "abandoned" literature. Apparently the only way to have a really big literary career in France was to tell everyone that you had given up writing!

In 1921 Breton was already shouldering Tzara aside to assume the real leadership of their little sect. Breton's writing was confined mostly to polemics published in *Littérature*, of which he became the sole editor in 1922. His prose style was classical, and much given to fine intellectual discriminations which made him seem ponderous at times, though he could be most eloquent in his vituperative vein.

He often talked of his erstwhile friend, Lieutenant Jacques Vaché, a dandy and opium addict, who had died of an overdose of drugs early in 1919. Vaché's war letters—he had been an art student of promise—published and edited by Breton after the war, had a very particular and casual tone of indifference to all things and a sort of bilious humor (*humour noir*) which disposed him to damn all the modern cults, such as Cubism, and indeed all the arts as *sottise*. What he admired most were the early American movies of the Western type. He also had something of the eccentric spirit of Alfred Jarry. In short, he was a proto-Dadaist. Breton liked to recall that Vaché had once appeared in Paris at the opening of an esoteric play by Apollinaire carrying a loaded revolver, which he brandished about and would have fired off in that crowded theater, if Breton had not withheld him. Though he saw a good deal of active combat in the war, Lieutenant Vaché manifested a fine contempt for the sentiment of patriotism that animated his fellow soldiers, and tried to preserve himself from death in battle. If he could help it he did not intend, as he said, "to get himself killed in *their* war," the war of fools, but would take his own way out, to oblivion in drugs and suicide.

I had come to France with all sorts of fixed ideas that were being changed for me: for example, the object of improving myself as a writer. The men of Aragon's and Breton's circle all seemed like accomplished poets and writers. But André Breton, the "sea-green incorruptible," steadfastly berated those who would earn their bread by writing for the commercial press. Had not the poet Rimbaud said: *"La main à plume vaut la main à charrue"*? Must they become mere "ploughmen" of literature? The other young men readily agreed they must be nothing of the sort. They occupied themselves in devising Dadaist handbills and flyers done with some humor. (In secret they were writing their own personal literature, in my belief.)

I was much impressed by the esprit de corps shown by members of the Dada movement. Each of them was supposed to be a "president"; "anyone can be a president of the Dadas," it was said, "there are already 391 of them." But André Breton was plainly more president than anybody else. It was quite apparent that the younger men, and the more pliant of the other apostles, took their cue from him. Whenever some new event took place that might be turned to the account of the Dada (or later the Surrealist) cause, or when some new personality appeared in their midst, they would wait to see how Breton reacted. Thus, these rebellious youths actually lived a very close-knit communal life resembling that of some religious order, such as the Franciscans or, more nearly, the Jesuit societies. They would meet at regular intervals almost every day, at the same hour of the afternoon, at the same café, Cintra's, or its annex, Le Petit Grillon, which were both as dim as the interior of an old church; and they would take their walks together.

While there were certain inconveniences in such a group life, one felt there was a warm spirit of comradeship ruling them. Whereas, in contrast, a gathering of avant-garde American writers and painters would have found everyone talking at cross-purposes, these men were in full accord in opposing the same stupidities, assailing the arrivistes of the arts as with one voice, and expressing a common enthusiasm for the program of action and intrigue by which they would spread confusion and disorder.

How did they live? Some of the younger ones were in the position of needy students dependent on their families. Breton vehemently opposed the idea that it was their *duty* to work. They were to live off society by their wits. "Go and marry a rich woman," was his advice to his friends. He himself had married Simone Kahn, the daughter of a banker from Strasbourg.

When his friends undertook to follow Breton's advice the results were indifferent. Aragon, who seemed always in the process of falling in love (prior to his long union with Elsa Triolet that began in 1929), formed an attachment at first with an American woman, and afterward with a young British heiress who was interested in all the avant-garde movements in art and politics. But these friendships did not last. Soupault, after a first marriage with a pretty woman of no fortune, divorced and then married Marie-Louise le Borgne, who was both intelligent and rich, but they too were separated after several years. Tzara, in his turn, eventually married a beautiful Swedish heiress related to the Nobel family, but they soon came to divorce. Even Breton remarried a young woman who was without means of any sort. Evidently there is no safety in connection with rich women nowadays.

Paul Éluard, well-to-do in his own right, had to work at his father's real estate business in the daytime, writing his poetry at night. His wife was a lively dark-eyed Russian émigré named Gala (later Mme Salvador Dali). Éluard, the self-conscious craftsman of poetry in this group, had formerly written under the influence of the Symbolists, but now contrived hundreds of "abstract" verses out of old clichés, nonsense words, and puns.

An odd one in this circle was Jacques Rigaut, handsome as a movie actor, a wit and man about town, always dressed in stylish British clothes and wearing rich cravats; he was then employed as the literary secretary of the old portrait painter, Jacques Émile Blanche, who was engaged in writing his endless memoirs. Like Philippe Soupault, Rigaut, the son of a bank official, had a family background of the comfortable middle class. He and I were on friendly terms during a year or two, and I saw him afterward when he came to live in America. Though he was a most pleasant companion, his humor was often sardonic. He pretended to be an idler; but he sometimes wrote sad and curious little notes showing that the subject of suicide was his special study and that he considered his life a preparation for the act of self-destruction.

A particular friend of Jacques Rigaut's and of Aragon's, who stood near the Dada camp but was not of it, was the aristocratic town-rounder Pierre Drieu la Rochelle; he had the repute of a war hero and was the author of a famous war journal, or rather, anti-war tract, *État-Civil*. Drieu used to boast that his wealthy mistresses provided him with ample funds, by grace of which he would stand us treats to rounds of champagne at the fashionable night club in the rue Boissy d'Anglas called (in honor of Jean Cocteau) Le Bœuf sur le Toit.

The one who was the true soul of Dadaism in this band, a youth of innumerable larks and, in fact, a regular ball of fire, was the poet Philippe Soupault. He had a long narrow head, sloping brows surmounted by curly brown hair, and yellow-brown eyes ("tiger's eyes") that were always laughing at you. Loving all things African, he collected records of Negro spirituals and jazz tunes, and once posed as an African when he appeared at a Dadaist soiree, his face daubed with burnt cork and splendidly costumed as the President of the Liberian Republic. In reality, he was of old French bourgeois stock, his father having been a famous doctor and a leading figure at the École de Médecine; Philippe was also the nephew of Louis Renault, the automobile king.

Philippe was probably the most worldly of the young rebels. He was forever on the run, like a man of great affairs, arriving breathlessly, doffing his hat, departing as swiftly—for he had many irons in the fire. Despite Breton's admonitions, he worked as an editor of a literary magazine, *La Revue Européene*, and had his wife run the bookshop of La Librairie Six, while he himself also held down a government job in the Bureau du Pétrole. With all that, he led a hectic social life, for according to legend, he had admiring lady friends in all the different quarters of Paris. If he had a point of weakness, it was his inability to resist a pretty face (a vice many of us share); but then most women also found it hard to resist Philippe, who had an infectious smile like the very devil, and a male beauty quite different from that of those Dapper Dans, Rigaut and Drieu la Rochelle.

He was often called "the heir of Apollinaire," whose particular style certainly influenced Soupault's own finely cadenced *vers libre*. Apollinaire used to dash off occasional verses on request. It happened that in 1918, while he was convalescing from his war wounds, Apollinaire wrote one of his last and most charming occasional poems for Philippe, who had come to his bedside. Not long after that, Apollinaire was carried away by the influenza epidemic, when he was but thirty-eight.

Soupault's verse was deceptively simple, often gossamer light, like the smoke of his perpetual cigarettes, yet composed of sharp images and dashes of strong color. Like Apollinaire, he wrote at great speed, under the impulse of the moment, a direct, terse, unfeigned poetry.

Why was Philippe Soupault always hurrying, and "where was he going so fast?" My wife and I used to call out to him in protest. His breathless rush (like his legendary "seven mistresses," no doubt) was the manifestation of his being "*alive*," he explained to us. He said:

... Those who in early youth were witnesses of nothing but death and destruction, those who survived that cataclysm of stupidity (which seemed as if it would never end) turned with a kind of fever toward life.

My generation wanted to be *alive* at all costs.

And again he said:

We wanted to love life—with which we had good reason to be disgusted. And we did love it. The greatest evil was to be dead. We

would always distinguish among persons we knew, by saying that
so and so was "alive," but so and so was "dead."

Soupault's fast pace was also related, no doubt, to his having
adopted what he regarded as the "American tempo," reflected in
the early Edison films that used to show everyone hopping about
madly because of the slow-timed motion-picture cameras. The
older generation in France, Philippe held, knew America only
as the Land of the Dollar; the literary group knew only of Whitman and Poe (who was practically a French product). But
Soupault and his Dada friends now wanted to discover the true
America, represented by our common soldiers in Europe, our
Negro jazz bands, and, above all, by our silent cinema, the
cinema of Mack Sennett, of *The Perils of Pauline,* of Douglas
Fairbanks, Tom Mix, Rio Jim, and all the bank robberies, the
swift abductions, the incredible gold strikes, and the cigar-chew-
ing tycoons in sumptuous offices "where the telephone rang with
the sound of a horn in the forest." The unreeling film, in Soupault's view, had revealed a new pictorial and dramatic beauty
to be seen in the gesture of a hand, a lock of hair, a drop of
water. Above all, the American cinema had give Chaplin to the
world—the beloved "Charlot" to the French—who created "a
sublime poetry, a new laughter," as Soupault wrote in his fine
essay on Chaplin.

French poetry strongly reflected the influence of the American cinema, as is shown by the work of Apollinaire, Blaise Cendrars, and Soupault himself. Even the learned André Breton
attended the silliest old American films, hoping to discover what
Jacques Vaché had seen in them: the surprising, the unexpected,
the incongruous in the action of a cowboy, the galloping of
Western ponies, the huge toothsome smile of Pearl White that
(for Soupault) "announced the beginning of a new order."
Soupault relates:

Those darkened halls . . . became the living theater of our
laughter, our anger, our pride. In those miraculous crimes and
farewells our eyes read the poetry of our age. We were living with

passion through a most beautiful period of which the U.S. cinema was the brightest ornament.[1]

Though I had come to France with other objects in view, I found myself giving serious study to a lot of old American films in the company of Soupault and Aragon, to whom I tried to convey some nuances of those silent film dramas that the French subtitles might have missed.

I also furnished them with a goodly store of recent "Americana" in the form of "Krazy Kat" cartoon serials by George Herriman, which had been brought to my attention by Slater Brown (who in turn may have got the idea from Gilbert Seldes). These were exhibited to my French friends as "pure American Dada humor." We also explored American newspaper and magazine advertisements for such "folklore" as they would yield us. Thus, without any premeditation, I found myself acting as a sort of "carrier" of American influences to France. For their own part, Aragon and Soupault, who both read English, had been devouring all the Nick Carter novels they could find.

In much the same spirit, and at an earlier period, Marcel Duchamp, having abandoned Cubist painting and gone to live in America, collected bits of rubbish, absurd machines, dummies, clothing racks, and other such disjecta membra of America's standardized civilization, and, naming them "ready-mades," offered them as artifacts selected and signed by himself. The troubling humor with which this great mystificator attacked the art of the past—a humor inspired largely by the American environment favoring such activity—made a profound impression upon the Dada and Surrealist cults in Europe.

Thus, a new life opened for me in which I spent days and nights with the young devotees of Dada in Paris, going to their homes and meeting their mothers, fathers, sisters, wives, and mistresses. (For months on end I lost sight of the American colony in Montparnasse.) The young French, who were of our own age, seemed to us normal and healthy folk; sometimes we even played tennis with them on Sundays!

The paradox of it all was that I had come here with certain preconceived ideas about exposing myself to the old literary culture of France: I was to have explored the collected letters of Flaubert, examined the technical innovations of Mallarmé, and investigated the decadents and Symbolists, following leads thrown out by the old literary critic, Remy de Gourmont. Instead, I was observing a young France that, to my surprise, was passionately concerned with the civilization of the U.S.A., and stood in a fair way to being *Americanized!* Looking into Apollinaire again, and with greater understanding of him than in earlier years, I found a posthumous essay, "L'Esprit Nouveau et les Poètes" (published in the *Mercure de France,* December, 1918), setting forth his visions of the new arts of the future that were nothing if not Whitmanesque and American in tone:

Is there nothing new under the sun? For the sun perhaps so—but for man everything! . . . The poet is to stop at nothing in his quest for novelty of form and material; he is to take advantage of all the infinite new combinations afforded by the mechanism of every-day life. . . . What he creates out of these new instruments, or the repercussions which these elements will have upon our lives, will form the material, the folklore, out of which the myths and fables of the future will be created. . . . The recent conquests of man over nature have in many cases surpassed the fables of ancient times. It is for the modern poet to create the fairy tales which are to be harvested in ages to come.

In my letters of February 4, 1922, I tried to communicate my new interests to my friends, Kenneth Burke and Hart Crane, in America. Apollinaire, I declared, had killed my interest in the classical realism of Flaubert, as in the comfortable ironies of Anatole France.

. . . We must write for *our age* . . . the poets should be no less daring or inventive than the mechanical engineers of wartime; our literature should reflect the influences of the cinema . . . the saxophone. . . .

Instead of invoking nightingales, poets should sing of those new birds that have giant wings of wood and canvas and gas engines for their hearts.

Hart Crane expressed complete bewilderment at my change of front, writing to one of his friends:

. . . But what has happened to Matty? And just why is Apollinaire so portentous a god? Will radios, flying-machines and cinemas have such a great effect on poetry in the end? Oh, Matty must be amusing himself perfectly in Paris.

However, Hart soon afterward proceeded to turn out one of his best poems, "Chaplinesque," under the direct inspiration of the cinema. After all, was there a more wonderful new poetry anywhere than in *The Kid?* Hart Crane soliloquized: "It made me feel myself, as a poet, 'in the same boat' with [Chaplin]."

Aragon arrived at our chilly studio apartment one morning in January, 1922, with big news. He had resolved that he must break off his career in medicine at the eleventh hour, prior to his final examinations to qualify for his doctor's license. This decision had rendered his mother and elder sister wild with anxiety, while his guardian, an eminent bureaucrat of the Prefecture of Paris, promised to cut him off from all further funds. Now he would really have to live by his wits. He was quite cool about this whole crisis. "Lend me thirty francs," he wound up. "I believe I shall be able to return them this evening." By some remarkable chance I had the money.

The same evening he returned, waving a bank note of one thousand francs (worth almost one hundred dollars). "We are going to celebrate the end of my medical career," he announced, and invited us to join him and other friends waiting outside in a taxi to take us to Montmartre. The youngest of the Dadaists were there, including the poet Jacques Baron, aged only seventeen, and Roger Vitrac, the future playwright, then aged twenty-one. So many persons arrived to join in the festivities that Aragon engaged a second taxi to hold them, and ordered them to

race each other as in a "movie chase" all about Paris, his guests
leaning out of the windows and yelling like redskins. We visited
"Zelli's," a new all-night jazz spot near the Place Blanche, whose
"sinister" atmosphere intrigued us. One could arrange to have
almost any conceivable vice humored in such a place, though
our young friends exhibited interest chiefly in pleasures of the
common or garden variety. At Zelli's my young wife and I
aroused admiration by dancing the new fox trots in an unaffected American style.

Alas, we soon ran out of champagne. What would we do now
to amuse ourselves? Our young men were soon engaged in a
contest to determine who could recite the longest passages from
Hugo's verses. Aragon, whose memory was uncanny, easily prevailed. Not only did we Americans enjoy the recitation, but all
about us demimondaines and dope peddlers listened for hours
to the ringing dodecasyllables of old Hugo.

From Aragon, Breton, and Tzara, also, I received, during
these evening gatherings, a piecemeal account of all their goings-
on during the preceding two years since Dadaism had burst forth
in Paris. I shall try to reconstruct their story partly from my
recollections of what they told me, partly from some verbatim
records of their "concerts," printed at the time in their reviews,
such as *Littérature*. The Paris Dadaists had acquired a strange
sort of glory—notoriety one might have called it—and as a
group already suffered from internal dissensions at the period
when I first met them.

After Tzara arrived in Paris from Switzerland, his French
colleagues, in January, 1920, hired the Salle des Fêtes of the
Grand Palais and decorated it with Dada poems mounted on the
wall like posters and machine-objects by Francis Picabia. (At
later exhibitions the "ready-mades" of Duchamp were represented, including his colored lithograph of the "Mona Lisa"
with a mustache painted on her upper lip; also the dreamlike

paintings of the Italian, Giorgio di Chirico, and the collages of
Max Ernst and Jean Arp.)

At these Dada festivals the proceedings would begin in disarming fashion: Tzara, Breton, and Aragon would solemnly pretend to be giving literary readings or lectures. Then, after a while,
their destructive humor would burst forth: six or ten would
commence shouting at once, while bells rang and drums rolled.
Tzara, for example, presented a play, *M. AA l'Anti-Philo-
sophe,* which was evidently made up of disconnected words or
ideas clipped from newspapers and whose personages appeared
in stovepipe hats of cardboard that masked their faces and
reached to their knees. On other occasions they read manifestoes
such as Picabia's *Manifeste Cannibale,* delivered by André
Breton in the darkened hall of the Théâtre de l'Oeuvre:

> You all stand accused here. Stand up, as for the Marseillaise,
> stand up . . . as for the raising of the flag. Stand before Dada,
> which represents life. . . . What are you all doing out there sitting
> about like dumb clucks—for you are serious aren't you? Death is
> a serious thing, isn't it? . . . You like death for other people, but not
> for yourselves. There is only money that does not die but just travels
> around. It is the only god you worship. . . . Well, whistle, laugh at
> me, hit me—and then what? I'll still say to you that you are all
> ASSES.

The audience would become restive and go storming out. Had
they counted on being improved? But when the newspapers reported these affairs in detail, the public came back, and they
came prepared, as at the next big soiree held in the Salle Gaveau,
the famous concert hall of Paris, on May, 1920.

On this occasion Breton and Soupault presented a "play" they
had written, *Vous m'oublierez,* which made mock of the theater,
since the characters all talked at cross-purposes. Philippe Soupault, impersonating a magician, was carried onto the stage in
a trunk, out of which he popped clad in a bathing suit. From
another trunk there issued colored balloons with names lettered
on them such as "Clemenceau," or "Poincaré," or "Jean Coc-

teau"; Soupault and Éluard then attacked these balloons with knives and hatchets, amid the din of bells and tom-toms. Then Georges Ribémont-Dessaignes, an older, baldpated member of the clan, delivered a harangue to the audience that was calculated to infuriate them:

> Before going down amongst you to pull out your rotten teeth, and your tongues full of sores—
> Before opening your bellies and pulling out your fatted livers—
> Before tearing out your abject sex organs, incontinent and slimy—
> Before spoiling your appetites for sweetness and light—
> We are going to take a big antiseptic bath.
> And we warn you: WE ARE KILLERS

During the entr'acte the audience had gone outside and purchased quantities of ripe tomatoes, eggs, and chopped meat; when they had had enough, they let loose a great volley of rotten eggs and tomatoes, overwhelming the performers. Philippe Soupault was knocked down by a well-aimed beefsteak, but staggered to his feet and challenged all comers to a duel. Mme Gaveau, wife of the proprietor of the concert hall, who occupied a box, had her dress splattered with tomatoes and cabbages. The police arrived and put an end to this disgraceful concert, while the Dadaists used their best arguments to divert the attention of the *commissaire* from themselves.

One of the troubling things about these public demonstrations was that the intellectual public of Paris began to favor them. Eminent authors such as André Gide and Jacques Rivière expressed their sympathetic concern for the angry young men of 1920, who seemed to be manifesting their disillusionment with the war and the postwar world. Reports of the Dada "concerts" appearing in the newspapers in all their grotesque details brought the public in increasing numbers to the next shows, a public equipped with whistles, horns, and even hammers and axes, showing by their attitude that they enjoyed being converted to

Dadaism, and were ready to do their duty by the works of Picabia, Max Ernst, *et al.*

To be tolerated, to be accepted spelled danger to André Breton. He cudgeled his brain for new inventions in the arts of provocation. Dadaism, now entering its second year in Paris, must never repeat itself, he insisted, but must advance into ever-new terrain, maintaining at full power its "disorganizing virtue." According to some of his associates, Breton intended to change the Dada movement into a secret society whose propaganda would make life miserable for many important public figures. In the spring of 1921 he staged a mock trial of Maurice Barrès, the sixty-year-old novelist and senator, who was one of the most distinguished of living French writers.

Barrès' earlier works had embodied the teachings of those iconoclasts, Stendhal and Nietzsche. But in middle life he had become the most rabid of nationalists and anti-Dreyfusards, urging the country on to a war of revenge against Germany and heading the Ligue des Patriotes, which corresponded to our American Legion. In truth, both Aragon and Breton admired Barrès for his prose style.

During preliminary discussions, Tristan Tzara vigorously opposed the idea of the mock trial of Barrès, on the ground that it might cause the Dadaists to be suspected of harboring liberal or humanitarian principles. Francis Picabia also protested that the whole business sounded "serious," and he would have no part in it. Breton argued, however, that his critics were being too rigidly negative, and that there were certain positive sentiments and tendencies that must be supported. In the end, Tzara, with reluctance, agreed to participate in the "trial," held before an audience of university students in a hall on the rue Danton.

M. Barrès was to be judged in absentia; on being invited to appear, he promptly left Paris for his country home at Aix-en-Provence. A clothing dummy made up to represent Barrès sat in the prisoner's box. Breton, naturally, served as President of the Tribunal, the members of the court being dressed in white robes, the counsels for defense, Soupault and Aragon, in red costumes, and the prosecuting attorney, Ribémont-Dessaignes, in black.

Reading the act of accusation, Breton charged M. Barrès with being guilty of "high crimes against the security of the human spirit"; Ribémont-Dessaignes, in the foulest language at his command, heaped contumely upon the great man. Tzara, wearing his monocle as on all public occasions, strove to maintain a proper Dadaist tone, testifying that Barrès, whom he had never hitherto read, was the greatest swine since Napoleon. He qualified his remarks, however, by adding that he had "no confidence in the process of justice even when administered by a Dada tribunal," adding: "We are all a bunch of swine, whether big ones or little, makes no difference." Questioning by the President elicited from the witness, Tzara, the opinion that, while he believed his friends (including the President) were swine, they were "sympathetic swine," whereas Barrès was a disgusting animal. On being asked if there were no one in the world whom he esteemed, Tzara answered: "Well, I myself am really a charming fellow."

Q. Is the witness trying to pass himself off as a perfect imbecile?
A. Yes, I am being an imbecile, but at least I am not trying to escape from the asylum in which I have spent my whole life.[2]

The high point of the trial was the appearance of the young Dadaist poet, Benjamin Péret, as a witness for the prosecution. A burly youth, he appeared wearing a gas mask and a German uniform covered with mud and filth, and gave his name as "The Unknown Soldier." In his own writings Péret invented a distinctively "brutal humor," achieved in part by assuming the air of a moron. Now he began to bellow hoarsely: "*Vivent la France et les pommes frites,*" and spoke of Barrès and all such patriots in terms of such vile abuse that his testimony became the climax of the affair, and precipitated the customary riot. The crowd, in an uproar, began to climb upon the stage and fell upon Péret, who managed to escape with his life.

After having done their duty by the conservatives and the

patriots, the Dadaists held their next meeting at the Place de la République before an open-air gathering of workers to whom they addressed speeches assailing both socialism and communism. The proletarian audience became unruly and made some threats of violence; but luckily, the Dada orators escaped without serious damage.

This was one of a series of "Dadaist excursions" to various quarters of Paris. A meeting I attended in January, 1922, was held in a restaurant before a special gathering of about a hundred Russian émigrés, among them admirals, dukes, and princes, and their ladies; we were supposed to expound the gospels of Dadaism for their benefit. Those titled Russians, in many cases, had been reduced to working as waiters or chauffeurs, but they were conservative nevertheless. We Dadaists sat together at some tables on a dais, behaving like vulgar clowns. In place of a speech, Philippe Soupault read the restaurant menu aloud, as a sort of incantation, sometimes interrupting his reading to direct an offensive aside at the distinguished audience. While reading, he continued to eat his dinner in a deliberately slovenly fashion, overturning his plate, throwing bits of food at the Russian aristocrats around us. Aragon, in his turn, tilting his nose in the air, castigated the guests as cowards and imbeciles. "Why don't you go back where you came from?" he exclaimed. At this moment, as the crowd became excited, I was persuaded to mount a table and read a tract in German on socialism. The Russian exiles began to boo and whistle at me, and threw pellets of bread and pieces of celery, one of which struck me in the eye. I reacted angrily, started to take off my coat and challenge my hecklers to put up their fists. But the proprietor and the waiters intervened and declared the meeting closed.

Not all our forays were imbued with the pure spirit of contrariness; some, indeed, were rescue parties, in which we played, by our own lights, a constructive role. There was a certain obscure author named Raymond Roussel (a contemporary of Al-

fred Jarry and Apollinaire), whom André Breton admired and
sought to revive. Roussel had traveled much in the equatorial
regions of Africa before the war, and in 1914 had produced a
play, evidently inspired by his African adventures, called *Locus
Solus*. The coming of war had interrupted its production; but
now the long-forgotten author, probably at his own expense,
had arranged for the revival of his play and turned over its
staging to the director of one of the popular theaters. The director, fearing that the public would make nothing of this esoteric
play, had decided to lure them to his theater with an added
attraction, a blood-and-thunder war drama in one act, by one of
the hack writers of the commercial theater. In any case, Roussel's play received no notice whatsoever in the press. My recollection of it is of a poetic drama whose action sequence seemed
as improbable as it was mystical; in one climactic scene a sea
siren swims about in a big glass tank filled with undersea foliage,
while her lover stands outside addressing interminable speeches
to her.

Breton suggested that we all go to the theater in a band and
make a fervent demonstration in favor of Roussel's play, which
was the curtain raiser, but register a powerful protest against
the patriotic melodrama that followed. He provided us with
free passes and assigned us to our battle stations, scattered
singly or in pairs around the hall, where, at the prearranged
signal, we were to go into action.

During the performance of Roussel we were just a happy
claque giving loud cries of admiration at certain passages of the
dialogue. The audience, which evidently could scarcely follow
this mystifying play, seemed diverted by our demonstrations and
tolerated them, assuming we were a claque paid for by the
author or theater manager, a common practice in Paris.

But once the second play went on, our band, to the surprise
of the audience, became a sort of anti-claque: booing, whistling,
crying catcalls. When one of the actors gave expression to some
patriotic sentiment, someone up in the balcony would call out:
"*À bas la France! Vive l'Allemagne!*" Or another agitator from

a box would exclaim: *"C'est faux!"* An actor coming to a pause, as indicated in the text, saying: *"Alors . . ."* would find one of our confederates suddenly breaking in, at the moment of silence, and crying out: *"Alors—merdes!"*

At last the actors could bear it no longer; they stopped; the lights went on, the ushers came to throw us out, and the whole theater was in an uproar, many persons in the crowd converging upon those of us who had been pointed out as disturbers. An usher spotted me and cried in protest: "Why, he didn't even pay for his ticket!" I protested that, at all events, I had paid the government tax.

Breton, accompanied by his wife, made his way slowly through the angry crowd down the stairs from an upper box, flanked by two policemen. He was thrashing his arms about and thundering forth a speech on the greatness of Roussel: "More beautiful than Corneille or even Bossuet!" He continued to protest at the addition of the second play as a "defamation of the human spirit!" The police seemed puzzled, and the crowd, as if bemused by Breton's theatrical air and reverberant periods, fell back. In the end he was released, and marched off proudly at the head of our band, none of us the worse for wear.

I was then writing every morning, but became quite *"engagé"* in these planned demonstrations organized by our young conspirators. My wife and I would meet the "enemies of order" for dinner in some simple bistro, then repair to Cintra's Café in the dim Passage de l'Opéra, prepare our line of march, and go off for the evening's sortie.

On occasions, when we had no more serious business on hand and if that indefatigable improviser, Philippe Soupault, were with us, we would amuse ourselves simply by following in his trail, as he wandered through the crowded streets on the Right Bank. He had a genius for improvising a sort of walking poetry, consisting in a series of spontaneous actions prompted by chance encounters. Was he a somnambulist or a harmless lunatic, people wondered? Pretending to have lost his identity, he would approach the concierge of an apartment house and ask: "Do you

know where Philippe Soupault lives?" Or he would address a
waiter at the terrace of a café on the Grands Boulevards, salute
him, and say: "*Bonjour*, Philippe Soupault." Accosting an old
beggar, he would borrow his hat and go about soliciting coins
for him, while talking the most charming nonsense to the passers-
by. Once, he entered a hardware shop to ask for a "climbing
vine" that would grow rapidly enough to permit him to mount
to the second-story window of a woman with whom he was madly
in love. On another occasion, he halted a bus on the Avenue de
l'Opéra late at night by extending a chain he carried with him
in its path, then entered it and asked all the passengers to tell
him the date of their birth.

With his bright smile and respectable air, he seemed not at
all offensive; most people responded to him politely or in the
spirit of play. Several times he was almost arrested, yet he continued to walk the streets, seeking everywhere the poetry of the
unexpected or the incongruous, looking for himself and even
saying hello to himself as in the poem "Westwego" (1921):

> *mais ce soir je suis seul je suis Philippe Soupault*
> *je descends lentement le boulevard Saint Michel*
> *je ne pense à rien*
> *Je compte les réverbères que je connais si bien . . .*
> *et je parle tout haut . . .*
> *Bonjour moi*
> *Les marchandes de tapis et les belles demoiselles*
> *qui traînent la nuit dans les rues*
> *ceux qui gardent dans les yeux la douceur des lampes . . .*
> *me connaissent sans savoir mon nom*
> *et me disent en passant Bonjour vous . . .*

On one occasion Soupault went rather far with his pleasant-
ries, and incurred the censure of his confreres. We were at
Cintra's one evening—Breton with his wife, Soupault with his
wife, I with mine; and Ribémont-Dessaignes, Vitrac, Baron,
and Péret also present, unaccompanied. It was a period of increasing tension; the Dada "conspiracy" was becoming repetitious, as Breton declared; he was insistently looking for "some-

thing new." Pounding the table with his fist, Breton exclaimed:
"But this is so dull; I am bored with everything. Who has any
idea?"

"*Allons à un bordel,*" one of those present, probably Vitrac,
said with a laugh.

At once the idea of transferring our meeting for that evening
to a brothel was voted on and passed. My wife and I had never
seen the inside of a bordello, but were agreeable to visiting one.
Breton reluctantly consented, though he too had never gone
to such a resort.

"I know a very proper one," said Soupault. "It is near here.
Let's go."

"With our wives?" I asked.

"Well it may amuse them!"

We set off, hardly believing that Philippe would seriously
carry out his idea. From the Avenue de l'Opéra we turned
into a side street, stopped before an elegant apartment house,
and, while Breton still remonstrated with Philippe, he rang the
bell. It was the favorite rendezvous of Senators and big politicians, Soupault remarked.

A pretty maid ushered us into a large reception room, full
of overstuffed sofas, easy chairs, mirrors and pink lights, and
the traditional mechanical piano. The madame appeared; she
looked us over coldly, finding us rather odd with three quietly
dressed and respectable-looking young matrons in our company.
"What would be the pleasure of the ladies and gentlemen? Champagne at seventy-five francs or at one hundred francs?"

Very authoritatively, Philippe ordered the lower-priced champagne. With the wine a flock of eight or ten courtesans of as-
sorted sizes and girths came tripping in, giving glad cries of
welcome, then, when they noticed our women companions, stared
in surprise. They lined up at one side of the room, half-nude,
wearing brief kirtles over their middles and some light bras-
sières which, however, they proceeded to remove.

"Show us your tricks," one of our party said. The girls in a
group knelt down on the floor and began to make lascivious

movements and gestures toward us, clumsily and mechanically. Soupault kept encouraging the girls in comic spirit; but Breton became, or pretended to become, angry. He had with him, as always, his heavy knobbed cane which he tapped on the floor impatiently. Everyone in our party felt uncomfortable, and no one knew what the next step was to be. Our own ladies, meanwhile, looked on politely with impeccable bourgeois manners.

"This is disgusting," Breton cried out at length, "a shameful spectacle—how could you take us to such a place?" addressing himself wrathfully to Soupault.

Philippe laughed, then said to the madame: "Take them away. Perhaps the 'champagne at one hundred francs' would be better?"

The madame, an imposing woman with a rather stern expression on her face, now looked as if she had had enough of us. "I hope you will leave quietly," she said. "We do not like disorder or noise here." Philippe took out a roll of bank notes, but she politely refused this, and said as we went out: "You needn't bother trying the house next door, because it belongs to the same management."

In truth, none of us felt very proud of that evening's "excursion," which left us with a sense of malaise. Breton's vexation was not at all feigned. Although he talked much of exercising freedom in every direction, and exhorted us to destroy the institutions of the family and the church, our learned young anarch admittedly had no taste for libertinage himself. As to his own romances with women, they were serious enough; in later years he was to have much to say on the theme of love, as in his famous autobiographical romance, *Nadja* (1928).

Aragon, who had not been of the party, rebuked us the next day, holding that we were wrong to disturb the peace of a decorous and well-ordered brothel. (He himself was more conversant with such places than any of us, though in a professional capacity. During the Armistice period he had been attached, as medical officer, to a body of occupying troops stationed at Saarbrücken, Germany, and had the duty of inspecting conditions in the city's two largest bordellos.) About three years earlier, when he had been a Decadent, Aragon used to frighten proper young ladies by assuring them that he had really lost his heart to an Egyptian mummy in the Louvre! Now he was all for "love"—romantic love, baroque love, but love at all events.

At this time Aragon happened to meet a dancer named "Floriane" who had raven black hair and affected Spanish costumes, with resplendent shawls, mantillas, and ornate combs. She used to appear in a small night club of Montparnasse in "Spanish dances" of her own devising. On seeing her dance and hearing her sing, in a harsh voice contrasting with her lovely physiognomy, one was quite ready to believe that she really came from Brussels, as people said.

The *maquillage* of Floriane required many hours of toil each day, for she used seven layers of cream, powder, and paint, making her face a complete mask in which only her dark eyes had movement. Hence, she was never ready to go out before 5:00 P.M. During a fortnight, Aragon professed to be wholly committed to the pursuit of this remarkable woman, so that his friends were regularly led by him to her little cabaret in that period. But why did he love her, we asked him? "Because," he replied, in somewhat mystifying manner, "she is perfectly the picture postcard of *la vie Parisienne*." He added smilingly, "Besides, I have always the need to be in love with The Queen."

Floriane was certainly one of the Queens of Montparnasse that season (it was spring). Yet she seemed to hold rather dim views on the future of art and poetry, and once assured me, with a laugh, that she preferred having a banker on the string rather than an impoverished poet. It was not long before Floriane and her poet were parted.

I happened to ask E.E. Cummings, around that time, to join me one evening and meet some of the Dadaists, particularly Aragon; and so we turned up at the dreary little night club where Floriane was dancing. The tall Roger Vitrac was with us, dressed in the handsome blue uniform of an *élève-officier;* and with him was the small, pink-cheeked Jacques Baron. Cummings, who

had been enjoying some of his favorite Calvados, suddenly exhibited a violent dislike for Vitrac because of his officer's uniform. "Down with the French Army," he cried; "I hate all
French officers!" I tried to explain that young Vitrac, like a
conscript, was under compulsion to undergo training as a student
officer, though he had no more love for the military life than
Cummings. But Cummings would not be pacified. Fortunately
for him, the oversized Vitrac knew no English at the time.

Floriane, meanwhile, came out to do her song and dance. She
was covered with paint and powder and wore only a few clusters
of beads. Her movements were graceless to the point of angu-
larity. Cummings disapproved of her too, and protested: "But she
has no breasts, no breasts at all!" Nothing pleased him that
evening.

However, he formed a high opinion of Aragon and his writings, and some years later did a remarkable translation of Aragon's long and celebrated poem, "Front rouge."

EIGHT

DECLINE AND FALL

OF DADA: 1922–1923

These daring young men, who seemed so amusing to me at the
time, were involved in nothing less than Nietzsche's old project
of the "transvaluation" of human values. They pretended to
occupy a high ground that, in moral affairs, was "beyond good
and evil," as on the aesthetic level it claimed to be "beyond the
beautiful and the ugly." Hence our gatherings at Cintra's or at
each other's homes often turned into impassioned debates over
experiments in *provocative actions*, in effect, moral exercises
that would serve to crystallize the "new" values we sought.

In short, we were a little freemasonry of "activists" absorbed
in schemes for undermining what Breton called "the bourgeois
moral plan." To be a writer, as such, was nothing, was passé; to
be engaged in a variety of moral experiments was everything.

In imposing revolutionary discipline on his band, Breton was
resolute to the point of fanaticism, which made him at times
intolerant and cruel to his most loyal friends. Louis Aragon, in
the days of his youth, could not help writing any more than the
birds can help singing. (Nor is he different now as a white-
haired sexagenarian.) He would come in every day with poems
he had written in a café, or stories done the night before. Breton,

like an autocrat, sometimes exclaimed: "Aragon, you write *too much!*" Though he was as fond of Louis as of anyone, Breton also tyrannized him. And Aragon—the "literary acrobat," as Breton called him, who always functioned with the greatest of ease—would appear cast down, because in those days he loved Breton like a brother or, if you prefer, like a young "father." Breton, doubtless, envied Aragon his great facility, for his own prose, though often much polished and intellectually provocative, was also pretentious and labored.

Tzara once remarked that "Breton, on going into the subway in Paris, would cry out in anger because there were so many people there and no place for him, Breton, to put his feet."

Early in 1922, my wife and I had been entertained at dinner by the Bretons at their apartment in the rue Fontaine, in Montmartre, a place filled with splendid pictures by Picasso, Braque, Chirico, and even the rare Seurat. (Some of them belonged to the couturier, Jacques Doucet, who employed Breton to help him form his collection of modern paintings and manuscripts.) Later, we invited the Bretons to an American meal at our austere apartment in Montparnasse. No sooner had we finished eating than Breton's younger disciples dropped in (as if they had been told to report there), and literally sat at the feet of the master, for there were few real chairs, while he reclined comfortably in the only armchair. The nonchalant young giant, Vitrac, sprawled full length; with him was Benjamin Péret, a troubled, sullen-looking youth; and together with two or three others there was Jacques Baron, a slight blue-eyed boy of seventeen, whose smile was both shy and engaging, and who already wrote and published poetry that was decidedly mature in style.

Breton used to catechize these young people with the air of a schoolmaster who was being kindly for the moment, but could be severe if he chose to. "And what have you been doing with your time?" he asked of each in turn. It was plain that he cast a spell over them with his probing intelligence and his air of stubborn strength. Having inquired about their news, he would then launch into a discourse upon the most recent project he had in view, often presented with eloquence and close-gripping argument. On this occasion there took place some colloquy between Breton and young Baron on the subject of the boy's difficulties with his father—he was playing the young rebel just then—and Breton offered him counsel and help.

A few days after the party at my house I heard that the "boy poet" had run away from his home and gone to the Rhineland as part of the entourage of a French pugilist and his sister—with whom Jacques was reported to be in love. His parents were frantic, and had the police hunting for him. Shortly, I heard through secret channels that Jacques had made his way back to Paris and remained hidden in André Breton's apartment. He had not a sou; Breton and his wife fed and sheltered him in their home, which the boy dared not leave for a time. At this period, as he told me later, he too came to regard Breton as his "father." The case of Jacques Baron offered a challenge to our deepest convictions about human freedom and "the right to love."

Jacques had been attending the Catholic College of St. Marie de Monceau as a day student, but he had been neglecting his school books while running about with his godless Dada friends and writing, even publishing, poetry. His father, a man of conservative ideas, determined to discipline him by having him become a full-time pensionnaire of the college, and live under the strictest surveillance. Jacques thought boarding in the Catholic school would drive him mad, and took flight. There was a pretty girl in the picture too.

When Breton became convinced that the police would soon be paying him a visit in search of Jacques—who was but a minor, after all—he arranged for the boy to slip away at night in the company of Aragon, who put him up in a cheap hotel in a working-class quarter. Meanwhile, Baron dared not venture out to seek work or even food.

Aragon then pressed all his friends for small contributions, in order to keep Jacques Baron alive. One day Aragon and I bought some cold food and chocolate, put it up in a parcel, and proceeded by tram and bus across Paris and out to its east end, where Jacques was domiciled under an incognito. As we neared the place, we looked about warily for police on our trail, then separated, each of us approaching the hotel by a different route, at an interval of ten minutes or so. Jacques had been shut up for days on end, and was overjoyed to see us. Opening a bottle of wine, we had a little celebration with him. We all talked in whispers, acting like great conspirators, and felt good about that.

A couple of days later, Aragon met with Jacques's father, through intermediaries, and arranged for the return of the boy to his home, on condition that he would no longer attend the same school.

Much of the group's discussion turned upon the matter of "unmotivated" crimes, or of those having a complex motivation: There was Julien Sorel, in Stendhal's *The Red and the Black*, shooting his beloved mistress; Stavrogin, in Dostoevski's *The Possessed*, instigating a young girl's suicide; and the "unprovoked" murder of a stranger by the hero of Gide's *Lafcadio's Adventures*. In much the same spirit as these literary personages, and reflecting the liberated moral values of his circle, Jacques Rigaut became an advocate of suicide as a fine art. The highest form of suicide would be the needless or unmotivated type which showed the most complete scorn of this life.

In some autobiographical notes and reflections published in *Littérature* in 1921, Rigaut maintained that only in killing himself did man attain that "unity of opposites, of life and death" which had so long fascinated so many philosophical minds. The consensus among his comrades at the time was that suicide was admissible.

Indeed, Rigaut stood in very high favor among them, because it was known that he had already made one attempt to end his life with a loaded revolver that failed to go off; though he had pressed the trigger firmly, the instrument had proved defective. The experiment had been made in the casual manner that he, as an expert, recommended for those who believed "that there was no more good reason for dying than for living." He added: "Naturally, it goes without saying that I did not, for a moment, think of firing a second bullet. What was important was that I should have taken the resolution to die, and not that I should die." The suicide of Breton's much-extolled friend, Jacques Vaché, had been carried out in the same debonair fashion, following an orgy of drugs; but Vaché had made rather an ugly joke of it by taking an unwitting friend along with him to his death.

I can no longer conceive what Breton hoped to accomplish by showing, in his writings, such interest in the act of suicide. Was it to his mind a supreme form of protest against society? Or was this special interest part of his unbridled nihilism? He certainly had a will to investigate the moral worth of every kind of anti-social act. Later, when members of his group did kill themselves, Breton stimulated a good deal of publicity about each of these events. At that period I did not take the talk of Jacques Rigaut's threats seriously, because he appeared so affable and charming on the surface.

After his first attempt at self-destruction, Rigaut acted as if he were living on borrowed time, until he came to the second trial. As Marcel Duchamp gathered "ready-made" artifacts from banal objects all about, so Rigaut became an "art collector" after his own fancy. He had hundreds of matchboxes of every type, as well as ash trays taken from bars, restaurants, and hotels in Paris and other cities. He also began collecting buttons, stealthily removed from the costumes of persons in every walk of life. Usually he had with him a tiny pair of sharp scissors; approaching, let us say, the doorman of the Ritz Hotel, Rigaut, always very well groomed, would address some question to him in the most polite tone, then quietly snip off a button of the man's uniform. It was said that he could perform the same trick in a salon with generals or deputies, or with some beggar encountered in the street. In exhibiting his collection to his friends, Rigaut had some drily amusing tale that went with each button. His action was a travesty on the role of the art collector; it also constituted a form of secret aggression.

Aragon, the thin young man with caressing manners, also wrote various stories which were exercises in the social nihilism affected at this period. One of these (which I translated for *Broom*), entitled "Lorsque Tout Est Fini," was based on the affair of the famous Bonnot gang of Paris anarchists who, after being betrayed by one of their comrades, shot it out with the police for days on end before blowing themselves up inside their fortified redoubt. The story is a study in the psychology of treason; one of its key sentences runs: "I found it infinitely voluptuous to contemplate the destruction of all that I loved"; and another: "The desire grew in me to commit the act which from every point of view would be indefensible."

Georges Ribémont-Dessaignes, one of the older members of the Paris Dadaist group, has described in his memoirs some other incidents illustrating the kind of moral intangibles the Dadaists played with in their experiments. He relates:

It was at Cintra's in the Passage [de l'Opéra] that another sensational episode in the secret annals of Dadaism took place. A waiter left his pocketbook on one of the benches after making change, and the Dadaists appropriated it.

They went off to another café down the street and heatedly discussed the question of whether they should keep the pocketbook and the money (which amounted to about twenty dollars). Their revolt against common morality required that they keep it. But it was the property of a poor worker, a waiter who would doubtless have to make good the sum to his boss. Was it not a cowardly action, according to Dadaist doctrine (which disapproved of cowardice, among other things)? If only it had been the purse of some rich man! Yet, if they now returned it they would be showing moral flabbiness, as if disapproving—out of absurdly conventional scruples—of the theft of property. Surely, one of them argued, it would be more interesting, more significant an action if they robbed a poor man instead of a rich one, which all common thieves tried to do. The discussion went on for hours; one would propose that they use the money to pay for a new Dada brochure, but another urged that they throw a big party and drink it all up. Finally, Paul Éluard volunteered to act as custodian of the purloined pocketbook until they made up their minds, and this was agreed upon.

The next day the pocketbook was returned by mail to the waiter. When this became known, the other Dadaists fell upon Éluard and heaped their contempt on his head. Breton was particularly severe in upbraiding him for what he called a display of "moral weakness."[1]

Francis Picabia, half-Cuban and half-French, had figured in the wars of art for about twenty years when I first saw him in 1922. He seemed driven by the urge to change and reinvent everything, but also by his love of *blague*. After having been, in turn, a Fauvist, a Cubist, and a Futurist, he naturally joined the Dadaist camp toward 1918. Presumably, he was a man of independent wealth; I remember his driving up to our meeting place at a café in an English sport car, clad in a white linen duster and looking like one of those South American millionaires one saw in Paris. In any case, he donated some money for the Dadaist publications, but complained that he often became bored with these younger rebels, accused them of being repetitious, and was not above playing hoaxes on them.

At times the Dadaists gathered at Picabia's spacious studio apartment on the Boulevard Raspail. Here occurred a strange incident known thereafter in Dadaist annals as the "Affair of the Anonymous Letter." The letter in question had been sent to Tristan Tzara. It was written in a highly offensive tone and was unsigned, though its style and knowledge of various details about Tzara indicated that it was by the hand of one who had been an intimate of the circle. Breton, Aragon, and Soupault were all in turn accused of authorship of the letter by Tzara, and each denied it. Then suspicion turned upon Francis Picabia, an inveterate practical joker, and a very likely suspect, but

he managed to convince the others of his innocence. Ribémont-
Dessaignes, who described the incident in his reminiscences,
has ventured the guess that Tzara "had perhaps written the
letter to himself in order to inspire his group of friends with
demoralizing suspicions."

At the time when Breton met with some of his younger disciples at my home he had talked, among other things, of a new
project that was very dear to his heart; the organization of a
sort of "congress" of intellectuals and artists to be held in Paris
in the summer of 1922 with the object of inquiring into the
principles of "modernism" in the arts. Part of its purpose
would be "to determine the directives for the defense of the
modern spirit." Eminent representatives of the avant-garde from
all over Europe would be invited to attend the Congress. André
himself would preside over their assembly, whose proceedings
would be released to the world's press and radio (something
new). Roger Vitrac, then associated with Marcel Arland as an
editor of the new literary review, *Aventure,* which had a very
promising group of youthful contributors, at first gave his enthusiastic support to Breton's plan.

However, the most heated disputes soon burst forth among
the Dadaists over this new and rather public-spirited enterprise.
Breton had written Tzara, formally inviting him to serve as a
member of the organizing committee, although these two prin-
cipals were already rivals and intensely suspicious of each
other's motives. Tzara wanted to keep Dada "pure"; that is,
purely destructive in its action, always ready for a big joke, and
keeping its powder dry for new surprise attacks. He did not
want Dadaism associated with other schools and isms, such as
Cubism or Futurism, and opposed holding a convention together with their spokesmen. "Dada is not modern," he used
to say mystifyingly. He also made the grave accusation against
Breton that he was "serious"; and in private, made mock of his

schemes. For the record, however, Tzara wrote Breton a formal letter of declination.

. . . I regret to say that the reservations I have felt about the very idea of the Congress would not be changed by my participating in it. I wish you, my friend, to believe that this is not an action of a personal nature directed against you or any others on the Committee, and I appreciate your desire to give representation to every tendency as I do the courtesy you have shown me.

As if to ward off further criticisms of his cherished project by the sharp-tongued Tzara, Breton quickly issued a press communiqué to one of the Paris newspapers (*Comoedia,* a widely read theatrical journal) published February 3, 1922, in which he warned the public against the machinations of a "certain personage who hailed from Zurich" and who was but "an impostor avid of publicity."

Breton's intemperate attack on Tzara was motivated in part by his domineering spirit and partly by his will to give a new and more positive direction to his following, in contrast with the negative spirit consistently manifested by Tzara. Dadaism and Tzara both must be destroyed. Dadaism had become futile, had been limiting itself to playing with velleities, and negated too many positive ideas and principles that Breton wished to fight for. He was en route toward a new faith that would be derived from the romantic traditions and the "proto-Surrealist" literature of France. For him, this episode marked the beginning of a life-long career of repeated "excommunications" of former friends and comrades.

Nevertheless, his sudden, venomous attack on the brilliant personality whom he had so eagerly invited to Paris two years before as "the new Rimbaud," and whom, a few days earlier, he had asked to join with him in the steering committee for his Congress, shocked the very persons whose support Breton solicited. The terms he had used in assailing Tzara (a Romanian Jew) as a *foreigner,* also suggested the xenophobe and the anti-

André Breton at the Dada Festival held at the
Salle Gaveau in Paris in 1920.

A performance of *Vous m'oublierez* with Philippe Soupault,
Paul Éluard, André Breton *(seated)*, and Théodore Fraenkel.

Le Coeur à barbe, pamphlet edited by Tristan Tzara in April of 1922.

Collage and photomontage prepared by André Breton and collaborators, including René Magritte, for the December 15, 1929, issue of *La Révolution Surréaliste*.

Louis Aragon and André Breton in a 1921 photograph
taken by Man Ray.

Tristan Tzara and Matthew Josephson in the Tirol
in 1922, photo by Jean Arp.

1   4

2   5

3   6

7

10

8

9

1 Jacques Rigaut

2 René Crevel
Photo by Man Ray

3 Benjamin Péret
Photo by Man Ray

4 Philippe Soupault
Photo by Berenice Abbott

5 Paul Éluard
Photo by Man Ray

6 Jacques Baron
Photo by Man Ray

7 E. E. Cummings
Photo by Edward Weston

8 Man Ray
Photo by Man Ray

9 Malcolm Cowley
Photo by James Casey

10 Edmund Wilson, Jr.
*Photo by White Studios,
from Vanity Fair*

The March, 1922, cover of *Littérature,*
which was designed by Man Ray.

Jean Arp's design for the August, 1922,
cover of *Secession* No. 3.

Tristan Tzara, Jean Arp, and Max Ernst in a 1922 snapshot.

Hart Crane,
Allen Tate,
and Slater Brown
at a New York
shooting gallery
in 1924.

Kenneth Burke in
full academic war paint.

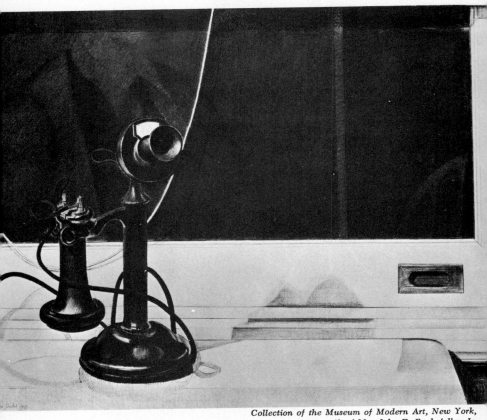

The black conté crayon "Self Portrait" of 1923 by Charles Sheeler.

Using oil on cardboard with cutouts, Jean Arp did
"Mountain, Table, Anchors, Navel," in 1925.

Jean Arp's "Collage with Squares Arranged According to the
Law of Chance" of the years 1916-1917.

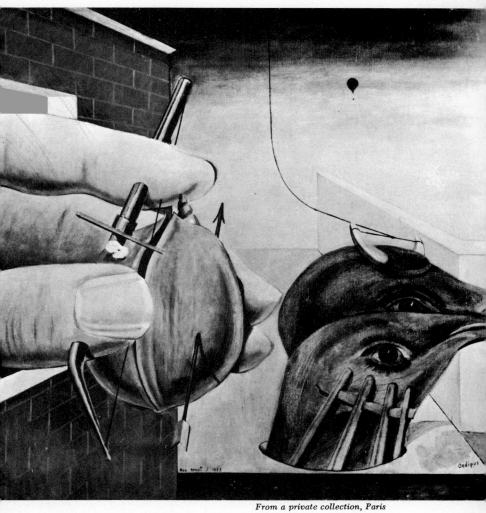

A 1922 oil on canvas by Max Ernst, called "Oedipus Rex."

Get Self Respect Like Taking a Pill
MENCKENIZE!

WE want smirks instead of piety.

We want to think it is intellectual to drink beer.

We want to laugh at our neighbours.

Who points out for us our national absurdities which are as glaring as electric signs?

Who consoles us if we prefer Stephen Benet to Plato?

Who has backed the rise of our national intelligence from that of a high school junior to that of a freshman co-ed?

It is said that Mencken is shaping public opinion. This is a DIRTY LIE. Mencken is *voicing* public opinion. Mencken's GROWING POWER is due to the fact that God sent him to express OUR AMERICA. That's why we want him.

We are for Mencken, editor and circulation-builder.

Mencken has been called a radical. This is a DIRTY LIE. Mencken is a conservative. Mencken expresses the conservatism of revolt.

Why Mencken is superior to Billy Sunday: Sunday wants us to go to church; Mencken makes it funny to stay away. Sunday wants us to avoid pretty girls; Mencken makes it charmingly naughty to look at the Follies. Sunday wants us to quit drinking; Mencken makes it intellectual to drink.

MENCKEN!

Up with MENCKEN — Down with BILLY SUNDAY

Can't you understand modern art?

Let Mencken show you the absurdity of the Ku Klux Klan.

Can't you follow modern philosophy?

Let Mencken snigger with you at William Jennings Bryan.

Did you flunk Trig?

Let Mencken ridicule professors for you.

MENCKEN!
will never betray you.

will never tax you.

will never talk above your heads.

gives you a standard product.

avoids all difficult thinking is for good sound common sense.

makes it clever to see the obvious.

says "damn" in public.

YOU CAN RELY ON MENCKEN

Since he has changed from *Smart Set* to *American Mercury* Mencken can be read without offence by women and children.

Would you like to be a snob without study? Look up Mencken.

Let Mencken cure your inferiority complex.

MENCKEN PROMOTION SOCIETY

"MENCKENIZE," a polemical "advertisement" in *Aesthete: 1925* by Kenneth Burke, with the collaboration of the other Aesthetes.

Dreyfusard. Breton himself afterward admitted that he had been "inept."

The organizing committee for the Congress included the artists Fernand Léger, Robert Delaunay, and Amédée Ozenfant; also the composers Erik Satie and Georges Auric; and the poets Jean Paulhan and Roger Vitrac. In an open letter to the press a number of these men now accused Breton of having issued his public statement assailing Tzara without their authorization, and of having done this in the spirit of a "narrow nationalist" and "reactionary." They also announced a meeting to be held at the Closerie des Lilas, February 17, 1922, where the question of the proposed Congress would be fully investigated. Breton was invited to appear at this meeting, and in effect to stand trial. He came, of course.

More than a hundred people were on hand when I entered the upstairs banquet room of the old café. Virtually all of artistic and literary Paris was excited over the "trial" of Breton—though such periodic cataclysms were a familiar part of its life. I remember seeing the chunky, bright-eyed Pablo Picasso, together with Henri Matisse and the sculptor Constantin Brancusi; also Jean Cocteau and his young friend Raymond Radiguet, the precocious novelist; and a good many of the *Nouvelle Revue Française* clan, as well as members of the press. I had come without any clear notions of what the conflict was all about; after witnessing the most tempestuous verbal brawl I had ever seen or heard, I said to myself: "The Revolution is devouring its sons!"

Never in my experience were words of such passion and flame hurled at each other by men without coming to blows. (If they had been Americans, they would have butchered one another.) Several of Breton's close friends, including Soupault, Éluard, and Ribémont-Dessaignes, expressed disapproval of his action. Aragon, as ever, was at Breton's side, a pale and eloquent advocate. Breton spoke in rolling periods in his own defense; while Tzara, leaping to the attack, fairly screamed in his high voice, talking so fast that I could not follow him. Erik Satie, the comic spirit of modern music, a paunchy man with gold-rimmed pince-

nez and a goatee, presided as "judge" and seemed to be laugh
ing over the affair all the time. Philippe Soupault, in one very
moving speech, strove in vain to reconcile the opposing parties
In the end—after all sorts of absurd charges had been hurled
back and forth—the consensus of the meeting was expressed in
a vote of nonconfidence in Breton and his proposed Congress
of Paris—which thus, in its preparatory stages, collapsed. It
was a humiliating reverse for that redoubtable man.

On the other hand, he had sounded the death knell for Dada
ism, the beginning of whose agonies I witnessed at the Closerie
des Lilas. After that day, Dada's bold lancers never rode to the
fray again as of old, as a unified band. Perhaps, as some ventured to say at the time, Dada could triumph only by dying.

Intellectual Paris has always loved such imbroglios and takes
them lightly. After it was over, several of us repaired to another
café. There were with us Erik Satie, Tzara, Éluard, and Robert
Delaunay. To my surprise, they rehashed the whole affair in
very reasonable terms. Satie busied himself, in consultation with
the others, in writing the terms of the majority resolution condemning Breton, which was to be handed to the press; he kept
gurgling into his beard with amusement, as he selected some
especially pompous phrases in the style in which André Breton
delighted.

In March, 1922, Tzara published a little brochure called *Le
Coeur à Barbe,* a polemic aimed at Breton. It was done on pink
newspaper stock, illustrated with little pictures of steamships,
balloons, camels, serpents, and even a urinal, done by Marcel
Duchamp.

Among those who contributed satirical notes, epigrams, and
doggerel to this pamphlet were Paul Éluard, Marcel Duchamp,
Philippe Soupault, Erik Satie, and the "mysterious" Dr. Théodore Fraenkel, a young man of wit who had been the comrade
of Breton and Aragon at medical school and in the Army. I, too,
was guilty of some doggerel included in this brochure, and was
promptly taken to task by Aragon, who assured me that I had
not the least understanding of what I was doing. I replied that

while I could not possibly follow all the raveled plots and counterplots of the warring factions, I did not believe they were serious, and, in any case, was resolved to live amongst them as a neutral party. This I managed to do for a long time, by meeting the "enemies" separately. In truth, they kept changing sides so rapidly that one could not distinguish friend from foe.

André Breton now revived the review *Littérature* (which had been suspended for several months) and in its April, 1922, issue published a memorable *envoi* to Dadaism. It had been, he declared, only a passing fashion, a "manner of sitting down." To be sure, it had been useful in fostering a certain "state of mind which served to keep us in a condition of readiness—from which we shall now start out, in all lucidity, toward that which calls to us." The call, it was hinted, would be uttered in good time by the prophet, André Breton.

He himself was preparing new ideas and new programs, which he was sure would be worth fighting and even dying for. In truth, he was turning back to old French traditions of esoteric romanticism and to the suggestions of "surrealism" left by Guillaume Apollinaire. This article of Breton's was entitled "Lâchez tout!" ("Abandon Everything!"), and had as its feature a remarkable epopee:

Abandon everything. Abandon Dada. Get rid of your wife. Give up your mistress. Give up your hopes and your fears. Sow your children out in the woods. Give up the substance for the shadow. Give up your easy way of life, and that which passes for a job with a future. Take to the roads. . . .

The war between the armies of Breton and Tzara did, after all, reach a stage of fisticuffs and bloodshed a year later, in 1923, when Tzara produced his play, *Le Coeur à Gaz*, at a Paris theater. A feature of the show was to be the reading of some poetry by Jean Cocteau, that melancholy dandy of the Right Bank, whom Breton regarded as his deadly enemy. Breton and his cohorts had threatened to start a riot if the play were put on; and Tzara, so it has been charged and also as stoutly denied, is said to have given the police warnings of their criminal intentions.

Breton and Aragon duly appeared in the orchestra of the theater; after they had heckled the actors awhile, both young men leaped to the stage, and Breton, wildly swinging his heavy knobbed cane, broke the arm of one of the players, the charming, pint-sized Pierre de Massot. Tzara hurled himself upon Breton and they rolled about the stage, while the audience was in a tumult, until the police arrived and threw Breton, Aragon, and their accomplices out into the street. Then, just as things had quieted down and the play had been resumed, Paul Éluard climbed up on the stage to create a new disturbance. But the distinguished poet was knocked about very rudely; during the melee he fell among the footlights, which exploded one by one and did some damage.

The next day the theater management sent a bailiff to Éluard with a bill for eight thousand francs. Thus the former brothers in Dadaism had reached the stage of waging lawsuits against each other!

NINE

HOW TO START

A LITERARY MOVEMENT

What I had seen of the French avant-garde groups prompted the thought that it might be great fun if we Americans, who were in Europe at the time, would start a literary movement of our own for the younger generation. Malcolm Cowley's essay for the New York *Post,* published a few months earlier, had spoken of the "youngest generation," rising out of the late war and their need for a literary organ of their own. It wasn't certain whether they shared many beliefs in common or would work together in such a unitary enterprise, but it seemed worth trying. We would enjoy publishing our own work, and at the same time throwing rocks at the Philistines, as our European contemporaries were so joyously doing.

Munson and I had been talking about starting a "little magazine" of our own in Europe. Before his departure for Vienna, I fired him with my own zeal for the idea, and set forth a whole program which he endorsed unreservedly.

In a letter of February 4, 1922, to one of my confreres in New York I wrote:

My reports on the lower cost of everything in Central Europe led Gorham B. Munson to contemplate starting a new review during the Spring months. *Broom* is not doing much sweeping. Beyond that you have *The Dial* and the *Saturday Evening Post.* Munson's plan is to reduce the economic pressure on art ad absurdum by going to the country bearing the lowest rate of exchange, say Austria. He has just left Paris with two large trunks. . . .

The review will cost no more than 30,000 Kronen per issue in Vienna ($20) and M. has about $500, so that a good time is assured for all.

I added that it was understood that I was "to bear some of the responsibility" for the proposed review, while "Munson bears the cost." All young writers, I argued, should publish their masterpieces in their own little magazines, and wound up: "My dear boy, if you don't have faith in little reviews what in hell can you have faith in?"

In an earlier letter I had described Munson as a former school-teacher who now fairly "yearned" to edit a literary magazine.[1] But while he was willing enough, he created some questions in my mind because of his evident lack of critical acumen and literary taste. When I first met him, he thought the style of Theodore Dreiser could hardly be improved upon, and that Waldo Frank was "the greatest American novelist." In a word (so it seemed to me), Munson scarcely knew the difference between Marianne Moore and Thomas Moore.

Now my own plan for our review was to raise a good deal of thunder on the left, by publishing and championing the adventurous experimenters of America, translating the work of the avant-garde in France and Germany, and vigorously assailing the Mrs. Grundies of literature. Aside from Hart Crane, Munson knew none of our young rebels.

Before Munson left Paris I wrote Kenneth Burke and Malcolm Cowley, soliciting their (unpaid) contributions to our new magazine. I also made out lists of persons like Marianne Moore, W.C. Williams, and Wallace Stevens, to whom Munson was to write; and put him in touch with E.E. Cummings and Slater Brown, who were then in Paris.

Cummings, after meeting Munson, permitted himself the

quizzical observation: "Munson's heart certainly bleeds for the younger generation of American writers." In any case, Cummings had a trunkful of unpublished poems, and kindly contributed a number of them that were done with his most intoxicated orthography, poems then considered too "modern" for publication by editors of magazines that paid for poetry. Miss Moore, Williams, and Stevens also had heaps of unpublished material for us; they were unwept, unsung and all but unread.

In writing to Kenneth Burke, I said that Gorham Munson would be returning to the United States in a few weeks and would probably look him up. In somewhat guarded terms I added that while Munson was an excellent comrade in arms, his taste might need guidance. "Be nice to him," I urged.

Malcolm Cowley, having heard from Munson, wrote Kenneth Burke in the same monitory spirit, saying:

This magazine Gorham B. Munson is starting may be the one we want—I don't know Gorham Munson, so I can't judge of it. When Munson comes to New York find out whether his taste is to be trusted, and if it is, entice him and his magazine into the green country. What do you know about him?[2]

In the meantime I labored to prepare the first two issues of our review; made translations of pieces by Aragon, Éluard, Soupault, Tzara, and Breton; and wrote a short essay on Apollinaire which embodied our "platform," our ideology of experiment and innovation:

Apollinaire . . . forerunner of almost everything of importance that will take place in the literature of the next generation, urged the poets of this age to be as daring as the mechanical inventors of the airplane, wireless, cinema and phonograph. . . . The modern folklore of which Apollinaire spoke is taking shape. . . .

In an exuberant prose I called on the poets of my generation to turn their thoughts to the realities of our Machine Age and to sing of our "new America," with its urbanized folkways, its mass entertainments, its violent dances, and its barbarous music.

Life in Europe had afforded some of us a new perspective of the United States, whose "marvelous young mechanical forces," I maintained, were destined to transform Europe herself. We must experiment or die; we must be audacious, and yet more audacious. My language may have been a little disheveled, my tone that of youthful overconfidence, but the spirit of affirmation was there, and my attempts at prophecy proved not too wide of the mark, considered in retrospect forty years later.

A statement by Munson, entitled "A Bow to the Adventurous," also promised that our magazine would be the organ of

those writers who are preoccupied with researches for new forms. It hopes that there is ready for it an American public which has advanced beyond the fiction and poetry of Sinclair Lewis and Sherwood Anderson . . .

To start a literary movement was one thing; to induce my confreres in America to join it was something else. I had seen how my French friends, though intensely individualistic and therefore much given to jealous strife, retained sufficient esprit de corps, at least in the beginning of their movement, to make the wars of art more interesting and amusing than anywhere else. Lacking the tradition of working (and also fighting) in artistic schools or groups, Americans, by comparison, seemed like lone wolves.

When I appealed to Burke, Cowley, and Crane to stand up and join our little movement and make war upon our home-grown Philistines with the new stratagems employed by the European Dadaists, notably their laughing-gas attacks, my friends at first only sniffed at me. Burke wrote that the Dadaists were "anti-reason" and therefore damned:

I am scandalized that words of all things are used in a way that denies their essential property, the property of ideological clarity. . . . How blatantly your own letter denies the whole Dadaist regime; for being moved by an authentic anxiety to express yourself, your first concern was with lucidity. It never even occurred to you to write it all Dadaistically.[3]

How in the world was I to bring my literary friends together so that they might serve the Republic of Letters as a more-or-less homogeneous group? Malcolm Cowley, for instance, wrote me avowing his present mistrust of the diverse "modernist" movements and his intention to write as a classicist either in the style of Alexander Pope or in the neoclassical manner of T.S. Eliot. I answered that T.S. Eliot had been "born dead"—his "Prufrock" was only a sad sack—a view that reflected an abrupt about-face on my part; for I too had felt, earlier, the attractive force of Eliot's impeccable verses. I also roundly accused Malcolm of having written (as of the spring of 1922) some "old-fashioned nature poetry"—a charge that was disconcerting to an enterprising young man. Malcolm replied with angry snorts; but soon came from Montpellier to Paris, looked me up, and went with me to meet my avant-garde Frenchmen: Aragon, Breton, and Soupault. He was impressed, as I had been, by the dead-earnestness with which they treated all issues of art and literature, as if they were matters of life or death—so that with them, the literary life seemed much more exciting than in New York. Breton was willing to wade through gore to make people appreciate Lautréamont or even M. Raymond Roussel; Aragon was ready to fight duels with some of his contemporaries because "they wrote French badly." Malcolm, falling under their spell, reversed himself, and in a letter to Burke wrote: "Matty is right about them [the Dada group]; they are the most amusing people in Paris." His style changed; the tempo of his verses now assumed something like a ragtime beat. He also became so enthusiastic a convert to the Dadaist cult of pure act that, a year later, amid the festivities of July 14, 1923, he punched the nose of the proprietor of the Café de la Rotonde—it was probably a well-deserved chastisement—and spent a night in jail before his friends could rescue him. The French, in truth, seldom liked to use their fists; but Malcolm was admired henceforth as a "man of action."

Hart Crane, then in Cleveland, Ohio, also wrote to Munson, airing his doubts about our undertaking: "dear Matty . . . is, it strikes me, altogether unsteady," he opined. Though he was amused and interested by my "performance," Crane was unable to embrace my newest theories.[4] Nevertheless he readily contributed several poems which other editors had rejected. There was a need for our review, for Hart had never before written verses as rich and ornate as those he sent me in 1922.

Cummings seemed closer than other Americans to contemporary movements in French poetry. He had a fondness (like the Dadaists and Surrealists) for juxtaposing the incongruous, and for "words that surprise each other" on finding themselves bedfellows. In any case, I felt that true Dada doctrine allowed for wide differences in personal style; and no scruples opposed my combining in our literary menagerie the cerebral fables of Kenneth Burke, the cacophonous music of Tzara's "collage-poetry," the "automatic writings" of Breton and Soupault, the neo-Elizabethan iambics of Hart Crane, and the lilting, expressionistic, and syntax-defying verses of E.E. Cummings.

Gorham Munson, meanwhile, journeyed toward Vienna, his trunks filled with manuscript material I had provided for the little magazine we were jointly issuing. Together we had selected several of my own experiments in verse and prose, some of which I signed with a *nom de guerre,* "Will Bray." Inasmuch as mail from the United States followed Munson rather slowly, he was obliged, for want of other manuscripts at the time, to make up the first two issues principally out of material supplied by either "Will Bray" or Matthew Josephson. Munson then named himself sole editor of the publication, though about sixty per cent of its text, at the start, consisted of my contributions. Even so, the new review almost failed to be born, owing to Munson's very capricious behavior (which I learned about several months later).

While en route to Vienna, he made a side trip to Rome to call on Harold Loeb, the editor and publisher of *Broom,* and applied for the job of associate editor of that publication. (From Rome, on February 7, 1922, Munson addressed a postcard to

Hart Crane saying: "I call on the *Broom* tomorrow.")[5] According to Loeb, Munson laid claim to having "the youngest generation in his pocket." In consideration of a job with *Broom*, he implied that he would turn over this advantageous property to Loeb—which consisted largely of literary material (and names of friends) I had assembled for the use of our own new review! Loeb, in his own recollections, has stated that he was unimpressed by Munson's claims to exclusive ownership of the "youngest generation," since he himself "had previously been in touch with Matthew Josephson, Malcolm Cowley, etc.," who were already being published in *Broom*.

It was understandable that Munson should have applied for a pleasant job that would have enabled him to remain for a long time in Europe. But it was disconcerting to learn afterward that he had shown himself willing and ready to dispose of the whole "movement" I had labored to "invent," without asking my leave and without even informing me of his action.

Munson's next halt was in Munich, where he visited an exhibition of the *"Sezession"* group of German artists—dating back twenty years—the forerunners of the Expressionists. As our review needed a name, he wrote me that he had conceived the idea of naming it *Secession*. I was taken aback, because in our own country the word would be associated with the American Civil War, while in Europe it had reference to a dated group of ante-bellum modernists. As he hurried to press before I could think of something else, the name stayed.

I have described in some detail the circumstances under which *Secession* was founded, in the first place, because numerous accounts of its history have been given by literary historians of the twenties who have not hitherto included all the little true facts of the affair; and in the second place, because Munson has made some very misleading statements about our brief literary collaboration in a whole series of articles he published many years ago. These included bitter personal attacks on my character, which I have never answered. The account given here is documented by my correspondence of the time, which has been deposited with the Yale University Library.

Secession's first and second numbers, of twenty-four pages each, were printed in Vienna and appeared in April and May, 1922; their cost was about twenty dollars per issue. Considering that it had a maximum circulation of three or four hundred copies, the little magazine aroused a surprising amount of interest among the literary public at home and abroad. In America, comment in the newspaper supplements and in such weeklies as *The New Republic* reflected some fear that we young Americans in Paris had lost our heads, had turned "expatriate," and were enacting a "new secessionist movement" away from the fatherland. Reviewing the contents of the new publication, in a mood both incredulous and disapproving, Louis Untermeyer concluded that it represented a search on the part of post-war youth for new values, but strongly deplored our interest in the subversive and "destructive" notions of the European Dadaists, naming me as the devil's advocate in our literary group, or "King of the American Dadaists." In those days it was common for Americans to treat anything claiming to be experimental or avant-garde as belonging to the "lunatic fringe"; some commentators singled out the poems of Cummings, Crane, and Tzara as specimens of our comical jargon. In reality, our small publication suggested to more discerning persons the abundance of talent and individuality to be found among new American writers who had been seldom published or read at the time. Among them were William Carlos Williams, Marianne Moore, and Wallace Stevens, as well as the still younger men, such as E.E. Cummings, Hart Crane, Malcolm Cowley, Kenneth Burke, Robert M. Coates, and Slater Brown.

Cummings' "Four Poems" in Secession 2 (not all of which seem to have been reprinted in his *Collected Poems*) conveys the nostalgia of those days when American literary tourists besieged Paris, and also commemorates the "suicide" of Dada in 1922:

what's become of (if you please)
all the glory that or which was Greece
all the grandja
that was dada
. . . waiter make me a child . . . so this is Paris
i will sit in the corner and drink thinks and think drinks
in memory of the grand old days
and of Amy Sandburge and Carl Algernon Swinburned

In London the literary critics, being more inured to manifestations of revolt in the arts, were tolerant and even friendly. Edith Sitwell, for example, found much that was interesting in the translations from the French Dadaists, observing that Louis Aragon's story was "literature of an exquisite order." My own claims for a program of aesthetic innovation, outlined in my essay on Apollinaire, were considered by Miss Sitwell provocative, if extravagant. "Will Bray" had been described by Munson, a heavy-minded jester, as a "youth of nineteen who has fought many duels on two continents," and so Miss Sitwell concluded sympathetically that "in the face of such critical promise we feel inclined to forgive him his mistaken jibes at Cocteau. . . . I shall subscribe to *Secession* for the purpose of reading its criticism and watching the career of Mr. Will Bray."[6]

Under the same nom de plume of "Will Bray" I had published a short poem entitled "In a Café," a bit of spoofing, mocking at "serious" poetry. Gorham Munson happened to make the poem the subject of his weighty critical comment, touching both on its "historic significance" (to his mind) and its treatment of "a subject hitherto condemned as unsuitable for literature" by means of "adroit evasions." In New York, Miss Marianne Moore also declared that this rather modest bit of work was, in her view, an achievement of the highest order, and expressed eagerness to learn the identity of the author. The poem runs:

He— You are a sweet girl
    and I shall throw you into the river
     you are a sweet girl

and I shall buy you narcissi
  you are a sweet girl
and I shall give you wormwood
  you are a sweet girl
and I shall chew your ear
  you are a sweet girl
and I shall leave you for a moment

She— I am going to leave *you* for a moment
He— I am going to leave *you* for a moment . . .
She— —a moment
He— —a moment

Marianne Moore, then working, as for many years past, as a librarian in one of the New York Public Library branches, was given to far-ranging and curious readings, but—greatly to her credit—seems to have had little knowledge of café-going, or of what happens when people have consumed a goodly quantity of wine. Thus she completely missed the slightly concealed allusions in the poem to natural functions. Her attitude toward me, at first, was most friendly and complimentary; while I admired (as I still do) her very strange and tense "observations," which occasionally rise to heights of true poetic statement. But, if I may be forgiven for saying as much, she was, and is to this day, a delightfully and determinedly old-fashioned person, even to her charmingly outmoded costumes—also an aspect of her particular individuality.

After some time, however, she did manage to discern the inner content of my small poem, was deeply shocked, and could hardly ever bring herself thereafter to forgive or to trust me again. On the occasion when I first met her (after my return to New York in 1923), she heaped reproaches upon me for hours on end for what she must have conceived as my perverse and wicked nature. And she can be most tenacious in argument. But if she is old-fashioned, she also has an old-fashioned integrity and generosity that is all too rare nowadays.

At the time of my return from Europe, I happened to meet a young poet, a Canadian, who was literally starving to death in

New York. I appealed to some people for help, among them Miss Moore. She donated money, though she had very small means; and thereafter, every Sunday on their way to church, during several weeks, Miss Moore and her mother would bring large parcels of food for that impecunious poet, until work was found for him.

At the end of nearly a year of our voluntary exile in Europe we all longed for more of the same. The old letters of my contemporaries who were in France then contain expressions of dismay at the thought of returning to the United States and exchanging their free, if poverty-ridden, way of life for some routine job in an office. For me, the society of the young Europeans with whom I lived on terms of comradeship had become very seductive. They might pretend to be moral nihilists and "anti-artists," but at heart they were true men of letters with a consuming passion for their métier, and who would wake up with new ideas about it every morning. What we were all doing was terribly important to us, even though the workaday world was indifferent. In the case of happily transplanted Americans like myself, our attitude toward our native land was much like that of Albrecht Dürer who, when asked why he tarried so long in Venice, replied: "Because here I am considered a gentleman, while at home I would be considered an idler."

The falling exchanges in Central Europe provided some of us with opportunities to prolong the time of our *Wanderjahre* by moving over to Austria or Germany. When Tristan Tzara informed me that an international group of French and German Dadaists would be gathering together at a little summer resort in the Tirol, and invited me to join them, I determined to go there for the summer and thus postpone my departure by several months.

My wife and I planned to begin our journey with a walking trip in southern France and a fortnight's visit to Italy, before going on to our Austrian refuge. I had amassed about two hundred dollars; with this we set off on our "grand tour," much of it done in short trips on hard third-class coaches, while our heavy baggage and books were sent on ahead of us to await our arrival (and customs' inspection) at the Italian border.

We traveled light: I carried a knapsack on my back and a spiked stick for climbing the mountains of the Savoie and Dauphiné. Halting at some town like Chambéry, we would tour the environs on foot, putting up at rude taverns or farmhouses along the road. During a week in May we marched twenty miles each day, climbing to the plateau of the Grande Chartreuse, traversing its snow-covered mountain passes in full view of the high Alps, and descending again to the valley of the Isère River at Grenoble, where we rejoined the railway line to Italy. In the mountains we gathered the violets of early spring in patches of grass showing through the snow; in the Isère valley we walked in a riot of flowers: blazing poppies and marguerites and fields of blossoming garlic. On one or two occasions, when a storm overtook us, we were forced to take refuge in the cottage of some poor Savoyard peasant, eating wretched food and sleeping in a broken bed, yet we never felt better in all our lives.

In Rome, the clear hard light reflected from the amber-colored walls of so many churches and palaces seemed blinding to us after the cloudy skies of Paris. As the city was then flooded with Catholic pilgrims, and had no accommodations, we found it best to continue our journey southward to Naples.

Naples with its great *chiamasso* of wildly expostulating people always reminded me of Dante's vision of hell. On its heights were orange orchards and perfumed gardens and the wide vista of pure sky and curving shores; down in the lower city, reached by streets that were but winding stone stairs, one arrived in a zone of immitigable squalor and all the variety of old Mediterranean stenches and a ragged people laughing and weeping at the same time—in short, Dante's Inferno, so conveniently situated just beneath paradise.

In those days my principles forbade "rubbernecking" among ruins and monuments, Baedeker in hand, as did the plodding

British and German tourists all about us. But Capri we must visit, for it was the island of the true lotus-eaters, and we must find out if we would be lotus-eaters; and so we sailed across the bay, ascended the funicular, and climbed the donkey path that led to a charming hotel then in a quite rural site on the ridge, or pass, between the town of Capri and Anacapri. We lunched under palms and lemon trees in its garden, walked about and gaped at all this Siren Land (as Norman Douglas, and Homer long before him, named it), and swam in the transparent sea full of colored stones.

In this sunlight and heat, among these subtropical plants and flowers, one felt oneself gradually dissolving into a protoplasmic happiness, and becoming only a sensual beast, as had happened to others on Tiberius' isle. Capri was then a quiet spot, inhabited by a colony of eccentric foreigners—English, Scandinavian, and Russian—as well as by its charming indigenous pagans. "No, it can't be true!" I would exclaim as I saw some seascape more theatrical than all that had gone before, or at the spectacular sunset that formed a backdrop for our garden terrace at the dinner hour.

The proprietor, seeing how much we were affected by his island, invited us to stay on by the week, naming a price that seemed more advantageous than the transient rate. "A week!" I exclaimed, "but I would like to stay here forever." Very obligingly our tempter quoted a monthly rate that seemed to us utterly minuscule. We could have enjoyed this excellent fare, all the blond Capri wine we wanted, our beautiful room with its balcony over the garden, and the blue sea merely by borrowing a moderate sum of money—and lived here in unending enchantment, forgetful of all the world outside.

That was what the foreign residents had done; one saw them in the piazza of the main village going to the English tearoom, a group of handsome bronzed young men who were the followers of Norman Douglas. At the beach there were also the mystical Russian disciples of Gurdjieff doing their yoga exercises, and Maxim Gorki among them at the time, as I was told. Persons of every sort and condition lived here. I was sorely tempted to stay, and send to Rome for our books and baggage.

The next morning, however, rising at six, I said to my wife, who was naturally as loath to leave the place as I: "Let's run away from here at once, by the early boat, and never look back, or we will surely be turned into swine." In any case, I had only enough in my purse to settle our bill and make the journey back to Rome. We were actually penniless and also hungry by nightfall, when we reached the terminal station in Rome.

Early the next day I set out by tram for the office of *Broom,* where some small funds in payment for several manuscripts awaited me. The special ceremonies at the Vatican, which had brought a horde of pilgrims to the city, were over; but now a crowd of a very different and less peaceful sort filled the streets in the neighborhood of the Piazza di Spagna, where *Broom's* office was located. These were mostly young collegians, of about the age of American high-school students, wearing black shirts and black armbands and carrying pistols! A big, fat, military-looking man sprawled in a partly armored limousine, with a sub-machine gun by his side, directing the groups of youngsters who were taking up positions around the square. As I had no idea of what they were up to, I did not take them seriously, and straight-armed my way through the crowd of small young agitators as if I were in a football scrimmage.

All unwitting, I had arrived at an historic moment, the eve of Mussolini's march on Rome, which was being prepared by his partisans there and was to be concluded several months later with the complaisance of the ruling government. On the outskirts of the city, in the suburbs populated by workers, there was an intermittent guerrilla war being waged by the young Fascisti against the "Reds"—principally Socialists in those days.

Three years after the end of the war, in 1922, Europe was as instable politically as it would be after World War II, in 1948, the time of the coup d'état in Prague and the Berlin airlift. Italy, we were made to understand, having emerged from the war with heavy casualties but no glory and almost no spoils, was torn by popular resentments and passions. The pressure of Mussolini's Black Shirts against a weak coalition ministry steadily increased. Rome was actually in a state of semi-martial order.

At our pension on the Pincian Hill, a respectable residential district, an Army captain was quartered, while his troops stood guard over several blocks in the vicinity. The Capitano was handsome, spoke French tolerably well, and was gallant to the ladies in the romantic Italian manner. When we questioned him about the growing disorders in Italy, he laughed like an opera singer. It was just a "jolly little brawl," he explained, offering no inconvenience to the tourist traffic, being confined to an area at the edge of the city, near the cemeteries, where the Fascists and Socialists scuffled a bit. "But here you are perfectly safe," he said with a sweeping bow, "so long as I am living in this house." Everything would work out peacefully, he assured us, because one of these days the Regular Army would sweep out all the quarreling Black Shirts and Reds together.

The Regular Army, however, never received such orders; and a few months later Mussolini entered Rome via the wagon-lits, and with the blessing of King and Parliament took over power.

Harold Loeb entertained us in the friendliest manner during our stay in Rome. We discussed the problems of his magazine, *Broom*, with passion. In recollections written many years later, he has tried to give some indication of how I appeared in my green and salad days:

Young Matty Josephson and his wife Hannah arrived in Rome, and I liked them immediately. Matty seemed a trifle brash, but then I could do with a little more of this quality. Of slender build, he was eager, earnest, energetic, and ambitious . . . his features, and especially his eyes, were animated by a lively intelligence. Hannah's . . . yellow hair, and wistful eyes had an attractiveness. . . . She shared her husband's interests and excitements.[7]

Certainly I was often tactless, and fitted well into the category of The Overzealous Young Man. Malcolm Cowley has also described me as one who had "a gift for making discoveries, for taking risks and for getting himself into hot water, as if he carried a steaming kettle with him through Europe."[8]

Although Harold was related to the family associated with the famous investment bank of Kuhn, Loeb & Company of New York, and his mother was an heiress of the Guggenheims, he himself had little of their money, and lived in Europe on an income provided by his mother. After graduating from Princeton, where he distinguished himself as a wrestler and boxer, he had worked on construction jobs in Western Canada, then at one of the Guggenheims' copper smelters in California, and more recently had run a modern bookshop in New York. There he had married Marjorie Content, a young woman of artistic tastes and independent income, but they had been divorced after several years. On the spur of the moment, Loeb had sold out his bookshop for about eleven thousand dollars, sailed to Europe and, with the collaboration of the poet-editor, Alfred Kreymborg, founded *Broom: An International Magazine of the Arts*. The name of the publication was taken from a passage in Melville's *Moby Dick:* "What of it, if some old hunks of a Sea-captain orders me to get a broom and sweep down the decks? . . ."

Harold Loeb had taken up this new role at nearly thirty, with very little training for the work of the literary editor or man of letters, except for having run a bookshop during a year or two. Alfred Kreymborg, in past years, had done excellent work in editing anthologies and little reviews devoted to modern poetry. But the opportunities that opened for *Broom* were those of creating a sort of bridge between the culture of two continents by presenting significant selections of the art and literature of contemporary Europe and America side by side. In this sphere Kreymborg had not appeared particularly knowledgeable. The Irish and British writers chosen by him and Loeb made *Broom* seem much like one of the contemporary literary periodicals in England. The Americans who represented the "Renaissance" of prewar vintage also did not help the review to make "a clean sweep" of things in its first year. Its literary tendency, in short, was all too catholic.

Part of Loeb's plan had been to take advantage of Italy's lower printing costs and to issue *Broom* as a large, beautifully illustrated publication on fine paper, to be sold mainly in America. Its circulation eventually rose to three thousand, which was not bad, considering that *The Dial,* backed by two free-spending young millionaires, attained only about six or seven thousand readers at the time.

The best part of *Broom* was its handsome reproductions of the School of Paris artists—Picasso, Matisse, Gleizes, Gris, Derain, and Léger—several of whom also designed remarkable covers for it. These great artists were almost unknown in America in 1921–1923; *Broom's* pioneering in this field helped win over a small but discriminating public.

Harold's friend, Kathleen Cannell (former wife of the American poet Skipwith Cannell), a tall blonde young woman who had frequented modern art circles in London and Paris for years, gave valuable aid to *Broom* by reading manuscripts and advising it on art matters. She was then living in Rome with her mother, and took an active part in our discussions of *Broom's* editorial problems.

In truth, Harold Loeb did not have enough money for such an ambitious enterprise, employing five or six paid assistants and maintaining a branch office in New York as well as in Rome. Despite its low rates for contributions—less than one-half a cent a word—and cheap printing costs in Europe, its deficit was almost one thousand dollars a month, and Harold was hard put to it to meet his bills after the first year. Kreymborg had departed from Rome following disagreements with Harold on policy; one of his new associates was an amiable English writer named Edward Storer.

During our talks in Rome, I urged that *Broom* should try to distinguish itself from other publications by presenting literary material that was as challenging as possible and at least as "modern" as the art of Picasso and the School of Paris. The Dadaist movement was reported to be expiring officially, but its French members, such as Aragon and Éluard, seemed to be at the beginning of great literary careers, and very suitable for inclusion in *Broom*. I also proposed translations from earlier authors, such as Apollinaire and Lautréamont.

I remember a very jolly evening in Rome at Harold's apartment, with my wife and Kathleen Cannell present, when we dug up a mass of Gertrude Stein's writings from a whole trunk of unpublished manuscripts she had sent *Broom*. Hitherto I had known her work but little; now, looking through a good deal of it, I read selections from *Tender Buttons* aloud and with such fervor that it made quite an impact on my hearers. Loeb and Kreymborg had previously published only a page or two of Miss Stein, but without conviction, Harold saying of it that it was "just blah." On first acquaintance she did seem rather dry; but I held that she was a "philosophical poet," with an extraordinary eye that saw all around things, and had a rare sense of humor as well. Her work, I urged, should be published at some length. Harold wrote Miss Stein that her writings were "enthusiastically hailed by Josephson," and *Broom* soon afterward printed some excellent shorter pieces of hers.[9]

The atmosphere of Rome, according to Harold, was desiccating; in those days it was like a provincial city. He now thought of moving the headquarters of *Broom* to another city where he could be in closer contact with contemporary activities in the arts. Berlin, under the Weimar Republic, seemed then one of the liveliest centers in Europe. If he decided to move to Germany, he said, he would like me to join him as associate editor. (It was the same job that Gorham Munson had applied for.) I had planned to spend the summer in the Tirolean Alps with friends, and counted on getting some writing done before returning to America in the autumn. On leaving Rome, I said that I would consider Harold's offer. He promised that he would come to the Tirol to pay us a visit during the late summer days, when he intended to look into printing arrangements in Germany, and we would take up the question of my joining the staff of *Broom* at that time.

My wife and I journeyed northward via Venice to Innsbruck, and then about thirty-one miles further to the town of Imst, where we arrived late at night, putting up at the Gasthof Post, an eighteenth-century château that had been converted into an hotel. The next morning, when we came down to breakfast on the veranda, overlooking the valleys of the Inn and the Gurgl Rivers at their confluence, it was cold after Italy, and a dense fog blotted out the Dolomites. Our friends had not yet arrived from Paris, but at the farther end of the veranda there were three young men at breakfast whose voices carried to me the accent of America. One of them turned out to be Virgil Thomson, a native of Kansas City and graduate of Harvard, who was undergoing his apprenticeship as a composer of music, in Paris, under the tutelage of Nadia Boulanger. Through a mutual friend, met in a Paris café, Thomson had learned of the little mountain retreat I had chosen for the summer, and its economic advantages, and had set out for Imst with two friends.

Paralleling the transatlantic movement of American writers and painters, there was a migration of young musical students in the early twenties, living on fellowships or on small remittances from their families, and learning their art from teachers in Berlin, Dresden, Vienna, and Milan, as well as Paris and Fontainebleau. Aaron Copland, my compatriot from Brooklyn, for example, had come to Europe in 1921 to study at Fontainebleau, where he, too, met Nadia Boulanger and became her pupil.

Thomson was a bouncing young man with a somewhat pugnacious turn of wit, whose early compositions, played for us on the ill-tuned piano of the Gasthof Post, were decidedly merry pieces, having something of the impudent humor of Satie.

The cold fog of our first morning in Imst lifted at noon and we saw a good deal of snow on the mountains in mid-June. Imst was a large country seat, with a lower and upper town, the upper part sprawling along the gentle slope of Mount Muttekopf and out toward the passes traversed by one of the historic road-ways between South Germany and Italy. The town also adjoined the east-west roads (and railway) running from Zürich to Vienna. This strategic site had seen much history; the swift Roman legions, the soldiers of the Holy Roman Empire and those of the Dukes of Tirol had all come and gone. Although the town had been destroyed by fire a century earlier, the existing earth-colored structures of stone and clay gave Imst a look of infinite age. In the neighboring villages the houses of an earlier period were often decorated with colorful religious paintings by peasant artists, and beautiful carvings of Madonnas and cherubs; in the fields there stood many fantastic crucifixes and wayside shrines guarding the crops and the peasants against evil.

Our large hotel room with its nine windows looked out on a deep Alpine valley enclosed on three sides by rugged peaks and sheer mountain walls. We had dropped into a backwater of European civilization, whose rustic inhabitants had changed their ways very little during a thousand years; they were ac-customed to tourists in winter as in summer, though these came here in smaller numbers than to the nearby Bavarian and Swiss resorts or the Salzburg region. The simple Tirolean peasants—a dark-haired, blue-eyed, long-headed Alpine people—many of them afflicted with goiters, were shy, but amiable enough, if one came to understand them, for their dialect was a strange kind of low German. They were deeply religious and had clung to their ancient folkways.

Almost every other day, it seemed, a religious procession blocked the winding main street for hours on end. It was pre-ceded by a band of rustic musicians and local militia in bright green uniforms and Tirolean hats, each sporting a feather; then came men in colorful peasant costume and women wearing velvet bodices, ornate lace collars, and flowered petticoats. Above them, borne on a palanquin, swayed a large, blue-robed, much-ornamented image of the Virgin Mary. The marchers usually halted in the upper town before the church near the

Rosengartlschlucht, where a waterfall tumbled into a rose garden. There, they would kneel during the service, the mountain peaks looming above them, the sun glancing off their brass wind instruments and rifles, while the choir boys sang high above the steady roar of the waterfall.

On a misty night in August we stood on the broad veranda of our hotel in Imst, having been advised to watch for the summer fires on the mountaintops. Suddenly people cried: "Look! Look!" On Muttekopf, on Heiterwand, to the north, east, and west, fires sprang up and seemed to leap from peak to peak, until they enclosed the wall of our valley in a wide semi-circle of flame. These were the St. John's Fires held at the harvest season, which comes early here; they also used to be called Luther's Fire (for it was thought they would have the effect of burning out the Lutheran heresies). The peasant youths were supposed to leap across the bonfires with lighted torches in their hands, thus ensuring the success of their harvests.

It was a great country for walking. There were dazzling blue lakes all about among the pine forests, especially the warm Blindsee, a very deep crater notable for its blind fish; and there were the long, sloping pastures around Muttekopf, which we once climbed to its summit, at nearly three thousand meters, to enjoy a vista embracing four nations: Germany, Switzerland, and Italy as well as Austria. When we descended from the heights at dusk, the cattle returning from their pastures would accompany us with tinkling bells all the way into town, where each animal, cow or goat, unerringly turned into its own gate, all of them knowing their own address quite well.

The Tirol was also an excellent place to get writing done. In the morning I would go off to a little gazebo set on a knoll facing the amphitheater of mountains, and work out of doors.

Our economy was at once very odd and very simple. The bill for our pension was usually fixed at the beginning of each month by the hotel manager in terms of Austrian currency, at something equal to fifty dollars a month for both of us. But at the end of the month, as the dollar would have risen one hundred per cent or more in paper *kronen*, I might be able to settle my account for twenty or twenty-five dollars. Then the rates would be doubled, and the process would be repeated. At this period I happened to receive twenty dollars for some poems I had sold, and thus was able to boast in a letter to one of my friends in America that at last I had succeeded in "living by poetry alone."

The government printing presses in Austria and Germany, which were making their currencies worthless, worked with fantastic effect and in many unforeseen ways. For a few of us Americans, who were apprentice writers or music students, inflation brought a relative freedom from economic pressure. It amounted, in some degree, to an award of a fellowship permitting us to live and study at leisure (like the Guggenheim Fellowships created for Americans some years later). For the little people, for the middle class in Austria and Germany, inflation was a disaster, raising prices of consumer goods sky high in ratio to incomes. At every step Austrians I met said to me in despair: "Our life savings, our pensions, our insurance policies have all been reduced to so much worthless paper!" On the other hand, native Capitalists and speculators garnered immense profits thanks to the export boom engendered by inflation, since prices of German goods and labor were abnormally low in terms of gold money. The sharp traders and the industrial cartels always know how to profit during such an emergency.

It is arrant nonsense to conclude, however, as some have done in writing of this period, that the few artistic tourists from America then visiting Austria and Germany played any important role in "exploiting" their bankrupt economy. Hardly any of us possessed the capital to buy and "profiteer" on the antique bric-a-brac or the art treasures being offered everywhere on the bargain counter. Rather, by bringing in our small sums of sound currency and spending them for the tourist services given us, we helped the Germans.

Nevertheless, there were some grotesque incidents that occurred at the height of the inflation crisis in Central Europe. We poets, formerly so needy, could, if we wished, and just for the hell of it, play at being grandees. Exchanging a modest traveler's check in dollars for a great bundle of nearly worthless paper money, we would exclaim: "Look, we are now *millionaires*—on paper."

Late in the summer Malcolm Cowley and his wife came to the Tirol to live near us for a fortnight; they afterward joined us for a week in Berlin. We would occasionally enter some palatial eating place or hotel, order luxurious food—including caviar, game, or wine—and pay for it all with a sum in American coin that would have bought a sandwich back in the States. Our caviar was weighed and given a price after the manager consulted the financial pages of his newspaper. We suspected that on some occasions the cost of our repast changed even before we had finished eating it. Once, Harold Loeb, visiting Munich during an industrial fair being held there, invited ten of us to dine with him at a sumptuous restaurant in the Exposition Park, the total bill coming to only $1.65. It was after witnessing such scenes that Malcolm Cowley (a square eater in those days) wrote his poem, "Valuta":

> Following the dollar O following the
> dollar I learned three fashions of eating
> with the knife and ordered beer in four
> languages . . . while
> following the dollar around the
> 48th degree of north latitude where it
> buys most there is the Fatherland—

These amusing lines have too often been misconstrued. We literary tourists had too few dollars to "follow" anything, and Malcolm Cowley had as little as any of us. After pretending to be the Count of Monte Cristo for an evening, we would return to the even tenor of our (lower middle-class) ways. Nor did many of us dream of abandoning our fatherland upon whose economy we were, after all, completely dependent.

A fair amount of political disorder accompanied the inflation madness that seized upon Central Europe. Munich, about three hours' journey from our Tirolean village, had been the center of a Bolshevist uprising for a few weeks in 1919, and by 1922 was the scene of Nazi riots. I was staying there for a few days, looking up printing establishments for *Broom*, while Adolf Hitler and his followers were engaged in some shooting affrays preliminary to his first attempt at a full-scale uprising, a year later, which was to end with his arrest and imprisonment. There was an air of tension in the city, and a good many police and soldiers patrolled the streets. Back in my Tirolean village, the men in the taverns would be whispering about their plots to invade the South Tirol, annexed to Italy after the war. Even in these remote mountains and forests (where the local hotheads drilled with arms) the disequilibrium of Europe was always visible. What was surprising about the Nazi movement was not that it won power over Germany and Austria, but that it took so long to accomplish this.

The summer before we arrived, the little mountain community of Imst had witnessed a gathering of French and German Dadaists, who had held some informal conferences and issued a brochure entitled *Dada au grand air*. Tzara and Éluard had come in from Paris; Hans Arp from Zürich, and Max Ernst from Cologne. The same group were supposed to meet here again in the summer of 1922.

Not long after my arrival I learned that Paul Éluard and his wife Gala had turned up and were staying at Tarrenz, just outside the village limits, with Max Ernst and his family. I walked over to Tarrenz, a tiny hamlet adjoining a pretty lake, about two miles away, and called on Éluard and Ernst, who impressed me as one of the most remarkable personalities of all the Dadaist clan. Ernst was slender and carried himself very straight; he had a thin Roman nose, keen blue eyes, and an alert, birdlike air. Although just turned thirty-one his curly, gold-brown hair was slightly flecked with gray; he was altogether of an extraordinary male beauty—that of a "fallen angel," the women used to say.

Maximilian Ernst was a Rhinelander, born in 1891 at Brühl, in the environs of Cologne, the son of an eccentric man who taught deaf mutes in a Catholic school off in the woods of Brühl. Max himself spoke but briefly of his early life. From what I have gathered through other sources, his father, though a very pious man, employed a subtle form of cruelty or malice toward his children, who lived in considerable isolation. It is not surprising that by the time he attended the University of Bonn, Max had turned into a complete Bohemian and rebel. He had taken up painting in boyhood, in imitation of his father, an amateur artist; then, as a university student, devoted himself mainly to philosophy and psychology. After a lapse of several years, he resumed painting just prior to World War I, becoming one of the most advanced of the "Young Rhineland" group at Cologne, which reflected Expressionist tendencies. During the war he had served in an artillery unit of the German Army, but had shown himself so insubordinate to discipline that he had narrowly escaped military trial. Paul Éluard said: "Though we were not acquainted with each other, Max and I were at Verdun together and used to shoot at each other." At the end of the war Max not only had a bad military record, but became a leading member of a scandalous Dadaist group in Cologne; one of their exhibitions in 1919 was suppressed by the police.

When I first saw Max Ernst he was living with his wife and infant son in a dilapidated apartment of a half-ruined villa by the lake at Tarrenz; he was clad in some worn Tirolian *Lederhosen* and sandals, looking very athletic and tanned. The extremely perturbing and coldly violent spirit of the collages he showed me stood in marked contrast to Ernst's reserved manner and mild speech. In their campaign against the old conventions about Art and the Beautiful, the Dadaists, like the Futurists, had perpetrated all sorts of outrageous artifacts, which have been labeled "anti-Art." But Ernst, with his devilish scissors and his pot of paste, gave one more of a shock than anyone else. Others

before him had used the collage device, Picasso, for example—
as part of a formal plastic organization on a canvas—but Max
Ernst had invented a technique of his own that wholly abandoned
the painterly effects of hand and brush.

The early work of Ernst, dating from 1919 to 1922, much like
the early Chiricos, used mechanical "signs" principally, as well
as clippings from old mail-order catalogues, technical encyclope-
dias, or illustrated volumes of Jules Verne. Illustrations of human and animal forms were cruelly dismembered; banal objects
were separated from their wonted place in nature and rearranged
in the most incongruous and fantastic relationships. The con-
triver of these collages had certainly nourished himself on the
fantasies of Matthias Grünewald and Hieronymus Bosch; but he
had also drawn his literary inspiration from the more halluci-
nated *Sturm und Drang* poets of Germany, as from Rimbaud,
who told himself that he "must change life." Ernst's collages
were not only provocative, they jarred the unprepared viewer.
Dadaists in Paris, and particularly their art philosopher, Breton,
saw a terrible power of revelation in them. Paul Éluard, who had
experimented a good deal with a poetry of dissociated words
and images, was so enthralled by the murderous kind of inven-
tion Ernst exhibited that he made a special visit to Cologne in
1921 to see him, and became his champion and first patron at a
time when none would buy such work.

The impassioned friendship between Paul Éluard and Max
had, in truth, an unexpected side effect after they arranged to
spend the summer together in 1922. A powerful electromagnetic
current sprang up between the handsome Max and the high-
powered Gala Éluard, with the consequence that Max separated
from his wife and child and moved into the Éluard quarters
right next door to his own. Paul Éluard, having obviously sacri-
ficed his attractive wife in his generous enthusiasm for his friend,
made such shift as he could to play the cheerful cuckold, but
sometimes looked restless and nervous. His Paris friends said
"he accepted everything Gala did."

These persons all paid homage to liberty, and (perhaps with

the exception of Frau Louise Ernst) regarded the marriage institution with indifference. Paul Éluard treated the business of
their *ménage à trois* lightly enough, saying with a brave grin:
"Well, I love Max Ernst much more than I do Gala." But we
knew he had been devoted to Gala; doubtless the readjustments
were awkward, and opportunities for distraction in the region
of Imst were limited. Moreover, because of the "emancipated"
views of the persons involved, this love affair of Gala and Max
(whom many women found irresistible) proceeded openly and
stormily, becoming quite a drama in the heavy Russian style—
hence somewhat wearisome for the rest of the company. Max
carried himself with much aplomb in a difficult situation, as he
is wont to do. But Gala showed all the manifestations of melancholy, emotional tension and changeable moods suited to her
position. "*Ah, vous ne savez pas ce que c'est d'être marié avec
une femme Russe!*" Éluard sometimes exclaimed.

Tzara arrived in July, put up at the Gasthof Post, and took
in the situation at a glance. Jean Arp (an old friend of Ernst and
Tzara) and his wife came from Zürich and stayed at our hotel.
Tzara and Arp had formed tentative plans to publish a new
Dadaist manifesto illustrated by Ernst and Arp; but now Max
and Gala's romance took precedence over everything else, and the
project was dropped.

Tzara was quite vexed over this business and, when alone with
me, expostulated: "Of course we don't give a damn what they
do, or who sleeps with whom. But why must that Gala Éluard
make it such a *Dostoevski drama!* It's boring, it's insufferable,
unheard of!"

He himself was accompanied by a lady friend of a more placid
disposition. Despite the recent warfare in Paris, Tzara was in
excellent spirits. He had no desire to act as Breton's rival or
contend with him for the leadership of an avant-garde "church"
in Paris, but felt "profoundly indifferent" even to the fate of the
Dadaist movement. Meanwhile, he was writing poetry, lyrical
poetry of a mock-sentimental kind, and nothing obscure about

it. Though he had come late to the French language, his poems were ingenious and fascinating.

Jean Arp, an Alsatian artist-poet, thirty-three years of age, was both one of the most lovable and fantastically comic companions I have ever had. He had a round shaven head, as smooth as one of his abstract sculptures, blue eyes full of quiet laughter, and fine wrinkles about his mouth and eyes. His fairly impassive and long face sometimes recalled that of a jolly priest or monk; but at other times, by very slight movements of his features, suggested one of the movie clowns of the Mack Sennett troupe. He told his best stories with a dead pan expression, but with a slightly mad glint in his eyes that had a devastating effect. Arp's very arrival at Imst brought cries of joy from all who knew him —one of the reputedly "wild men" of the Dada revolt against culture, yet outwardly so gentle of manner that he seemed almost a timid soul.

One of his best stories was of the remarkable and unheroic experience he had had at the beginning of the late war. An Alsatian with a German mother and French father, he became convinced that "the war between France and Germany was no good for me." Alsace being then part of the Reich, he promptly took refuge in France; but on learning that he would be expected to serve in the French Army, he made his way to neutral Switzerland. Even there the long arm of Germany reached for him; the German consul at Zürich called him in and told him he must undergo a physical examination prior to being deported and drafted. He was then given a form to fill in, listing about thirty questions starting with his birth. He wrote down the day, month, and year—1889—on the first line, repeated this for all the rest of the questions, then drew a line at the bottom of the page, and added it all up to the grand total of something like 56,610! Then he stripped off all his clothes and, with a supremely idiotic expression, handed the paper to the examining official. This person, in some alarm, said quickly: "That's all right, now, Herr Arp; you may put on your clothes. We will get in touch with you in due course." But the Germans never bothered him again.

We had a merry table at the Gasthof Post, with Tzara and his *amie* and Arp and his big wife, Sophie Taeuber, a Swiss physical-culturist who took up art, under her husband's tutelage, with considerable success. Though 'a revolutionary in his field, Hans preferred order in his domestic life, and was married to the good Sophie for twenty years, until her death. When our talk once broached the romance at Lake Tarrenz, Arp observed un-expectedly (for a Dadaist), though with an oblique reflection upon Max Ernst: "I could never make love to a woman unless I were married to her." In truth, he was devoted to Sophie; she had helped him through difficult times, and he often said that he owed everything to her.

On one occasion, however, he violated his own precepts about conducting himself in proper bourgeois fashion. Something of a fetishist about shoes, he wore very heavy and costly English brogues. One day there was a flock of American women tourists wandering about the town, dressed in sober business suits that made them all look like Salvation Army lasses, and wearing flat walking shoes. Arp was fascinated by their shoes, followed them about, and, approaching one of them, politely introduced himself in French, and asked her where she had bought her shoes. The woman turned a look of withering scorn at poor Arp, and he fled as fast as he could all the way down the main street. "Terrible, the look she gave me," he told us afterward. "It froze me to my heart. *C'était la Vierge d'Alaska, même!*"

In his room at the hotel Arp busied himself every day making collages and "reliefs" out of colored bits of paper. Sometimes he would tear up little pieces of paper and shuffle them about, or drop them at random, making a montage out of the chance arrangement in which they fell. He also tried to teach me how to make an "automatic" painting: taking an open ink bottle and white sheet of paper, he overturned the ink bottle on the paper, making a large blot which was certainly the product of accident. However, my own efforts at automatic painting were not as deft as Arp's. Was it possible that it was not the ink bottle that made the good automatic picture—just as it was said of Max Ernst's collages (by himself) that "it was not the *colle* (paste) that made the collage." Overturning another ink bottle, Arp with a neat movement made a lovely blot resembling the contours of a pair of female buttocks.

A few weeks earlier I had told Max Ernst about our new review, *Secession*, and invited him to design a simple cover for us in black and white. The next day he handed me a tiny collage the size of a large postage stamp, made up of cuttings from an old volume on medicine cunningly arranged in the form of a medallion. By examining this work closely one could discern that it was a foetus emerging from a womb, but a smiling foetus dressed in evening clothes and top hat. It seemed an appropriate enough image of our new "movement," and I mailed it to New York; but soon heard from Munson that it was considered censorable, and had been discarded. I wrote to our new co-editor, Kenneth Burke:

. . . What is the logic of chucking our playful Max Ernst cover design for a perfectly indifferent still life . . . from fear of censorship, when page 11 of your story is a howling obscenity and will not fail to get us suppressed. I am very glad that Kay Boyle and Gilbert Seldes were consulted about such an urgent question. Postmaster-General Burleson's successor might have been more to the point.[10]

However, I replaced Ernst's collage, with Arp's "abstract" ink blot as the cover design for *Secession* Number 3. Despite its suggestion of a voluptuous nude it was passed by the U.S. postal authorities.

Arp's poems in German, one of which I translated for *Secession*, possessed the highest interest for me. He said that in his poetry he "tore apart sentences, words, syllables, and tried to break down the language into atoms, in order to approach the creative."

So many of us in those days, like Miss Gertrude Stein, seemed to be busy experimenting, dissecting, and "breaking down" all sorts of things in the hope of approaching our creative goal more closely. Arp told me that in his view the object of Dadaism as a movement was to destroy all "illusions," or at least illusionistic representations of Nature; instead the artist was himself to become an agent, or force of Nature, creating "pure movement," or rivaling Nature in working out the beautifully erosive effect of sea or weather on rock or wood, or achieving the effect of chance or accident in the processes of Nature! Yet out of the drastic Dadaist experiments, such as Éluard's or Tzara's with "pure words," there have endured for us only those pieces that approximated true poetry, in essence not very different from old models of good poetry. The same could be said of Arp's montages and sculptures which also evolved steadily, for he was a remarkable student of his craft, until they became ever purer variations or "re-inventions" of the natural forms he so closely observed.

There was much talk in our circle at Imst of the reputed "death" of Dada, and of rumors that the French, under the lead of André Breton, were planning a new departure. I told Arp about the Battle of the Closerie des Lilas a few months before. He declared that he, for his part, would never change his allegiance. Dada was a spirit that was perhaps indefinable; it had appeared long years before there were twentieth-century Dadaists, and would ride again. "They may call us by any names they please: Surrealists or something else," he concluded, "but they will find that underneath my skin I am always and forever a dyed-in-the-wool Dadaist." (*Echtgewaschener Dadaiste* was the expression he used.)

When we parted at the end of the summer Arp gave me most explicit instructions about what to look for in German museums: those of Vienna, Dresden, and Berlin. He also assured me that he felt a keen desire to visit America, and believed it would be inspiring for him. In 1924, after I had returned home, a note came from him asking me if I "could help him find a job in a deaf-mute publishing house," since he knew no English. He did not come, however, until some years after World War II, when he was an old man, given exhibitions everywhere, loaded down with honors, and acclaimed as one of the world's foremost sculptors, which, in fact, he is.

At the end of August our friends from Paris returned to their homes, among them Paul and Gala Éluard. Max Ernst, after conducting his wife and son, Ulrich (now "Jimmy" Ernst, a well-known artist himself), to Cologne, took leave of them and went to Paris, staying for a time at the Éluards, which was where I found the three of them again when I visited Paris in the winter of 1923.

Max Ernst endured great poverty in Paris for several years, before his collages and oil canvases were brought to market by one or two small art galleries toward 1925. To maintain himself at first, he worked in some dreary shop in a slum quarter of Paris, designing and making trinkets for tourists—souvenirs of Paris. Though poor and threadbare, he bore himself with his habitual pride; when success came to him he was no different, remaining both gracious and reserved in manner, but ever driven by the somnambulist within him to produce his truly Surrealist pictorial visions with unending inventiveness.

We, too, prepared to leave the Tirol at summer's end. After bringing in their harvest the peasants, normally very shy, seemed to be seized with the spirit of jollification and went about eating, drinking, and yodeling their heads off. One of the local youths we had come to know, after many entreaties, agreed to conduct a party of the Americans staying at the Gasthof Post to a forest tavern up on a shelf of the Muttekopf, where the merry-makers of the community were to celebrate the harvest festival. We set off on a Sunday afternoon, our party consisting of two other Americans as well as my wife and myself. Our guide, clad in *Lederhosen* hung by suspenders and having the motto *Grüss Gott,* led us in a rapid climb up the long slope to a small mountain lake in the woods, with the secluded *Berghütte* at its edge. As we came into view of the place, our Tirolean ut

tered a long quavering yodel, and from across the lake came a
beautiful chorus of herdsman's yodels in answer.

On the terrace of the tavern, which had the form of a chalet,
a crowd of peasants sat guzzling beer, or pranced about to the
music of an accordion; the women among them, stout and red-
faced, matched drink for drink with their boisterous swains, the
couples sometimes embracing each other and rolling in the
grass. There was also the Unterbürgermeister himself, a learned
village philosopher I had met before, bald, pot-bellied, his spectacles slipping down his nose, now completely befuddled, and
with a stout female sitting in his lap. As we came to the door of
the *Hütte*, a man appeared on the balcony above the terrace and
poured a whole beaker of beer on the group below. We managed
to evade this sudden shower, but the old assistant mayor was
drenched, and collapsed on the ground, to the great amusement
of his constituents. It was like some old Dutch painting of a
peasant carnival.

Inside the dimly lit tavern the dance of the Tirolese was in
progress. A musician kept playing the same refrain on his accordion with a heavy beat, and the dense crowd in *Lederhosen*
or dirndls went stomping round and round at top speed—until
the women lost their balance and were dragged away by their
perspiring mates.

The pace was dizzy, the merrymaking seemed to be growing
louder and rougher all the time, and the air was terribly close.
I began to feel some misgivings about how it would all end; it
would be either a bloody brawl or a rude sort of orgy. My wife,
who had been circling about with a burly peasant, constantly
turning in the same direction, looked ashen pale and seemed
about to faint, when I rescued her, and called my American
companions to leave with us. One of the American visitors had
got thoroughly drunk, after dancing like a madman, and it looked
as if the peasant boys might give him a bad beating. We got
him away in time, and in the deep twilight hastened down the
mountain toward the lights of the village. The next day we

learned that the night of revelry in the *Berghütte* had, after all, ended with some bloody brawling among the natives.

The shadows cast by the steep walls of our valley were growing long, and the nights almost frosty, in early September, as we entrained for Berlin.

TEN

THE LOST

REPUBLIC

Our plans had called for returning home after a year's absence, and here we were riding eastward to Berlin, preparing to spend our second winter in Europe. This was because Harold Loeb had written me that he had definitely decided to move the head-quarters of *Broom* to Germany; and, at the end of August, had visited us in the Tirol and renewed his proposal that I join him as associate editor. We had then reached an agreement allowing me an equal voice in the direction of the magazine. In his relations with me subsequently, Harold showed himself one of the most considerate men with whom I have ever worked. I was, of course, delighted to prolong my stay in Europe; although, unfortunately, *Broom's* weak exchequer provided no security beyond three or six months ahead.

Conditions in Rome, of late, had been somewhat nerve-wracking: the Fascisti increased their agitation, the printers went out on strike, shipments of the magazine were held up, and its pages were filled with fantastic errors. The Italian printers, in truth, seemed to take joy in mixing up the table of contents and changing the names signed at the end of stories or poems. In Berlin, which Loeb chose as his next center of operations, he was given assurance that the technique of print-ing and especially the lithography was of the highest order. The somewhat lower costs and superior facilities we would find in Germany, in my view, would help to prolong *Broom's* existence. After it became more firmly established, it was our intention to bring it home to the U.S.A.

Harold Loeb, admittedly, had begun with some "vague eclec-tic program" in mind for his magazine. It was to be a forum in which a variety of artistic tendencies, European as well as American, would be presented. During our discussions of policy that summer we agreed that, instead of pursuing an educational function, as others, such as *The Dial,* were then doing, *Broom* should become in essence a *tendenz* magazine, expounding a militant modernism in literature as well as the plastic arts. We would become a "fighting organ," sponsoring the avant-garde of postwar Europe, the German as well as the French experimenters, and the youth of America.

Gertrude Stein has said that it is a very good thing for a writer to have the experience of comparing another civilization with his own. Living in Europe for some length of time did pro-vide one with a new perspective on America and its evolving machine-age culture, which underwent revaluation in our minds —with results quite different from those of Harold Stearns and his associates in their recent symposium, *Civilization in the United States.* Instead of condemning the onset of mechaniza-tion and mass entertainment, we would "accept" it and give it welcome. Were not the new machine-objects, created by industry, things of beauty in themselves, whether sculptures in steel or images made by a camera? The modern artist must learn to "compete" and live with the machine, I wrote in a spirit of buoyant optimism in an article: "After, and Beyond, Dada" (*Broom,* June, 1922). "We must be friend to the skyscraper and the subterranean railway" and make of the machine "our magnificent slave."

Harold Loeb, during the summer, had worked up an essay on "The Mysticism of Money" (*Broom,* September, 1922), which is interesting as a record of our preoccupations in that period. Americans, he argued, were no mere dollar-chasers; their overwhelming concern with money-making had become a *mystique* replacing traditional religion. The rich drove on at their money-getting with unflagging élan, even when they had no more need to do so. But on the other hand, Americans were the freest spending people in the world, addicted, as Thorstein Veblen had said, to "conspicuous consumption." Hope for the advancement of our culture resided, in Loeb's view, in such consumption being directed to new objects. New art works, without academic blessings, were actually being created by our democratic mass-life, our commerce, and our commercial entertainment: the popular arts of the new dances, the cinema, the jazz music that was originally the expression of our Negro peasants, as well as the vertical and "functional" structures of the Chicago School of American architecture.

My own sketchy contribution to the theory of the popular arts was an essay entitled "The Great American Bill-Poster" (*Broom*, November, 1922), a study of the language and mythology of our advertisement literature. This, I held, contained a core of "primitive" or folk poetry, both reflecting and appealing to the appetites, sentiments, and values of the common people. Poetry was to be found not in rose gardens but in testimonials for canned soups and motor cars. Thus the line:

MEATY, MARROWY, OXTAIL JOINTS

might be compared favorably with that of John Keats celebrating the virtues of good wine:

WITH BEADED BUBBLES WINKING AT THE BRIM, . . .

And what an expression of delicate, if unconscious, irony in the phrase:

FRIGIDAIRE ADDS THE FINE TOUCH TO HOSPITALITY

I ended by proposing that our poets should try to write verses in the style of advertisement slogans that might be "published" by sky-writing airplanes. E.E. Cummings was already attempting something of the sort by inserting occasionally in his poetry some banal advertising slogans for automobiles:

Ask the Man who Owns One—ask Dad He Knows!

Some of my friends and detractors in the United States held that I was trying to inaugurate a cult of "skyscraper primitivism." My suggestions, however, pointed toward the exploration of material that was a familiar part of our lives and which Art with a capital "A" always ignored—certain modern painters had taken this same path ever since the Armory Show of 1913 in New York. There had been, for example, the superb photography of Alfred Stieglitz, offering its challenge to the representational paintings of academicians. And Marcel Duchamp and Francis Picabia, as long ago as 1915, had made objets d'art not only out of machines but out of junk. Besides his "ready-mades," Duchamp had mounted an old bicycle wheel on a metal kitchen stool and presented it for exhibition as a piece of mobile sculpture. The American Dadaist, Man Ray, had also invented machine-objects, sometimes infernal-looking, usually inoperative.

In 1916, Robert Coady, whom Loeb and I regarded as an important precursor in the field of popular arts, had published a few numbers of the highly original magazine, *The Soil,* in which selections from Nick Carter's dime novels, scenes from Chaplin's slapstick movies, and photographs of the pugilist Jack Johnson in combat, as well as pictures of new skyscrapers and naked machines, had all been printed together as a medley of native art. "The true American art," Coady declared, "is as yet outside our art world"; it was growing up "out of the soil," out of the folkways of our people, and not as an "exotic" product for the pleasure of a few snobs.

The new "ideology" of *Broom* certainly owed much to the stimulus received from contact with the new men of France and Germany. But Dadaism itself, as we have seen, was derived in great part from American source materials.

As if in reply to the exuberant polemics published in *Broom,*

Edmund Wilson, in the literary section of *Vanity Fair* (of which he was then an editor), wrote a warning to the young avant-garde of France and their American sympathizers:

Do not try to make pets of the machines! Be careful that the elephants do not crush you! . . . The buildings are flattening us out; the machines are tearing us to pieces. . . . The electric signs in Times Square make the Dadaists look timid; it is the masterpiece of Dadaism, produced naturally by our race, and without premeditation that makes your own horrors self-conscious.[1]

To my mind Wilson at that time, like others whom I liked to refer to as members of the Uplift School, wished that Americans would embrace a genteel form of culture that harked back to Victorian England, and whose chief apologist was John Ruskin. Their hope lay in our people and our society becoming ever more "refined," or better educated and humane in the Ruskinian sense. On the other hand, our own consisted in exploring the arts naturally propagated in our society.

At all events, as Malcolm Cowley remarked at this time, *Broom* now had produced a sort of manifesto, which might help to revitalize the current discussion of the arts. Harold Loeb wrote to the editor in charge of the New York office, Miss Lola Ridge:

Broom is no longer a forum, as Waldo Frank put it, where anyone can hold forth who commands the English idiom. It is becoming an organ with a *strongly held* point of view.[2]

I certainly enjoyed the controversies *Broom* was arousing in our own country and abroad. Discussion of the "lively" arts was stimulated again (as in Coady's time) among the American *literati*. Some of these, such as Gilbert Seldes, expressed approval of our program; Seldes had lately found high art in Krazy Kat cartoons, vaudeville shows, and jazz music, and was to incorporate these findings in his book, *The Seven Lively Arts*, published in 1924. Others assailed us (justly, as I now perceive) for unconsidered and over-optimistic pronouncements on the culture of the Machine Age, which ignored its human costs.

At the beginning of our stay in Berlin I was in a great bustle, opening an office and making new arrangements for printing and shipping the magazine, while Harold closed up the headquarters at Rome. At the same time I was arranging to have new German and Russian authors translated for us; and twice during that winter I went back to Paris to gather material there too.

Throughout the autumn, after Harold arrived in Berlin, we worked over a special American issue to be made up of contributions by William Carlos Williams, Marianne Moore, Gertrude Stein, Hart Crane, Kenneth Burke, Malcolm Cowley, and myself. Our art consisted of some elegant machine photographs by Paul Strand, specimens of the photography and the painting of Charles Sheeler, and half-tones of some ancient Mayan sculptures.

On leaving the Tirol we had been warned that, because of the inflationary boom in Germany, we would find Berlin crowded with tourists and commercial travelers from all over the world and hotel space all but unobtainable. One of our friends—it may have been Arp or Tzara—had therefore recommended a cheap hotel in an uptown district of Berlin, near the Zoologische Garten Station, where we might stop for a few days until we located permanent quarters. This advice, as it proved, was certainly given us in a mischievous spirit.

Our hearts sank at the Berlin we saw then; this sprawling metropolis of recent growth had never known the elegance of old Paris, nor did it have the sympathetic homeliness of London. In the late war it had seen hard days; its buildings, most of which had ugly stucco façades, had their paint peeling off. Even the Germans, comparing Berlin with their older, more beautiful cities, sometimes thought of it, in the terms of the artist George Grosz, as "a stone-grey corpse." It was in its own way stridently and offensively "modern," with big electric signs, gaudy shops for people of fashion, and dreary slums that were interchangeable with those of Liverpool or Chicago—in short Everyman's City of modern times.

My wife and I succeeded in finding a room at the Hotel am

Zoo, located in the upper stories of a big musty building whose street floor housed a school for waiters. It was with consternation, however, that we soon discovered that our temporary domicile was unmistakably a *maison de passe*. Although we traveled with considerable luggage, the surly concierge demanded that we pay for the night in advance, and seemed irritated when I explained that we intended to stay the whole night and perhaps the next day as well. His establishment, in fact, was mainly patronized by a troupe of West End Berlin streetwalkers; they and their clients went clicking in and out through a turnstile at the entrance every hour or half-hour with faces averted and hat brims turned down—sometimes casting a look of astonishment at the innocent-looking young thing I had brought with me to this mournful bagnio.

A day later we cleared out, first taking a room in a very proper pension in Charlottenburg, and shortly thereafter moving to a sumptuous apartment in the Tiergarten section. We knew that the Cowleys, who were due to arrive from the Tirol a few days after us, had been given the same destination, but like good Americans did nothing to spoil the surprise they would meet with at the shady Hotel am Zoo.

Malcolm and Peggy Cowley, however, found this *Lokal* highly diverting, and managed to put themselves on a friendly footing with its surly proprietor, who even permitted them to keep the big German shepherd dog Peggy had acquired as her pet during their week's sojourn in Berlin. It was droll to see the faces their respectable friends made when they called for the Cowleys; Harold Loeb evinced shock at first, then mirth; Kathleen Cannell, also visiting Berlin, dressed in the height of Paris fashion, peered at the place in surprise through the lorgnon she always carried; and the poet Mina Loy, all unsuspecting, arrived to take dinner with the Cowleys accompanied by Joella, her lovely golden-haired daughter of fourteen. Indeed the merriment of Malcolm and of Peggy, as they played at being Monte Cristos for a week with their small store of *Valuta*, made a bright note for us in the rather grim Berlin scene.

This huge city was still shaken by its recent catastrophes and insurrections, part of the populace half-famished, the other wallowing in fleshpots. To provide currency, with no gold reserve to back it, the government had unloosed its printing presses, as if deliberately engendering an inflationary crisis. With its fiscal system in ruins, Germany could pay nothing in reparations to the Allies, for the time. Meanwhile her whole society, as well as her economy, suffered profound change. The seemingly indestructible faith of people in money was destroyed, and many of them, especially the peasants, returned to a primitive scheme of barter. The money crisis, in truth, was changing the social order before our eyes; the old human values, as well as social conventions, were being cast away. As money became progressively worthless day by day, most sensible persons hastened to rid themselves of it by spending; but on the part of those who were in need, everything was *for sale* at bargain prices, even body and soul.

The streets fairly roared with life. There were thousands of street girls hustling for customers; many of them, recent recruits to the harlot's trade, had no style, used no rouge, wore shapeless hats and dowdy garments of wartime *Ersatz* material, looking more like threadbare, bespectacled schoolteachers than women of pleasure. Thanks to the long war, when young men were deprived of normal relations with women, the increased numbers of homosexuals was all too evident. Male prostitutes in their war paint mingled with the crowds on the boulevards, competing with the professional women. And at almost every corner there were war cripples hopping about on their wooden pegs, and offering, with their metallic arms, foreign cigarettes or other contraband, or even opium and cocaine; some did service as panders. Berlin, in the aftermath of war, showed us human creatures with souls laid bare, a people brutalized, as in the steel-hard drawings of George Grosz, or utterly forlorn, as in the pictures of Käthe Kollwitz. (A few years later, when economic stability was restored, some decorum, and even a certain chic, reappeared in Berlin.)

One winter evening my wife and another American woman were walking along the Kurfuerstendamm, looking at shop windows displaying fur coats and trying to calculate their prices. The mark had dropped from a value of two hundred to five hundred to the dollar shortly after our arrival, then had fallen to one thousand, and recently to three thousand per dollar, so that it was not easy to estimate the cost of things.

"Seventy thousand marks," said the other woman; "I wonder how much money that is in our money?"

A little German boy of about ten had been standing near them. Though the night was sharp and it was snowing, he was without coat or hat; his shoes were broken. He had a sweet, idiotic face. Hearing the foreign ladies speaking English, he echoed the telling word that so often recurred in people's talk: "Money-money-money-money." They tried to give him a few hundred marks. He refused and answered only: "Money-money-money." They moved on, but he followed them, repeating his song until they got rid of him by entering a nearby café.

The Romanisches Kaffeehaus on the Kurfuerstendamm, the focus of Bohemian life in the West End, was as good a center as any in which to meet friends and set off for an evening's entertainment, or merely to look at the human conglomeration. It was a huge, imitation-Gothic structure like many of the city's beer halls, accommodating fully a thousand clients or more. (In 1945 it was bombed out.) A most curious international mob of people—with long hair, short hair, or shaven skulls, in rags or in furs—filled the place to bursting. George Grosz, who was then both a Dadaist and a Marxist, often appeared there dressed as an American cowboy, booted and spurred. In one part of the Kaffeehaus one heard nothing but Russian spoken—these were the White émigrés—and in another only Hungarian—by the "Red" exiles from Budapest. The distinguished Russian sculptor, Alexander Archipenko, sometimes came here; as did his young compatriot, Ilya Ehrenburg, the novelist, who sat out the revolution of Lenin in Berlin and Paris for some years, but afterward returned to Moscow.

There were even some distinguished German literary personages in this crowd, including Alfred Kerr, dramatic critic of the
Berliner Tageblatt, the Expressionist novelists Gottfried Benn
and Alfred Döblin, and the art critic Carl Einstein. Among the
Americans in residence I used to meet Marsden Hartley in the
Romanisches. This talented artist, after an unhappy period in
New York, where his work received poor support, had recently
auctioned off all his unsold paintings at low prices and settled
in Berlin, where he lived at very modest cost and produced some
of the best canvases of his later years. There was also a crowd
of American music students, some of whom practiced twelve
hours a day at the piano under an exacting master like Artur
Schnabel.

The night places of Berlin flourished in astonishing profusion
and variety, serving up an imitation American jazz with imitation champagne. They were usually decorated in Expressionist
style and in color schemes so depressing as to diminish one's
appetite for drink or pleasure. The awkward females who performed esoteric dances at these *Nacht Lokale* reinforced our
resolution to shun these places of amusement—after a few visits
—in favor of the opera and especially the theater which, under
the inspiration of Max Reinhardt, offered the finest dramatic
productions in Europe.

One of my letters of the time runs:

The slush is mean and thick outside the Kurfuerstendamm Palast.
A car skids, and backfires. The corks of bottles of *Deutscher Sekt*
pop into the air at the same time toward the rose and emerald lights.
The parade of the whores begins. The band (dead drunk) plays
Mammy. A concerted rush is made for the floor by all the guests.
How the thousands of marks go! . . .

Louis Aragon arrived in Berlin, unexpectedly, and felt all the
dreadful fascination of the place. We had encountered him by
chance a few weeks earlier at a railway station in Austria, where
he had been summering in the company of his mother and sister.
He had made what seemed only a half-serious promise to visit

with us for a few days; then, growing weary of the company
of his family, had suddenly fled northward by the night train
which deposited him in Berlin early on a Sunday morning.

"As I had only the office address of *Broom,* which you had
given me," he related in his carefree manner, "but did not
know where you lived, I set out on foot through the streets of
Berlin in order to find you. Hoping to attract attention, I dressed
in a dinner jacket and a cap; and wherever something happened
in the street, such as an automobile collision, and a knot of
people gathered, I would rush in among them to see if you, by
some chance, were there."

In truth, having nothing left in his purse, he had fasted for
twenty-four hours before he found me at the office early on
Monday morning, though he seemed none the worse for it. It
was a delight to see his animated French face, to hear news of
our friends in Paris, and to prowl with him. In some notes he
wrote at the time, which were published in *Littérature* (November, 1922), he reported:

Berlin is becoming the most modern city of Europe. Its residential
quarters spread out widely among the former potato fields. . . .
Advertising is everything here. The electric signs are luminous over
the Potsdamer Platz; the radio blares everywhere in this town. At
the sign of an imitation Arp *Rückforth Liquöre* are sold; and an
imitation Picabia also promotes

MINIMAX

TO KEEP FIRES WITHIN BOUNDS

HAVE MINIMAX IN YOUR HOME

MINIMAX

I recommend a visit to the arcade of the Passage Panoptikum
where a sign heralds "The World's Greatest Abnormalities" and one
may see women of all nations, nude, with bellies opened to show
the infinite variations of their organs. . . . The bars and music halls,
such as The Scala, are decorated with an applied form of Cubist
or Expressionist art, while the subway stations must have been
designed by Arnold Boecklin. In the luxurious West End millionaires
and prostitutes jostle each other. And in the early hours of the
morning, after the trains have stopped, an old fashioned horse-

drawn omnibus gathers up all the flotsam of pleasure seekers who have become belated playing with the boys and girls along the Kurfuerstendamm.

During his stay of several days, Aragon wrote a story, "Paris la nuit, ou les plaisirs de la capitale," which was actually inspired by his rambles through Berlin. At his request my wife oversaw the printing of this booklet, in a limited edition of two hundred copies, and shipped it to him in Paris. His preoccupation with the urban landscape also gave rise, three years later, to his essay-novel, *Le Paysan de Paris* (1926), a remarkable example of his early writing of the Surrealist period.

Inquiring about the Berlin Dada group, which had flourished in spectacular fashion at the end of the war, I learned that their movement was dead and their leading spirits had left for distant parts. Richard Huelsenbeck, the man with the monocle, had gone to sea as a ship's doctor; others had found it advisable to depart also, for the German Dadas, in contrast with those of France, had been highly "political" and acted in sympathy with the Spartacist and Communist insurrectionists of 1919. At the time of the armistice they had staged some of the most frantic Dada "concerts" ever seen, as if with a view to spreading disorder and confusion that the revolutionists could turn to account.

One of the most notable of the Berlin Dadaists, George Grosz, a most prepossessing and eloquent young man, described in retrospect the season of despair in which the Dadas took to the hustings. After long training at art schools his own career had been interrupted by three horrible years of combat, which ended in his case with a siege of brain fever.

"I thought the war would never end, and I think it never really did end," he wrote afterward in his autobiography. After the armistice, when he came back to Berlin in the early winter of 1919, he found a city plunged in darkness and freezing for want of fuel. A Leftist insurrection carried on by guerrilla bands sputtered along, with snipers on rooftops firing at random into the blacked-out streets, infested with prostitutes, dope peddlers, and thieves.

The Red uprisings were soon put down with extreme brutality; but the prolonged money crisis had a more terrible effect than any social revolution. Men thought and dreamed only of food and drink. Grosz drew pictures of the famished, standing before illuminated shop windows filled with hams, sausages, cheese, and wine, while policemen came to drive them away with clubs. Side by side with the hungry ones were the hoarders of food and goods who seemed no less insane than the others, and who, after filling their cellars to bursting with provisions, stood guard over them night and day.

The people of Berlin were certainly of a mind to welcome the nihilistic demonstrations of the Dadas of 1919, directed by their mystical "Ober-Dada" Johannes Baader. Huelsenbeck and Walter Mehring acted as satirical entertainers, armed with noise-makers of all sorts. Kurt Schwitters (among others) exhibited his works of *Merzkunst*, collages ingeniously made of colored rags and bits of scrap metal. One such opus was a pyramidal "Garbage Monument" by Baader, dedicated to "Germany's Greatness and Downfall." For their soirees, Grosz devised placards with slogans in which they abused and insulted their public: "*Dada über alles!*" and "Dada kicks you in the behind and you like it." Strangely enough, some of the war profiteers and *Valuta* speculators in the audience offered the performers money and champagne, calling for more "toasts to *our* downfall" or bidding George Grosz "to please say some more about us bestial capitalists." These concerts usually ended in violent brawls, which were broken up by the police.

In those days, Grosz said, the earth always seemed to be trembling underneath Berlin, as secret armies of the Left and Right constantly prepared themselves for trouble. One of these armies was led by the proto-Nazi, General Wolfgang Kapp, whose putsch in March, 1920, was foiled by the general strike of all the Socialist trade unions. The people, meanwhile, seethed with undirected passions of fear and hatred, hatred of the Allies and of their own militarists who had led them to disaster; hatred, now, of the Weimar Republic, or the Jews, or the Bolsheviki. The early Nazis assassinated the "Red" leaders Karl Liebknecht and Rosa Luxemburg; and not long afterward (just before I came to Berlin), the brilliant Foreign Minister, Walther Rathenau, who was a liberal Capitalist and a Jew. They would also have dearly loved to assassinate George Grosz for his savage drawings and paintings portraying both the "exploiting class" and the frozen-faced military boys, whom he named "the pimps of Death."

Under the spell of this angry city I gathered material for a special number of *Broom* that would pay its respects to the artists and writers of postwar Germany. For illustrations, we had drawings by George Grosz taken from his recently published collection, *Ecce Homo;* also, probably for one of the first times in an English-language publication, the delicate and terrible fantasies of Paul Klee. (When I first met this great artist-poet of the Expressionist-Dadaist era, I was surprised to find him a very simple and gentle soul; his chief distraction was playing Beethoven on the piano; his home was filled with Biedermeier furniture.) In this German number we also included, very appropriately, a group of remarkable madmen's drawings, collected in 1922 by Dr. Karl Prinzhorn from institutions for the mentally diseased, drawings that mirrored the lunatic spirit of Germany in that era.

In the Germany of 1922–1923 my earnings of thrity dollars a week definitely placed me in the millionaire class. We occupied an apartment of seven rooms in the most fashionable quarter of Berlin, near the Kaiserallee, and had the services of an excellent cook who came with the establishment. Our life was extremely comfortable, and my wife could go riding occasionally in the beautiful park outside our door. Our monthly rent of twenty dollars, paid in United States currency, was enough to support our landlord, a feckless and shell-shocked Baron von O—, veteran of Richthofen's famous air squadron. To spend the rest of the "millions" I earned, we also entertained many of the local artists and writers, as well as visitors from Paris and New York.

All would have gone well that winter, if the French government had not decided to invade the Ruhr Valley when Germany stopped reparations payments, with the result that coal supplies for Berlin were entirely cut off. Now the earliest of the Nazi street bands made their appearance in Berlin and went tramping about our quarter at all hours of the night roaring their bloodthirsty songs. My letters of the time describe the *grosser Wirr-Warr* of those youthful gangs, for my study window gave on the street:

Feb. 25, 1923—finds me still in Berlin with an iron ring of French *Panzers* barring the way to Paris. Believe me there is a lot of *chi-chi* going on in your old Europe. . . . The little flock who have been living off the rotting corpse of *Kultur* may have to fly to happier climes. . . .

They have forgotten how to keep the peace. One becomes peculiarly sensitive to political developments when, as a result of them, a boiler blows up in the cellar and central heating is off for the rest of the winter. From a cozy spacious apartment, one is reduced to huddling in a single room that can be heated by a little coke stove.

I am sitting on the lid of a crater, getting my book of poems out. . . .

It was at this moment that the tremendous trifler and suicidal dandy, Jacques Rigaut—he who collected coat buttons and matchboxes—arrived from Paris with his new employer, André Germain, and came to dinner. Germain was a rather brittle specimen of the French upper class who, thanks to the millions of francs he had inherited from his family's holdings in the Crédit Lyonnais bank, supported a monthly literary review in Paris called *La Revue Européenne*.

Another of our dinner guests that evening was Mina Loy who, as widow of the legendary Arthur Cravan, aroused the intense interest of these French literary men. Cravan, an Anglo-Irishman who claimed to have been the nephew of Oscar Wilde, had been associated with Apollinaire, Picabia, and the Cubists in Paris before the war, and wrote some "Futurist" poetry in French. A large and athletic man, he had sometimes earned money as a heavyweight pugilist, and once, when in desperate straits, dared to enter a prize ring in Paris with America's Jack Johnson, who, of course, knocked him cold in a few seconds, Cravan having arrived dead drunk. Later, during the war, Cravan and Mina made their way to New York, and eventually to Mexico, where he was drowned somewhere in the Gulf (or so it is presumed). Mina Loy gave us a fascinating account of this celebrated character, and delivered it in her most studied duchess manner.

In the street outside, the nightly racket of our juvenile Nazis began as usual; their loud threats to "cut the throats of forty million Frenchmen next time" floated through the window. Louis Aragon, a few weeks earlier, had listened to such boasts and had laughed at them. But the tiny, sad M. Germain, who suffered from nervous indigestion—he was on his way to the spa of Karlsbad—looked ill. We proposed having him stay at our place for the night. Jacques Rigaut agitated him still more by affirming that the streets outside were alive with murderous German bandits. In the end M. Germain bravely opted to return to his hotel, and I offered to accompany him and Jacques. I went out, hailed a taxi, and conducted them to the Adlon without incident.

I came to know the Germans well and to appreciate their patient strength, their kindness toward children and dogs, and their passion for music. (When the average German hears music he becomes a poet, was a common saying.) Moreover, they appeared to be among the best-educated and best-informed people of Europe, showing a gift for idealistic or metaphysical reasoning that I found attractive. The pleasure-seekers and wastrels of postwar Berlin were, after all, a minority, though a noisy one; all about us there was a great mass of honest workers, now threadbare and hungry, but laboring as always with discipline and skill to build up their country anew. I enjoyed my daily business with some of these faithful craftsmen, who did the beautiful printing and engraving of *Broom's* Berlin issues.

In the days of crisis over the occupation of the Ruhr, when the city was freezing for lack of coal, I attended a concert of the Berlin Philharmonic Orchestra and heard a performance of Mozart's *Requiem Mass* by a chorus of three hundred singers. The people in the chorus looked very thin and worn, yet for hours on end they sang in the most perfect ensemble I have ever heard, and gave themselves with religious fervor to Mozart's unearthly choral music.

Oddly enough many members of the audience, though wearing looks of rapture, kept munching sausages which they drew from their pockets throughout the concert—it was one of those *petits faits vrais* that was very revealing. At the State Opera they also drank beer with their Wagner.

The case of my wife's piano teacher illustrated the plight of a large part of the German middle class. She was none other than Adele aus der Ohe, one of the world-famous pianists of the nineteenth century; through one of our friends we learned that she would consent to give lessons to my wife, a musical novice. Fräulein aus der Ohe, a tall, dignified spinster of fifty-nine, had been a pupil of Liszt, and a friend of Clara Schumann, Brahms, and Tchaikovsky—whose great piano concerto she had performed for the first time in America at the opening of Carnegie Hall in 1891 under the direction of the composer. Now the large fortune she had accumulated during a lifetime of giving concerts before millions of people was all gone, for it had been loyally invested in government war bonds all made worthless by inflation. She subsisted half-famished in her once luxurious, now musty, apartment, surrounded by the memorabilia of her public career; and survived only because her two servants, whom she could no longer pay, retained their lodgings in her place while going out to work elsewhere, yet with beautiful devotion brought in a little food each day which they shared with her.

Fräulein aus der Ohe knew nothing of the kind of world in which she was living. She was an exceedingly proud and high-minded woman; when my wife kept raising her fee (because of the fall of the mark), leaving her increasingly large bundles of paper money, the old lady could make nothing of it and would not even look at the money left for her.

One evening we invited her to dinner and fed her red meat and Burgundy. She seemed so weak and crippled by arthritis that we wondered if she would be able to play for us. But after eating and drinking, she marched, with flushed face, to the piano and performed Schubert's "Wanderer Phantasie" as we had never heard it played before or since. What was remarkable was that the untuned piano had at least a half-dozen dead keys; yet she was able to improvise something that to us sounded faithful to Schubert's score!

I met another idealistic German, a young man of only twenty-five, who was the leader of the German Social-Democratic Youth Association. All that he worried about was carrying on the moral and physical improvement of some astronomical number (300,000 or 400,000) of young men and women. A considerable fraction of this number, whose parents were dead or separated, had taken to wandering about the country in small bands during the spring and summer, and were known as *Wandervögel*. I used to see a few of these *Wandervögel* occasionally in Bavaria and Austria, wearing ragged shorts and sandals, but looking clean and bronzed as they marched along the roads, always singing. The leader of the Youth Association told me that he used to gather these young people together at huge summer camps centered in the Harz mountains, where they were sheltered in tents, fed, and organized for sports and great sing fests sometimes made up of choruses of ten thousand voices.

The object of our earnest idealist was to provide these foot-loose youths with some social guidance, and ultimately to di-

rect their political support to the still new and weak Weimar
Republic. Unfortunately, he was given too little help by the old
trade-union bureaucrats. It was the Nazi organization that
persistently wooed the *Wandervögel* later on and recruited them
for the Hitler Jugend.

A very accomplished German woman, whom I met some
years later, told me a good deal about her experiences during
this period, when she had been one of the *Wondervögel*. At
the end of the war family life had become insupportable for
her, as for many restless youths in impoverished homes, with the
male parent in many cases dead or gone. Leaving her home
in East Prussia, the girl, an art student, had joined a band of
fellow students and they had gone hiking along the roads for
the summer, pitching camp in the woods and literally living like
birds. When they needed food they would come down from the
hills to some big town, dress up in impromptu costumes, and improvise some entertainment, singing and dancing together in
the street outside of some café; then they would take up a collection and thus provide themselves with enough to eat and some
beer to drink.

A shy little man with pale blue eyes and sandy hair, dressed
in neat but worn clothes, appeared at the office of *Broom* one
afternoon. He introduced himself as Edwin Muir, whose name I
remembered because a charming prose piece of his called
"Aphorisms" had appeared in our magazine a few months before. Now with a timid air he drew forth some poems, done
somewhat in the style of the old Scottish ballads, that he
wished to submit for publication. He also made proposals for
translating certain German authors, in particular Franz Kafka,
whose work he earnestly recommended. (There was a long delay
before Edwin Muir and his wife completed their English version
of *The Castle*, so that Kafka's work failed, after all, to appear
in *Broom*.) Muir, then about thirty-five, proved so delightful a
companion, so unmistakably and orginally himself in all his

views of life and letters, that I held him in talk for hours, then set off with him to collect his wife and bring them home to my place for dinner.

Muir was a native of the Orkneys; his blue-eyed, black-haired wife was from the island of Shetland; and they left no doubt that they were Scottish born and bred. We used to call them our "wild Scottish Highlanders." Before meeting them I had not been aware that something like a "war" was still being waged between Scotland and England, though a bloodless one, as manifested in Muir's case by his will to write poetry in a style unlike that of the present-day English, but endowed with the raciness of the old Scottish speech.

He would begin to recite the Scottish ballads, which I had read with pleasure as a boy, yet never understood so well as when he rendered them, while making informal comments as he went along. During these recitals, he and Willa would also toss off many a tumbler of German-substitute "Scotch" neat—as they used to do in their cold native islands —and would become worked up both by the spirit of the ballads and that of the whisky. Then, together, this nimble little pair would execute the most fiery of sword dances.

Edwin Muir was all the more interesting for having been almost entirely self-taught. Having left the Orkney Islands with his ruined parents, who came of a long line of crofters, he had worked since his early youth in hideous factories near Glasgow, yet by his reading had made himself a true man of letters; and though taking up writing late in life, he had taught himself to be a poet of the first order. He was just beginning, toward 1922, to strike his real vein. There were tragic undertones in his verse, for misfortune had beset his family, and he himself, dogged by poverty, had been afflicted with long illnesses. In politics he was an ardent Socialist, but his was a socialism curiously molded by his innate Christian sense of pity, and a visionary spirit that permitted him, as he often assured me, to "hear voices." His mystic visions, he believed, derived from old race memories of the island Scotsmen that went far back

in time before Christianity. Perhaps I did not appreciate suffi-
ciently, in earlier years, those esoteric qualities of Muir that
so delighted and moved me in his later poems.

He possessed, moreover, both a highly critical intelligence
and a quality of intellectual honesty that was most appealing.
Reading our avant-garde reviews, *Broom* and *Secession,* he
gave hearty approval to our will for experiment and change, but
declared that he, for his part, must work in the old traditions
of poetry. He saw clearly the limitations as well as the technical
value of the art of Gertrude Stein and James Joyce.

At the time he had made only a beginning of publishing
articles in the newspapers and literary weeklies, and had managed to exist in London with difficulty. By coming to Germany,
he and Willa were able to live with some security. Willa, who
was university-educated and had taught languages at various
schools, provided much help to Edwin in the work of translation
they now pursued together. They lived in the charming village
of Hellerau, an art colony set in the low, picturesque mountains
outside of Dresden. Here there was a theater of the dance
and a progressive and bilingual school for children, where Mrs.
Muir taught German and English during part of her time, receiving in return for her services a diminutive cottage with a
lovely garden. There was a lively group of foreign residents at
Hellerau, including some Irish Republicans and a few unre-
constructed Scottish Nationalists. A young friend of Edwin's,
named John Holms, had also settled there for a while and
occupied himself with some writing. Holms, who had been an
heroic officer in the British Army during the war, in later years
was destined to play a leading part among the English sup-
porters of the Spanish Loyalists, up to the time of his death in
1937.

Muir invited me to visit him for a weekend, and I set off for
Dresden a few weeks later. After the false-front world of Berlin,
Dresden seemed a marvelous baroque city of old palaces, foun-
tains, tasteful dwellings, and romantic *Bierstuben* beside the
Elbe River. Five miles away, up in the high hills called the

Saxon Switzerland, was Hellerau, where the Muirs lived cheerfully on two or three pounds sterling per week earned by their
combined labors.

They had two eccentric German philosopher-poets for dinner
the evening I arrived; one was wiry and dark, the other a stout
giant with pink complexion and a mane of white hair. We talked
of the postwar crisis in Germany and the chaos of her social
order and finances.

"It is the most *wonderful thing* that could have happened to
our people," the white-haired philosopher asserted, "and has
made Germany far better off than any other nation. Why so?
Because men at last have learned to live *without money*, the
most corrosive element in modern society. Here in Hellerau I
give a few lessons, and in payment accept no money, but
only food—packages of rice, tins of cocoa and coffee—and so
I live very well, as free as a bird!"

The large man taught, among other things, Sanskrit; both
men ardently pursued studies in Indian and other Oriental re-
ligions. To sustain himself, the smaller man, who was something
of an artist as well as a poet, worked a few hours in an atelier
where rugs and tapestries were produced by ancient methods
of handicraft. He, too, received only his food and lodging as
wages. He spoke, nevertheless, like an exalted poet, indifferent
to his poverty, expounding his method for attaining mental and
physical discipline, and, finally, accord with the universal spirit
—in a word yoga. Germany in those days proliferated a variety
of mystical cults whose enraptured advocates thus turned their
own and others' minds away from present realities.

In the field of the arts there was a great ferment of ideas
among members of the different schools in Germany. During
the early twenties certain of the Central European artists'
groups were engaged in rather bolder thinking and planning
than their contemporaries of the School of Paris. The Expressionist painters were still in high fashion and on display at

centers such as the Sturm Galerie, directed by Herwarth Walden, when I arrived in Berlin. However, the movement toward abstraction of a later, or "classical," type was now exceedingly vigorous. A strong contingent of Russian talent also showed itself in the international group that had congregated recently in Berlin.

At the suggestion of one of *Broom's* advisers on art, Eliezer Lissitzky, the brilliant Russian abstract painter, had been commissioned to design a cover for the magazine (February, 1923), which he executed beautifully in three colors. When he arrived with his drawing, he asked me to conduct him to the lithography department of our print shop and himself supervised the preparation of the lithographic stone and the mixing of the colors. During my stay in Germany I saw much of this small Russian, a man with a wonderfully symmetrical bald head, delicate features and hands, and keen brown eyes that had a very searching gaze. We became good friends; I was allowed to watch him in his studio working precisely with the instruments of a mechanical draftsman to organize, or rather "construct," his superbly logical compositions. With those pure mechanical forms he would carry off remarkable feats of equilibrium, a magician and an engineer in one. His machine-images, unlike those of the Dadaists, were not intended to disturb or shock the viewer, but were clean, purposeful, and well-balanced constructions. Lissitzky could speak of his ideas in a fair German; he was a good deal of a theoretician and teacher among his fellows.

At the time when Cubism and Futurism first appeared in Western Europe, he told me, the Russians, too, had developed an avant-garde group tending toward abstraction, headed by Vasili Kandinski. Another faction, however, under the influence of the French "purist," Albert Gleizes, toward 1914 became absorbed in experiments with pure two-dimensional forms, as represented in the "Suprematist" paintings of Kazimir Malevich. It was at this period that Lissitzky, formerly trained as an engineer, had taken up painting and joined the group led by

Malevich. After the Bolshevist Revolution of 1917, Malevich, Anton Pevsner, and Lissitzky assumed leading roles as teachers at the Art Institute of Moscow. In the winters of the Civil War, when famine raged in Russia and there was no fuel, Lissitzky used to conduct his unheated art classes clad in a raccoon coat, and expounded the principles of modern industrial design and of "Constructivism" until he contracted tuberculosis as a consequence of his privations.

The Constructivists, he held, were buoyed by a utopian spirit and conceived of an aesthetics of order and functional beauty attuned to "the brave new world we were building"—so he actually expressed it to me in a letter in German (written in 1925) that used the same terms employed ironically by Aldous Huxley several years later. (Lissitzky himself had a decidedly ironic vein in his speech.) Unfortunately, the rulers of Soviet Russia saw no virtue in the teachings of this advanced group of artists who tended to reduce all design to the square or to a few simple two-dimensional forms. They were eventually ousted from the academies, to be replaced by old-fashioned art teachers; thus Malevich, Pevsner, Naum Gabo, and Lissitzky wound up in Germany, where the latter underwent a cure. Kandinski had previously left for Weimar.

In the late summer of 1922, as I arrived in Berlin, an important conference of modern artists had been called together by Theo van Doesburg, the Dutch abstract artist (long associated with Piet Mondrian), which was held at Weimar. Several Russian and Central European members of the Constructivist School attended, including Lissitzky and László Moholy-Nagy, a Hungarian, as well as the German motion-picture experimenter, Hans Richter. It was probably no accident that Tristan Tzara and Hans Arp had also journeyed to this conference from the Tirol in order to speak for Dadaism, but their presence created a near riot. The faction led by Lissitzky and Moholy-Nagy made bitter protests at the policy of the chairman, Van Doesburg, who then favored the Dadaists, and the protesting group angrily withdrew from the conference. To them the Dadaists were a purely *de-*

structive element, while they were resolved to *construct* the shining new cities of the future in accordance with their ideals of abstract design. One of the Constructivists' German colleagues, Walter Gropius, not long afterward established the Bauhaus-Dessau as a center for teaching their ideas of modern industrial design.

One evening in the winter of 1923, Lissitzky accompanied us to a lively gathering of the Constructivists of Berlin in the barnlike studio of his friend Moholy-Nagy, an exile from Budapest since the counterrevolution of 1919. Though Moholy lived in dire poverty at the time and boasted no furniture in his big studio, he was a most gallant host. The place was decorated with abstract paintings of his own as well as with machine-sculptures by the Russians Lissitzky, Gabo, and Vladimir Tatlin. These artists had the support of a few speculative patrons who, with some packets of worthless currency, were purchasing works of theirs which, today, are considered almost invaluable museum pieces.

The Constructivists were threadbare; their women were dressed in shapeless clothes; but they were gay and full of hope and big ideas. Moholy had us all sit down on packing boxes covered with some colored cloth, which were arranged in a circle around a huge bowl of soup in the center of the floor space. We guests advanced with our smaller bowls, filled them with the excellent mess, and returned to our packing boxes, making merry the whole evening over some weak table wine.

In truth, the future was to belong to these devout abstractionists. Much of the inspiration for the new "international" style of architecture and design, which gained ascendancy not only in Western Europe but in the United States as well, was derived from the young persons in that cold studio loft in Berlin —men like Lissitzky, Gabo, Moholy, and the architect Walter Gropius (whom I met somewhat later). When I visited Germany again in December, 1927, I found the new art center of the Bauhaus-Dessau flourishing, and in it several of my Berlin friends, who were busily designing houses, rugs, furniture, lamps, and kitchen utensils. As their guest, I slept in a lovely and aseptic Constructivist bedchamber and was none the worse for it.

In the early twenties, Lissitzky, preëminently the engineer-architect, made magnificent models of new skyscrapers, airports, hangars, and theaters, and gradually won an international renown among Europe's cognoscenti, though he was somewhat in disfavor in Soviet Russia. An important exhibition of his work was given by Katherine Dreier in 1925 at her gallery, the Société Anonyme, in New York. But Lissitzky returned to Russia in the late twenties and gave his adherence to the Communist regime, abandoning his abstract art and performing only technical services thereafter for the government's publications. Though he had become a legendary figure in the art world outside, he disappeared from sight within Russia.

During a Cook's tour I made to Russia in 1934, I managed to find him again, not without some difficulty. He was then living with his German wife and children in a country house outside of Moscow, not far from Tolstoi's country seat at Yasnaya Polyana, and was as engaging and animated as ever. He was well treated by the Soviet government, but admitted to me that he had made a "voluntary sacrifice" of his abstract art. During the invasion of Russia in 1941, the village in which he lived was overrun by the German Armies. Lissitzky and his family were swept up in the massive eastward migration of millions; feeble in health and unable to endure the sufferings of that retreat, Lissitzky died soon afterward.

ELEVEN

THE ROAD

TO SURREALISM

The adventures of my French friends continued to hold my attention more than almost anything else, even when I was far away in Berlin. With what eagerness I would await letters reporting their most recent caperings! I also renewed direct contact with them during two visits to Paris of a fortnight or more in the winter and early spring of 1923.

When I had left them about six months earlier they had been all agog over their innovation of "automatic writing," inspired by a work Breton and Soupault had published in 1921 entitled *Les Champs magnétiques*. This consisted of a series of prose pieces without intrigue or characters or ordered discussion of any subject, which the authors declared they had written *automatically* under the dictation of their subconscious minds. Soupault had always been disposed to write on the spur of the moment, in the unstudied and effortless way of Apollinaire. Breton, as an amateur of psychoanalysis, was much occupied with writing down fragments of his dreams or daytime reveries. They had worked together on *Les Champs magnétiques*: one would give the other a substantive clause or some verb, and each would write as swiftly as possible whatever words came into his head "automatically" and without regard for its literary effect. The most bizarre images or phrases went into this mixed salad, and there was no suite of ideas from one sentence to another. Breton's confreres soon became absorbed in similar experiments of their own.

I, too, had sometimes joined in the game of automatic writing, usually staged in some noisy café, together with Aragon and two or three others, all of us scribbling whatever free associations of thought came to us, although my own libido often gave forth only the feeblest stutterings. As I remarked around that time: "By drinking quantities of beer and writing as fast as you could, in competition with others, after three or four hours you became so dazed that your subconscious began working a little."[1]

The painters, too, were encouraged to attempt automatic drawing or doodling; in my opinion they performed much better than the writers. Picasso himself attempted such experiments at the time—though these may have been scarcely new stunts for this resourceful and inventive man. But when I rode into Paris again in the early winter, my friends had already abandoned their automatic writings and were off on something new.

Aragon gave us warm welcome at the station and informed us that we were to dine quickly and accompany him to Paul Éluard's house where there was to be a séance of psychoanalysis among our friends, each of whom would recite his dreams and submit to their being analyzed by the others.

I laughed aloud, and exclaimed: "But everybody in Greenwich Village, New York, was doing just that—they were having themselves 'psyched'—six or seven years ago!"

"It is different with us, you will see," Aragon promised.

Here again was the trio we had found so diverting in Imst-in-Tirol the summer before: Paul and Gala Éluard and Max Ernst. Ernst had been received by his literary admirers in Paris with open arms; in such free time as he had, while working at his dreary job in a toy factory, he had completed some striking compositions. On one of the walls of Éluard's parlor a large

group portrait by Ernst had been recently hung which represented all the members of the circle present that evening. They
were ten in number, those whom one might call the apostles
of André Breton and their prophet, the initiator of most of their
intellectual enterprises. This canvas, *"Au Rendez-vous des amis,"*
was partly painted and partly built up by the method of photo-
montage. Breton occupied the center of the picture, and around
him, seated or standing, were Aragon, Éluard, Ernst, Péret,
Vitrac, Baron, Max Morise, René Crevel, and Robert Desnos—
a newcomer to this circle. On two pedestals in the background
were also the busts (in photo-montage) of the two patron saints
of Surrealism, Dostoevski and Chirico. Most of the persons in
this picture were to be known for some years to come as "Surrealists," a term already in use at the end of 1922 but destined
to become memorable as the name of the school of artists and
writers officially established in 1924.

France had seen many different schools during the century
that passed since Hugo's romantic cenacle had appeared. The
Romanticists had affected the most flambuoyant costumes, such as
the historic red vest of Théophile Gautier. Our band of Surrealists were no less romantic than their predecessors of 1829;
they too would flaunt the red vest, figuratively at any rate, before the Philistines of this world. They would try to "change
life," as Rimbaud had proposed doing, by escaping from every-
day realities to the zone of the "super-real" and the occult. They
were to be united by their identical tastes for the most audacious
liberties and by the ardors they shared in making war upon
bourgeois morality. Perhaps nothing so cohesive as the group
Breton gathered about himself between 1922 and 1929 had
ever been seen. A later commentator, Jules Monnerot, in his
sociological study of their movement, went so far as to call
them a *Bund*. However, as Breton argued, if its members accepted a common discipline and worked together toward the
same objectives, their association in this *Bund* was purely voluntary. In truth, they were held together by Breton's magnetism,
strength of will, and his overweening need for proselytes. It was

as if the man feared being alone, and demanded always the favoring milieu of a group of young disciples.

The newcomer, Robert Desnos, had been introduced to the circle by me, as it happened, about a year earlier. He was a conscript soldier in a shapeless blue uniform and a red fez, recently discharged from the Army of Morocco, who had come to my table at a café where I regularly met my French friends, saying that he had seen me with Aragon and Breton, and earnestly begged me to present him to them. Being a poet himself, he admired these young men above all others. I obliged him by performing the introduction the following day, and Desnos thenceforth became one of the Surrealists' most valued recruits, enjoying the favor of Breton in particular, to whom he showed passionate loyalty. Desnos was not only a highly original fellow in his own right, but, when the spirit moved him, could play the clown in marvelous style.

On the night when I came in from Berlin, the Surrealists were raptly reciting their dreams. As I arrived in the midst of their séance, I could scarcely follow what they were talking about—there was no attempt at systematic analysis—though I recall that their unconscious thoughts, as reported on this occasion, seemed to be full of expressions of violent hatred or love for one another. But none could *embroider* his dreams like Desnos!

He would go off into a transport, his protuberant eyes taking on a strange light, while the account of his marvelous chimeras gushed from his lips. There were the pursuers and the possessors; visions of the Apocalypse and the procession of its prophets; scenes of mythical violence filled with anguished cries; and "wizards" who now assumed the shape of "Fantômas" (as in the serial thriller of the movies) or now that of Nicholas Flamel, the thirteenth-century alchemist. How like an acrobat, with the greatest of ease, Desnos swung from one millennium to another, or from one continent to another. (Someone in the room was taking it all down stenographically, so that these dreams could be printed afterward.) Whereas the dream recitals of others were mostly boring, Desnos' seemed to come out of a real trance, and were narrated without clichés; they had, in fact, the quality of genius.

Were they going to practice therapy upon each other, I wondered? Or would they treat their recorded dreams as so much "literature"? Breton explained that their object was to explore the dreamwork of man, the world of the undirected subconscious mind, in "scientific spirit," thus to learn something of that *surréalité* which men of prosaic and rational ways were unable to attain or enjoy.

Some of the Surrealists, however, forgot their dreams, or their recitals lacked—shall we say—verisimilitude? One or two, long afterward, confessed that they sometimes faked their "sleep." In any case, Breton, eager to pursue his researches, soon persuaded his friends to take up the practice of occultism in different forms.

René Crevel, the golden-haired young man with the face of a laughing cupid, was the one who initiated them into the procedures of spiritism, of which it seemed he had some experience. By the beginning of 1923 they were holding séances in a dark room around a table, joining hands and working themselves up to a state of high tension and expectation. But instead of rapping the table with his hands, Crevel, decidedly a neurotic type, would suddenly bump his head against it, crying out incoherent tirades that resembled his own rather elliptical writings. Once more it was Robert Desnos who was the greatest "medium" of them all. At these table-turning séances he would detect the voices of invisible spirits or of telepathic communications as unfailingly as a Marconi receiver.

On one occasion in the darkened room, Desnos, completely unconscious or in a trance—in the presence of his friends— entered into communication with Marcel Duchamp, then residing in New York. That famous mystificator, at the time used to contrive word games made up of puns and double-entendres, conceived in a spirit of delightful folly and having his own very particular wit. Some of these he forwarded to his friends in

Paris, who published them in *Littérature* under his pseudonym
"Rrose Sélavy" (*Eros c'est la vie?*) Specimens are:

Ovaire toute la nuit (in place of *Ouvert toute la nuit*) ; and *Il faut
mettre la moelle de l'épée dans le poil de l'aimée.*

To the astonishment of his fellow occultists, Desnos, while
mesmerized, began to write rapidly on a piece of paper before
him a series of rhymed plays on words "dictated" from New
York by "Rrose Sélavy." Moreover, they seemed at least as
good as the original models, if not better:

*Rrose Sélavy se demande si la mort des saisons fait tomber un
sort sur les maisons.*
*Croyez-vous que Rrose Sélavy connaisse ces jeux des fous qui
mettent le feu aux joues?*
Est-ce que la caresse des putains excuse la paresse des culs teints?

The "telepathic communications" of young Desnos inspired
much excited comment when published not long afterward in
the Surrealists' review. Was he not merely simulating sleep,
some asked? Yet expressions of similar literary power or wit
had been recorded in the circles of spiritists and theosophers
since the 1840's; more recently the modern medium Mme
Helena Blavatsky and the poet W.B. Yeats had obtained similar
results. Such phenomena have been attributed by psychiatrists
to the mechanism of the unconscious mind in the cases of persons of exceptional talent during sleep real or feigned. Now the
young Desnos had rare gifts of improvisation and mimicry,
shown in his published verse and prose, which, like his dreams,
soon surprised and delighted the literary world. They were an
amalgam of poetic obscenities, of fear-and-sex-obsessed nightmares, and of gay nonsense in the style of Lewis Carroll.

Louis Aragon, in replying to those who expressed doubts
about the authenticity of Desnos' dream writings, declared that
even if the poet had been simulating unconsciousness, he had
achieved a clear expression of "the genius of the subconscious
mind." In a later, more public phase of his literary career,

Robert Desnos showed himself in fact a remarkable improviser, performing in night clubs and at radio broadcasting stations, now inventing or now reciting from memory his fantastic and often clownish songs.

In reality, he had no need of the mesmerist or the turning table in a dark room, for he had other means of stimulating himself to a condition of autohypnosis and uninhibited improvisation. A regular dosage of opium—and an audience of at least one—was all this highly narcissistic personality required in order to function. (The truth about his drug addiction came out some years later, in 1929, on the occasion of a resounding public quarrel between him and his once-beloved master, Breton, to whom he had confessed his private vices.) For all his vices and his periodic outbursts of violence, Desnos was one of the most lovable and entertaining of men.[2]

By 1923 André Breton was unquestionably on his way to the new faith, "Surrealism," whose gospel he was shaping. (The term itself had first been employed as defining the new direction of literature by Guillaume Apollinaire.) For years I myself was half under the spell of Breton's power of intellectual innovation and the passion for morally dangerous experiment which he communicated to others and by which he attracted them. What was he doing now with his explorations of the occult and the thoughts that come during sleep?

To my mind, Breton's critical faculties outweighed the creative element in him. His interest in the creative process itself led him to experiments with automatism and the subconscious mind, as if to compensate for his own want of spontaneous qualities— such as made Aragon and Desnos "natural" poets. Both Taine and Nietzsche, long before Breton, had furnished important psychological clues to the role of the automatic, or unconscious, in artistic creation; the writings of Sigmund Freud also shed new light on the same problem. In the summer of 1921 Breton had made a journey to Vienna to interview Dr. Freud. Breton may have indicated that he intended to apply the methods of psychoanalysis to artistic experimentation, but it would seem that he received scant encouragement from Freud himself, judging from Breton's published account of their conversation (in *Littérature*).

I was told in Paris in 1923 about the spiritist séances Breton was holding with his friends, but feeling no spirit for such things, failed to attend any of them. I admit to having felt repelled, even a little dismayed at the plunge into the subconscious, the occult, and the irrational my friends were taking. It seemed to me that Breton was misusing psychoanalytic methods (essentially a therapy for the mentally ill), and, like a dilettante, was trying to extract literature from the minds of persons in a state of hypnosis or sleep. A reasoning fellow myself, and with some slight knowledge of Freud's high-minded purpose, I had the conviction that Freud would never have countenanced what the Surrealists were trying to do. Freud's own practice of mental therapy was designed to locate hidden sources of disturbance evidenced in his patients' dreams, and thus to effect a harmonious adjustment of the sick personality. But Freud never believed, as Breton seemed to assume, that subconscious thought was more "true" or "better" than consciously reasoning thought. It was *balance* between the two forms of mental activity that Freud sought.

Besides the inquiries of the earlier psychologists into the relationship of the "automatic" mind and the creative arts, there were also suggestions that came from the poet Baudelaire. In his occasional efforts to attain an occult condition of correspondence with the universe, Baudelaire had not only indulged in hashish, but had flirted with Swedenborgian mysticism as well. His observations of the "unknown and the invisible" were set forth in *Paradis Artificiels*. And after Baudelaire there had been Rimbaud, who also used drugs at one period of his life, while proclaiming the mission of the poet to be that of a "clairvoyant" and "an alchemist of the word."

Now came Breton with his call to the artists and poets of modern times to put their dreams to work for them, to make, so to speak, a *conscious* effort to exploit their unconscious minds for the sake of their art. "We must burst the bonds of reason—of narrow rationalism," Breton urged, and, immersed in the state of dream, project ourselves toward that higher zone of "absolute reality or super-reality" where we would encounter always "the marvelous." ("I believe in the future resolution of those two states of mind, dream and reality, in appearance so contradictory . . . into a super-reality," he boldly avowed in 1924.) By abolishing reason and logic, and with them the social and sexual taboos of bourgeois society, Breton continued, man would liberate himself from the considerations of the material world as from the chains of duty and convention. Thus he would arrive at a new system of values (not defined as yet) which would restore him to "the innocence of the human word . . . and its pristine creative virtue."

I have tried in this brief résumé to make some sense of the chain of unreason Breton pursued as he worked to convert his little band of rebellious artists into a "church," making them adepts of a religion that was antinomian or gnostic, and hence, anti-Christian, judging from the "First Surrealist manifesto," published in December, 1924. What filled my mind at the time with trouble and doubt was the feeling that under Breton's lead Surrealism was taking the empire of the irrational for its future province. It followed, naturally, that he would proceed to offer (in imitation of Nietzsche's scheme of master morality) every variety of nonconformism, in fact a program of "total subversion," anti-social and anti-patriotic.

Meanwhile, in pursuance of his search for truths occult, marvelous or incongruous, Breton began hypnotizing persons like Desnos. Robert was extremely responsive, loved the treatment, and came through with some extraordinary verbal effusions. But Robert also began to be violent. (I would certainly not have cared to be responsible for the troubled soul of a man like Desnos or one or two others in Breton's entourage who were plainly psychotic.)

One day in 1923 Desnos appeared at a dinner party given at a restaurant on the Place de l'Odéon in honor of Ezra Pound. Jean Cocteau, whom Pound greatly admired, had also been invited to this dinner but had not come. Desnos had gone looking for Cocteau whom, he said, he hated and would kill on sight. Cocteau being absent, he evidently decided to finish off Mr. Pound instead. Drawing a long sharp knife from under his coat, he suddenly made a pass as if to stab the author of the *Cantos* from behind. Fortunately he was seized before he could strike, and overpowered by Pound's friends, who threw him out of the place. News of the incident was kept from the newspapers and no charges were preferred against Desnos, who was plainly under the influence of drugs that day.

A good many years later, in 1952, André Breton published some troubling confessions about his experiments in hypnotism between 1922 and 1924, and told why he felt forced to abandon them. One night a large party of the Surrealists and their friends, including several young women, were gathered in a spacious villa somewhere near Paris that belonged to one of their number, and held a séance during which they subjected each other to hypnosis. In this state they wandered about the darkened rooms of that big house in a collective trance, saying and doing all sorts of incredible things or just falling asleep. Breton himself finally awoke from his slumbers at two in the morning, to find that he had been lying on a strange bed in an upper room of the house, and everyone else had disappeared. He began to feel worried about some of the young women who had come as guests. Hearing voices down below, he descended the stairs to the entrance hall; there, under a great chandelier, two or three of the women, urged on by René Crevel, were trying to hang themselves with some wire they had tied around their necks. Breton put a stop to all that and sent them home.

Meanwhile, in another room Robert Desnos, in a fine frenzy rolling and armed with a big kitchen knife, pursued his fellow-poet Paul Éluard—whom he really loved to his dying day. Coming to Éluard's help, Breton managed to disarm Desnos. But later on Desnos, who regarded Breton as both his "father" and his favorite mesmerist, repeatedly came to Breton's house and begged to be put to sleep. On one occasion, when Breton yielded and mesmerized him, he found after awhile that it was impossible to waken Desnos by the usual methods. In great alarm he called a doctor, though it was late at night, had him revived, and sent him away. After that Breton gave up the hypnotic séances and turned to other games.

Another facet of Breton's many-sided career in the twenties was his activity as a critic and philosopher of art. His polemical essays on the problems of modern painting, gathered together in his book, *Le Surréalisme et la peinture* (1926), had a notable influence on the artists themselves. One explanation for this is that his sermons were very timely; he was telling the modern artists the things they wanted very much to hear.

By 1922 Cubism was apparently played out (although abstract art itself was not), and the artists were wondering where to go. I remember being at Breton's house in the spring of 1922, after he had just returned from the auction rooms in the rue Druot, bringing the sensational news that the leading Cubist painters of the School of Paris—Picasso, Braque, Gris, and company— had suddenly announced their abandonment of the Cubist method and turned to experiments in a more figurative and "neoclassical" style. There was a temporary collapse in the prices of Cubist pictures that season; Breton, who was interested in market values as well as aesthetic values, shrewdly resolved to buy up some of those historic paintings, as he told us, both on his own account and for that of his patron, Jacques Doucet.

From 1922 on, Breton urged modern artists to carry out a sweeping revaluation of the classical conceptions that still ruled their various schools. He was, of course, opposed to the merely representational; the painters must give up trying to do what a machine like a camera could do better than they with mere hands. For Breton, the primitive artifacts of African and Ocean-

ian craftsmen, like those of the various archaic periods, constituted an art that penetrated to "the internal object," and freed
itself from the limitations of the laws of perspective, gravity,
extension, and so forth. Whether they were primitives of recent
times or ancient Minoans, such artists had truly liberated their
imagination, surrendered themselves to their dreams, and
achieved that "innocent vision" which the men of modern art
must now somehow reacquire.

How were modern men to accomplish this? By occultation,
by seeking to recover man's psychic powers, "by a giddy descent
into our own depths, by the gradual illumination of hidden
places and forbidden zones." Thus the artist also would be attuned "to the psychic secrets of the cosmos and the universal
flux of things." The artist was exhorted to become a magician, a
"seer," and a prophet. The idea of abandoning oneself to the
play of the subconscious mind and working from a state of
psychic automatism made a powerful appeal to the young artists
whose minds were open to Surrealist doctrine.

Moreover, Breton assured his artist followers that in liberat-
ing themselves they would also help to overturn the foundations
of our stupid bourgeois culture, would revolutionize our moral
and social values. They were to be, henceforth, no mere daubers
of pigment on canvas, but an elite of cultural insurgents: Pro-
metheans, "stealers of fire." (A quarter of a century later I perceived with consternation that members of the new cult of
Abstract-Expressionism in America were plunged into the same
welter of automatic and unconscious thought that the Surrealists
had initiated. The Americans who were influenced by Surrealist
and Dadaist art, however, avoided the social subversiveness of
their predecessors.)

It was not surprising that—inspired by Breton's eloquent
call—numerous young artists of talent flocked to the banner of
Surrealism. Breton had extolled first of all Chirico and then
Max Ernst as artists whose works embodied in poetic form that
"meeting of incompatibles" to be discovered usually in the
dream state. Max Ernst, André Masson, and Joan Miró appeared

at about the same period as adepts of Surrealism to create the original body of its paintings; and were followed some years later by Yves Tanguy, Salvador Dali, and others. Formerly they had been poor devils who could scarcely sell their canvases for a few hundred francs; now they were "supermen," in effect, or so designated by their prophet Breton, who not only carried on a tireless propaganda in their behalf, but opened an art gallery for them exclusively, so that in the end some of them were made famous and became richer than himself. In the field of art, Surrealism was a success.

In times past poets and artists had often envisioned some utopian myth into which they might escape, leaving this workaday world in order to live and create at liberty. Now the cult of Surrealism and its intellectual autocrat offered them the most agreeable of utopias, indeed all the wide landscape of freedom and even love without constraint.

The publications of the Surrealists, from 1924 on, expounded almost every form of heresy; even the "duty to work" was ridiculed, as was the concept of "bourgeois honor." At the same time, the quaint notions of the Marquis de Sade about sexual felicity were rescued from oblivion and made fashionable anew. Human love itself must be refashioned, like everything else, Breton pontificated; only by indulging in all his caprices, and exploring the darkest caverns of human passion and eroticism, could man rediscover the true sense of "inner life." One of the novel intellectual entertainments of the Surrealists was their collection of "beautiful crimes," reports of which were culled from the Paris newspapers, and "reviewed" or analyzed for their psychological or aesthetic values in their literary organ.

Breton, in truth, showed an abiding, if academic, interest in acts of violence. He found it a matter of significance that his wartime friend, Jacques Vaché, should have drawn a revolver in a crowded theater out of disgust with a public absorbing what purported to be culture. At one of the early Dada concerts in Paris Breton himself came on stage with two revolvers strapped to his temples.

There was much talk of the "allure" of "unprovoked crimes," as exemplified in André Gide's *Lafcadio's Adventures,* in Surrealist circles. In 1929 Breton, in an outburst of spleen at the spectacle of vulgarity and corruption all about him, wrote: "The simplest Surrealist act would consist of going out into the street, revolver in hand, and firing at random into the crowd as long as one could." (*Deuxième Manifeste Surréaliste,* December, 1929.)

This *boutade* caused Albert Camus to liken André Breton to the Nazi leader Hermann Göring who was reported to have said, "When I hear the word 'culture' I always feel like taking out my revolver." Breton later expressed regret at his own remark about firing a revolver at random, saying it was written in a "moment of giddiness."

The young Surrealist artists of the 1920's were enchanted by André Breton and his subversive ideas. The charming Yves Tanguy called him "Papa"; the poet Benjamin Péret sometimes acted as if he were Breton's bodyguard; and Jacques Prévert (after leaving the *Bund*) wrote: "We loved him like a woman!"

André Masson was one of the new artists whose experiments in automatic painting, executed with innate imagination and skill, won him acclaim in the art world at this period. I watched him in his studio one day performing beautiful linear acrobatics with his pencil, but throwing away sixty to a hundred sheets of paper before he achieved the free and vibrant movement he sought. In later years Masson ruefully admitted to me: "When one went in for automatic drawing it was like going fishing; you never knew what you might bring back. Sometimes you caught a big fine carp; but other times, just as likely, you would only fetch up with an old shoe!"

These young men had been repeatedly exhorted by their spiritual leader to oppose family, church, and state, and "throw over everything," including wife, job, and career. (The leader himself seldom traveled far from his comfortable apartment near the Place Blanche in Paris.) Some of them took him at his word. One day in 1924, after withdrawing without authorization a considerable sum of money belonging to the construction business in which he was employed by his father, Paul Éluard fled to Monte Carlo, gambled successfully, then took ship for Polynesia. His sudden disappearance created a buzz of excited conversation in Paris; he was likened to those earlier fugitives from Western civilization, Rimbaud and Gauguin. Unlike them, however, after only a few weeks he became bored with Tahiti, and dispatched a cablegram to his wife Gala, saying: "Come and join me with Max." He was starting west by boat and would meet them at Saigon, he added.[3]

Max Ernst, who two years before had already taken flight from his fatherland and his family to come to Paris, now disposed of such possessions and pictures as he could sell and embarked for the Far East in the company of Gala Éluard. They met Paul in Indochina, and spent some time observing the monuments and ruins of that country. Paul Éluard, having been pardoned by his father, now decided to hasten back to France by the first fast boat. Max and Gala, like Paul had become weary of the Orient and also left, taking a slow boat whose engines broke down so that she almost sank in a storm in the Red Sea. Months passed before they saw Marseilles again.

At about the same period the dapper Jacques Rigaut, who had been working at some business job in Paris, also absconded with some money, which his father, however, made good. The father, in return for his financial aid, demanded that his son now remove himself to America (where I later found Jacques again).

Thus the Surrealists did commit a number of anti-social acts, though they usually managed to avoid the serious attentions of the police, with the help of their families or some other means. In any case, the anti-social acts of Éluard and Rigaut seem to us unimpressive as manifestations of the Surrealist Weltanschauung. Surrealism always held out the promise of daring and violent actions to its followers, and the thrill of danger; but on the whole, the adepts avoided going too far (as Robert Desnos himself observed). Some of their critics later accused them of treating their "Surrealist Revolution" as a mere war of words. Breton pointed out that they were trying, in the main, to create a movement of minds. In truth, much of their interest in homicide, incendiarism, and sadism appears to have been academic. (The chief of the school himself is said to have been singularly free of any but "normal" vices.) Thus they had all the fun of carrying on a "war" against society from within, while avoiding the hardships usually visited upon members of a rebellious sect.

A typical outburst of the Surrealists, of which I heard a good deal shortly after I returned to the United States, occurred early in October, 1924, when they launched a virulent attack on the character and repute of Anatole France—in the form of a scurrilous brochure—on the very occasion of the great public funeral given the recently deceased author, whose remains were placed in the Pantheon. The famous man was atrociously abused and pilloried as the prime example of one given to moral and artistic compromise. "Have You Ever Slapped a Corpse?" was the gruesome title of Aragon's part in this pamphlet. In France, everyone takes off his hat when the dead pass by; and so the behavior of the Surrealists in speaking evil of the late Anatole France appeared so outrageous that they were characterized in the metropolitan press as "jackals." Indeed, the newspapers now reached an agreement to give only the silent treatment thereafter to the activities of these young aesthetic nihilists whom they regarded as perpetrators of bad jokes.

Our charming friend Aragon contributed further to the silencing of the press when two years later he issued his book, *Le Paysan de Paris*, a sort of essay-novel or reverie about Paris, together with a stern public warning that anyone who reviewed it would be horsewhipped by the author. The well-known weekly *Les Nouvelles Littéraires* accepted the challenge, printed a review of the book, and a rather favorable one at that. Aragon, one of the most sensitive of creatures in private life, then went into action as a true Surrealist. He arrived at the office of the literary newspaper armed with a heavy cane, beat up its editor,

M. Maurice Martin Du Gard (cousin of the novelist), threw his typewriter out of the window, and departed. His victim, however, refrained from preferring criminal charges against his attacker.

One read less about the Surrealists in the newspapers; and Breton was not happy under these circumstances. Their "revolution" must expand or die. It was becoming, at the end of the twenties, rather a platonic affair. But where would they go next?

TWELVE

RETREAT

FROM BERLIN

In the early winter of 1923 I was back in Berlin seeing new issues of *Broom* through the press. As our *pièces de résistance,* we offered translations of the previously unpublished chapters of Dostoevski's *The Possessed* ("Stavrogin's Confession"), Lautré-amont's *Les Chants de Maldoror,* and Apollinaire's *Le Poète Assassiné,* as well as prose and verse by Aragon, Paul Éluard, Philippe Soupault, and Roger Vitrac. In the January issue, an "All-American Number," we published the poems of Marianne Moore, William Carlos Williams, Wallace Stevens, and Hart Crane; also such young newcomers as Glenway Wescott and Kay Boyle; as well as more Gertrude Stein, which led to trouble.

Since I had become an associate editor of the magazine we had been at loggerheads with Lola Ridge, the American editor, an excellent woman who wrote rather dull free verse. Miss Ridge's position was difficult at best. She was supposed to be in charge of the New York office, gathering and selecting copy and sending it on to us with her recommendations. There she also conducted a modest salon attended by a group of writers and poets to whom she gave encouragement as well as tea and cakes each week at the *Broom* office, 3 East 9th Street. It made her unhappy when the manuscripts of writers she had recommended were rejected by the editors in Europe. Harold Loeb had not accorded her a free hand, although she had gathered most of the material by American writers that made up the January, 1923, issue. I, for my part, had the feeling that her literary taste was retrograde and usually counseled against her selections. Miss Ridge, on the other hand, declared herself opposed to our ideas about giving reflection to the Machine-Age culture of our time, holding that artists would survive only by fighting against the machine and capitalism. Moreover, she had no liking for the work of Gertrude Stein, whom I found so intriguing and whose publication I strongly favored.

Lola Ridge had been doing her uttermost to promote the magazine in the face of great difficulties. For this she earned a very small salary, and sometimes did not even draw that. But when Loeb and I insisted on publishing more of Gertrude Stein in the American number of *Broom*—over Miss Ridge's protests that her work was "mostly blah!" and "would soon be forgotten"— then Lola Ridge, as a woman of principle, decided she was through, and cabled us on November 15, 1922:

Resign on inclusion of Gertrude Stein in American number.

Our next move (at my unfortunate suggestion) was to write Gorham Munson a letter, at the end of November, inquiring in confidence if he would be willing to replace Miss Ridge. I wrote the letter with Harold's approval. To be sure, Munson already had his own little magazine, *Secession*, which appeared irregularly, paid nothing, and had about three hundred readers, but my thought was that we might combine forces and put *les jeunes* together—they were in fact the same group—into the larger magazine, *Broom*, which at least paid small fees to writers and had a circulation of almost three thousand readers. We also believed Munson was in accord with our own thinking, for after his return home he had written Harold: ". . . What America needs is some violent Dadaism to save us from our art worshipers."[1]

But it happened that we had recently rejected a hundred-page monograph Munson had written on Waldo Frank, in which he eulogized Frank as though he were Tolstoi and Walt Whitman in one. To make matters worse, I myself, not knowing or considering Munson's feelings in the matter, had lately published in *Broom* a disparaging review of Frank's latest book in the form of a rather harsh satire of that author. I now realize, in age and repentance, that instead of trying to amuse myself and my readers by parodying Frank's overblown style and deriding his Messianic ideas about sexual freedom and the New Dawn, I might have chided him with a kindlier humor, inasmuch as he is, leaving his novels to one side, an intellectual of much character and moral courage. At any rate, Munson was livid when he found his own monograph rejected and then read my unkind review of Frank.

He promptly dispatched a thunderous letter of protest to me, consisting mainly of abuse of Harold Loeb as a sort of mindless playboy, a letter which I refused to show Harold, as it was private, none of it was true, and it would have made Harold unhappy to read it. Meanwhile, my own letter offering Munson a job at our New York office had already gone out, crossing Munson's angry letter by the slow ship mail of those days. I had mentioned in confidence our differences with Lola Ridge on editorial grounds, adding also some criticisms of her management of the New York office—as I understood things then—statements which were for Munson's benefit and not intended for Miss Ridge's. What was my consternation on learning, a few weeks later, that Gorham Munson had taken my letter and shown it to Miss Ridge! When Harold heard of this he said that Munson had behaved like a "dirty politician," by seeking to create more bad feeling between Lola Ridge and ourselves.[2]

A week later came a second letter from Munson, no longer wrathful, but exceedingly polite, acknowledging my "feeler" about the position in New York and saying that he would accept it, though he now feared he might have disqualified himself by his peevish outburst at us in his preceding letter. He reported that he now had "the beginnings of a critical reputation," which perhaps justified his being allowed some voice in our editorial councils. But in truth he had been earning only forty dollars a month by his writing, was weary of living with his wife's parents, and would welcome the position under any circumstances as the "first congenial job" that had ever been offered him. Finally he said he was "damned thankful" to me for proposing it.[3]

Despite his contrition both Harold and I decided to give no more thought to Munson as a possible associate. Earlier, on returning to America in April, 1922, Munson had gone out to New Jersey to meet my old friend Kenneth Burke, as I had advised him to do. It was my wish then that Burke join us as a third member of *Secession's* editorial board, to which Munson agreed. At the little whistle stop of Cranberry Lake, Munson was met by Kenneth. Looking at the old freight cars that studded the scene of the little water town, Munson remarked: "Not much like Paris!" According to Munson's own recollections, Kenneth appeared rather glum at this specimen of the Munson wit.[4]

Nonetheless, Kenneth soon opened up conversationally, as he usually does, and in forthright language declared that he would have no part in our Dadaist experiments or in our proposed exegesis of the culture of the Machine Age. He expressed strong disapproval of the tendencies I had manifested after living in France, which were reflected also by his friend Malcolm Cowley. Burke was hell-bent on leading American literature and criticism back to the true path of Spinoza and Goethe, his literary idols of the moment. In fact he was saying the same things to us in his letters; but in the heat of argument Burke's voice often became a deep bellow, so that Munson was all the more impressed and was persuaded that the Dadaist tendencies which had once appealed to him so strongly should now be cast off. He could not comprehend that in talking uninhibitedly about his friends, Kenneth was only behaving as one of the charter members of our old Anti-Logrolling Society.

Thus rescued from the perils of Dadaism, Munson now became in effect Burke's "disciple." However, the next season, after being exposed to the conversation of Waldo Frank and George Ivanovich Gurdjieff, he would become momentarily a mystic, a devotee of yoga, a Buddhist. Having invested about twenty dollars to begin with in the literature of America's Youngest Generation, and armed with a few letters of introduction from me, Munson had come to regard himself seriously as a sort of Magister Artium. Despite my recommendations, he and Burke rejected the prose of Gertrude Stein, which might have added to the interest of our little review.

In the meantime, I was still committed to help publish *Secession* in my spare time while I was in Europe. I had edited *Secession* No. 3 (August, 1922) while in the Tirol, and printed it in Berlin at my own expense.[5] In addition I was to work on the fourth issue. This was being prepared during my vacation trip to France, just before Christmas, 1922, when we visited with Malcolm and Peggy Cowley at Giverny for a few days. Giverny was the site of Claude Monet's residence—with its fabulous flower gardens—and was again becoming something of an art colony. Jim Butler, our naturist friend, was there; and among others, the poet John Brooks Wheelwright, a very odd and amusing classmate of Malcolm's at Harvard. Now Wheelwright, as it happened, had met Kenneth Burke and Gorham Munson in New York, prior to sailing for Europe; they had given him most of the material for *Secession* No. 4, which he turned over to Malcolm and me. Since he was going to be in Italy that year, Wheelwright had kindly offered to attend to the printing of *Secession* and also to pay for one or two of its issues out of his own pocket.

Munson had written me about him in very hopeful terms, saying that Jack Wheelwright and young Glenway Wescott—just arrived in New York from Wisconsin—were going to serve as "our arm of social penetration" at literary teas in New York and Boston and would thus advance our cause. I thought that was absurd, and twitted Munson about it at the time.

Jack Wheelwright was indeed an eccentric son of old Boston. A thin, long-legged, blond youth with pale blue eyes and a long nose, he would always appear in tight-fitting, sharply creased suits, a bowler, and carrying a Malacca cane, when we all set off for a walk in the country clad in comfortable old clothes. He traveled about Europe, moreover, with fully fourteen pairs of shoes, every inch of him the dandy nonconformist; and held forth as both a social rebel and a devoutly religious Anglican. Oddity that he was, we found him lovable nevertheless; his verbal sallies, which concealed his underlying melancholy, amused us; while his poetry, which at first glance showed a poor ear for language, on further acquaintance revealed depths of feeling and an authentic voice. Wheelwright and I remained good friends for many years, up to the time of his death in an automobile accident in 1940.

Our editorial conference in Giverny, over the material for the new number of *Secession* sent us by Munson and Burke, was an hilarious affair. Most of the material seemed uncommonly dull. We took exception in particular to a series of poems by someone who wrote under the pen name of "Richard Ashton," though our colleagues on the home front had approved of him. Reading these poems aloud, we came at last to the final verses of the one entitled "The Jilted Moon":

> O moon,
> Thou art naught but Chinese,
> Only Chinese.

All of it seemed bad except for those last three lines, which we agreed were neutral and so passable. "Why don't we cut out all that junk and print just those last three lines," one of us daringly proposed—it may have been I, it may have been Wheelwright; I no longer remember. All of us laughed at the idea. It was irresponsible; it was not editing; it was murder. But it was done, on the impulse of the moment, and perhaps after a good many potations of red wine. We were far away from our *Secessionist* colleagues in New York, and, at all events, felt that we were all "presidents" in this movement. Moreover, Jack Wheelwright, having agreed to pay the printing bill, evidently conceived that he had some seignorial rights in accomplishing the final touches of cutting and editing.

Wheelwright himself later wrote in some autobiographical notes he left with me:

> Though I had no use for little art papers when other people ran them, now I had my own. So I behaved the way all people do who have little art papers, only more so, and so made trouble for everybody including myself.

What was worse, poor Wheelwright, like other poets, was shaky in his spelling and had not the slightest experience of proofreading.

When Munson saw the fourth and fifth issues of *Secession,* he bellowed with rage. It seemed that Wheelwright had "butchered" the copy of several contributors—Munson himself had not been spared—while poor Mr. "Ashton's" work had been clean killed. The Editorial Director now demanded that a public apology by Wheelwright be inserted in the next issue, and proceeded to write out the terms of such an apology. Wheelwright, however, printed his own explanation, declaring that he could offer no apology since our misdeeds had not been in error but intentional:

> The two who were responsible for *Secession* No. 4 persevered in the distasteful task of printing Richard Ashton's poem. Then their intelligence rebelled. Very deftly, if somewhat drastically, they cut all but the last two lines [three], which thus became a comment on the preceding.

Munson afterward held that he had "blundered" in choosing me as a collaborator; and so he has stated (but falsely) that he "fired" me from an office that required unpaid labor and had ceased to be amusing. He had blundered again in asking Wheelwright to serve as his deputy, and now severed all relations with him. Then Kenneth Burke, after a few months, became fed up and resigned. Wherever Munson turned, apparently he could find no one he could trust or who could work with him—truly the

young literary people were a bad lot! As a result he reigned
thereafter in lonely splendor as Editorial Director of the last
two issues of *Secession*.

Afterward, Munson spread the report that several of us who
were associated with the review were "literary assassins." Yet
some years later, when I happened to meet the ill-used author of
"The Jilted Moon," whose real name was Donald B. Axton
Clarke, he laughed heartily when recalling the massacre of his
verses in *Secession*, and remarked amiably enough: "As I look
back at it now, you might have done no harm if you had gone on
to cut out those last three lines that you did manage to print."
Munson however remained unforgiving in his attitude toward
me, and later extended his displeasure to Malcolm Cowley also.

Several years later Malcolm wrote an ironical account of
the "wars of *Secession*" in the form of an article for the *New
Republic* (used later as a chapter of his book *Exile's Return*).
In reply Munson published a whole series of polemical articles
accusing Malcolm and myself of all sorts of evil doing, and
charging that, while helping him to edit *Secession*, we had acted
as "unscrupulous Machiavellians" who schemed to "manipulate
him" and to operate as "powers behind the throne." But there
was no throne and very little power in *Secession*.

The truth of the matter is that since Munson appeared to us
so ill-equipped for his duties as editor or literary critic, we occasionally tried to manage him a little. In other words, we
wanted to prevent him from making us all look like hams. Munson naturally resented our ill-concealed interventions. Of course,
we were young sparks then, often tactless or even at times a
little malicious with each other. But Munson saw wickedness or
double-dealing in actions that were but sportive. For years he
continued to fulminate against us; as a consequence some literary historians have taken his animadversions seriously and
treated our altercations with Munson as "disgraceful" and "jealous" quarrels. In reality we enjoyed having Munson as our
"enemy," and continued the pretense of a quarrel with him as
long as it seemed entertaining. Unwittingly, in spite of himself,

Gorham Munson was a priceless comic figure of the literary scene in that period, which is the principal reason for my having given him some space in these reminiscences.

In Berlin, *Broom* carried on from day to day as if the sheriff were expected to come in at any moment and foreclose the mortgage. Although the magazine was doing tolerably well, its original capital was gone, and a few thousand dollars Harold had obtained in addition was also nearly exhausted. While buying supplies of paper I happened to make a lucky speculation and was able to sell a part of our consignment, that we did not need, at a profit of nearly a thousand dollars, which paid for printing two issues of *Broom*. Harold Loeb, very pleased, wrote me at the time: "You're some business man—thanks. Your saving certainly helps."[6]

At the end of December, 1922, a cablegram arrived from his younger brother Willard E. Loeb urging Harold to come to New York for a visit with his family and a conference over the question of financing *Broom*. Harold departed at once by fast steamer, leaving me in charge at Berlin.

The results of his voyage were nil. Harold was told that no more funds for the support of his magazine would be advanced from his mother's estate. He then wrote letters to his immensely wealthy uncles, Simon and Solomon Guggenheim, sending them some copies of the magazine and appealing for the sum of ten thousand dollars a year to cover *Broom's* deficit. It is my impression that if Harold had gone to see his Uncle Simon in person the situation might have been saved. But the two copper barons could understand neither the pictures nor the printed matter in *Broom*. After a cursory investigation by one of his "efficiency experts," Simon Guggenheim took the trouble to inform Harold that his was just another losing venture and he would be wise to abandon it altogether.

In his family circle Harold Loeb's rating as a man of affairs was very low. In my own view, however, it is much to his credit that he broke away from the Guggenheim and Wall Street way of life after 1919 when he started his bookshop in New York and later his transatlantic magazine.

The curious thing about this episode is that a while later those same hard-boiled Guggenheim uncles of his wound up by imitating their poor relation, Harold Loeb, and becoming patrons of the arts on a gigantic scale. Beginning in 1924, Uncle Simon donated some eighteen millions (now grown to fifty millions) to the John Simon Guggenheim Memorial Foundation which provided fellowships for hundreds of artists and writers, including quite a number of contributors to *Broom* whom Simon Guggenheim had formerly been unable to "understand." Not to be outdone, Solomon Guggenheim afterward spent almost as much in founding the Guggenheim Museum of Non-Objective Art in New York and filling it with pictures by the very same avant-garde artists whose works were reproduced in *Broom* from 1921 to 1924.

In the early twenties you could not have got a nickel for modern art from all the Rockefeller clan. Truly the leopards of Wall Street have changed their spots. But then the income tax picture has also changed drastically, so that it is now in the material interests of millionaires to "lose" money on art and win it back again as a tax rebate.

After only a few days in New York, Harold hurried back and —after stopping off in Paris—arrived in Berlin in late January, empty-handed and looking very blue. His anxiety over the reported illness of his fiancée, whom he calls "Lily" in his autobiography, had made him curtail his stay in New York, he explained. Now he imparted to me the melancholy news that we would have to close up shop and that our March, 1923, issue was to be our last. At the New York office he had found things in a state of confusion, he reported, chiefly because Miss Ridge was ill and tired and was merely waiting for someone to supplant her. He suggested that when I returned to the States I might try to untangle the magazine's affairs in New York and distribute its last issues.

I had expected that I might soon be leaving my desk in our office in the old Friedrichstadt quarter of downtown Berlin. But while Harold seemed resigned to the demise of the magazine, everything in me rebelled at the thought of allowing *Broom* to die without a last ditch effort to save "her." Little "art papers," as Wheelwright called them, usually lost money; but ours had a loyal public of three thousand readers, was developing a group of new and talented writers, and was becoming known from Brooklyn to San Francisco for its vigorous support of the experimental in the arts. I had heard that *The Dial*, which then had only two or three thousand more readers than we did, required as much as forty thousand dollars a year to cover its deficit. We, however, needed only a moderate subsidy. Our prospects seemed good enough to warrant a renewed effort to raise a few thousand dollars. I offered to go back to New York and try to do that myself. Harold gave me his blessings—though he felt the outlook was almost hopeless.

Now some question arose about continuing *Broom* for one or two more issues (beyond March), so as to keep its monthly distribution uninterrupted during the time I would need to return to New York and reorganize things. Our exchequer had about a thousand dollars left in reserve, or enough for one or two months more; for a short while Harold was undecided about what should be done. At this point Lily entered the picture.

She was a charming and intelligent woman, but liked neither the climate nor the social atmosphere of Berlin; her heart pined for Paris where she had lived for years since the breakup of her first marriage. When it came to disposing of Harold's last reserve of surplus cash merely to have *Broom* appear for another month or two—which seemed to her like throwing good money after bad—she entered polite but firm objections which prevailed.

Lily made very entertaining company at our evening meals when she visited Berlin; and I remember gratefully her fund of good stories about all sorts of personalities we knew or had read about, stories she told in an ironical tone and with a world-weary smile. Her spirits drooped, however, as Harold continued to postpone the date of their marriage, and she assumed a complaining habit. The trouble was that Harold was now enjoying his bachelorhood after years of marriage and child-raising, and could hardly help showing himself playful and romantic every time some pretty female appeared in our midst. He would scrutinize them all carefully in his myopic way, through his horn-rimmed spectacles. There was no harm in it; most of us chaps are like that. But Lily, who was becoming ever more petulant in manner—used to kick Harold under the table; and sometimes, aiming at him, she would give *me* a hard kick in the shins. Seeing my look of surprise, she would take more accurate aim the next time and hit Harold, who always looked hurt. The second time I got kicked by mistake I remarked to my wife, though in private, that I intended to provide myself with a base-ball catcher's shin guards the next time we dined out with our two ever-loving friends.

My relations with Harold remained excellent; he had promised me an equal voice in editorial matters and always lived up to his promise. He has also testified that he found me extremely independent. Though not a man of letters by disposition, Harold had native abilities which he displayed some years later, in the 1930's, when he became the head of a small government agency in Washington and carried out important studies of national economic planning for the New Deal administration.

I headed for Paris, en route to New York, armed with full authority from Harold Loeb to do what I could to save *Broom* from an early death. Harold chose to stay in Paris where he was to occupy himself by writing novels. There he met Ernest Hemingway, who was already winning a modest reputation in trans-atlantic literary circles, though he had published only a few sketches and short stories. They became good friends for about two years—until Hemingway's novel *The Sun Also Rises* appeared in 1926 with its "real-life photographs" of Hemingway's circle in Paris and Harold Loeb very much in the foreground, which caused the rupture of their friendship. I was to learn more about that story (which makes a curious footnote to American literary history) during my second visit to France.

The trees in Paris were turning bright green in early April; the streets were thronged with people who seemed always to be smiling, in contrast with our Prussians in Berlin. Many Americans who could never live anywhere but in France repeatedly said that the French were real s.o.b's. But I always answered: "Well they are my s.o.b.'s and I love them just as they are."

With the coming of spring our French friends were busy separating from their wives or their mistresses and falling in love again or preparing to be remarried. The American colony in the Montparnasse cafés moved out into the open air of the terraces and carried on their philandering amid the familiar Paris odors of blossoming trees, coffee grounds, and the open-air *pissotières* along the street.

Evenings we dined out a great deal with the Surrealists, informing ourselves of their latest pranks or depredations, and sometimes going out to attend little riots they staged. In the daytime we were buying French hats for my wife, such as we would never find again anywhere else.

We were saying good-bye to people over and over again, with broken hearts. "Why do you leave when you are happy here?" Louis Aragon asked, but we had no answer.

Only at the last moment did I notice that the two or three Paris frocks and the little hats we had purchased for my wife had taken our last sous, and we had no money even for the taxi to the boat train. Philippe Soupault, the last person to see us off, insisted on lending me five hundred francs for our *menus besoins* on board ship. "But I may not be back for years," I warned him. "It doesn't matter, you will need it for tips and the bar," he said. It was with this kindly parting gesture that he took leave of us, and we proceeded to catch the boat for New York.

THIRTEEN

"THE POET'S

RETURN"

"When you are back in American life again I
do not know if you will be able to . . . enjoy the
'great funny time being had by all.' "
—EDMUND WILSON, JR.

We approached New York harbor in the late afternoon, so that
the white towers of Manhattan rising from the water were rose
tipped and made the place look for a moment like Venice. Once
we were in the city's dark resounding streets, however, the effect was more oppressive than beautiful. Sending my wife and
our baggage ahead by taxi to her parents' home, where we
were to stay a few days, I set off in the subway to visit my family
out in Brooklyn. After an absence of two years the New York
subway gave me a certain shock: at the end of the day the
people all looked stupefied and never glanced at anybody as if he
were a human being, but stared at the floor of the car or de-
voured their newspapers. Later, when I myself began to move at
the American tempo, I never gave a thought to the faceless
people in the subway.

I found my father partly disabled as a result of a coronary
attack suffered a year earlier, which left him with one arm and

leg semi-paralized. I now understood the reason for his delay in sending me a sum of money I had cabled for at about the time when he became ill. He still went to his office every day, though he was, of course, much less active than before. I felt some pangs of remorse at the thought that I had never been willing to enter his business and learn all about it and give up writing, as he would have wished me to; and that he, nevertheless, always remained very tolerant and kindly toward me. He certainly thought I was an odd one, but said only that he continued to be amused by me. My mother was unreserved both in her display of affection and in her reproaches to me for the harum-scarum life I led.

Soon I was busy day and night with the tangled affairs of *Broom*. My wife and I, with two hired boys, went through the drudgery of shipping out 2,500 copies of the magazine's latest issue, which had been stacked up for several weeks in the New York office. Thereafter I gave all my thought to seeking means for continuing *Broom's* publication. Harold Loeb had already tentatively accepted a very fair offer by the business manager of *The Dial* to turn over to them our paid-up subscribers, and thus discharge our obligations. At my insistence this arrangement was now canceled.

The New York office of *Broom* had occupied, rent free, the spacious basement rooms of an old mansion at 3 East 9th Street, in the neighborhood of Washington Square, which belonged to Harold's former wife, Marjorie Content, daughter of a prominent stockbroker. When I first came to work at the office I found myself confronted by two long faces: those of the former Mrs. Loeb and of Lola Ridge. Miss Ridge still lived in the rear rooms of the basement apartment as a nonpaying tenant, thanks to the kindness of the proprietor, who greatly admired her. Marjorie Content was not only very unforgiving toward her former husband, but also showed some displeasure toward me as his associate and friend, and made it plain that she wanted me to clear out at once, together with *Broom* and all its clutter of papers. I reported to Harold: "The most crushing disappointment is that we are being ejected by your former wife. . . . By giving her a long harangue I got eight more days to quit the premises."

Lola Ridge had good reason to be displeased with Harold, "who changed his mind too often," as she said. She had arranged to liquidate the magazine's affairs, then had been forced to send out notices that we were resuming publication. She also had some grounds for being vexed with me. There was, for one thing, the business of Munson's having shown her my confidential letter with its sharp criticisms of her policies. In the second place, she was a very high-minded woman, who wanted to discharge the debts of the magazine in honorable fashion, and felt doubts about the ability of a light-waisted young fellow like me to find money and keep the magazine going. A few hundred dollars had recently come in from bookshops and new subscribers, but she insisted on keeping this money in escrow in our bank account, which she alone had authority to draw upon. I was forced to borrow seventy-five dollars for posting the last issue of *Broom,* while waiting for a proper power of attorney to arrive from Harold Loeb in Paris.

I thought that Miss Ridge would prove less obstructive if I could only reach a better understanding with her—leaving aside our differences over Gertrude Stein or Picasso. I therefore invited her to have lunch with me at one of the tea shoppes in the neighborhood, and she accepted. In a frankly apologetic tone I declared that I felt I had misjudged her work at the New York office, for now, after a week in charge of things here, I could appreciate what difficulties she had faced and what strenuous efforts she must have made to promote our magazine. Miss Ridge, who had been very cold, now began to relent toward me.

Various persons had been spreading rumors that *Broom* would soon give up the ghost. I told Miss Ridge that my determination to raise money and save the magazine was unyielding, and said this with so much force that Lola Ridge felt I meant business. She unbent, assumed a very coöperative attitude, and began to give me some detailed information about the problems I faced, and about what I could or could not do to mend things.

There was one passage in our conversation which now seems amusing to recall. We had been discussing our different views of art and literature. With much emphasis Miss Ridge put the question: "Mr. Josephson, what is *your* definition of poetry?"

"You know very well," I replied, "that up to this day the greatest of poets and men of letters have failed to provide us in the English language with a concise definition that is adequate. No more can I do so in few words, although I can tell you what my preferences in poetry are."

"I will tell you *my* definition," she went on very sweetly, narrowing her fine dark eyes and assuming a faraway expression. "My idea of the poem is a snowflake sparkling and melting in the sun."

I said nothing, but bowed in acknowledgement of her metaphor. What could I have said to this excellent woman who had lived an arduous life up to middle age, suffered much poverty, and given expression to her experience in some poems that had the fire of a true idealist. There was a gulf between us. To my mind, the trouble with her and with a good many like her in America was that they still belonged to the "snowflake school" of poetry. We younger men, therefore, had a real job of modernization cut out for us.

In the first few weeks after my return I talked with many persons about this whole problem, often speaking impetuously, and sometimes, I fear, provocatively. One evening my wife and I, for example, attended a dinner party at the home of her brother, Maxwell Geffen, who had shown some friendly interest in my activities. After having worked as a newspaper reporter on a New York daily, he had taken a job with a printing firm and advanced himself so swiftly that within a few years, though still in his twenties, he practically owned the big firm. One of the other guests was a young public-relations man, M.L. Schuster, who was then planning to go in for magazine or book publishing together with my brother-in-law and several other investors. That evening they were looking me over, as I realized later, while they leafed through some copies of *Broom* I had placed before them.

Schuster almost upset the applecart for me when he came upon a picture in *Broom* that filled his soul with trouble and even anger, for he exclaimed, with feeling: "I am sure this Picasso is no artist; he is a *fake!*"

I replied with a vehement speech in defense of Picasso; I was a David fighting alone in this parlor against all the Philistines, for in those days there was no Museum of Modern Art in New York to educate them. However, to my great relief, my brother-in-law, that rising young tycoon of the printing trade, promised that he would undertake a study of *Broom*'s affairs, and after a few days—despite the warnings of his friends—came forward with an offer to help continue the publication of *Broom* for a year or two longer. The essence of his proposal was that we would be given a line of printing credit by his firm amounting to half of our manufacturing costs, and that he would also help us raise four thousand dollars in new capital.

I felt as if a miracle had been wrought! The greatest problem was to keep printing. What do struggling young editors of struggling literary papers dream of if not printing credit? And to my own surprise I had found this after having been back in America only about two weeks. Although our new patron relished neither our prose nor our poetry, let alone our art, he showed a good deal of sporting spirit in this case, for he was a hard-headed man of business, and estimated that we would lose money for at least two years more. At the time, he thought *Broom* eventually might be combined with a larger enterprise.

We drew up papers of incorporation for the "Broom Publishing Company" and sent them off to Harold Loeb, who cabled his hearty assent. Our plans called for reducing the quarto format of our magazine to a page of seven and a half by nine inches and the number of pages from ninety-six to sixty-four, as a measure of economy. Even with its shrunken size our magazine would cost fifty per cent more to print in the United States than in Europe, but we would eliminate the cost of shipping across the ocean, cut out one of two offices, and gain second-class mail privileges. Geffen was to raise most of the new money and command a half-interest in our venture, while Harold and I were to control the other half and also enjoy a free hand editorially. As Harold made it plain that he did not wish to take an active part in editing the review, since he was going to stay in Paris, it meant that direction of the magazine would be left entirely in my hands.

I was thoroughly happy at having been able to bring our review to America. In optimistic terms I wrote Harold: "The place for everybody is here; after all Europe is for repose, for leisure. But to put something over we have to be here."[1] I had never taken the business of being an "exile" very seriously. We who had learned a few things during our apprentice years abroad would now apply ourselves to the challenging American scene and bring to bear upon it the new insights we had gained. America, for all its Babbitts, was our frontier; the idea of putting our artistic roots down here again was deeply satisfying.

The new office of *Broom*, at first in the parlor of my small "Village" apartment, became a scene of frenzied activity, the activity of a single person, myself, serving as editor in chief, business manager, advertising director, stenographer, and errand boy all in one. With one hand I would write an essay discharging a broadside at the reactionaries of literature and championing what Kenneth Burke laughingly called "our Great Young New American Movement"; with the other hand I would dash off correspondence with authors from whom material was solicited, rejections of unwanted manuscripts, circulars and advertisement copy designed to win subscribers, as well as bills to retail shops that sold our magazine. Then toward the end of the day I would sometimes take to my legs and run about the city collecting funds owing us from bookshops. I would find one that had sold twenty-five copies and another thirty-five, and return with forty or fifty dollars. The booksellers said to me:

"If you advertised that magazine, it would sell more." The only advertising we did was by exchange of space with other small publications.

Broom had friendly readers in the West as well as in the East. "There is a great interest in the revival of *Broom* among persons who regard it as an open door to young writers and new stuff," I reported too hopefully.

The editorial program I drew up—with Malcolm Cowley's active help, after he returned to New York in August—now involved the presentation of more literary and art works originating in America and less translated material from Europe. For example, we planned to give prominence to such American artists as Charles Sheeler, Charles Demuth, John Marin, and Joseph Stella. A survey of the motion picture in America was to be the major theme of another issue. Robert Alden Sanborn, who had been associated with Coady's magazine, *The Soil*, contributed an article on this subject. At the happy suggestion of Edmund Wilson, Jr., whom I met shortly after my return to New York, I scouted the Broadway music halls to gather material on the "nuthouse" comedians, Joe Cook and the Four Marx Brothers, who, as unwitting Dadaists, had invented a new laughter of their own.

Wilson, a short, plump, pink-cheeked young man of about twenty-seven, was then one of the editors of *Vanity Fair*, and showed himself both cordial and helpful. It was he and his friend and fellow poet, John Peale Bishop, also on the staff of *Vanity Fair*, who kept the cultural departments in the back pages of that very fashionable journal *au courant* with the latest modes in art and letters. Wilson had learning, a wide-ranging curiosity, and, at the same time, a hard-headed skeptical spirit. He was forward-looking and all for "stunning" the American bourgeoisie; but on the other hand, when I showed him some of the experimental writings of the European Dadaists, he remarked doubtfully: "I wonder if they aren't pulling our leg."

One of Wilson's proposals was that we should give representation to, or at least report the writing of, some of our popular humorists, such as Ring Lardner, as worth-while contributions to literature. At the same time he called my attention to the work of his Princeton friend, F. Scott Fitzgerald, whose "Tales of the Jazz Age" had recently appeared in *The Saturday Evening Post*. Fitzgerald, already a glamorous figure among our *jeunesse dorée*, was described by Wilson at this period as "the man who made America Younger-Generation-Conscious." At any rate he had recently jumped into the fountain outside the Plaza Hotel in New York while fully dressed, and thus, in his own manner, uttered a great resounding "Yes" to life in the United States.

Nowadays Wilson plays the stout crusty old literary pundit, but performs his Johnsonian role with a rare intellectual independence; everyone knows that under his crust there is really a very gentle soul. In the early twenties he sported orange neckties and looked like an Ivy League collegian, but when he chose he could be as roistering as his friend Scott Fitzgerald. Wilson was equal to setting forth at night in a taxi, clad in a bright-colored bathrobe, with his wife, Mary Blair, an actress, in pajamas and raincoat, and Tallulah Bankhead in a bathing suit, to attend a bathtub-gin party and enact a vaudeville show after their own fancy; the ladies would do parodies of Sarah Bernhardt and Gilda Gray, while "Bunny" Wilson performed conjuring and card tricks with skill and aplomb.[2]

Thus various allies and helpmates gathered to give support to the American edition of *Broom*, though, as will be seen, they scarcely made up a unitary group. Among those I remember was the golden-haired, twenty-one-year-old Glenway Wescott, who was soon to lead the Wisconsin contingent to Paris and the Riviera for a long sojourn. ("The young people dream only of getting away," he wrote in *Good-Bye Wisconsin*, adding that a great many Midwesterners like himself were to be found wandering about all over Europe "as a sort of vagrant race like the Jews.") There were also in our circle the gifted Negro novelist, Jean Toomer, and Isidor Schneider, the poet, who was employed at Boni & Liveright, and who made helpful suggestions for promoting our magazine.

One of these new acquaintances, who was very different from the rest of us, was an older fellow, the artist and photographer Charles Sheeler, a tall, thin, gray man with very keen blue eyes, drily humorous of speech, and as pithy in his talk about art as were the lines of his drawings. Sheeler, a native of Pennsylvania, had had some ties with the modern movement in painting since the Armory Show of 1913, having been associated with the Cubist-Futurists of that period, including Marcel Duchamp. Together we worked to prepare a "Sheeler number" of *Broom*, illustrated by his admirable paintings of Bucks County barns and his photographs, and having as its frontispiece his strangely impressive and now historic conté crayon drawing of a telephone, entitled "Self Portrait."

At an art gallery where this picture was exhibited, Sheeler was asked by one of the viewers, the Irish literary critic and translator Ernest A. Boyd: "Can you tell me why telephones are always *black?*"

"Well, when they were young they must have been green," Sheeler drawled, "but after they got older they all turned black."

The "Village" was still a quiet backwater of Manhattan, though speak-easies were mushrooming up everywhere about us. South of Washington Square, in the quarter called "Little Italy," there were delicatessen or grocery shops in whose back rooms a crude wine or rum was served for as little as fifteen or twenty cents a drink. On Sullivan Street there was a cheap Italian restaurant decorated with bird cages and aspidistras, with its basement bar open to the street. "We sit in the sun in the late afternoon drinking 'California Chianti' from coffee cups," I reported to my friends in Paris, "while little children play nearby, and a policeman comes in to sit beside us and sip wine peacefully."[3] The "Village" speak-easies were not always peaceful resorts in the twenties. When the staff of *Broom* left the Sullivan Street tavern at a late hour one night, a band of neighborhood gangsters lay in wait for us and we were forced to run hard to avoid their knife play. On another occasion, Slater Brown received a knife wound in the chest when a gangster held up one of our speak-easies.

I often dined, nevertheless, at the Sullivan Street place, with Slater Brown, Edward Nagle (a young painter who wrote for us on art), Kenneth Burke, Hart Crane, and sometimes John Dos Passos and E.E. Cummings, who had lately returned from Paris.

One day Brown answered a curious newspaper advertisement calling for a "literary secretary," and got the job. His employer proved to be an aged and eccentric millionaire named J.J. Manning, who was one of the famous Wall Street operators of his era. On dull afternoons in the market, Bill would read Shakespeare to Mr. Manning; thus he had some free mornings to finish some of the charming prose pieces he wrote for *Broom*. He used to tell us delightful stories of his employer, who lived in a mansion on Fifth Avenue next to one of the Vanderbilt houses. Manning, it seems, though passing rich, was frightfully stingy about his wife's allowance, so that she was reduced to stealing his cigar coupons and exchanging them for cash. Catching her in the act late one night, Mr. Manning proceeded to berate his wife in such loud tones that she exclaimed: "Hush, hush, the Vanderbilts will hear you!" (After Brown gave up that job, Clifton P. Fadiman, then a Columbia College undergraduate, replaced him for a while.)

Hart Crane appeared at our speak-easy one evening accompanied by a wispy, blond young man with an enormous cranium and diminutive and delicate features, whom he presented as Allen Tate of Nashville, Tennessee. They had become acquainted by correspondence, in the course of which Tate had assured Crane that he was the greatest of living poets. Allen was even then very well informed about contemporary literary movements in France and England, as well as America. In those days he was as blasphemous as any of our young scapegraces who had fled from the hinterland of America to Greenwich Village. He used to ridicule the pretensions of Southerners to culture, holding that all they did was "second-rate"; and even tried to suppress his Southern accent. "At Vanderbilt University they used to call me the 'Yankee,' " he told us proudly. Nor did he give much thought then to glorifying the Confederate dead of the Civil War, or reviving the doctrines of social reaction and aristocracy that he embraced in later years. At the time, Allen had published only a few poems in little magazines; yet his wit, his critical spirit, and his individual poetic style were already in evidence, and quickly won him the favor of his New York friends.

For a few weeks, Cummings used to eat with us every few days at the Sullivan Street tavern. Then he suddenly disappeared and we missed his rapid-fire table talk. His absence, I was informed, resulted from his having married the very attractive Mrs. Elaine Orr Thayer, who had lately been divorced from Cummings' friend, Scofield Thayer, one of the owners of *The Dial*. A fortnight later, great was our surprise when Cummings reappeared at our favorite speak-easy, but alone, looking very gloomy, and avoiding us. For some time after that he ate at a corner table all by himself. This odd behavior was explained to me in whispers: following a marriage of only a few weeks he was now separated from his wife, from whom he was divorced not long afterward.

"New York is lively, drink is plentiful and varied," I reported to one of my transatlantic correspondents. "But you have to sell your soul to pay the bills."[4] I was drawing a salary that was only enough to cover the rent of my small apartment at 45 King Street on the southern border of the "Village." My wife found work as a proofreader and later as an editorial assistant on the staff of one of the so-called "pulp magazines," so that she provided us with food, but we had almost no furniture. I wanted to arrange for my older friends, William Carlos Williams and Charles Sheeler, to meet each other; and so we held a Dutch Treat dinner in a speak-easy, after which Williams,

Sheeler, and their wives returned to our house, each guest bringing his own bottle of wine. We all sat on the floor not out of any Bohemian affectation, but because we had no chairs.

As I was usually occupied from ten to twelve hours a day, there were only one or two evenings a week for social life. For economy's sake I was doing the work of five people, handling the several "departments" of *Broom*, but I was gradually obliged to give more and more time to promoting its circulation. That, as I wrote to Harold Loeb, was "the ONE WAY to advance Art in America."

Malcolm Cowley, my co-editor, returned from France in August, 1923, in the highest spirits, but absolutely flat broke. He was improvising ditties to be sung to ragtime, and chanted one in honor of *Broom* that ran:

> We got a movement, a little movement,
> And our movement she's all right!—

But Malcolm was obliged to take a job at once, a job that involved arduous labor with late hours at a technical publisher's. For several months he could not help me with the editing of *Broom*. He observed at the time that I had certainly taken hold of the management of the magazine and thought I was doing it well.[5]

The slim American series of *Broom* that began with the August, 1923, issue and continued up to January of 1924 made a brave show, despite our small means. We had our Message to deliver; we had the conservatives of literature to dispose of; and our "new poets" to champion.

One of our literary conservatives, Stuart P. Sherman, had recently published an essay entitled "The Genius of America," in which he assailed such novelists as Theodore Dreiser for being Realists and ignoring that "profound moral idealism" which Sherman believed constituted the true genius of our nation. In a polemic piece on Stuart P. Sherman I denied that we in America were just a bunch of idealists:

> The genius of America is rather for economic organization and expresses itself in quantity production and national sales. It creates an inspiring enough spectacle for poets and novelists to ruminate over. It is certainly their business to define, somehow or other their present environment . . . inasmuch as their own lives are enmeshed in it all. But that they should go about crying: "Oh beautiful my country," as Professor Sherman urges, is an appalling proposal which offers horrible consequences.

In letting fly at the literary conservatives in America I happened to include the poet Elinor Wylie among those I dared to censure, holding that her etiolated verses reflected her own preciosity but not the facts of modern life in the United States—"and so had nothing to say to us which would place them in this time rather than in Heine's or Landor's time."

The charming Mrs. Wylie was then one of the reigning hostesses in literary New York, and many influential literary people adored her; in consequence of my outspoken criticisms of her some of these persons, for years thereafter, treated me as an unspeakable scoundrel. At the time, John Dos Passos told me that while he agreed with my views, he feared I had gained for myself some powerful enemies who would not soon forget me.

The rather sharp-tempered, one might even say ill-natured, polemics of *Broom*, contrasting with the usually polite or complaisant tone of literary talk in this country, stirred up little controversies here and there which were most pleasing to the egos of young writers like ourselves. An article in the *New Republic*, for example, roundly condemned us as prime examples of "Young Anarchy" in the field of letters. (The writer of it, Louis Untermeyer, several years later recanted, saying: "Today I rather think Matthew Josephson was right in his championship of youth and its right to play, no matter how recklessly.")

Burton Rascoe, the indefatigable literary columnist of the New York *Tribune,* who made news of everything that happened in the republic of letters, also paid his respects to the "youthful iconoclasts" of the *"Broom* group" (in his "Bookman's Daybook" column for September 17, 1923). With the persiflage of a knowing old journalist of thirty, he reports that I gave him an interview (which I no longer remember) and that I kindly undertook to explain the unorthodox views of the "youngest articulate generation" on life and art:

"First of all," Matthew Josephson told me rather abruptly, "we are against all the dead lumber which critics like you have been touting." (He may not have been so blunt as that: Mr. Josephson is a courteous well-mannered young man, and had a proper respect for my years; but though he softened his thrusts with tips of velvet, his poniarding was to the heart and so intended.)

He then relates that I advised him to give no serious consideration any longer to such "shopworn" authors as Anatole France, Joseph Hergesheimer, Elinor Wylie, and Sinclair Lewis. "Diamond Dick" provided much better literature than theirs; and the writing to be found in our commercial advertising matter was still better. Rascoe continues:

Mr. Josephson is of the generation of writers [who] went to Europe after the hostilities and . . . found that, whereas Americans were turning to Europe for inspiration and guidance, the younger writers of Europe were looking toward America. . . . They were welcoming our jazz tunes as authentic new music, praising our architectural triumphs which made the finest cathedrals uninteresting; they found in our billboards new and suggestive forms of literary and pictorial design; and in our engines, derricks, cranes and machines a new source of life, and an unexplored field of expression. . . .

Rascoe, however, was skeptical of our idea of the Machine. A battery of steam-riveters going outside his office window all summer had given him a long headache, and he refused to believe that their "music" constituted high art.

Edmund Wilson next entered the discussion with a long article in the *New Republic* (cast in the form of a symposium) on the rather novel and affirmative attitude, expounded in *Broom,* toward our technological society—the world Thomas A. Edison and Henry Ford had made for us.

It must be remembered that at the time intellectuals and liberals held the fairly consistent view that undirected industrialism was the curse of American life; that we were being turned into barbarians bent only on accumulating money and material things, and that the development of a true culture in such a brutalized society was an impossibility. Sherwood Anderson, for example, in *A Story Teller's Story*, went so far as to assert that "the giving of itself by an entire generation to mechanical things was surely making all men impotent." In order to live a full life sexually as a child of nature and be a poet, Anderson had quit his own profitable advertising business, for he was convinced that the spirit of industrialism tended to "kill life."

Similar views were reflected by Van Wyck Brooks, Waldo Frank, Paul Rosenfeld, and their younger colleague, Lewis Mumford—whom I, in doubting spirit, used to call "the Uplifters." To be sure, I esteemed Brooks's real gifts for literary and social history, which offered a fascinating record of the movement of ideas in America's past. But it seemed that he now lived only in the hope of reviving the Golden Age of New England; and, as Edmund Wilson remarked, wrote like a sort of gloomy dean of letters, rejecting Henry James because he had been an expatriate in Europe, and Mark Twain, too, as one corroded by our puritan-commercial ethics.

Meeting Van Wyck Brooks in the office of *The Freeman*, I found him one of the most high-minded writers of the time, but held a long dispute with him—it was decidedly my habit in youth, and still is now—on the score of his pessimism about America's civilization. His views have changed a good deal since then, but I now realize there was much premonitory truth in what he was saying in 1923.

The whole controversy over Man and The Machine in

America has since been resolved in terms that none of the debaters of the early twenties could have foretold. We have had, in any case, to build up our culture, such as it is, within the the craters left by our technological revolution.

Of this group Paul Rosenfeld in particular, because of his impressionistic method of criticism and his inflated style, had often served as the target for our polemics in *Broom* and *Secession*. Now came Edmund Wilson's essay entitled "The Poet's Return," which treated of the experience of a young American who had gone to live abroad for some time and then come home; it used the form of an imaginary dialogue presenting me as one of its protagonists and Rosenfeld as the other. This dialogue was concocted by paraphrasing things we had each written from our opposing points of view. While taking some liberties with us and parodying some of our statements, Wilson assumed an attitude of impartiality.

The imaginary Paul Rosenfeld begins by taking me to task for my criticisms of Mrs. Wylie's poetry, and also for my notions that vulgar music-hall comedies and advertisement copy might contain the germs of true literature. He declares that Mrs. Wylie's poetry "is the pang of the heart that is transfixed by the splinter-sharp ice of lack, the woman-cry in its sheerest bell-timbres . . . " while I on the other hand am represented as a hard-bitten young skeptic scoffing at his terms: ". . . but I hope you don't consider it criticism." Wilson's dialogue continues:

MR. JOSEPHSON: That is precisely the kind of thing that has compelled my colleagues and me to write about you so much and so bitterly. The day for irresponsible rhapsody as a substitute for exact analysis has now long passed. What you publish as critical essays are, of course merely opium visions . . . your outburst just now has nothing to do with Elinor Wylie, . . . Neither you nor Elinor Wylie exists in the face of the great American Fact!

Mr. Rosenfeld then argues that, after living abroad, I have come back with the same mistaken ideas formed by some Europeans, and especially the Dadaists, who have made a cult of a new exotic America of dizzy skyscrapers, Chaplinesque (or comic) movies, and Negro jazz. "When you are back in American life again," he warns, "I do not know if you will be able to preserve [your view of things]—I do not know if you will enjoy 'the great funny time . . . ' " (A shrewd thrust by the author of this imaginary dialogue?)

Neither the writers of advertisements nor the workers in our assembly lines are truly happy, Rosenfeld is made to contend; and men like Sherwood Anderson at least show the courage to oppose themselves to this world of automatic production without end, and of haste and toil that blights so many lives. They speak at least "for the honor of the human spirit!"

MR. JOSEPHSON: The Honor of the Human Spirit . . . the Principles of Justice and Humanity . . . the Dawn of a New Day . . . E.E. Cummings could make an amusing poem by mixing them all up together . . .

Instead of worrying about the Human Spirit, I am reported as saying, we should give way to Dada laughter at the scene before us, and . . .

plunge into that effervescent, cacophonous milieu . . . where the Billposters enunciate their freedom, the cinema transports us, and the newspapers intone their gaudy jargon.

My protagonist, however, concludes on a sad admonitory note:

MR. ROSENFELD: For me, it is a serious matter, but for you, it is only a game. . . . You can only get yourself cut to pieces by prostrating yourself before Juggernaut. . . .

The taste for experiment, at all events, dominated the American issues of our magazine. It was exemplified by Cummings' lyrics in small capitals and an inebriated typography, by Cowley's burlesque songs arranged to be sung to well-known ragtime or jazz melodies, and also by Hart Crane's "words in flaming collision." There was also Robert M. Coates doing short stories in the manner of the American dime novelist Nick Carter. Kenneth Burke contributed some moral tales in the form of poetic fantasies written in a rather classical style, while Jean Toomer's studies of Negro life in America were essentially naturalistic; on the other hand, Kay Boyle's and Glenway Wescott's poems recalled the mode of the Imagists.

One of my own contributions at the time was an attempt to give expression to the modern myth of America. Using the language of advertising copy, with the terms of its clichés somewhat misplaced or rearranged, I tried to write an ode in honor of Henry Ford, entitled "The Brain at the Wheel," of which some specimen lines run:

> With the brain at the wheel
> the eye on the road
> and the hand to the left
> pleasant be your progress
> explorer, producer, stoic after your fashion.
> Change
> CHANGE
> to what speed?—
> to what underwear?
> . . . nothing suprises you, old horseface
> guzzle-guzzle goes the siren . . .

We were all of us different, we did not really agree on any approved recipe for literature. Furthermore, some of us at any rate were bent on being young insurrectos, ready to wage war on the stuffed shirts, the literary puffers, and the commercial hacks in our field. Owing to the contagious effect of our contact with the young Europeans, and especially the French, Malcolm Cowley and I were also eager to introduce a certain excitement into the rather dull literary scene of New York, and make the practice of our medium in some wise a "life of action" and sometimes pure act. We also wanted to tell the world of the moral indignation we felt at certain eminent publicists, even such as H.L. Mencken who, while pretending to chastise our

Babbitts, at times pandered to their lowest prejudices by assuring them that the exponents of new methods in art and literature —the Picassos and James Joyces—were worthless, inasmuch as they "made no sense." More often than not Mencken was good clean fun, but there were others who, in our view, lent themselves to dishonest and venal writing, and we talked of insulting and challenging them. Sometimes we wrote letters of protest to the New York newspapers, a few of which were printed; sometimes we jested with our opponents. On one occasion, when Mencken announced his candidacy for the office of President, we sent him a telegram promising we would come to his support in a big way if he would stop publishing inane and commonplace poetry in his magazine *Smart Set*. Mencken genially agreed to our terms if we would "throw him our ward." We also had the idea of staging hilarious "concerts" (like the Dadaists) or inviting the public to attend mock trials of important personages. Some of these schemes were conceived in the hope of attracting the attention of the public and raising funds for our review, whose deficits harrowed us. Little or nothing came of them.

In truth, those of us who returned after a year or two of life abroad, a life that was impecunious yet graced with leisure and the sense of personal freedom, found the problem of adjustment to the homeland harassing. We had bravely announced our "acceptance" of the Machine Age, without much analysis or thinking through the matter, I dare say. In the long run, I believe, we were right: we could not become New England Transcendentalists in 1923, nor try to live in the woods and make our own lead pencils like old Thoreau. But who cared about our ideas?—least of all the Chamber of Commerce element. We had the effect of a few people firing off peashooters at the unbreakable plate glass-and-steel façade of our civilization. Meanwhile, there were no generous patrons to be found, it seemed; no sinecures or comfortable posts that might have permitted us time for our literary undertakings. We ourselves, in effect, were being flung to the machines. Our young poets were forced to

give most of their waking hours to selling or glorifying machine-
made goods, and in the process they were becoming fatigued
and enervated.

Malcolm Cowley, a country boy who pined to live on a farm,
was pent up all day in an office, editing a vast catalogue which
advertised machinery of all sorts. Hart Crane, returning to New
York from Ohio at the beginning of 1923, found employment
as an advertising copywriter at the J. Walter Thompson agency.
He was assigned to writing the literature of cosmetics. Thinking
to inspire him, his superiors placed on his desk numerous vials
of strong perfume, whose odor he was supposed to capture in
words. But the perfumes nauseated him and so one day, when
he had come to work with a bad hangover, he snatched up
the whole collection and threw them out of his office window.
After that he was done for at the agency and forced to take
refuge in the country, at Woodstock, New York, where he lived
on about ten dollars a week, while beginning to write the long
series of poems to be known as *The Bridge*.

"You have no idea of the pressure under which we live," I
wrote to Harold Loeb in September, 1923. *Broom* had a small
trickle of receipts from subscribers and newsstands, which at
first covered about sixty per cent of our running expenses; but
this dwindled, and our small capital again disappeared. By
October, 1923, when it seemed that we could not pay even half
our printer's bill, our last "angel" drew a long face and prepared
to give up his part in our venture.

I could have borne everything, I thought, except the mood
of indifference or apathy that sometimes seized our circle of
writers. They knew hardships of their own and had to save their
skins as well as they could, but too often they failed to produce
the sort of material we needed. "The 'group' associated with
Broom is in a remarkably sterile condition," I reported in the
autumn of 1923.

Malcolm's job after a while allowed him more leisure, and he
now gave many hours to editing the magazine and to fund-
seeking. We discussed the alternatives of reducing *Broom* to a

quarterly issue and working on it in our spare time, while I took some business job; or allowing it to come to its end, as many other little magazines with noble intentions had done before it. If so, Malcolm urged, "it should have a spectacular end."[6]

He now proposed calling a meeting of the writers who contributed to various vanguard reviews like *Broom* and *Secession,* at which we would discuss our common problems and consider combining forces, so that we might work more effectively both at publishing and fund-raising. In order to make it a non-partisan gathering, Malcolm decided to invite Gorham Munson and Waldo Frank—though they had had their differences with us. It was Malcolm's purpose to compose factious quarrels and bring about a union of a larger group of our confreres. I went along with him, but expressed little confidence in the outcome of the meeting.

Some twenty writers came, several of them with their wives, to dine together at a tavern in "Little Italy." A few declined our invitation, among them Frank and also Munson, who was convalescing from a recent illness; Munson, however, sent a long "public letter" to Malcolm, which he wished to have read before our gathering.

I had attended numerous literary debating sessions in Paris that were by no means polite tea parties. But Americans, unlike the French, are given to drinking strong spirits. Our guests gulped down their cups of bootleg liquor or raw wine hurriedly, because of their vile taste and stunning force, and soon turned the meeting into a riotous party. Attempts by Cowley or me to keep order during the after-dinner discussion were set to nought by interruptions or outcries on the part of the intoxicated ones (especially Hart Crane), who took exception to everything or began to quarrel heatedly with each other.

Some of those on hand and others who, unable to come, had written letters, expressed their approval of the management of *Broom* in America. Then Malcolm Cowley began to read aloud Munson's letter, which provided the climax of the affair. I had not seen it previously. Munson denounced *Broom* and its managing editor in particular, charging that I was a low, cunning, self-seeking, and dishonest character, a "fakir" as a writer and moreover one who showed "disrespect for literary criticism." Any movement of the American vanguard "must part from Josephson," else Munson and his allies would shun it like the plague.

Midway in the reading of this long-winded manifesto, written with studied effort and with pompous rhetorical flourishes, Malcolm was overcome by his sense of its absurdity, as he related afterward, and began to declaim it in the manner of a ham actor reciting Shakespeare. Thereupon, Munson's friends loudly protested that Malcolm was doing an injustice to the author of the letter. For the moment, the fickle Crane opposed me and championed Munson; Hart Crane described himself as "the only delegate present from the Higher Spaces"—referring thereby to the new cult of yoga which Munson and his friends had recently embraced. Others shouted Hart down, crying out that the Munson letter could not possibly be made to appear more ridiculous than it was. I tried to make a statement to the effect that I would say nothing in answer to Munson's accusations, and urged that the meeting should return to reasoned discussion of its agenda, avoiding disputes over personalities. But everyone shouted everybody else down, as the guests believed they were privileged to create a "Dadaist uproar," forgetting that the French Dadaists usually worked with great discipline at their preliminaries. Isidor Schneider, a gentle soul, expressed sorrow at so much disorder; a woman present burst into tears; and Glenway Wescott protested indignantly: "You people can't even preserve ordinary parlor manners!" With this, he swept out of the place. Hart Crane was still making impassioned speeches against me when the managers of the tavern firmly bade us all to depart.

Hart Crane actually tried to keep on good terms with both the Munson-Frank faction and that of *Broom,* although Gorham Munson "forebade" him to see any of us. Crane insisted that if he gave up seeing Cowley, Brown, Burke, and myself, he feared he would become frightfully bored. He also lampooned Munson in some verses touching on his addiction to the mystical doctrines of Ouspensky and Gurdjieff:

Chanson

"I"
said Mr. M. as we crossed the street together
"am compelled to reject this
poem . . ."
At that moment a terrific detonation interrupted his
dictum
and Mr. M. soared into space astride
the lid of a
man-hole
The last I saw of him he was miles high
trying to climb off
In suchwise did Mr. M. ride into Heaven.
Hallelujah!

Malcolm Cowley and Kenneth Burke had earnestly sought a reconciliation between the *Broom* group" and the Munson-Frank faction. As Cowley has related, after his return to America he felt inspired by his contacts with Young France with the hope that we returned "exiles" might, by working together, introduce better standards and new ideals of literary life in the United States. Yet the "exiles" were defeated, he says, mainly because they could not agree among themselves, and were led by "their jealousies into a war of secession."

I had not manifested any "jealousy" of anyone, and least of all of Munson. Nor had I written any libelous letters about him. Yet after his letter pronouncing my interdiction (!), he continued his slanderous campaign by saying or writing unpleasant things about me. I got fed up and talked with some of my friends about what one might do with such an unreasonable fellow. "There's no use discussing things with the man, I would give him a good beating," one of them advised.

As Munson was then staying at Woodstock, New York, I arranged to spend a few days there with my friends, Slater Brown and   Edward Nagle, and use the opportunity to settle accounts with Gorham. He has written in recollection of these events:

> I had heard rumors of his coming . . . but dismissed the reports as only bluster . . . I was mistaken. Here he was knocking at the door, after traveling 100 miles to avenge himself. . . . I had some guest for tea, when Josephson burst in shouting for battle. The guest dispersed hastily, leaving Josephson and my host William Murrell Fisher to parley. . . . Fisher said there was nothing to do but fight.[7]

It was he who had wanted to "parley" with me. As I really disliked this business of fisticuffs and wished to get it over with, I became all the angrier.

It was a cloudy afternoon in early November; as it had just stopped raining, the meadow where we squared off was mucky. Neither of us knew anything about the manly art. Munson, who had been convalescing for several weeks after a siege of "flu," had become very fat, outweighing me by about fifty pounds. His fists felt like pillows. He stood still; I hauled off and hit him a first roundhouse blow in the mouth that left a slight scratch. "The scuffle was brief, but not bloody, and at one moment exceedingly funny," he wrote afterward. The slow-moving Munson, after a few exchanges, clinched with me and we fell to the wet ground, rolling about a while and becoming well covered with mud. I struggled to break from him. We were both out of breath as we got to our feet and could scarcely swing at each other. Fisher, who was very good-humored about our little imbroglio, forgot to call off the rounds; and after about five minutes we both halted our hostilities. Fisher told me later that I was sitting on Munson's chest when we stopped. Munson sent out a telegram, as I heard, declaring that he had fought me to a draw.

I returned to my friends, Slater Brown and Ed Nagle, saying nothing but showing a slight bruise above one eye, which I had got only by bumping against my adversary's head. However, news of our Duel in the Mud promptly spread to New York and the press, whose literary columnists published excited conjecture and rumor about the "fratricidal strife" among the literati of the "left wing." It was set down as (possibly?) the first time in the history of America that two men of letters came to blows over their opposing critical or aesthetic doctrines. Munson, several years later, in one of the numerous articles consecrated to his differences with me, bragged that his fisticuffs with me at Woodstock had "put such a crimp in *Broom* that the magazine expired a few months later. . . ." *Broom's* suspension, however, had nothing whatsoever to do with the flabby blows directed at me by Munson.

That delightful comedian of letters, H.L. Mencken, continued to make fun of the young men of *Broom* and all their avant-garde works, though with a kindly humor. In the *Smart Set*, as later in *American Mercury*, he assured his middlebrow readers that we were "phoney," and what was worse, "highbrow." It was in this clownish spirit that Mencken wrote a hilarious review of my translation of Guillaume Apollinaire's *The Poet Assassinated*, published serially in *Broom* and brought out afterward in a limited edition. He solemnly pretended that [1] there was no such French author as Apollinaire; [2] his real name was "Wilhelm Sprudelwasser" (a take-off on the European mineral water named Apollinaris); [3] the book was a "hoax" which I myself had concocted, while pretending to be its editor and translator. A fine piece of buffoonery, in short.

At about the same time, Burton Rascoe conducted me to the home of Ernest A. Boyd, who had said he wanted to meet me. Boyd was a garrulous man with a brown beard, who held forth on the subject of French literature. I was informed that he acted as an expert adviser to New York publishers on French books which were to be translated into English, and that he possessed "vast learning" in twelve languages. But perceiving that he really knew or cared nothing for any French writer who came after Anatole France (b. 1844), I fell to teasing or provoking him, as was my habit. Our conversation rose to the pitch of a shouting match. In the course of the evening Boyd had expressed some curiosity about the people who wrote for *Broom;* he was then closely associated with H.L. Mencken and I soon learned why he was interested in us.

The much-publicized first number of the *American Mercury,* edited by Mencken, reached us at the end of December, 1923. Its leading article was a literary tract by Ernest Boyd entitled "Aesthete: Model 1924," which purported to be a "composite portrait" of the Younger Generation coming into the literary field. In a tone of heavy irony it combined the tag ends of facts and hearsay relating to the careers of such diverse persons as Gilbert Seldes, E.E. Cummings, John Dos Passos, Harold A. Loeb, Malcolm Cowley, Waldo Frank, and (possibly) myself, together with some insinuations referring (perhaps) to Hart Crane. This composite but inchoate creature was described as the emasculate product of one of the old Eastern universities, who carried a yellow cane, avoided combat service in the late war, lived in Europe a while, then in Greenwich Village where he flirted with certain mystical cults and published his own prose and poetry in his own little magazine. That is, he put down words and sounds as they came out of his head, so that "he seemed to have lost the faculty of making sense." This ill-humored caricature was calculated to arouse the prejudice of the "booboisie" while giving strong offense to those at whom it was aimed.

Malcolm Cowley was greatly exasperated, believing that some of the unjust implications of the "composite portrait" might be thought to refer to himself. "We must do something about this," he said; and added in afterthought, "Perhaps someone ought to punch Boyd in the jaw."

It must be remembered that the report of Malcolm's affray with an unlovable café proprieter in Paris on Bastille Day some months earlier had reached New York; and there had been gossip published of my recent Duel in the Mud. Thus, when Malcolm telephoned Ernest Boyd and asked him for an appointment, saying that he wished to set forth his objections to the

offending article, Boyd, as if in great fear, replied that he could
see no occasion for the visit. Thereupon Malcolm swore a mighty
oath and hung up.

A week later we had a gathering of Malcolm, Kenneth
Burke, and Hart Crane in my apartment, and we all took turns
at calling up Mr. Boyd and delivering our poor opinion of his
composite portrait and his own character. Hart Crane excelled
us all in invective. But while strong language may have been
used, no one, to my knowledge, actually threatened Boyd. Nevertheless Boyd announced to all and sundry that he had been subjected to abuse and threats by a whole gang of muscular, aggres-
sive, and bullying "Aesthetes," who, he believed, intended to
break into his house and beat him to within an inch of his life.

Soon the literary press buzzed with the great stir created by
Boyd's satire in the *American Mercury*. With some obvious
hyperbole Burton Rascoe reported the affair in the *Tribune*:

Two hours after the edition of the *American Mercury* appeared on
the stands, Greenwich Village was in an uproar. The whole literary
left wing, which had hitherto been disorganized by internecine strife,
solidified against the perpetrator of the article. Obscure poets and
art theorists . . . began collaring people and . . . saying that Boyd
had them especially in mind, and they meant to have his blood.

East 19th Street swarmed with younger poets and when the vener-
able Boyd set out on his morning constitutional he was greeted with
a fusillade of ripe tomatoes, eggs, sticks . . . and barely escaped with
his life back into his house.

There he was kept a prisoner for three days while the Dadaists
pushed his doorbell, kept his telephone abuzz, scaled the walls to
his apartment and cast old cabbages and odor bombs through the
windows. Barricaded behind his books, subsisting on depleted
rations, grown wan and weary under the assaults . . . Boyd called
Heaven to witness that he had never heard or read anything of the
assailants who besieged him.

We had come to love our little magazine, *Broom*, which we
struggled to bring out every month, though it seldom arrived on

time. Its end was to be spectacular, but in a way we had not quite foreseen—that is to say, it was totally unrelated to the quarrels of the literary factions.

In the November, 1923, issue we had printed a story, found in our pile of unsolicited manuscripts, entitled "An Awful Storming Fire," by a Chicago paper hanger named Charles L. Durboraw. It seemed to Cowley and me that the work was inherently interesting as a "primitive"; the author had preserved himself from the vices of literary affectation. It is the story of a banal street-corner pickup by a workingman of a girl with "dreaming purple eyes," and of the temptations and unearthly trials he undergoes:

. . . I got up and sat down in her lap and kissed her again and again . . . So we changed positions and she threw her leg up over the arm of the chair. I said: "Do you know that the finest artists' models in the world are in factories and offices. Rats on the society and rich stuff!"

But the pair are suddenly interrupted at the moment of consummation by all the lights going out and the appearance of the Devil in shadowy and hideous form, who draws them up into the air toward a great red "storm of fire in a fire." Voices cry: "Beware, repent!" The hero, whose hand has been clutched by the "witch-girl," fortunately remembers that he wishes to roll a Bull Durham cigarette, relinquishes her hand, and manages to escape from his nightmare world back to his familiar street corner again, and thence to his little flat and his wife. He concludes with the homily: "Nature's Laws punish us for our sins." This work of naïve Surrealism aroused some interest and its author was invited to write for other literary reviews.

What was our surprise at receiving, on December 8, 1923, a letter of warning from the United States Post Office Department at Washington, citing Section 480, Postal Laws on Printing and Mailing of Lewd Filthy Matter, etc., and informing us that upon repetition of an offense similar to the one in our November issue, the second-class mail privileges of *Broom* would be revoked.

At this period, my wife, with the help of our friends, had obtained employment as assistant editor of a "pulp magazine" called *Telling Tales,* which specialized in risqué fiction and "true confessions." Despite the solicitous activities of the Society for the Prevention of Vice, there was a great vogue in America for popular magazines such as *Snappy Stories* and *Telling Tales,* printing specimens of illicit sex experience—or more usually near misses of them—written in a suggestive manner. It was one of the paradoxes of the time that our supposedly puritanical nation produced more of such stuff than any other, and that those who wrote and published it were very busy and prosperous, while the literary eggheads of *Broom* and *The Dial* were in tatters. All of this sex literature of the early twenties, however, would be considered entirely innocuous by the readers of today.

My wife's job was agreeable enough; but one of its less pleasing features was the regular visits of a special inspector from the United States Post Office Department, who was the de facto censor of magazines published in New York. He would come in on one day each month, read proofs of the forthcoming issue, and advise the managing editor in advance on what must be emended or what might be printed as it was. This was a convenient way of protecting a large publishing firm, whose magazines had readers in the hundred thousands, from the loss that would follow if whole issues were denied the mailing privilege. For such protection the executives of the firm covertly paid bribes to the said inspector, who was known only to the rest of the personnel as "Mr. Smith."

It happened that one morning my wife learned from her superior at *Telling Tales* that "Mr. Smith" had talked, during his visit at the office, of having recently read a "fancy" literary magazine called *Broom,* which had published, as he alleged, "some off-color stuff." He had seen it too late to take action, but had promised himself that the next time it came out he would read it before it was mailed, and if it had anything censorable in his view he would order its mailing privileges revoked. At the time, however, because the relations between the magazine and "Smith" were a business secret, neither my wife nor the editor in chief, who was a friend of ours, said anything about this matter to Malcolm Cowley or to me. It seemed improbable that our small "highbrow" publication would be molested.

Before receiving the warning letter from the post office in early December, we had had a passing moment of anxiety when we considered material for the next issue of *Broom*. We had undertaken to print a story by Kenneth Burke, "Prince Llan: an Ethical Masque," and I had written, promising that we would publish it without revisions. "We are not afraid of the Vice Society. In any case, I believe, they are illiterate . . . and find *Broom* too dull to investigate," I wrote him.

On the first page of this rather intellectual fable—so different from that of Mr. Durboraw's—there was, to be sure, a reference to the hero's "buying women," and mention of their having "breasts" and "sitters that undulated." These phrases were about all that, conceivably, might have drawn the attention of the watchful "Mr. Smith."

The story was to appear in the January, 1924, *Broom,* which was in press when the letter of warning had come from the post office. We had cut down the size of our magazine from ninety-six to sixty-four pages, and now again (after skipping a month) reduced it to forty-eight pages; we were also using a cheaper printer, most of whose bill we paid in advance by raising the money ourselves.

On January 10, 1924, a letter came from the Postmaster of New York City informing us that the January issue of *Broom* had been withheld from dispatch pending decision as to its mailability by the Solicitor for the Post Office Department at Washington. A week later came a letter announcing that this issue of our magazine had been found "unmailable" and that bundles of some fifteen hundred copies would be returned to us upon receipt of our pledge that we would not attempt to send any copies through the mails. In striking at our small publication

"Mr. Smith" had made a show of action, which undoubtedly won him credit in his office.

It was a sheer disaster; payments from out-of-town dealers and subscribers would have enabled us to carry on, although Cowley and I now had only our evenings to give *Broom*. Nor did we have means or time to dispatch copies by railway, as a last resort. We were able to deliver some bundles of a few hundred copies by taxi to bookshops in New York, which sold them out with a rush. The rest of the edition had to be disposed of as waste paper.

The newspapers and press services aired the affair; the New York *Times* in particular published a detailed account by a reporter who read the supposedly offending passages and indicated concern at the drastic action of the post office. We were offered free legal aid by the American Civil Liberties Union if we wished to contest the ruling in the courts; but the editors, battle-weary and dead broke, felt unable to take advantage of the sudden newspaper fame their magazine had achieved, or even to answer the many letters of sympathy from readers.

Just when the troubles of *Broom* were at their height, the eccentric little Joe Gould fell upon me with demands for money—providing Shakespearean comic relief against the tension of our literary tragedy. We had published a few pages of his so-called *History* in one of our last issues, but had announced at the same time that our magazine had no money to pay for contributions. Greatly excited at being put into print at last, Joe Gould refused to believe that he would not be paid an honorarium of some kind, and kept telephoning me at all hours. Beside myself with exasperation, I swore at him; whereupon this tiniest and most impecunious of historical scholars began to address me in a tone of severe formality, declaring that I had grossly insulted him and he was obliged to challenge me to a "duel"—a duel, with the midget Gould! Since it was he who issued the challenge, he requested that I name the weapons to be used.

"*Pillows!*" I roared into the telephone. "I'll meet you with pillows at sunset tomorrow." But he never came.

Denial of the mails to *Broom* was but one of a series of such repressive actions; the banning of Joyce's *Ulysses* and of D.H. Lawrence's novels had gone before; the celebrated "Monkey Trial" of Darwin's theory of evolution was to follow within a few months in Tennessee. In reality, American civilization was not at all as regressive and corrupt as appearances suggested during the "cultural lag" of the Harding-Coolidge era. But the truth was that we young men of *Broom* felt we had come to the end of a phase of our own progress.

Harold Loeb wrote me a letter of condolence and of warm appreciation for "all that I had tried to do for others."[8] I had been so preoccupied in my struggles to raise money, make ends meet for our publication, and pay our writers their small fees, that I had had no time to write anything of my own for many months.

Several of us who were in the first wave of literary tourism in Europe had returned to the United States with the hope of putting our Great Young New American Movement into high gear. We had tried to give expression to some elements of the modern myth of America as a machine economy and a society of the *Masse Mensch*. But there were as yet no helpful social arrangements by which the artist himself might escape the peril of being caught and mangled by the assembly lines. At any rate, our affirmations had won us too little public support; our amusing perturbations had raised up only some small tempests.

Now in their middle twenties, the men in our sector of the Young Generation turned to mending their own fences. We dispersed to take up business jobs in Madison Avenue or Wall Street or wherever opportunity led us; for it was time to make a home, beget a child, and plant a tree.

FOURTEEN

CONFESSIONS OF

A "WALL STREET MAN"

It was spring and I sat at my desk in my luxuriously furnished office high in a tower of the financial district looking down into the well formed by old Trinity Church and its mellow graveyard. I was in reflective mood, and doodled:

> I.T.&T.: high 21½; low: 19⅞; close: 20¼
> Buy Jones' Tea @ 37½; buy Bessie 55⅞
> A very good buy. The directors will declare dividends—

A partner of the brokerage firm that employed me stepped into my office, and I arranged a smile for him. Promptly I brought forth from my desk drawer a statistical report on U.S. Cast Iron Pipe, which he had asked me to prepare. It showed the trend of that company's sales and earnings, and the price range of its stock over the last ten-year period. I had been given, after only a few months' experience, the title of "statistician" and was supposed to gather financial data on various stock corporations. But this work occupied only part of my time; far more important was my activity in guiding the speculations of a little clan of margin-account speculators who, under my supervision, traded—in fact gambled—in all sorts of Stock Exchange securities.

275

I had two telephones, one of which often rang while I talked to a client over the other: "Yes, I am to buy two hundred Can at the market, at once . . ." "No, Mr. B., we cannot hold Mexican Pete for you any longer unless you put up five hundred more as margin . . ."

Financial research in the twenties was primitive. The key sentence placed at the bottom of every statistical report I dictated to my secretary was the qualifying statement that "The information supplied herein is taken from sources considered reliable, but not guaranteed." What counted for us was the business of keeping our customers trading in and out of securities, so that win or lose we gathered our broker's fees at fifteen dollars for each hundred shares.

My office adjoined the board room, a spacious, clublike lounge, furnished with upholstered chairs, and having on one wall a large stock board where a clerk rapidly chalked up stock quotations as they came in on the ticker tape, and at the other end a glass-enclosed booth where an order clerk received orders to buy or sell and telegraphed them to our floor broker on the Exchange. A crowd of day-to-day speculators sat here always watching the panorama of the stock board, making a buzz of talk or sometimes expressing themselves in laughter, jeers, or oaths, depending on how the wheel of fortune turned for them. The tickers' metallic voices sputtered steadily, telephones rang repeatedly, "customers' men" shouted prices into telephones for clients and rushed to the window of the order clerk with their orders on little slips of paper.

The board room was the heart of the firm's business. In a thousand such board rooms in New York a network of wires led to the floor of the New York Stock Exchange, as well as to the grain and cotton markets in New York, Chicago, New Orleans, and, in fact, to all the great cities of the world. These board rooms and their branches throughout the United States made up the nation's financial nerve system along which innumerable distinct impulses moved constantly at the speed of electric current to "make the market."

Can anything have been more fantastic than my abrupt change from the sedentary and impecunious position of a young man of letters to my post in a nerve-wracking board room in the great casino of Wall Street?

During the early twenties the chances of winning one's bread as a free-lance writer who took his art seriously were almost zero. Sinclair Lewis, to be sure, had won a popular success with social novels such as *Main Street* and better still *Babbitt,* which represented honest and creditable work; yet he had gone to school at the *Saturday Evening Post* and his writing showed it. Though Lewis' achievement was perhaps a good augury, he was far surpassed by the author of *The Sheik,* the big best seller of 1922. Along New York's Grub Street, then still on Fourth Avenue, commercial book publishers sold their standard merchandise under definite categories, such as Romantic Adventure, Humor, or Religious Inspiration. To succeed as a writer one evidently had to believe in oneself as a sheik or a "Pollyanna," or perhaps a sky pilot producing religious tracts.

"I utterly hate and despise the trade and the tradesman of letters," Malcolm Cowley, my companion of Paris days, wrote after returning to New York. To take a job with one of the book firms or women's magazines on Grub Street meant either editing or writing a purely commercialized literature. In the end would one not become commercialized in every fiber and brain cell? We used to call the writers of light fiction for mass magazines "touts," since their stories were always strung out in the back pages to lead the reader through a maze of display advertisements of every kind of merchandise.

One way of remaining a practitioner of belles-lettres was to be wealthy like Amy Lowell, or at least to enjoy a small income like Ezra Pound. But failing that, being forced to earn our own livings and yet desiring to preserve the amateur spirit in our writing, we believed that we should seek our livelihood as far away as possible from the commercial press.

A good many of us had tried to live on the margin of society, in a basement of the "Village" or a cottage in the country, contenting ourselves with a pittance so that we might continue the work we thought we were called to and which we enjoyed. But our position grew always more untenable. We were the Forgotten Men; no one here "owed us a living."

In the crisis of my penury, which was accompanied by the end of *Broom*, I determined to make a complete about-face and take a business job. Since it was to be business, then, like so many others who dreamed of quick fortune I thought a career in Wall Street might offer a short cut to some of the folding money I had long dispensed with, but now required in the most immediate sense. I thought I would put aside all the agreeable mental furnishings accumulated during years of travel and education as no longer useful, and stake out my claim in the great financial community of New York that was just around the corner. Had there been some frontier to open up or new mines to dig, doubtless I would have gone there. But I knew that since the 1890's, from coast to coast the soil of America had all gone into the hands of realtors.

We had come to the Fat Years of the Coolidge Administration; a Bull Market was in full swing in Wall Street; I supposed anyone with his wits about him might profit by this new gold rush. There, we were told, lay the real power in the land, in that community of big industrialists and financiers who seemingly manipulated the entire body politic at will. Even the reputed "wickedness" of the Street gave it a certain glamor in the twenties.

A newspaperman of my acquaintance, who had "covered" the financial district for many years, sent me with his warm recommendations to a friend who was a member of the Stock Exchange; and so I was engaged. I had to borrow money in order to make my appearance in Wall Street in a new, well-creased suit of clothes.

During a fortnight of orientation I familiarized myself with the machinery of the security markets, finding it complex but very neatly rationalized. Then I was put to work at the top instead of at the bottom, after receiving some tutelage from an aged partner who planned to retire soon. Mr. T. was a crusty fellow, very ruddy and stout, dressed in a morning suit and square derby and very much a nineteenth-century figure, even down to his waxed mustaches. Like many Wall Street men he cultivated a hobby, in his case that of collecting rare Americana; he also wrote on finance for the Wall Street press. Once he showed me how to get up the weekly market letters, containing recommendations of investments for the customers, I quickly adopted the vocabulary of the Street, took note of the senior partners' opinions of the trend, and turned out a page or two of this stuff in an afternoon. I also memorized the symbols, or abbreviations, for the names of hundreds of active stocks, and soon posted myself in the board room to begin trading in the market for a few clients.

The old traders, habitués of the board room from the opening gong at 10:00 A.M. to 3:00 in the afternoon, were a colorful lot, much like racing men; they ate, drank, and breathed only with the pulsations of the ticker tape and had their professional lingo and mythology, which was remarkably superstitious. These were not the Big Fish—who seldom appeared, but kept contact with my superiors by telephone—they were inveterate small speculators, usually hard-faced, middle-aged, and gray-headed, but with young eyes. William Butler Yeats once wrote very perceptively that the gambler, like the hunter or the lover, must be ever-youthful and eager for the chase. Some of these men acted as the eyes and legs of bigger speculators, watching for some signal or waiting for orders by telephone before taking swift action; others played for themselves. I observed their complete cycles of buying and selling operations in quick trades. A man who had the market in his blood would suddenly leap to his feet and buy with all he had even at high prices some stock that showed "good action" on the tape and which had crossed a "point of resistance." If he sold for a short turn after a few days when the momentum had slowed down, he would stroll over to the cage of the cashier next to the order clerk and draw some money from his account to live on for awhile. If, however, he had been deceived by the variety of feinting maneuvers used by those who manipulated stocks behind the scenes—the managers of "pools" or syndicates associated with each corporation —then our professional speculator would pocket his losses and wait, chewing his fingernails, for the next chance to recoup.

It was not long before I was directing the speculations of a little group of customers I had accumulated. They would be required to deposit as a margin of their equity in an account only ten per cent of the value of some stock, the other ninety per cent being supplied as a loan at call-money interest rates through the firm and its bank. A man might start with as little as five hundred to a thousand dollars. In imitation of one of the knowing veterans in the board room, I purchased three hundred shares of an active oil stock at thirty-three dollars a share for a client who deposited one thousand dollars as margin. Within three days the same stock had reached 36½, and we sold, gaining approximately a thousand dollars profit after paying brokerage fees and interest. My man now had two thousand dollars to his credit, or a gain of a hundred per cent in three days. For the next turn, I would buy more shares for him and increase the rate of our profit.

It was a beautiful game, I said to myself. I wondered why more people did not enter into it, rather than go on slaving in their dreary shops or just hoeing potatoes.

We were then following a seasonal movement of the oil stocks in the early spring, in anticipation of increased motoring and hence consumption of gasoline. With a flash of beginner's luck I made another turn of three or four points the next week, and then another. Several of my customers were now, with my encouragement, doubling their bets. A few others were mired in disappointing speculations whose value declined a little or which did not move at all. The lucky ones grew excited, showing emotions both of greed and vanity; they told their wives and friends how clever *they* were in winning money quickly and without pain—and brought me interested friends of theirs as new clients.

"You are getting *action*," one of my firm's executives said to me approvingly. "That is the main thing here, action." He meant that by turning over securities rapidly I was netting fees in good volume—a third of which was credited toward my salary. Within several weeks my salary was raised from a beginner's pay to a more comfortable sum. I was assured that I was an apt pupil. My growing confidence and zeal increased my following; as my activity expanded I became accustomed to take quick advantage of short-term movements; then my salary was raised again, so that I earned more in a week than my wife and I had sometimes lived on during three months while in Europe.

A younger partner of my firm, a very pleasant-spoken man, now favored me with his friendship and advice. He encouraged me to pursue an active social life and make new acquaintances, by entertaining or dining out, joining clubs, and going to the races as he did. Most well-to-do-Americans possessed the gambling instinct and when persons like ourselves, who were considered well posted, discussed our market operations or, upon request, gave our advice, the interest of such men could be easily won and they could be persuaded to open accounts with us. M.'s method was to talk with an air of quiet confidence as an Insider. He might casually drop a suggestion, that is a tip or a "point" on some stock. If it went up, the prospective client who had not acted on the tip would be reminded of the fact. (If it went down, you talked of something else.) The potential customer would perceive that he might have garnered five thousand dollars on a fast move in Baldwin Locomotive as he had been advised to do last week; the next time he would rise to the bait.

In the language of the professionals M. explained to me that stocks did not go up or down of themselves, but were "put up" or "sold down." By whom? "*They*," he replied; it was a superstitious nomenclature often invoked by our veteran speculators to describe the powers behind the scenes—that is, the Insiders who manipulated everything. In a show of friendship M. now confided to me that just the night before he had dined with a certain tobacco magnate to whom he was related, and learned from this great man that his corporation would certainly increase its dividend from three to four dollars annually at the next directors' meeting. I was enchanted at being entrusted with this advance information (a "hot tip") and felt that I was now getting very close to the Insiders.

In a little campaign initiated the next day I whispered my "inside information" to my clients, placing about half their resources and that of a couple of new accounts in the favored stock, which we shall call "Tobacco Stores." It was then at about 60, but within a week, on the basis of a higher dividend, was expected to reach 75 a share. My customers felt unquestioning confidence in me as a member of the Wall Street establishment. "*You* should know; *you* are the man who is watching the market," they would say.

Without warning the squall struck. Older eyes than mine had missed the signs of evil weather approaching. All the market "leaders"—American Can, General Motors, General Electric, U.S. Steel—suddenly went down under heavy selling, and the majority of stocks declined in sympathy with them. The next day urgent selling continued and values retreated on a broad front. We now heard rumors of "Bears raiding the market" and of bad news impending.

I looked at the stock board in amazement; all the corporations that two days earlier supposedly enjoyed the most pleasing prospects were now worth five or ten per cent less, and looked sick. I saw also that most of my clients were in twice as deep as before and could be two-fold losers if they sold at these lower values. I tried to cheer them in my reports on the telephone, offering the hope that the morrow would bring a rally. In truth, I was overcome with fear and could not sleep that night as I tried to calculate what I could do to extricate my clients if things got worse.

On the third day of the "bear drive" the market suddenly plunged downward under furious selling. I had thought of salvaging what I could for my clients, but now realized with

horror that it was too late. By rough estimates my lightly mar-
gined accounts had not only lost their paper profits, but were
reduced to only a fraction of their original capital. Worst of
all was the behavior of "Tobacco Stores," in whose basket I
had, so to speak, put about half of our eggs. To my great grief
the news about its dividend, when flashed over the wire service,
proved to be the reverse of what I expected; instead of increasing, the directors *reduced* it! We had been gulled and the stock
was down by all of ten points from yesterday's close! When I
went to the sleek young broker who had imparted his "inside
information" to me and sought an explanation of the matter, he
simply brushed me off saying he was busy, and thereafter avoided
me.

It was a day of disaster. In the crowded board room most of
the regular traders and many other visitors sat watching the
changing stock board, as tense, pale, and silent as I was.

Only a small group seemed not at all distressed by the continuing massacre, but full of merriment. They were the "bears"
who had been "selling short," that is selling stocks they did not
own (but had borrowed temporarily for delivery) with the idea
of buying them back at much lower prices. They were laughing
over the calamitous news story about "Tobacco Stores" which
some of them had been astute enough to sell short, having made
the shrewd guess that the rumors about its future profits and
dividends were false.

"I have been waiting for this day for twelve months," one of
them cried exultantly. "Look how much faster things go down
than they go up!" A strange place this, where the misfortunes
of one group of speculators, such as my own clients, brought
gain and happiness to another group.

At the close of that melancholy session I slunk away at an
early hour together with one of the old hands who had invited
me to join him at a downtown speak-easy. He had been through
the wars and tried to cheer me up with his tall tales. "Don't
worry," he said. "It's *only money*." But I could not forget my
poor clients, and rued the day that had brought me to the pit-

falls of Wall Street. It seemed to me that the whole setup was false and there was nothing to lean upon here—where big operators treacherously manipulated the stocks in which I risked the funds of my clients. And what of that well-spoken young broker? Had he been a party to this deception or had he, too, been gulled by the big man he supped with? Was everyone's hand turned against the other in this jungle?

The first bear market is the hardest, like the first battle action for the raw recruit in an army. Most new hands at this business, I was told, usually failed to survive the first real shakeout. Speculation on the narrow margins then allowed was far more dangerous than people realized, because a sharp decline of about ten per cent on average would wipe out the light-waisted gamblers. We small operatives always worked with our clients for the rise on the "long" side, but the market went in two directions, down as well as up. The bears, or short-sellers, were usually professionals with big money; they were well-informed and would attack the market on a big scale until all the lambs were shorn. There was no Federal regulation or policing of the markets then; only the officers of the Stock Exchange, that great private club of brokers, had authority to enforce some of the rules of the game.

When I turned up at my office late the next morning, and with a bad headache too, the office manager and the margin clerk (a sour-faced individual) were lying in wait for me and were thoroughly angry. "Where have you been at a time like this?" they exclaimed. They had been trying to reach me since the afternoon before to warn me about the condition of my clients' accounts. "Margin! They all need margin right away," the manager said sternly.

I remarked that my clients no doubt would be feeling unhappy about their heavy losses and I preferred not to disturb them. At this, the manager turned purple and yelled: "Get out and see them right away. Bring cash, gold, checks, anything, or

we will sell them all out!" The fine print in our contracts with
customers allowed the broker full liberty of action; to protect his
loans against their stocks he could sell them out even at the low
prevailing prices without giving them a chance to recoup.

Only a few days earlier I had been congratulating myself
upon having forsaken the literary life and found an easy road to
riches. Now I was on the hot seat, forced to hound my clients for
cash, and working to get rid of the financially wounded and dying, those who no longer had the means to stay in the game.
Some laughed at their own folly; others who had lost their savings of many years were bitter in their reproaches, or seemed
distracted at what were for them ruinous losses. I remember one
who told me with a long face that his wife kept him up all night
with her complaints at his reckless gambling. In the language
of the Street this process of cleaning out weak accounts was
termed "shoving the corpses overboard."

As I sat in the board room looking rather blue, the eldest
partner of the firm, who had been my tutor, said to me gruffly:
"You are very foolish to be sorry for your clients; they only
come down here to get something for nothing." The managing
partner, noting that my business in brokerage fees had shrunk
alarmingly, observed: "It seems you will need some new blood."
A veteran telegraph clerk on overhearing this, explained to me:
"He means new suckers. Anyway, there's one born every minute."

After a while the market began to recover. My luckier customers, who had been able to hang on, flourished again. I also
gathered in several new accounts, for I regularly solicited many
persons who had money for speculation—we kept making lists
of them—and who had heard nothing of my recent setbacks.

I was beginning to know my way around and becoming hardened to the dangers and losses. This was like war; each one
fought for his own financial life, either going it alone or in wolf
packs. And the Wolves of Wall Street had an old-fashioned habit
of eating up the pack leader if he happened to fall. With added
experience I began to discern the character of the forces at

work behind the scenes in the securities markets, and the differences between deceptive tactics and "constructive" operations by which one might profit. Luck played a part here, but not much more than it would in a game of chess between a novice and a master.

The financial community gradually assumed in my mind the form of a hierarchy. At the top were the powerful groups controlling great reservoirs of money through their banks and corporations, for whom the "free and liquid" market in securities was an economic necessity. These big people were the Insiders who knew in advance what was going to happen; with them was associated the army of brokers and dealers who distributed stocks or maintained a free market in America's corporate securities, in return for a commission. Lower down in the scale were the day-to-day traders and the small speculators, such as my own clients, who were constantly recruited on a nationwide scale to complete the cycle of distribution at the retail level.

By constant scanning of the market horizon I became more familiar with the weather conditions; the credit standing, the biographies of the different corporations became known to me, and I could gauge somewhat the characteristic actions of their stocks in response to certain news developments, calculating, for instance, the effect of a coal miners' strike upon the railroads or the impact of a revolution in South America upon copper shares.

In my mind the lore of old Wall Street was also being stored away. One who taught me a good deal was an eccentric old fellow who often came into our board room. He was a short, stout, white-haired man whose face, once handsome, was now deeply lined; he was dressed, however, in castoff, outsized clothes, so that I marked him as one of those human wrecks one saw occasionally in the Street. Formerly he had held some high position here, but, it was said, he had become addicted to drugs and wound up as a defaulter. Now "Jimmy the Scout," as he was called, apparently had no means of support, but wandered in and out of brokers' board rooms every day, meeting other men of his kind who transmitted rumors and tips to each other in whispers, thus making up a sort of grapevine. His role was to go about and circulate dubious or even false information, with which some of the sportive element in our board room provided him, and to bring back gossip of the same sort. Indeed, Wall Street was a huge whispering gallery. As one of my employers remarked: "This stock market is made up of gossip, among other things—even false gossip."

The livelier habitués of our place used to treat Jimmy as their clown, greeting him with shouts of joy or obscene oaths, according to their estimate of his usefulness on different occasions. But when the closing gong rang and they rose from their chairs, they would often take up a collection of a few dollars for him.

This sad clown of Wall Street interested me; meeting him in the street on occasion I would buy him a sandwich; we would converse in friendly manner and he would tell me endless anecdotes about the old days and the Wolves of the Street. Some gossip he gave me concerned high banking officers in the downtown institutions, who sometimes betrayed the confidences of their banking clients and profited richly thereby. A big plunger in stocks who had become overextended might have his loans suddenly called and his securities thrown on the market at a heavy sacrifice—in such cases advance information "leaking out" would offer glittering profit opportunities for those in on the secret. (In the 1930's, under the New Deal, the detailed reports of committees of Congress fully documented the frequency of such treacherous actions.)

Old Jimmy remembered all the great panics going back to 1873, and also knew the Big Fish of Wall Street by sight. Standing near Trinity Church, he would watch those who were going in and out of the First National Bank at the corner or J.P. Morgan's offices farther down the street. "There goes George F. Baker," he exclaimed in excitement. I saw an octogenarian wearing sideburns in Civil War style, dressed in a cutaway and a square derby, walking out of his bank with firm stride. The old banker had been Morgan's close ally in some of the historic market struggles of former times. I must read about these people someday, and about the Vanderbilts and Goulds too, I told myself. Some years later, when I came to write my book *The Robber Barons,* my background knowledge of the financial community and its warlords stood me in good stead.

As the boom cycle was resumed in the summer of 1924, I began to center my efforts on the flotation of new issues of stock coming on the open market for distribution. These represented the capitalized wealth of what were formerly family-owned concerns, now being merged into large units—as in the later case of the Dodge Brothers Motor Company being taken over by the Chrysler Corporation. New issues of electric utility securities were also being floated by important financial syndicates, such as those headed by the Morgan and Rockefeller interests or Samuel Insull or Harrison Williams. I was able to operate in such shares, during this prosperous period, with comparative safety and by some rule of reason I evolved; for the time being it seemed imperative for those big financiers to create "a good market" for their new capital issues, and I had my clients subscribe for them as heavily as possible with excellent results. In one case I executed a single order for two thousand shares of a certain public utility, large enough to have our firm's name announced over the financial news ticker as buyer of that stock. A few weeks later we were able to dispose of these securities at a profit of about sixty per cent. The Big Fish were certainly pushing things at the time.

By the summer of 1924 I wrote to one of my friends:

There has been a turn for the better, and I am moving ahead a little. I guide my clan of speculators steadily, taking a few lickings now and then, but eking out small wins regularly enough, and once in a while making a major move.[1]

In the course of a year I had survived one bear market, regained more than the ground lost, and had my starting salary tripled. I had also built up an investment account of my own, as a prudent "long-pull" affair, which eventually netted enough for a down-payment on a cottage in northern Westchester County. My dream was to gather in enough fish so that I could quit the Street, and New York as well, and live in the country with my wife and infant son, who arrived in the autumn.

"A whole year has passed and not a poem written," I noted regretfully on New Year's Day of 1925. In truth I was living my life as a schizoid personality. From ten in the morning to about four in the afternoon I worked over ciphers and Stock Exchange symbols, representing quantities of money in the most ephemeral form, and dealt with the crassest men of business, stockbrokers and their underlings, or with clients who dreamed only of winning riches without pain. I felt no dislike for these people, but a profound indifference to them. Talking with them over the telephone or handling the routine part of my work, I would often think of subjects that were as far away as possible from the market.

Returning to my apartment I would take up some reading, often in those days the later novels of Henry James. My wife and child used to retire very early then, and I would work at night at some writing in a small room set aside as my study. On one or two evenings a week I would turn with immense relief to the society of my fellow poets.

In the winter of 1924 to 1925 we used to meet for dinner at fairly regular intervals at an Italian table d'hôte in Perry Street operated by a genial Neapolitan named John Squarcialupi. Cowley, Burke, Brown, Hart Crane, and Allen Tate were usually there, as well as some new acquaintances one of us would bring to meet the others. Often we had the basement dining room to ourselves for those weekly gatherings, which we called "the dinner of the Aesthetes" in honor of Ernest Boyd's polemic against us.

That Boyd, and Mencken too, should not forget us, we devoted part of our time at these gatherings to preparing a broad-side against them in the form of a thirty-two page pamphlet, which we embellished with all the wit and humor we could contrive. Putting our heads together, we helped each other polish aphorisms and couplets with which we proposed to demolish our literary adversaries. After a while we had the idea of finishing the whole pamphlet by working together in an all day-and-night session. On one afternoon I left my office early and joined the others—including the inimitable Jack Wheelwright, who had just then returned from Europe—at an old hotel in the downtown section, where we had engaged a large room for the day. There, working in excellent ensemble, we produced most of the copy for our "little magazine" (having only one issue) which we entitled *Aesthete: 1925*. Some who were unable to appear, such as Dr. Williams, Edmund Wilson, and Hart Crane, sent in their contributions by mail. Wheelwright concocted a satirical anthology called "Little Moments with Great Critics"; Charles Sheeler provided us with a drawing of New York skyscrapers for our cover; while the rest of us worked up squibs about such persons as William Lyon Phelps, Irving Babbitt, Ernest Boyd, H.L. Mencken, Henry S. Canby, and others in the form of mock newspaper headlines and advertising slogans:

> Vast Crowds Storm Algonquin Hotel—Cultured Mob Jams
> 44th Street as Critics Meet for Witty Luncheon—
> Prominent Brokers and Actresses Narrowly Escape
> Trampling in Throng—Woman Nearly Swoons

> Mencken Jibes at Rotary Clubs—Youthful Sociologist
> and Circulation Builder Also Mentions
> Chatauqua—Humorously

> Yes and No Says Canby—Editor Outlines Middle
> Course Between Heaven and Hell

The best of our pseudo advertisements was printed in behalf of the "Mencken Promotion Society" and headed by the slogan: "MENCKENIZE."

We even included a satire of ourselves as former "expatriates" in a "French Letter" (written by Kenneth Burke):

Richard! At last, I am in Paris! Great God, man, how I detest you back there among the Rotary Clubs and the grape juice!

Last night I walked the streets until morning, content with just the feel of Paree, . . . I shall never forget the surge of triumph as I stepped out of the gare (station) and realized that at last I was alive!

In this instance we avoided having a "sponsor," such as Gorham Munson had been for *Secession,* but invented a mythical Maecenas, gave him a nom de guerre, "Walter S. Hankel," wrote epigrams in his name, and also published what purported to be a picture of him with bald head and curling mustachios (so that he looked like the corpulent ghost of Munson). At subsequent meetings at Squarcialupi's we always kept one chair vacant at the head of our long table in honor of our ghostly "sponsor." The three hundred copies of *Aesthete: 1925* that were sent to a few bookstores were well received and quickly sold out.

Aesthete: 1925 attracted the attention of Miss Jane Heap, who was then compiling an issue of *The Little Review,* which was to be made up of new writers from France and America. Miss Heap invited me to make a selection of work by the "Aesthetes" for her publication. "It would be fun to publish your group and the French group against each other," she wrote.[2] Thus our little company performed together again in the Spring, 1926, *Little Review;* and repeated its performance two years later in a special "New York number" of the new magazine *transition.*

My own article for *The Little Review* consisted in an "Open Letter to My Friends," in which I attacked the Surrealists of Paris, some of whom were included in the French section of the same issue. Certainly I had experienced a great change of heart toward the esthetic nihilists who had so long fascinated me— a change which was related to the two years just spent in the front-line trenches of Wall Street. I now expressed a vehement dislike for their anti-social and irrational tendencies, as for their preoccupations with nightmares and day dreams; all the spiritist séances and pseudo-Freudian experiments, I declared, yielded only the dullest records of the subconscious mind. "Of what value are these tepid dreams?" I asked. Their other "games," such as questionnaires about each other's sex life, seemed equally value-less. In contrast, I pictured the situation of American artists and poets as "precarious and desperate"; some, indeed, were being driven into "storm cellars or country retreats" in order to sur-vive. But at least we were facing the facts of life. We sought to "accept" modern society in the United States, instead of trying to escape from it, and hoped to discover and commemorate its new myths. We also stood in danger of being crushed out in the process.

In Paris, André Breton, the Surrealist "pope," turned livid on reading my offending remarks and pronounced me eternally damned, that is, excommunicated.

At this period Hart Crane knew all the reverses and disap-pointments that might be experienced by a young American of immense talent who devoted himself to poetry in its purest form. Nor did neurosis, alcoholic and sexual, make his problem of ad-justment easier to solve. Recognition came to him slowly, though in the years from 1924 to 1927 he touched the heights of his poetic powers. The opulence and sonority of his language in such poems as "Voyages" (1925) were a continual surprise to his friends, though they had come to expect a good deal of him.

Was there anyone in America who could create such poetry as Hart's, we asked ourselves when we read such lines as:

> Where icy and bright dungeons lift
> Of swimmers their lost morning eyes,
> And ocean rivers, churning, shift
> Green borders under stranger skies, . . .
>
> O rivers mingling toward the sky
> And harbor of the phoenix' breast—

> My eyes pressed black against the prow,
> —Thy derelict and blinded guest
>
> Waiting, afire, what name, unspoke,
> I cannot claim, let thy waves rear
> More savage than the death of kings,
> Some splintered garland for the seer. . . .

All the drama of Hart's turbulent personality was there in the strange images of those verses. We admired him at one moment, and in the next would feel troubled by him, even consternated by his extravagant behavior. It would only be truthful to say that he was often a trial to his friends.

When he was only partly filled with alcohol his talk might flow in a torrent, full, to be sure, of perceptive comment and imagery. He would station himself before a painting, a photograph, or one of those Oceanian carvings he loved, and begin to verbalize with exuberance. At times he would grow so eloquent, as he described the plan of the symbolic poem he was writing that was to encompass the past and the present of America, that we would hail him as our Whitman, nay our Byron! But if someone jested with him or dropped some incautious or reproving remark, the hysteric in him would appear, he might burst into tears, or in a rage begin to break up the furniture around him. After a few drinks he would swing easily from an overflow of joyous spirits to the blackest melancholy. It was on one occasion when he was in such a mood (both sad and violent) that a friend of his remarked: "Yes, Hart's like Lord Byron all right, and we will all appreciate him much more after he's dead and gone."

In retrospect, one realizes that the chances of his becoming a happy and fulfilled being were on the whole slight. He was nowadays frankly the "masculine" homosexual, but remained unreconciled to the anxieties of his position. A part of his burden was his sense of guilt as the child of unhappy, divided parents and his awareness of his own "sterility," for which at times he "hated" himself.

> But some are twisted with the love
> Of things irreconcilable—
> The slant moon with the slanting hill . . .

The Dionysiac in Hart often drove him to the underworld region of the Brooklyn docks, where he cultivated all sorts of shifty characters by whom he was sometimes beaten and robbed. I once urged him to "settle down and become monogamous" like other more tractable men of his kind. It was true that when he lived with one of the amiable and sympathetic breed Hart became tranquil—for a while.

On the other hand, the poet in him drove Hart to seek the company of his literary friends—though their sex was "normal" and they had wives, children, mistresses—he needed them too. They gave their admiration to his poems, they fed him, or looked for jobs for him, and when he could not hold those jobs even found patrons who gave him money so that he might have time to write. At various periods Waldo Frank, the Cowleys, Slater Brown and his wife, and Allen and Caroline Tate were most generous friends to Hart, though it was not easy to maintain oneself on terms of intimacy with him. We helped him, and we also failed to help him enough.

Though Hart attacked his medium with great boldness and tried to work on an heroic scale, he lacked a sure command of his art such as less intoxicated poets sometimes achieve; or at any rate, despite his tall talk, he wanted confidence in himself. The "epic" of *The Bridge* was a daring effort at poetic exegesis, exuberant in color, rich in orchestration, and beyond a doubt one of the memorable poems of our literature. It is, however, uncompleted; it remains, after all, a ruin, even if a magnificent ruin, for we know it contains only a part of what the poet endeavored to say. He himself was aware of losing momentum during the last years, as he wrestled with this work; his life was increasingly disorganized and he himself befogged in alcohol at the time when he halted.

There had been a cloud over our friendship that soon passed.

It arose in 1923 from Hart's misunderstanding or ignorance of my difficulties with the ship's mails between America and Europe. He had sent me the second part of a long poem for *Broom* (then in Berlin) before sending on the first part, so that before he could warn me, I had published the poem in *Broom* in the wrong order and under the provisory title he had given it ("The Sirens of the Springs of Guilty Song," which he afterward changed to "For the Marriage of Faustus and Helen").

In the winter of 1926 he came to my home for dinner and talked with his characteristic rapture about the idea of *The Bridge*. As he did not have any manuscript with him, he sat down at my typewriter and very quickly, from memory, typed out a hundred lines or more of the section he called "Powhatan's Daughter." Each subdivision of his long poem was then very clear in his mind. That night I told Hart he was writing like an angel.

Then, with one of his sudden changes of mood, he began to tell us of the great trouble he was having with *The Dial* over one of his recent short pieces, though it had been accepted for publication. Our old acquaintance Marianne Moore had lately become editor of that periodical; but from the beginning of her service there created many difficulties for people, because she conceived it her duty to rewrite many contributions in conformity with her own idea of style. (!) Miss Moore is a woman of rare talent, and very dedicated too; she would work long hours to change a manuscript. However, she had had no experience as an editor acting in collaboration with other writers. Moreover, she was decidedly different in temperament from the lyrical, uninhibited Crane; one would have said she was almost puritanical.

The poem Hart called "Wine Menagerie" was an excellent example of his work; but it was impossible for Miss Moore, no matter how well-meaning, to enter into its spirit and improve on him. Nonetheless, she had set about changing the order of his verses, paraphrasing many of them, and cutting out almost half of what remained, so that Hart could no longer recognize the

thing as his own. She also changed his charming title to something quite dull: "Again."

"I would never have consented to this outrageous mutilation,"
Hart cried, with tears starting in his eyes, "if I hadn't so desperately needed the money—only twenty dollars." When he
was overcome by emotion and wept, my wife and I asked him
to lie down and rest in a little guest room we had. (As this happened several times, we came to call that room "Hart Crane's
Crying Room.")

When he had recovered his spirits, he typed out his own version of "Wine Menagerie," and also some passages of it as revised by Miss Moore, which gave me an idea of how drastic her
editing had been. I was then full of emotion over the parts of
The Bridge Crane had shown us, and felt deep indignation at
the outrage done to his new poem. "Let me try to buy your
poem back from *The Dial,* and we will manage to print it elsewhere just as you wrote it," I said to him impulsively. At the
moment he agreed that I might make such an offer to Miss
Moore on my own responsibility.

The next morning I wrote her saying that while I had always
felt great esteem for her own writing and for her integrity as a
critic, I had learned from Hart Crane of the sweeping changes
she had introduced into the poem he had submitted to her and
felt she did him great injustice. In effect, she had taken all the
"wine" out of the "Wine Menagerie." It was as if the director
of an art gallery, before exhibiting an artist's painting, insisted
upon retouching the work according to his own ideas of the art.
Would Miss Moore have liked it if Hart Crane, or another, had
demanded the right to change her own poems before printing
them? "Either you have faith in a man's whole work or reject
him completely," I argued. In his grief, I wrote, Crane had un-
burdened himself to me, saying that he had only yielded to her
because of his need for money. I had therefore decided to write
to her on my own responsibility, offering to pay *The Dial* twenty
dollars, and asking that his poem be sent to me.

Nothing, I suppose, could have seemed to Miss Moore more

meddling and offensive than my letter. Through mutual friends I learned that she was greatly put out, though she did not reply to me. Instead, she called Hart back to her office and questioned him closely, receiving his assurances that he had not "authorized" me to make such protest or proposal, and approved of her "corrections."

Such was Hart. Nor was it easy for his friends to forgive his waverings. Miss Moore, on the other hand, is a woman of great moral strength and most tenacious in argument. The poem appeared as she had rewritten it in *The Dial* for May, 1926.[3] However, talk of the affair spread, and Miss Moore's editorial interventions gradually diminished thereafter. Hart reported gaily that as a result of my "meddling" the next poems he submitted were printed in *The Dial* in full, without change even as to punctuation.

For a while Hart's fortunes improved; he found a rich patron. Otto Kahn, a senior partner of the famous banking firm of Kuhn, Loeb & Company, kept bobbing up here and there, during the twenties, as a Maecenas. The Provincetown Players, among other theater groups, was one of the beneficiaries of his charity, and thus Eugene O'Neill and James Light, director of the Provincetown, came to know the multimillionaire. O'Neill, who had been greatly impressed by Hart Crane's poetry and touched by his plight, prevailed upon Mr. Kahn to donate some funds in support of the poet. Waldo Frank also used his good offices with Mr. Kahn. The banker then agreed to furnish Hart with a grant-in-aid of two thousand dollars, half to be paid in the autumn of 1925 and the rest the following year.

At this bit of fortune Hart was lifted up to the heavens. Earlier, he had submitted in a letter to Otto Kahn a long outline of *The Bridge* (a document of remarkable interest); he now called on him in person, gave his thanks, and proceeded to tell him all about his proposed "mystical synthesis" of America's legends. The old financier was polite, but made it plain, as Hart reported with keen amusement, that while he was ready to pay the poet a small subsidy he could make nothing either of his outline or of his poems, and did not want to hear anything about the work in progress.

Putting money in Hart's hands was no solution. Released from dire poverty for the moment, he went careening about the bars in the "Village" and Brooklyn Heights, and within a few weeks had squandered most of the funds received. Then he went off to the country to stay with Allen Tate and his wife in an old house about sixty miles north of New York, his share of the rent being ten dollars a month. He proved to be a difficult neighbor, even though he had an upper floor to himself. Once he had begun drinking hard cider he would become so boisterous that the Tates found it impossible to work at their own writing.

In the early spring of 1926, after a row with the Tates, Hart packed up and went off to the Isle of Pines in Cuba. These frequent explosions of Hart in no way affected the friendship Allen and Caroline felt for him; they were, indeed, most forgiving.

Hart's first volume, *White Buildings*, was published in the autumn of 1926 by Boni & Liveright. The head of the firm, Horace Liveright, had reluctantly consented to bring out the book on the condition that Eugene O'Neill, who had been Hart's sponsor, would write a preface for it. When O'Neill, however, found himself unable to write even a brief critical foreword, Allen Tate undertook to "ghost" it for him, which was a most generous action. In the end, O'Neill insisted that Allen's foreword, an analytical study of Crane's poetic method, sounded so unlike his, O'Neill's, writing that Allen should sign it himself. While Tate eulogized his friend as one who worked in the grand manner, he also permitted himself the privilege of dissecting Crane's shortcomings as an artist, calling attention to the "discrepancy between sensuous fact and . . . organizing symbol" in the structure of these poems, as well as their obscurities. Moreover, he went on to announce in advance that Crane had in preparation an epic poem on the subject of the greatness of America, and ventured to predict that the poet would fail in his undertaking. He argued that America was "static" [!] and therefore "it was no longer possible for a poetic myth to be constructed on the American theme."

One would have thought that in prefatory remarks inviting the public to read a new poet, it would be appropriate for the sponsor-friend to confine himself to an affirmative view of the volume's worth, given without exaggeration but also without cavil over the details of its artistic imperfections, and leaving the duty of negative criticism to the reviewers. Poor Hart Crane was agonized enough by the fear of failure at every step and scarcely needed his friend's reminders of such dangers. How disconcerting it must have been to be told, in public, even before one had finished a new and difficult project, that it was bound to fail. No doubt Allen Tate was young then and full of certainty that the things he was saying of his friend were improving, for I am sure he meant no harm. Heaven preserve us, I have often said to myself, from having our friends write introductions to our books.

That epigone among literary critics, Gorham Munson, also chose to make public his disappointment in the still-youthful Crane, in an essay written in the autumn of 1925, wherein he holds that the poet's ideas are "unsystematic," that his poetry "would not stand the test of time," and that its occasional fine passages are achieved by accident. *En moraliste*, Munson made pointed reference to Hart's disordered life. At the time, Hart seemed greatly troubled by such blundering efforts at evaluation. Writing long afterward, one of Crane's biographers remarked that the attitude of the poet's friends "was unfavorable to a project like *The Bridge*."[4] But aside from Tate and Munson, Hart's other friends seem to have been judicious in passing judgment on his work.

I do not believe that Hart Crane (who had his faults as a poet) was one who might have been helped by criticism to achieve clarity and the spirit of logic. He was self-taught; the play of image and symbol in his poetry was contrived by an intuitive process. The different themes and historical epochs of Pocahontas, Walt Whitman, Wilbur Wright, and John A. Roebling are set together as in a large mosaic or an historical mural painting executed in a marvelously baroque style.

The symbolism of the bridge, in Hart Crane—as in Poe, Kafka, and others—has been analyzed as a representation of sexual joy fulfilled.[5] A clue is given us in one of Hart's letters, referring to the ecstasy he felt at the beginning of a love affair during which he and a beloved companion walked arm in arm from the Brooklyn shore "across the most beautiful bridge of the world, the cables enclosing us and pulling us upward in such a dance as I have never walked and never can walk with another." But love failed, the bridge failed him—he never reached the farther shore by way of the "unifying" bridge. One of the last lines of his poem is prophetic in its image of the poet sinking into the sea:

Atlantis,—hold thy floating singer late!

(It was from the bridge of a steamship that Hart was to make his final dive into the Gulf of Mexico on April 27, 1932.)

In our sector of the Younger Generation a number of us were again trying to "escape," this time to the country outside the metropolis of New York. Some had done their apprentice years in Europe and returned, others had stayed here; but most of us found the condition of poverty in which men of letters lived in large cities both irksome and depressing.

Several years earlier, in 1922, Kenneth Burke had fled from a grimy basement in the "Village" where he had been living with wife and child, in constant fear that he might become a chronic invalid. (This sturdy *malade imaginaire* always boasted a large repertory of incipient diseases.) The summers spent happily in upstate New York and Maine had given him ideas. He now proposed to live as a Noble Savage in the remote suburbs, purchasing a dilapidated farmhouse and eighty acres of run-down land in the New Jersey Highlands, some fifty-five miles from New York. Its modest initial cost of fifteen hundred dollars was soon paid off by the writing of essays and the translation of books. By owning a roof over his head and planting a kitchen garden, the penurious man of letters could render his life both more salutary and more dignified; the severe economies of the rustic life would also enable him to gain more time for the serious pursuit of his art. Kenneth, moreover, hoped that in time several of his friends would help colonize his corner of rural New Jersey, for he could not live without conversation.

His reports fairly glowed with the joy of life in that season of pioneering; soon his friends came for weekends to the green hills of New Jersey to inspect his gardens, the new-sown lawns, and the siding of fresh shingles that he and his wife had provided for their old house. After passing in review all his lares and penates, I ventured the thought that the place needed a flush bowl water closet.

Kenneth reared up in indignation, crying out that flush bowls were the curse of our benighted country and to hell with 'em; he would not have 'em. "All the damn fools in the cities just flush everything down the drain and believe that is the end of their problems," he exclaimed with fine scorn. The outhouse became the shield of his rustic honor and the water bucket the insigne of his Spartan way of life.

Soon his friends followed his example, although they did not, as it happened, put down their roots in New Jersey, but found tumble-down houses here and there in New York and Connecticut beyond the commuting zone, sixty miles or so from the city limits. With much hammering and sawing of timber, or sweeping of rubbish and old cans, and cutting of sumac, the young writers toward 1925 began to establish themselves in the country, usually in run-down farmhouses.

Eleanor Fitzgerald, the business manager of the Provincetown Players, who had owned a small summer home at Sherman, Connecticut, for several years, brought many of her friends there and found them places that could be rented or purchased cheaply. Thus, in 1925, Slater Brown who had recently married my old acquaintance of Clemenceau Cottage, the former Susan Light, acquired a run-down farmhouse of Revolutionary War vintage and a sizable acreage of second-growth woods and rocks in the village of Patterson, New York, just outside the Connecticut line at Sherman township, near Quaker Hill. Hart Crane came to stay a while with the Browns at "Tory Hill," as the place was called, and helped with the carpentry and painting their house needed. After a few weeks he found space at the old rooming house of Miss Addie Turner a half-mile from the Browns, where Allen and Caroline Tate, with their infant daughter, Nancy, occupied the lower floor during the winter of 1926. Malcolm Cowley also rented a small cottage on Quaker Hill in Sherman, Connecticut, a mile from the Browns and Tates, using it for weekends and summers.

In this hilly community our friends lived in the frugal style of rural Americans of the nineteenth century, cutting their own cordwood for heat, using ten cents worth of kerosene for cooking and light, and brewing their own ale or obtaining hard cider from their rustic neighbors.

In the spring of 1925 I also found a country cottage, at Katonah, New York, in northern Westchester County, which I purchased with some money the stock market had not yet taken back from me. Though my friend Kenneth jeered at me as a "backslider," I cravenly installed a 1910-model bathroom in the house and wired it for electric light. My place was an hour from New York and somewhat less than that by car from the literary community near Quaker Hill (the title of one of Hart Crane's lyrics in his last volume).

We lived near the reservoir lakes in what was then fairly open country dotted here and there with suburban homes. Although sparsely populated, Katonah was within commuting distance, but typified the wealthy suburbs, our own being one of the few small cottages in the neighborhood then still distinguished for its "gentleman farms" and stables of saddle horses. I did not mind being a neighbor of industrial barons and Wall Street financiers, but it was a trial to come in contact occasionally with their English gardeners and liveried chauffeurs, who looked down their noses at us with a class spirit their American masters would never have affected so openly.

One day, unhappily, my rickety Model-T Ford grazed the body of one of my neighbor's stout, chauffeur-driven limousines. A little later the owner himself came riding down on his big white horse and presented me with a bill for five dollars to repair the scratch on his car. This I refused to pay, because the road past our house was extremely narrow and it was not clear who had been at fault. My own car had also lost some of its paint, though one could hardly tell where. After an unpleasant discussion the man dropped the matter; but his British chauffeur used to look at me with withering scorn whenever we met at the village store, and would sniff something in a cockney accent about my poor driving. Eventually I decided that I would sell the Katonah place and move farther out to the deep countryside, which I did two years later.

The only literary figure in Katonah, so far as I knew, proved to be the long-legged, red-haired Sinclair Lewis, who rented one of the large estates in the neighborhood during the summer of 1925. With Malcolm Cowley, who was visiting me at the time, I went over to call on Lewis one evening, and found him with his wife and two guests. The house was a big, overstuffed Victorian mansion. They were sitting at dinner on stiff-backed Italian Renaissance chairs, Lewis looking almost feverish with discomfort, but very cordial and evidently happy to see Malcolm and me.

In truth, "Red" Lewis was drunk, as oftentimes happened. His handsome, Junoesque wife, Grace Hegger Lewis, seemed constrained and unhappy; a few weeks later Lewis was to leave the Katonah house and begin proceedings for a divorce. After a while the master rose unsteadily to his feet, brusquely made his excuses to the others, and asked Malcolm and me to accompany him to his room upstairs. There, still in his dinner jacket and with his shoes on, he flung himself upon his sumptuous bed and ordered a servant to bring us some whisky.

"I don't like those people, don't want them; they're stuffed shirts," he exclaimed. "I much prefer to spend a little time with you boys." He then settled back and talked with us in a very friendly and sensible manner.

Lewis had been a nonconformist in earlier life, and even a Socialist for a while. Now that he was America's "millionaire novelist," his wife would have liked him to behave with the decorum of other members of the high-income class into which they had risen, or somewhat like the "old New York families" of Westchester County. But sudden fortune had made "Red" less tractable and more opinionated than before. What was the use of selling a million copies of your books if you could not tell people you disliked to go to hell? I used to see Lewis occasionally thereafter, roaring about the offices of Hartcourt, Brace & Company like a very egotistical literary lion, exploding with anger because his last book had not received sufficient publicity or even having a row with his old friend Alfred Harcourt. "Send me a check for fifty thousand this afternoon at the Hotel Plaza," he would demand suddenly, and Harcourt would almost jump out of his skin.

On the other hand, although he was very impetuous and contrasuggestive by nature, Lewis had a lively intelligence and showed a warm interest in other writers. After blowing off steam at the editors of Harcourt, Brace, he would take me aside and in a gentle and avuncular manner talk with me about something I had written, expressing disapproval, or sometimes approval, in a very forthright and heartening way.

At Katonah both Malcolm and I had expressed admiration for *Babbitt* as a trenchant satire of America's business class. Lewis counseled us against becoming "too literary" and "too intellectual" in our writing. He thought that the Younger Generation who went to Paris were given to affectation, and felt aggrieved at some of them who criticized his novels as poor imitations of Zola's naturalistic works.

When my wife and I drove up to see the Browns on occasion at "Tory Hill" we would constitute, together with Slater and the

Cowleys, a quorum of the group of "exiles" who had lived in France for a while but now existed as a curiously isolated band in the rural backwaters of America. According to Hart Crane, reporting on our cheerful gatherings in one of his letters from Patterson, New York, we used to "drink and talk all night long" at the Browns.

In the country, friendship could be more leisurely and expansive than in the big town. One felt this when we occasionally journeyed in a body to the hills of New Jersey for a reunion weekend with Kenneth Burke. Though he lived on what many would have considered a pittance, his hospitality to his friends was charming and thoughtful. We warmed ourselves with the rude rice wine his wife brewed and listened to Burke's "theories" of the semantics of literature, which he had all ready for us, as if impatient for listeners after having been long alone. Sometimes he spoke with so much verve and at such great length that afterward, as he said, he had neither strength nor will to write down the big ideas he had "talked out."

I remember one winter night at the Browns when Hart Crane, overflowing with the spirits of hard cider and applejack, flared up in angry dispute with the rest of us, so that we had to sit on his chest to quiet him. Then he broke away and ran through the deep snow to the Turner house, where he was then living. The next morning as I happened to walk down the road past his house I heard the phonograph going in very loud volume, playing Brahms' Fourth Symphony as it had been doing all night, I was told, while Hart worked at his poems. At that very moment Hart came to the window and brusquely flung out his portable typewriter, which landed in the soft snow beside me. This meant, presumably, that he was "blocked" and in a rage. A minute or two later Hart, chewing a cigar, his face flushed, came down and retrieved his much-abused typewriter; soon I could hear it ticking away again upstairs. It was not long afterward that he removed himself at first to Cuba, then to a room in Brooklyn Heights.

The Tates stayed at the Turner house in the winter of 1926,

when the heavy snow isolated them, as well as the Browns, from the world for days on end. To live in those hills under such conditions with a young child proved too arduous; the next autumn they returned to New York to stay in a basement apartment of a brownstone house on Bank Street in Greenwich Village, where Allen, in lieu of paying rent, served as janitor. It was not time-consuming work, and so he was able to continue writing book reviews and critical essays for newspaper supplements and weekly magazines.

"Think of it, Allen a janitor!" Hart Crane wrote in one of his letters of the time. That so accomplished a poet and essayist should be reduced to such a role struck me as a curious commentary on our kind of civilization.

The thought came to me that I might try to call people's attention to Allen's plight, hoping that this would bring help to him, or that publicity in the press might beget him such a grant-in-aid as Hart had received from Otto Kahn. I did, one day, talk over the telephone with an acquaintance on the city desk of a New York newspaper about the case of the young poet and philosopher who, burdened with wife and child, was reduced to tending a furnace. He promised to do something about this.

At the time, though I was ignorant of it, Allen had gradually changed his views. Formerly he had been as a Yankee among Yankees; he used to assure me that most of the so-called aristocratic families in the South were descended from British indentured servants or deported criminals convicted of having stolen a sheep or something of the sort. But lately he had come under the influence of that future royalist, T.S. Eliot; reading Spengler's *The Decline of the West* also tended to make him skeptical about contemporary America and its idea of "equality." Moreover, his wife, Caroline, was very proud of being a descendant of the Meriwethers. Allen also began to be interested in his own lineage, discovering with pleasure that he, too, was kin to some of the "old" families of the South, and he resolved to return to their cultural traditions. (I had then only the vaguest idea of what these traditions were, associating them with the ceremonious drinking of mint juleps by moonlight in a garden of camellias.) To be a good poet, Allen now believed, one must put down his roots in the ideas of his ancestors, even though they were medieval-minded. I heard of this change of front only a while later, and am simplifying his doctrines a good deal, for Allen is quite a subtle fellow.

But when I tipped off my friend at the newspaper I had no idea that Allen was now ashamed of his part-time occupation—though to any Yankee what he did was perfectly useful and honorable. Sinclair Lewis had also worked as a janitor, and Hemingway in early youth was a dishwasher and waiter.

When a newspaper reporter and photographer called to interview Allen as a likely subject for a Sunday feature article —under some headline such as "Poet-Janitor Composes Sonnets While Stoking Boiler"—Allen at first was extremely angry. But being a quick-thinking young man, he kept his wits about him and smoothly talked those newspapermen out of their idea of using him as the hero of a Sunday article. He was bitterly offended with me, when he learned of my role in the affair, and for a long time would not forgive what he regarded as a wicked and shocking intrusion on my part, though I was but trying to use my good offices in his behalf. Our mutual friends laughed a good deal over the incident which they regarded as a Dadaist prank; however, they judged that I had been thoughtless in not consulting Allen in advance, an oversight for which I realized afterward I deserved to be censured.

My days spent in Wall Street grew more and more tedious for me. Though I tried to match my wits against those of the animals with superior cunning—bears, bulls, or wolves—who prowled the financial regions, I managed only to survive. Sometimes I thought of myself as an "anarchist," preying on society in a small way while performing no useful service as far as I could tell. Of course, my "anarchism" was not related to any utopian cause, but was merely a rationalization of my circumstances, from which I derived neither pleasure nor pride. In reality I found many intelligent and enlightened people in Wall Street, even stockbrokers who read *The New Republic* every week. Most of them believed that they performed a vital function within our capitalist economy by maintaining an open market in the nation's corporate securities, which was true enough.

One of the more interesting features of my life in a board room was the news ticker that carried reports to us of everything happening in the world before most other people knew of these events. On one day in 1925 I read a foreign dispatch about the bombing of an American consulate at Buenos Aires as a protest at the impending execution in Boston of two real-life anarchists, Sacco and Vanzetti. I knew nothing of their case, for I scarcely ever thought of politics in those days.

On another morning the news ticker carried the story of the defeat of a lengthy strike by half-a-million coal miners, under President John L. Lewis of the United Mine Workers' Union, which had been fighting to unionize the big coal fields of the Southern states. The speculators in our board room, reading this news, gave a great shout of joy, and began to buy the leading railway and steel company stocks in great haste. The defeat of that strike was celebrated by a spectacular rise in the market. For a moment the thought passed through my mind that the people around me were cheering for the wrong side; I was not happy because the lot of the mine workers would be all the worse and the steel workers would go on toiling twelve hours a day. "What am *I* doing here in this galley?" I wondered.

My business flourished for a while in 1925, but the work was losing its savor for me; I became increasingly indifferent to profits and losses shown in the accounts I handled. There came a time when the crowd of marginal speculators were "loaded up," for the bull market of the Coolidge Era had been riding high. At such a moment, when many people hold stock in which they hope to take big profits, a deluge of selling often arrives and they end by taking losses instead. Fear spreads among this mob, and they create wave after wave of liquidation. Again I saw most of my clients trapped on the "long" side; it was too late for them to sell and their equities were dwindling fast. This was my second bear market; I was at the telephone hour after hour reporting the battle, desperately trying to save a few shreds of my customers' capital. My duties at this time kept me on the go late at night, calling on clients in different quarters of the city. On one of those nights I was caught in a drenching rain, and returned home greatly fatigued and suffering from a cold which developed into a painful earache, and then, as I learned afterward, an abscess. In the morning I was back at my telephones, when suddenly I felt the pain in my head become unbearable and at the same time could scarcely hear anything of what was being said to me. I had to turn my telephone over to a clerk so that he could take orders accurately. Many of my accounts were being foreclosed, that is, sold for whatever they could bring; I was supposed to go out and bring in new "suckers," but by now I cared no longer about what would happen in the market, for I realized that by continuing this work in a state of concealed mental depression I was letting my health run down.

On examination by an eminent physician and specialist it was found that, for the moment, I could not walk in a straight line, that I must have rest and treatment for several weeks and prepare for some drastic surgery. I arranged for a long leave from my office, so that others would handle my accounts, but made the resolve never to return to the Street. In the early autumn, while suffering great pain, I spent my days in a hammock in the garden at Katonah. Near me my infant son lay in his pram, laughing aloud as he often did, the wind blowing on his cheek and the rustling of fallen leaves keeping him continually amused. I thought to myself that I must somehow simplify my life and find again the secret of happiness that my child possessed.

After a few weeks I recovered sufficient strength to undertake some writing again. This, as well as visits to my doctor, required occasional journeys to the city by train. Returning to Katonah one evening, I found a telegram had come for me announcing that my father had been stricken by another heart attack. As we had no telephone then, a taxicab had brought the message after long delay. I started back to the city and went on to my parents' home in Brooklyn, reaching it too late to see my father alive.

My mother's turn came not long afterward. She had confided to me a year earlier that she had cancer, though she had decided not to tell my father about it at the moment because of his weakened condition. From time to time, while feeling very poorly myself, I had accompanied her in secret visits to doctors' offices and to hospitals. Now, only a few months after my father's death, she took to her bed and with much self-command waited for the end—which came in the spring of 1926—while I, who had been much away from her, was now often by her side; she talked with me calmly and with good sense about my future and of the duties I owed to the other children.

Not long after my mother's death I myself underwent a rather arduous operation, then awoke from my ether dreams with a marvelous sense of relief and that surge of hope which comes when the doctor's victim discovers that he is alive again. I heard that the market was now rising strongly; such news of good hunting usually stirs the blood of the confirmed addict. But nothing in the world could have been farther from my wishes than a return to the carrousel of Wall Street.

FIFTEEN

FRANCE

REVISITED

Once more, in April, 1927, we were pitching and rolling over blue water in an old ship that pointed its nose toward the coast of France. Four years had passed since my return from Paris; I felt, however, more than four years older.

The twelve months after the autumn of 1925 marked perhaps the most unhappy period of my life, my nadir. I had been turned into a sick man by the brutal business I carried on in Wall Street; only later did I realize how much I had struggled to conceal the depression I felt while working there. In that same year I had seen both my parents die, and I myself had nearly followed them. In the post-operational period one of the surgeons who had given me a working-over explained that for a time I had stood in serious danger of meningitis.

By the winter of 1927 I had won back all my strength and was cheerfully occupied with the planning and research for a book. A small inheritance left by my parents to each of their four heirs provided me with a modicum of security for the present, so that I was able to run the risk of low earnings by the writer's trade. Now, as I walked the deck of the S.S. *Suffren*, I felt not only stronger and happier but impatient to land and begin work on the book I would be writing during the next year in France.

The thought of returning to Paris gave me in anticipation a joy not unmixed with a sense of anxiety. I had been so utterly happy there in my youth that I feared to return to those same scenes, feared that the boundless pleasure I had known in the past, when very young, could never be refound; for I knew I had changed and I feared the friends I had loved must have changed no less.

That I was engaged in writing a book, under contract with a New York publisher, and provided with an advance against my future royalties to help me survive while writing it, was in itself an event that marked a new stage of the literary trade in America. The postwar economic boom had gone so far that by 1926 little wavelets of prosperity reached even to Grub Street. New publishing firms were opening their doors on Fourth and Madison Avenues and were bidding against each other for new authors.

Something amounting to a revolution in the public's taste seemed to occur after 1924 or 1925; undoubtedly this change of heart on the part of the reading public was owing in great measure to the courageous activities of men like Sinclair Lewis, Theodore Dreiser, Sherwood Anderson, Eugene O'Neill, and above all H.L. Mencken—carrying on his laughing-gas attacks on Prohibition, Piety, and Puritanism year after year. As a consequence, novels imbued with the spirit of realism and naturalism—to the average reader those treating the subject of sex with frankness—were now in high favor, as were also general books of a critical or even controversial spirit written by so-called De-bunkers. The morally and mentally genteel was done with; the new men, moreover, brought added prosperity to the booksellers. A popular sensation of the autumn of 1926 was young Ernest Hemingway's novel, *The Sun Also Rises,* whose heroine, Lady Brett, was both alcoholic and libertine.

Publishers now favored authors of "advanced" tendencies whom they had formerly neglected, and invited them to those lavish "literary teas" which became one of the features of social life in New York in the late twenties, where rivers of synthetic gin were dispensed in place of tea and cakes. Some of these boisterous parties in honor of the musical comedy actress, Peggy Hopkins Joyce, the author of a work of candid memoirs, or of a travel writer like Richard Halliburton—who appeared before his admirers in a hotel ballroom mounted on a white horse— were examples of pure American ballyhoo introduced into the bookselling field. It was at one of these so-called literary "teas" in the late autumn of 1926 that I encountered the heads of a new publishing firm, who cornered me and—'mid the sounds of revelry by night, and people guzzling bootleg gin or whisky, or shouting and dancing all about us—offered me a commission to write a literary biography.

The next morning I was closeted with Mr. Lee S. Furman, head of the newly organized Macaulay Company, who proved to be a very genial man of business with much experience of the publishing trade as a book salesman. We discussed various subjects, the most appealing of which turned out to be the life of Émile Zola, the French master of the naturalistic novel. No complete biography of Zola existed in English, and, though much had been written of him, there was no adequate life in French either. The subject was agreed upon; the publisher then offered to pay my passage to France and to advance me a small drawing account against future royalties that would add up to about a thousand dollars. I accepted his terms with alacrity, and soon hurried off to the French Line boat with my small family in tow.

Formerly, in my Dadaist years, the long humanitarian saga of *Les Rougon-Macquart* would not have been to my taste. But a good deal had been happening to me of late. My two years in Wall Street had taught me to think in terms of power and of the struggle for material power; as a result I had become more rather than less social-minded. I had also lost some of my illusions about the purists of literature, symbolists or neoclassicists, who believed with T.S. Eliot that the poet "should not be a thinker" but could remain indifferent to great public issues and seek only the perfection of literary form. I suspected that we would need to do a good deal of thinking through of our relations as human beings and artists with the real world, with the world of modern industry and power politics, with our swiftly changing society. Could it be that men with the cast of mind of Eliot and Pound were no longer concerned with the *truth,* the living truth? (Even Flaubert had said that it was, after all, the truth that he had sought all his life.) In their literary criticism they were turning "clerkly"; they were becoming obscurantists. The same reproach could be directed at my French friends, the Surrealists, whom I had recently assailed.

Zola, moreover, led me back to the great nineteenth century in French literature. A taste for historical research was awakened in me through my preliminary readings in his period. I had had no proper notion of the large stature Zola had achieved by his immense literary labors, and was to discover that in the later phase of his life he had crowned his long career by his heroic action in the cause of the unjustly condemned Jewish officer, Alfred Dreyfus. Zola had believed fervently in the idea of liberty and justice and risked everything to make known to the world the truth about the Dreyfus Affair. The image of the writer turned public man appealed to me powerfully in Zola, as it did also in the figures of Rousseau and Hugo of whom I wrote later.

The American invasion was seemingly at its flood tide when we arrived in Paris again in the spring of 1927; our ship alone had brought 531 American tourists in cabin class. The most eminent of these was undoubtedly a husky-voiced torch singer named Helen Morgan, then a large-bodied, vivacious girl of twenty, who was accompanied by an expert jazz band from Chicago. The importation of a big American jazz troupe from the Middle West, which was scheduled to play that summer in the night clubs of Paris, was a foretaste of the changes I would witness.

There were certain quarters of Paris that summer where one

heard nothing but English, spoken with an American accent. The whole city was refurbished; the old dim-lit cafés in Montparnasse were now brilliantly illuminated, and their old black-hatted poets were gone. In their place an army of American café-goers held forth, counting its writers, artists, dilletantes, and camp followers by the hundreds or thousands, where there had been only dozens before. New establishments had been built to receive these hordes of pleasure-and-culture seekers, such as the neon-lighted Coupole on the Boulevard Montparnasse, a brewery hall that could house a regiment of people.

Ernest Hemingway's novel of the previous season, *The Sun Also Rises*, with its informal Baedeker of the Montparnasse cafés, gave clear reflections of the changes that had come over Paris recently. The barmen in the places his hero visits are shown to be mixing powerful cocktails, dry martinis, such as one never saw there in 1921 or 1922. The personages in the novel are also described as going to lunch at quaint old restaurants in the Ile de la Cité, where one is obliged to wait forty-five minutes in order to have a table. In earlier days there were no such crowds and no waiting at the excellent small restaurants we frequented. Had all the Americans I now saw in Paris come here under the inspiration of Hemingway's bibulous "exiles"? I wondered. My ever-thirsty friend, Hart Crane, said that merely reading about all the drinks consumed by the characters in *The Sun Also Rises* gave him "an attack of acidosis."

Soon we were meeting and dining out with old American cronies. Laurence and Peggy Vail still ruled as informal social leaders of the "American quarter." We had seen something of them the year before, when they came to New York with their two children to visit Peggy's mother. In those days Peggy was very much the young matron, somewhat shy in manner and plain in appearance, but beautifully dressed. Though not yet a patron of the arts, she had begun to use part of her large income to help certain writers such as Mina Loy, who was given a little capital with which to open a shop in Paris where she sold lampshades of her own manufacture. Peggy used to declare, frankly enough, that she considered her inheritance an accident and felt strong sympathies for the Socialists. In 1926, for example, she donated ten thousand dollars to the relief fund for the British General Strike. Her husband disapproved of Peggy's Socialist tendencies, holding that all political movements, and especially those of the Left, were "*so* boring." But Laurence never interfered with her benefactions, because he allowed no restraints upon his own freedom of action.

The Vails now lived most of the time in fairly quiet fashion in a Mediterranean villa near Hyères. But when they came up to Paris, Laurence would begin drinking heavily and would soon be up to his old tricks. A few weeks before we arrived in Paris Laurence had got himself into a scrape with the police. He had been dining in a restaurant one evening with Peggy, his sister Clotilde, and two friends, when he became greatly agitated over something that was said and began hurling bottles of wine toward the mirrors on the wall. A group of four French Army officers sitting at a nearby table took strong exception to Laurence's sport, one of them having been grazed by a flying bottle. They called the police and Laurence was seized, beaten while resisting arrest, handcuffed, and dragged off to jail. Only after Laurence's devoted sister Clotilde made the most impassioned pleas to one of the offended officers and induced him to withdraw his complaint was poor Laurence released on the following morning. The officer, Captain Alain Lemerdy, meanwhile, declared that he had fallen in love with Clotilde and asked her hand in marriage. All this went to explain the presence of a large, ramrod-backed French Army officer, a typical product of St. Cyr and a Royalist as well, in constant attendance on the charming Clotilde, whenever we dined with the Vails. The Captain did his best to accommodate himself to the Bohemian spirit ruling this circle, though it was not easy; but he was a persistent man and eventually, after several years, persuaded Clotilde to marry him.

My old comrade in arms, Harold Loeb, had also stayed on in Paris. He had renounced marriage with Lily and now usually appeared with a younger person, a handsome Dutch girl named Suzanne, whom in good time he married and later divorced. During lunch with us the pair had some trivial disagreement, and Suzanne, by misdirection, kicked my leg under the table. I swore under my breath and said to myself: "But this is where I came in before!"

Earlier, during a visit to New York, Harold had told me a good deal about his friend Ernest Hemingway and his group of Serious Drinkers. Hemingway, according to Harold, was refreshingly different from the rather nervous or effeminate sort of American writer one usually met in Europe, being a red-blooded, Teddy Roosevelt type who enjoyed hunting, fishing, tennis, bullfighting, and poker. In an expansive moment Hemingway said to one of his acquaintances at that period that for him the "three most exciting things in life were flying, skiing, and sexual intercourse."[1]

After *The Sun Also Rises* came out, Harold said no more about Hemingway. Their friendship was ruptured. It seemed that in composing his story of the so-called "Lost Generation" the young novelist had painted his circle of friends in Paris from life, or one might say he had reproduced them in sharp-focus photograph. In exposition of his method he remarked, in 1926: "I was just knocking around with the bunch and I tried to put it down. If you're a . . . good writer, you write about things you know."[2]

After the publication of *The Sun Also Rises* there were at least six of its characters who recognized themselves in its pages and set off in search of the author in order to settle accounts with him, according to the reminiscences of James Charters, a retired English pugilist who was Hemingway's favorite barman in Paris.

At any rate, it seems highly coincidental that the protagonist of the novel, Robert Cohn, is represented as having a "flattened nose," wearing spectacles, and being the scion of a wealthy Jewish family in New York who has been recently divorced, and

has occupied himself in publishing an avant-garde literary review. The novelist did not even take the precaution to change
the name of his friend's college, which was Princeton. Moreover,
those of us who knew Harold's former fiancée, Lily, found quite
remarkable resemblances between her and the sharply satirized
personage of Frances Clyne; she is pictured as a "forceful
woman" of complaining habits, who is also much given to
kicking Robert Cohn under the table.

The protagonist Cohn, however, is represented as one who
can let fly with his fists in vigorous style, and thus makes his
way, despite numerous rivals, to the bed of the lovely, but ever
alcoholized, Lady Brett Ashley. In Ernest Hemingway's ontology,
fornication is ranked together with bullfighting, boxing, and
elephant hunting as one of the competitive sports in which the
palm goes to the man of courage; thus we may assume that the
novelist intended to represent Robert Cohn as one who acquits
himself with honor. Whereas the pathetic hero, Jake Barnes,
who serves as the author's narrator, is portrayed—o rara avis—
as an impotent man, having become thus cruelly afflicted as a
result of wounds suffered in the late war. What a singular hero
to have chosen! In explanation it has been pointed out that
Hemingway was very much involved with his first wife, Hadley,
at the time when the actual prototype of Lady Brett appeared in
the pubs of Montparnasse, fascinating the Bohemian characters
she met and setting off jealous conflicts among them.

That there may have been a living model for the American-
Jewish Don Juan in *The Sun Also Rises* was a thought that occurred to many persons in Paris and New York who knew
Harold and to whom the secrets of this *roman à clef* were transparent. (A picture of Loeb mounted on a wild bull in the ring
at Pamplona, Spain, in 1925, at the time he was there with
Hemingway's party, happened to appear in the rotogravure section of the New York *Times*.) Harold had not previously appealed to his friends as being typically a Lovelace or a Don
Giovanni. But still, the whisperings about the dramatis personae
of Hemingway's novel wrought no harm for Harold, who was

free and unattached. Often, persons who have been publicly
caricatured, in a way that proves unexpectedly flattering rather
than injurious, try to act in real life as they have been represented in fiction. With the popular fame of Hemingway's novel,
Harold also gained a sort of *succès de scandale*. At the time he
chose to make no complaint, but curiously enough waited about
thirty years and only then published a memoir giving his own
account of the relations between himself, Hemingway, "Lady
Brett," and the other models of Hemingway's personages, and
of their expedition to the bullfighting fiesta at Pamplona, an account honest enough—though less entertaining than Hemingway's romance.

We soon met up with Lily herself, who spoke ruefully of
having been, unwittingly, a sitter for one of the ironic portraits
in *The Sun Also Rises*. She was then attached to a young French-
man who happened to be about six foot three inches in height,
and told us that she sometimes toyed with the idea of sending
her new fiancé around to interview Mr. Hemingway. He, however, was not in Paris at the time.

I tried to commiserate with her, remarking: "Hemingway
may be a most gifted writer, but it hardly seems safe to be a
friend of his, since he might take it into his head any day to
put you down in one of his books."

In truth, when I met Ernest Hemingway some years later,
during a winter I spent at Key West, Florida, he appeared
—at least in private life—a delightful companion and a hospitable neighbor. He was both high-spirited and self-centered,
undereducated and yet widely read in his field, and had an
entertaining way of telling stories as well as writing them. Nor
was he Gargantuan in his drinking habits, as one might infer,
but rose at six in the morning to begin work. Neither was he
preëminently the womanizing type, though he had his follies. In
the winter of 1937, as he prepared to leave his second wife—
while setting off for the wars in Spain with the prospective third
—he said to me with an air that was only half-jesting: "The
trouble is I'm a fool for women; I always have to marry 'em."

To revert to the Paris of 1927, it was borne in upon me how accurately Hemingway had drawn his friends and acquaintances in his first novel when, one afternoon, I happened to walk into the whole circle of them in the flesh; meeting them gave me the uncanny feeling of having dropped right into the pages of *The Sun Also Rises.*

I had paused for a moment at the bar of the Dôme for an apéritif, and stood beside a tall slender woman who was also having something and who engaged me in conversation, at once informal and reserved. She had a rather long face, auburn hair, and wore an old green felt hat that came down over her eyes; moreover, she was dressed in tweeds and talked with an English accent. We were soon joined by a handsome but tired-looking Englishman whom she called "Mike," evidently her companion. They drank steadily, chatted with me, and then asked me to go along with them to Jimmy's Bar near the Place de l'Odéon, a place that had aquired some fame during my absence from France. In a relaxed way we carried on a light conversation, having three or four drinks and feeling ourselves all the more charming for that. Then Laurence Vail came into the bar and hailed the lady as "Duff." At this, I began to recall having heard about certain people in Paris who were supposed to be the models of Hemingway's "lost ones"; the very accent of their speech, the way they downed a drink ("Drink-up-cheerio"), and the bantering manner with its undertone of depression; it was all there.

Suddenly Harold Loeb himself strode in vigorously, saw Duff, and stook stock-still; he had evidently heard she was in town and gone looking for her. He sat down at our table and said little, but looked his feelings much as Robert Cohn was described as doing. Duff's English friend then made little signs of irritation at Harold's presence (quite as in the novel). Laurence Vail ventured the remark: "Well now, all we need is to have Ernest drop in to make it a quorum." Duff laughed that one off bravely, and took another drink. But Ernest did not come. The talk ran down and the gathering broke up; I had an appointment for dinner with Laurence and went along with him.

That was a spooky sort of cocktail hour, as I look back at it. The characters were all familiar to me because I had recently read the novel; they seemed real enough and definitely were not ghosts. But I wondered whether I was real, or was merely acting a part in a play or caught between the pages of a book. Lady Duff Twysden had a certain charm and had been, no doubt, very lovely once, though she now seemed somewhat worn or run-down. Nothing apparently could stop her drinking. Many years later I happened to meet her again, at the beginning of World War II when she wandered out to my corner of northern Connecticut and stayed with friends of mine. I came there one morning to drive one of them to the train, and Duff sat drinking coffee and gin in quantities, looking more haggard than ever. Not long after that I heard she was dead.

By 1927 there was a noticeable increase of activity on the part of the American literary tourists in Paris, not to mention the artists and musicians. Young men or women from Grand Rapids or Cincinnati or Brooklyn sat in damp little hotel rooms writing their novels with a distracted air. Where there had been one or two literary reviews published in Paris, there were now three or four. The *transatlantic review,* edited by the seasoned English novelist and literary critic, Ford Madox Ford, appeared in 1924 after *Broom* expired. Hemingway, like many others, was seized with the fever for little magazines, and actively assisted Ford for awhile, though publication of the magazine was suspended in 1925. *This Quarter,* another excellent review, edited by Ernest Walsh and Ethel Moorhead, dedicated itself to the religion of literature, and acknowledged Ezra Pound as its patron saint—but soon the editors angrily disavowed Mr. Pound. One of the writers it published, together with Joyce, Hemingway, and "Bryher," was the young Kay Boyle, who had left the office of *Broom* and New York to live in France in 1923. Kay Boyle's early novel, *Year Before Last*

(1931), gives us an interesting portrait of a brilliant young amateur of letters, said to have been inspired by the short-lived Ernest Walsh.

The most important of the new American reviews being issued in Paris was *transition*, whose first number appeared in April, 1927, just as I arrived. With its 150 pages of small type it appeared almost encyclopedic, and gave representation to every tendency in the literary spectrum of modern Europe, America, and the antipodes. So inclusive was it that one often came upon unexpectedly good things in it: translations from Franz Kafka or from the Russian of Vladimir Mayakovski and stories by an unknown American from the South named William Faulkner appeared together with the Dadaist detonations of Tzara and the classical-symbolist verses of St.-John Perse. Moreover, *transition* also made a specialty of printing selections from Joyce's *Finnegans Wake* and a whole medley of Gertrude Stein's works.

I soon met the editors, Eugene Jolas and Elliot Paul, who showed much interest in my own earlier experience with little magazines. Jolas, about thirty-three, born in New Jersey of a French father and German mother, had been taken back to his parents' native Lorraine where he spent his boyhood before immigrating again to the United States at sixteen. It was not surprising, therefore, that he wrote poetry in three languages: German, French, and English. If he was trilingual, it was also apparent that he knew English less well than his other languages; yet he was hell-bent on revolutionizing the English language and literature, as well as the French and German. Inspired by Joyce's later hermetic writings, Jolas concocted some rather ill-digested theories about the "mysticism of language" and the "revolution of the word." Like the Surrealists, with whom he also sympathized, Jolas was going to transcribe dreams into a new poetry. But by now such esoteric doctrine wearied and irritated me; I was up in arms against the Surrealists and found myself opposing Jolas with what I held were the counsels of good sense, though our discussions were always carried on

amiably over steins of dark beer at Lipp's Café, Jolas being a
very lovable man.

For him Joyce's *Work in Progress* (as *Finnegans Wake* was
first titled) represented the highest peak of literary art, whereas
I had my doubts about the value of Joyce's experiments in ren-
dering the myth of the Irish race-mind in his private Jabber-
wocky.

"It seems to me that through excess of self-love or the *délire
de grandeur*," I told Jolas one day, "Joyce, a veritable lord of
language, is writing his saga in an Esperanto of his own device
that will provide much labor for the critics and lexicographers
who try to decipher it." In other words, Joyce was making himself "hard to get" and becoming boring in the process, though
there were brilliant details. My predictions have beeen borne
out by the appearance of a battalion of scholars who have composed elaborate glosses for the dreams of Joyce's Everyman of
Dublin. (Joyce himself once promised that he would keep the
critics busy for "three hundred years.")

The salon of the Jolases, however, toward 1927 and 1928,
became a chapel for the idolaters of James Joyce; several American women, including Eugene Jolas' wife, donated a good deal
of money to support the great man and his family when he was
growing blind. My words, therefore, were sacrilege. I remember
that during a heated discussion one evening, Elliot Paul, an
eccentric and bearded Bostonian, became so excited that he
tried to gulp down a whole bottle of cognac and fell into a
dead faint.

Nevertheless, Jolas was so tolerant, or so catholic in spirit,
that he allowed me to write whatever I wished in his magazine
in opposition to the Joyceans and the Surrealists; to my surprise he also appointed me a contributing editor of *transition*,
and charged me with gathering American material for his
review after my return home.

transition, which achieved a circulation of four thousand
copies, also did much to arouse interest in Gertrude Stein, who
appeared to be even more mystifying than Joyce. Her old

things were being reprinted, and readers in America now were hotly engaged in debate over whether she was a genius or a fraud. Meanwhile, in the late spring of 1927, a great tea party in Miss Stein's honor was given by Nathalie Clifford Barney, an heiress from Cincinnati and an old resident of Paris, who belonged to the generation of "exiles" preceding my own. This party really marked the coming out of Miss Stein, formerly somewhat retiring.

Miss Barney's mansion in the rue Jacob was one of the most beautiful in the old St. Germain quarter; behind its austere seventeenth-century façade were spacious rooms and salons where she had entertained many distinguished French writers who were her friends. In late middle age she was still the beautiful blonde Amazon to whom Rémy de Gourmont had long years ago addressed his *Lettres à l'amazone*. The tall rear windows of the house looked out on a large walled garden, with ornate flower beds arranged around a petrified oak log and a sort of gazebo of glass—actually a little colonnaded "Temple of Venus."

The ceremonies took place in the garden, where some two hundred guests from every walk of life were gathered. As the principal speaker of the day, Ford Madox Ford, a man of considerable girth, stationed himself in the "temple" and read a paper entitled: "Homage to Gertrude Stein." Afterward, in one of the salons, Virgil Thomson (my old acquaintance of Tirolian days in 1922) sang and played at the piano a number of his compositions that provided a musical setting for some of Miss Stein's prose pieces. The crush of Americans was so great that most of Miss Barney's aged French writers, among them Paul Valéry and Léon-Paul Fargue, soon beat a retreat.

Miss Stein, a solid block of a woman, was there in the midst of the crowd, talking with many of us, taking everything in with her characteristic aplomb. She was elegantly dressed, after her fashion, in a simple gray costume; her finely shaped, masculine head with its short-cropped, grizzled hair and expressive blue eyes gave her the appearance of an old Roman senator. We

talked about Thomson's music, which was very humorous; Miss
Stein allowed that it was decidedly spiritual, and described, with
amusing touches, her collaboration with the composer. She
was very well-spoken, carried herself with poise, and her keen
eyes now regarded her interlocutor closely or now roved about
the room. A formidable woman, in short, and with quite an ego.

For nigh on twenty years she had fought to publish her work,
printing most of it herself, and all but resigned to live in the
shade. The quotation of her chance remark about the "lost
generation" as an epigraph for Hemingway's recent novel had
caused widespread discussion of Miss Stein. By now she was
on the offensive and was telling the tourists from America who
came to her house in the rue de Fleurus that there had been
only one American writer of genius before her: Henry James.
To those who complained that her prose was obscure, she was
reported to have said that it was obscure only to the lazy-
minded. "My prose is a well, a deep well, well it is like a well,
and that is well." There were many such stories told about her.
But how, then, could a good writer or artist function without
egotism, without the burning conviction that he alone, and not
somebody else, could "save the world" by means of his books
or pictures?

I have often thought since then of the observation of John
Peale Bishop that Gertrude Stein was probably "a great artist
without a subject." Since her early work, *Three Lives*, she had
avoided using directly the materials of her own rather singular
life experience, and written an ingenious prose, "Cubist" or
repetitive, but calculated to conceal rather than to communicate
her ideas. (The ideas were there, but you had to dig for them.)
Not until she wrote *The Autobiography of Alice B. Toklas* did
she speak her mind freely; and that very ironic memoir is filled
with misstatements, some of them expressed with a malice
that caused outcries of rage among her friends in Paris.

Miss Barney entertained her guests not only with excellent
food and tea, but also with liberal quantities of champagne. The
Americans relaxed more and more; the sound of jazz music

filled the stately house in the rue Jacob. As I left, my last glimpse was of a small salon where some young women, transported by literature and champagne, danced madly about in each other's arms.

One of my objects in returning to France had been to renew my friendships with the young writers who had been my comrades in 1921–1923. Whatever others might say of the French "national character" those gifted young men possessed the art of friendship in the highest degree; life with them had been enormously stimulating and would surely be so again. What was my disappointment to learn, almost immediately after my arrival, that the ban pronounced upon me by André Breton was final and absolute. No one in the *Bund* was permitted to see me or talk with me; I was to be given no opportunity to present my own side of the case. In the street I passed one of the group whom I had once helped with a little money; he stared at me in sudden recognition, then made a grim face and hurried on. Louis Aragon and I had been as brothers (the word was his). I wrote to him immediately upon my arrival; no reply came from him.

As I was extremely curious to learn what my old friends had been up to, I took my life in my hands and went in search of these violent young men at the Galérie Surréaliste, recently opened in the rue Jacques Callot in that labyrinth of narrow old streets by the left bank of the Seine, near the École des Beaux Arts. With the help of his wife, Breton had become a dealer in pictures; in his writings he sang the praises of the Surrealist painters—Chirico, Ernst, Arp, Miró, and Masson—and he also sold their pictures at a profit, or at any rate to earn his living. As I entered, Breton was busy hanging some pictures; he saw me come in, scowled, and turned his back. Benjamin Péret, that humorous brute, glowered at me as if he would have liked to throw himself upon me. I looked about at my leisure, then left the place, somewhat diverted by the incident. I learned after-

ward that Breton had remarked: "There's Josephson, who thinks
we are going to take him back to our bosom after all that he
wrote against us!"

The outlook for enjoyment of the literary life in Paris seemed
very poor. Was I to be cut off forever from my most entertaining
friends? However, it soon appeared that André Breton's intolerant and autocratic spirit helped to arrange things just as I would
have wished, making his auto-da-fés harmless. He squabbled
fiercely with one after another of the men who had formed the
original Surrealist sect, until a majority were excommunicated
by his decree. And so I soon saw most of them, and we all
enjoyed life again as men adjudged and damned by Monsieur B.

Philippe Soupault, one of the closest of my friends, had been
out of town when I arrived, but soon hastened to greet me and
take me off to his new home and new wife in the nearby suburb
of Neuilly.

Philippe had been the very soul of mischief and deviltry in
the time of the Dadaists. But after trying to go along with Surrealism he had found it impossible to endure the oppressive
moral discipline of this new church. He said that the magic of
the great days of 1919–1922 was gone, and with it the old team
spirit. It was like playing cards every day at the same hour
with the same players in the same café on the central square
of some provincial town. Soupault worked as an editor and
book publisher for part of his day; in the morning he wrote
novels and biographies. More rarely nowadays did he write
poems, though he read us a recent love poem entitled "Georgia"
that seemed to me one of the greatest things of its kind, consisting in the repeated utterance of the name Georgia in different connotations, accompanied by different metaphors, which
gave the effect of a constantly rising stress of passion.

At all events, Soupault had been formally "expelled" from
the Surrealist cenacle (for the second time!) about six months
earlier, on charges of "venality" and "corruption"—*id est*,
earning his living by writing and editing. He had been divorced
from his first wife and had married a tall young Frenchwoman

of a rich bourgeois family, who was also very cultivated. Marie-Louise Soupault had a personality of great charm and warmth, and was our good friend.

The roster of those who had been condemned and excommunicated, with or without trial, was impressive: besides Soupault, there were Roger Vitrac, Jacques Baron, Robert Desnos, Antonin Artaud, Raymond Queneau, Jacques Prévert, Joseph Delteil, Pierre de Massot, and the painter André Masson. Of the old group, Louis Aragon remained virtually alone at Breton's side as his faithful vassal, which was why he had not communicated with me. Paul Éluard for various reasons remained apart from the Surrealist group; while Tristan Tzara had never really joined it. In short, I found myself in excellent company, and Paris became as amusing as ever.

In the last years of World War I and soon after its end the Dadaists had tried to laugh at a world they never wanted and whose insanity they brilliantly mimicked. But Breton, thereafter, had chosen to turn away from the real world and create one that was "super-real," composed of the occult visions, the hallucinations, and the automatic or unconscious expressions of artists and poets. Moreover, he desired that his group of adepts and subversives should serve as a "communal" movement, standing apart from the bourgeois herd, sometimes waging a sort of guerrilla warfare against society, yet also, somehow, functioning, surviving within its bosom.

"It was not easy," he himself confessed afterward, "to find people who would hold to the requisite standards and make the sacrifices needed for such a common cause."[3] And so it was said that he often "changed his friends as one changes a pair of shoes." For in order to lead such a "collective intellectual action" as theirs was, Breton held that he must take the hard course of "subordinating consideration of human sympathy" and executing "even those who had been his companions along the road, even those in whom he had placed the highest confidence."

André Breton's almost tyrannical sway over his followers

and his mania for punishing their "heresies" aroused wondering comment in the press, where he was described as

Surely one of the most seductive figures of the generation about to reach the age of thirty. . . . He has the bearing of an Inquisitor; how tragic and slow is his regard and even his gestures. And he is a magus too. Perhaps a little in the manner of Epinal; and he wields over his faithful flock the magnetic authority of an Oscar Wilde. . . .[4]

Such were the rumors that circulated about the man. Yet André Breton resembled Oscar Wilde only in the physical appearance of the lower part of his face. His nonconformist principles made him tolerant of one or two homosexuals in his entourage (which was always reinforced by new men) and also of two or three avowed drug addicts, but the chief of the band was innocent of the sort of evil-doing sometimes charged to him slanderously by such persons as M. Paul Claudel, the Catholic poet who was France's Ambassador to the United States.

In this close circle clashes of personality occurred frequently enough; these people sometimes ate each other up. Their efforts to keep themselves pure in their Surrealist faith, in a world of unbelievers, made their whole situation paradoxical. For example, Breton extolled certain painters as the truly elect among modern artists, but at the same time he made money by selling their canvases to snobs who could afford to buy them. The writings of Breton and Aragon were often published in limited editions as *objets de luxe;* thus they were constrained to living off the very same snobs whom they always affected to despise. By shocking or frightening people they aroused interest in themselves; as Aragon admitted, the literary public regarded them as "wild beasts in a cage"—interesting because they *looked* dangerous, but harmless so long as they stayed in their cage. How would they get out of their cage? That was the question.

A typical outburst of discord had arisen among them in May, 1926. The Ballet Russe, directed by Sergei Diaghilev, had engaged Pablo Picasso to design their stage sets not long before—

a commission he executed with éclat. The next season Picasso recommended that Diaghilev employ the new Surrealist artists Max Ernst and Joan Miró to design the ballet's stage sets, and they were given the commission, which involved a generous payment. Ernst and Miró were then far from rich. On learning of this, Breton flew into a great passion, denouncing Miró and particularly his beloved Max Ernst for betraying the principles of Surrealist art to a "commercial enterprise."

At the opening night of this highly fashionable ballet the Surrealists, under the command of Breton and Aragon, staged a rousing protest that began just as the curtain rose to show Max Ernst's stage set. In a box near the stage Aragon stood up, lifted his thin Roman nose in the air, and yelled invectives at the public; Breton, Desnos, and the others likewise blew whistles and used noise-making machines to drown the overture, and fought the police who came to eject them. The protest was aimed not at the music nor at the corps de ballet, but chiefly at Max Ernst.

Ever since Ernst had first come to live in Paris, Breton had "built him up" as the Surrealist painter par excellence. But by 1926, when he was awarded the commission for the Ballet Russe stage sets, Max had come into a measure of prosperity and begun to receive a little recognition in the big art market of Paris. In other words, Breton's protégé—if one could conceive of the independent-minded Max being that—could now walk by himself.

My wife and I met Max Ernst again at a café, and he cordially invited us to dine with him at his home. Remembering how desperately poor he had been in 1922, I was agreeably surprised to see him established in a magnificent studio high up on Montmartre overlooking all Paris. With him was his young wife, Marie-Berthe, whom he had recently married; she was a most beautiful child of eighteen—less than half his age—looking like a starlet of the cinema.

Their marriage made quite a romance. Max had met Marie-Berthe in 1925; they had fallen in love, but the girl's wealthy and pious family absolutely opposed their marriage. There was Max's age, his previous divorce, his being a German and an artist—and a penniless and scandalous one at that. Marie-Berthe, however, eloped with him; as she was a minor, Max was charged with abduction. The case was somewhat similar to that of Jacques Baron, whose friends had kept him in hiding from his family; the Surrealists now did the same with Max and Marie-Berthe.

For several days detectives hunted them throughout France; pictures of the couple were published in the papers. But instead of leaving Paris, the two lovers had remained within the city, living virtually day and night in taxis, cruising about from one quarter to another, never stopping long, but managing to meet with their friends at secret rendezvous that were changed each time. In this way they were able to keep in touch with their lawyers, who were negotiating with the irate father, and also to obtain funds for their non-stop taxi fare.

At one of the secret halting places where they alighted to meet Breton *et al*, the father, accompanied by a detective, suddenly appeared—for he had been hot on the trail—and cried: "Arrest that man, the abductor, Max Ernst!" As police gathered to surround the taxi, Breton suddenly came forward and declared: "You are mistaken—I am Max Ernst." Several of his friends came up to testify that what he said was correct, blocking the movement of the policemen and creating a momentary confusion, during which Max and Marie-Berthe managed to escape again. After a few days of the chase the father was conciliated, and the pair were permitted to be married.

As to the imbroglio over his commission for the Diaghilev ballet, Max Ernst had refused to be disconcerted by the attacks his friends had made upon him—unjust as they were—for none of them had ever dared to reproach Picasso and others for earning a living by their art. Ernst and André Breton had composed their quarrel and renewed their collaboration. But Max felt a strong distaste for the "communal" spirit of the Surrealist group, which he found confining and irksome. He now gave Breton to understand that he would remain of the Surrealist camp, but not in it. When it pleased him to do so he paid no attention to Breton's terrible edicts against men and things; nevertheless, Breton continued to show Ernst's pictures in his gallery. It was Breton who was forced to compromise, for Ernst was now in the stronger position, yet remained magnanimous. Long afterward, in 1941, when both men were driven to seek refuge in the United States during World War II, it was Ernst who was in the fortunate position to help André Breton survive in this country, and he did so generously.

On the occasion when we visited Max Ernst, he had in his studio his big oil painting, "The Virgin Mary Spanking the Infant Jesus before Three Witnesses," which had made a sensation when shown at the Salon des Indépendants the year before. The Virgin is shown in the foreground, seated on a stool with the Infant in her lap and her hand raised to strike. At a small high window in the background the faces of André Breton, Paul Éluard, and Max himself are shown, staring at the scene with beady eyes. The subject of the painting is said to have been proposed by Breton and is the only instance of Ernst's having represented anything but his own fantasies.

We who had been excommunicated from the Surrealist camp formed a large rump, perhaps a majority, of its original contingent. As the wild actions of Breton and his flock continued to afford me amusement, I gathered from the banished ones, as also from the current surrealist publications, the record of their recent doings. It seemed that after having given up their experiments in spiritism and dreams, they had established a Bureau Central de Recherches Surréalistes in a ground floor apartment at 15 rue de Grenelle in the center of the city, where all sorts of strangers and crackpots were invited to come in and make depositions or confessions of strange behavior, or their dreams or even crimes they had committed. These were solemnly written down, studied, and classified, some of them being published in the official journal of the group, *La Révolution Surréaliste,* which was printed in the sober format of a scientific review. Some of the Bureau's material was released to the Paris daily press.

The person put in charge of this work, however, was the young poet and actor Antonin Artaud, who, as Breton noticed, was often subject to "paroxysms" which were no doubt manic-depressive. In *La Révolution Surréaliste,* Artaud published an open letter, in terms of execration, to the Pope of Rome; he addressed another open letter to the Dalai Lama of Tibet declaring that he, Artaud, and others who signed the letter, had found that their Surrealist faith had many points of correspondence with the spiritual cult of the Tibetan Buddhists. Finally, another open letter was addressed by Artaud to the superintendents of asylums for the mentally ill all over Europe, urging them to open their doors and set free their inmates who were so unjustly detained. (Several years later Artaud himself was confined in a public institution for the insane.) At this point, Breton stepped in and fired poor Artaud, then closed down the Bureau of Surrealist Research.

My own recollection of poor Artaud, who was a professional actor as well as a theater director, is of a thin young man with glittering eyes, carrying on wild talk with such brilliance of language as no ordinary lunatic could have equaled. He also kept breaking up the dishes at our dinner table or, in his paranoid way, threatening to stab me with a fork—though he did not know who I was—until he was led away by his friends; at the moment he appeared to be either under the influence of opium or badly in need of it to calm him down.

One of the exploits of the short-lived Bureau of Surrealist Research was its discovery of a defrocked priest, the Abbé Gengenbach, who had recently been expelled from the Society of Jesus for having an affair with an actress. He turned up one day to testify that he had renounced his religion and was ready to embrace the doctrines of the Surrealist faith. Furthermore he offered to reveal and publish in their journal all that he knew about the alleged conspiracies of the Jesuits and the Catholic

Church against the people of France. The odd man also created amusement when he appeared, always in a worn black cassock, at the café terraces of Montparnasse, where he sat tippling with little demimondaines in his lap. For a while the Surrealists made loud boasts about their convert. But nothing came of the ex-Jesuit's revelations; he soon quarreled with his new associates; the fear of God also returned to him and he recanted his charges against the Church, while denouncing Breton and company as "the sons of Anti-Christ."

The recent activities of the Surrealists also included questionnaires on a variety of subjects answered by their membership and recorded in their official journal. Certain aspects of the sex problem, for example, are covered in verbatim reports of two conferences held in January, 1928; the questions put to the Surrealists by themselves touch upon "the awareness of giving pleasure to the woman during the act of love," upon their preferences as to "sexual positions," and upon the matter of "physical impotence manifesting itself during sexual intercourse." With regard to the phenomenon of impotence, Breton's authoritative pronouncement was: "That can only happen with a woman one loves."

Other questions and answers ran:

Q: What is the role of speech in the act of love?
A: More and more important nowadays . . .
Q: What do you think of houses of prostitution?
A: So-so. Not very good, but always there!
A: They could be improved and perhaps give better service.
A: [By Breton] I dream of closing them all up. Why? Because they remind me of hospitals and prisons. Do you like to sleep with a woman who must be paid?
A: Not at all; wouldn't think of it.
A: I never tried it. But I've had them pay *me*.
Q: How necessary to you is erection in the accomplishment of the sexual act?
A: A certain degree is necessary, but as far as I am concerned, I have had only incomplete erections.

Q: Do you consider that a matter of regret?

A: In so far as any physical debility is to be regretted, yes, but no more than that. I do not regret it any more than the fact that I cannot lift a piano with my fingers.[5]

Although they may have been somewhat diverting, these conferences could scarcely lay claim to having made any scientific approach to the subjects they treated. I had a strong feeling that the Surrealists were becoming mired down. Even the "savage objects" exhibited at their gallery, such as Duchamp's "ready-mades" or Man Ray's "snowballs," signed by him and offered in a limited edition, no longer seemed novel.

At this stage of things, toward 1927, the Surrealists, by their manifold experiments—in the words of Aragon—believed they were groping toward "a new Declaration of the Rights of Man." (In later years, after his own views had changed decidedly, he summed up their whole movement as a "continuation of Romanticism.")

About a year earlier their chieftain himself had indicated that the great "moral revolution" the Surrealists advocated and tried to exemplify by their own behavior might not be effectual unless the conditions of society itself were changed. At the time the colonial warfare raging in Morocco was a lively political issue before the country; a goodly number of intellectuals were joining the group led by the famous pacifist writer, Henri Barbusse, and the Communist Party in their agitation against the war. Breton, though formerly indifferent to political action, now issued a new manifesto calling upon the Surrealists to make common cause with the parties of the Left. In other words, they would no longer limit themselves to transforming men's minds but would carry their movement onto the social plane and, in alliance with the proletarians, endeavor to "change the world." Breton admitted that he had "little talent for economics" and knew even less of Marx or Lenin's teachings at the time. Aragon had recently called the Bolshevist Revolution in Russia a "mere ministerial crisis." But they were willing to learn; and so Breton and his confreres made approaches to the Communist Party of France.

The Communist intellectuals, then associated with the weekly journal *Clarté*, were quite ready to welcome this distinguished group into their midst. But the high Party officials insisted upon examining them thoroughly before accepting them as recruits. When they came to read the Surrealist publications and noted their views on sexual liberty and sadism and the illustrations by such "madmen" as Picasso and Max Ernst, those sober-sided Communist officials were deeply shocked. The stern Michel Marty is said to have asked André Breton the most humiliating questions. "What do all these things *mean?*" he kept reiterating. Were not the Surrealists really counterrevolutionaries?

Breton, undergoing a severe catechism, insisted that while he wished to coöperate with them, he could not accept Communist Party discipline; his group must preserve its autonomy in any joint actions, and their "experiments in inward life" must be continued without control by the Marxists. To show his good faith, however, Breton undertook to serve as a Party organizer among the gas workers of Paris, an assignment for which, after a while, he showed the greatest repugnance and which he soon abandoned.

Meanwhile, many of the Surrealists had split with Breton over the proposal to join forces with the Communists, among them Soupault, Max Ernst, Éluard, Vitrac, Masson, Prévert, Artaud, and Queneau; and so they had been excommunicated singly or in pairs.

At the time of my second visit to France most of them were up in arms against the leader. After my return to America I heard reports, in 1929, that the schism had become public. Adopting Breton's style of vituperation the dissidents published a pamphlet, *Un Cadavre: André Breton*, in which they subjected the "pope" of Surrealism to the sort of calumny he had dispensed for the benefit of the dead Anatole France. "The great commandant of the Palace of Mirages is dead," Jacques Prévert announced. He had prated of love, revolution, poetry, and a whole salad of ideas, and like a musician he "had played the *lute* of the classes under the window of the Communist Party only to be greeted with a shower of brickbats." (Prévert's amusing pun read: *luth des classes* instead of *lutte,* or "struggle.")

Artaud declared that whereas Surrealism had meant for him pure moral revolt, especially against the coercions of the father, Breton had violated the principles he had professed by acting "like a curate" and watching over everyone's morals. The sons of the Surrealist Revolution were evidently bent on devouring their "father."

In replying to the heretics with his second manifesto of Surrealism (December, 1929), Breton made mincemeat of his former friends; for him they were nothing but "literary pimps" and *"viveurs."* He reaffirmed his faith in the dogma of "absolute revolt," declaring further that his ultimate purpose was to achieve "the occultation of Surrealism." It became, in truth, a form of religious belief for whose adepts "life and death, the real and the imaginary, the past and the future, the communicable and the incommunicable," in the words of its leader, were all blended together. Many former adherents who were opposed to the spread of superstition found this movement no longer amusing.

As to the activities of Breton and his school in the political field, it is not surprising that at an early stage Breton found Stalinist communism repugnant and came out for Leon Trotsky and his dissident faction, who were much more to his taste. Trotskyism and the Fourth International played a mainly negative role during the 1930's; affiliation with this minority movement in no way disturbed the interior life of the Surrealists. Thus, as Jean-Paul Sartre has written, social revolution for Breton remained a rather Platonic affair. On the other hand, his old comrade in arms, Louis Aragon, was fated to break away, become a fervent Marxist, and, in highly professional and orthodox fashion, a leading personage in the Communist Party of France.

I was quite ready to believe that Surrealism was all washed

up by 1929–1930, the time of its worst schisms. But André Breton was a most willful and resourceful man; during two or three decades he continued to display his inspirational qualities before new flocks of young talent. After Ernst, Miró, and Masson had left his side, the clever, sensation-seeking Salvador Dali reigned as a favorite in Breton's circle; after Aragon and Éluard departed, new poets such as René Char joined him. Over the years Breton continued to organize international expositions of Surrealist art in Venice and New York, as well as in Paris, and to publish its literature.

Choosing to leave France after her defeat in World War II and the German occupation, Breton came to New York in 1941 and resided in America for five years. He continued to attract some snobs and gilded youths to his séances, at which they carried on experiments in pseudo-psychoanalysis, occultism, and in some peaceful forms of nihilism. But Breton also enjoyed a serious influence over a number of our avant-garde painters. At the end of the last war American artists of the "Abstract-Expressionist" or "Action" group felt greatly attracted by Breton's preachments and the gospels of Surrealism, which urged them to take "the great plunge into the subconscious mind" and to paint "automatically." It was a recurrence of our own youthful interest in the planned disorders of Dadaism a generation earlier, after World War I. Thus Breton and Surrealism experienced a revival chiefly because of the historical interest many felt in the man and the cult.

As late as September, 1959, on the eve of the vernissage of the latest International Surrealist Exposition held in Paris, a Canadian artist named Bénoit performed a special Surrealist ceremony the like of which one might not see again very often. Appearing before a select audience in a darkened hall, dressed in a fantastic costume of robes, feathers and mask—somewhat like an American Indian—he went through some mummery to the accompaniment of sound effects and solemn readings from the last testament of the Marquis de Sade, then took up a red-hot iron and baring his chest branded himself with the letters s-a-d-e. Thus a young North American celebrant of the Surrealist cult ritualized the symbolic transference of the spirit of Sade to himself and his co-worshipers. He also created sensational publicity for the exhibition in which, incidentally, his own work was shown. To such a state had Surrealism been reduced thirty years after many believed we were finished with it.

My thumbnail history of the later era of Surrealism, meanwhile, has led us far ahead of the time of my second visit to France. In the autumn of 1927, quite by chance, I finally encountered my old friend Louis Aragon, who had been keeping away from me (under stern orders to do so!), and at last we had an opportunity to take up the differences that had arisen between us.

I had just returned from a vacation trip to the Riviera during which I had visited Laurence and Peggy Vail for several days. Laurence and I used to disagree in our opinions of almost everything, yet so long as I was a guest under his roof he was so much the gentleman that he would never dispute with me. But once we were back in Paris together, on neutral ground, the case was different. In a restaurant one night in October we came to angry words. Pushing our chairs aside, we rose and drew back our fists, while Peggy, also present, gave forth little agonized screams that drew the attention of the crowd. Suddenly a tall figure stepped between us. It was Aragon, who led me to a table at the other end of the room where he had been dining with a companion.

"I am so sorry, I have been away from Paris; I wanted so much to see Hannah and you . . ." he began. There was too much we had to say to each other for that evening and we continued our talk the next morning when he came to my hotel in secret, that is, without the permission of André Breton, as he confessed. He had experienced much trouble on my account because of what I had written against the Surrealists. Why had I done that? I explained that life had changed, my views had changed; we were learning to face the realities of existence in America.

Aragon could not prevail upon me to change my attitude and appeared distressed as he left. He came to meet me only once more before I returned to the United States in the winter of 1928, and again covertly. At the time he felt powerful bonds of love and loyalty to Breton. From the hints in one of his novels, *Aurélian* (1947), which describes this period of the 1920's, it seems that he feared he would die of boredom if he could no longer take part in the new "games" that Breton constantly invented. Yet he himself must have had his doubts, for only two years later he left the Surrealist camp for good and all. Years afterward Aragon recognized that theirs had only been a war of "words, words, words"; he also wrote me that his own literary generation had "occupied itself mainly in saying *nothing* magnificently and with the greatest freedom of expression. And now that we have found what we have to say . . . can we ever say it well enough?"[6]

Just before World War II began, he came to America in the spring of 1939 for a few weeks to write some articles for the Paris daily *Ce Soir,* of which he was managing editor. During this stay, he and his wife, the novelist Elsa Triolet, spent a week in June with us at our house in Connecticut. The times were threatening; Louis was trying to finish all sorts of things he was writing, including a long novel which he carried in his head, sometimes reciting to us its yet unwritten chapters (which later appeared exactly as he had narrated them verbally). He remarked at the time that the French had such queer ideas about Americans that they "would scarcely believe we knew how to live so well and so peacefully in the country with our children, our dogs, and our flowers." Often during the day he and Elsa sat on the garden terrace overlooking our valley in a mood of tranquil joy that he assured me could not last long. "War is coming soon," he said. "I do believe these are the last happy days I will ever enjoy."

A few weeks later he was back in France and was drafted for

war service as a reserve officer, though he was then forty-two. Serving in a tank regiment during the battle of France and the subsequent retreat, he conducted himself in such wise that after being once surrounded by the Germans and later captured by them, he managed to escape both times (with a good many of his command), and after the armistice was awarded two military decorations. In the years that followed, during the Occupation, he became the national poet of the Resistance Movement in France, publishing his own and other patriots' writing secretly, and constantly engaged in clandestine activities aimed at stirring his people to revolt against the Nazis. At that dangerous period he wrote us a letter in guarded terms which wonderfully conveys the atmosphere of the time:

In the Occupied Zone my books, like those of many French writers, can no longer be sold . . . I can see no possibility of my earning my living as a writer [or finding] any other work. By being very careful with what remains of my army pay we can live here until November 1. After that who knows? . . .

I am writing poems, and as long as the fighting lasted, I was still able to publish them. I still write them but I keep them for myself. . . . It takes a great deal of courage to write without knowing what will happen to one's work. What a terrible road since the days we spent together! Note that the rest of this letter would be false to my meaning if you concluded from it that I have become pessimistic. I believe on the contrary that God moves in a mysterious way and that the gate is straight through which we must pass. In my country, even when it is unfortunate, even crushed, I have a confident hope that there is no way of expressing, except by deeds; and there is nothing to change in what I told you there in your country house, of which I dream today as if it were some image of childhood or a scene from a novel. . . .

Your old friend (my hair is now completely white) who hasn't forgotten you.

Louis

Although Aragon is a very high-strung and sensitive person, he is both quick-thinking and very cool in time of danger. I never worried about him; but feared only for friends of mine who might suffer all the more because they wanted the resolute courage such men as he possess.

In the meantime, a whole community of persons who were uprooted from conquered Paris, both American "expatriates" and French refugees who were old friends of ours, arrived in America, a good many of them settling down to wait out the war in country cottages in our section of Connecticut. Among the later crop of "exiles," this time moving in a reverse direction, were my friends André Masson and Max Ernst, also the Surrealist painter Yves Tanguy, and finally André Breton himself, with his second wife and a young child. I thought it was time to forget all past differences between Breton and myself and received him and other French friends as my guests. We had a very jolly party one weekend in 1941 for Breton and other refugees; it would all have passed off most agreeably were it not that at one instant, while we were sitting in the garden, I remarked that just two years before Louis Aragon had been here with us—and now I wondered if he were alive or dead. (We and other friends in America were in communication with Aragon only at intervals.)

André Breton is a good hater. He had become inconceivably bitter toward Aragon, the military hero and national poet. At mention of Aragon's name Breton exploded in one of his characteristic outbursts: "If I had power I would have Aragon shot tomorrow at dawn!"

We were so appalled at his words that we were speechless. With great deliberation I changed the subject of conversation.

Through most of that year in France I really felt somewhat remote from the wars of art that were going on around me because I was spending my days in Paris in the old Bibliothèque Nationale, immersed in the nineteenth-century world of Émile Zola. I found myself completely absorbed in the voluminous and fairly complete collection of Zola's manuscripts, letters, and posthumous papers deposited in the library by his widow. In the twenties the master novelist of the Naturalist School had fallen into neglect, and his work was decried by fashionable literary commentators, though it was still read by the multitude. Several years later, in the 1930's and 1940's, the critics would reverse themselves on Zola's merit; even André Gide "rediscovered" with great satisfaction the man who had been perhaps more widely read than any other author of his era, and whom a whole generation in France—because of the bitter controversies surrounding him—had wanted to forget since 1902, the year of Zola's accidental death.

Notable among these little-explored private papers of Zola's were the detailed, precise outline notes he had written in 1868, when still a young man, in which he set forth the entire plan of a long family novel, *Les Rougon-Macquart,* that eventually expanded itself to twenty volumes completed in almost a quarter of a century. Thus most of Zola's working life had been consumed in carrying out that one plan, in building up that vast literary edifice stone by stone with unflagging will and energy. Henry James, so different from Zola, admired in him a genius for organization and ranked him as one of the great architects of literature.

Zola's famous circle of friends included Flaubert, Turgenev, Daudet, the Goncourt brothers, Maupassant, Huysmans, and the painter Paul Cézanne, who was his boyhood friend. Through their correspondence, notes, and autobiographical writings, found in the Zola papers, I came to know them very well, as if they were present before me; there were even a good many verbatim accounts of the periodic dinner meetings of "The Big Four," attended by Flaubert, Daudet, Edmond de Goncourt, and Zola, available in the *Goncourt Journals.* In imagination I used to converse with them as I walked about the old narrow streets of the Palais Royal quarter near the library. In a measure, I lived Zola's life vicariously. Malcolm Cowley, in describing my method of writing biography, defined it as that of "immersion" in each subject I took up. He went so far as to claim that I tended to imitate each character I wrote about, in their bad as in their good traits—which is an amusing exaggeration.

After a period of accumulation I left Paris with my wife and child and a store of books and notes to establish myself in a little country house at Éragny on the Oise River, a rather dull village some twenty miles from the capital, where I concentrated entirely on the task of writing.

My first thought had been to write an ironic portrait of Zola; it was the fashion in the twenties, inspired by Lytton Strachey. Moreover, I felt somewhat skeptical about my great man's philosophy, which derived from the humanitarian and positivist ideas of the Second Empire and early Victorian period; he had been nourished on the theories of Claude Bernard, Darwin, and Taine. Thinking of himself as something of a scientist in his own field, Zola used to take up, one by one, his "slices of life," submit them to the laws of heredity, environment, and social force, and what followed would make up the "natural history of a family" during a given era. It was much too pat!

Closer acquaintance with Zola and his work, however, removed my doubts and won me over. Like most great artists he exceeded his own plans; his methodically documented novels emerged as powerful dramas, composing in their totality a new *Comédie Humaine*, for Zola was the true heir of Balzac, and like him essentially a poet, and a *romantic* poet at that. After all, he was a product of the nineteenth century, and at the same time one of the key figures in the literary movement in France that had brought the novel to this stage of culmination. The Russian as well as the American novelists, from James to Dreiser and Sinclair Lewis, had learned their trade in Zola's school.

In the end the biography I was writing followed the older English models rather than that of Strachey. I tried to make *Zola and His Time* a sort of literary banquet, whose entertainment was furnished by the wisdom and humor of the master and his friends, gathered from their letters and their talk.

For purposes of information I kept in touch with the family of Zola and particularly his daughter, Denise Leblond-Zola, who

was as beautiful as her mother, the mistress of Zola's middle
years. One of the excommunicated Surrealists, the charming
Pierre de Massot, was employed by me for research in the bibli-
ography of Zola, a service he performed very well. Another person who was of great assistance to me was Léon Deffoux, an
eminent literary critic, who was one of the editors of the Havas
Agency in Paris and who in early youth had been the secretary
of J.K. Huysmans. Deffoux had written a volume on Zola's
circle of friends, *Le Groupe de Médan*—Médan was the site of
Zola's country house on the Seine river, where Daudet, Maupassant, and company often came as guests, and was only a few
miles west of the village in which I lived. I was aware that Deffoux, a Catholic and Royalist, disliked Zola and the Dreyfusards;
he told me all the indiscretions he knew of in Zola's life and
showed me unpublished papers of Huysmans filled with unpleasant and intolerant reflections on Zola's moral character.
Both Huysmans and Alphonse Daudet had broken relations
with Zola at the time of his action in the Dreyfus Case in 1894.
Like them, Deffoux belonged to the anti-Semitic party, and I
felt I must beware of his advice, although his first-hand knowledge of the period was useful.[7]

From the back windows of my house I had a view of the narrow, canalized Oise winding about the flat saucer of our valley
and among the fields of asparagus; the river carried barges filled
with coal, steered by old women smoking pipes, who had the
family wash hanging out on deck. I was going along every day
with an absolute regularity of which Zola would have approved,
writing during three sessions day and night, halting only for
meals. For exercise I would walk along the Oise Canal in the
rain that was unfailing that year, often in the company of two
local friends, the village schoolmaster and the cobbler. The
latter, an aged man, had a basement shop on the Grande Rue
that was filled with bird cages, fully fifty of them, and boasted
of a library with the complete works of Zola, among other books.

Our housekeeper had gossiped about what I was writing and so many of the residents of Éragny were aware of what I was doing.

Another local friend was the proprietor of the café at the railroad depot, where I often stopped for a glass of Pernod before dinner. He was a well-spoken man and the leading Socialist politician in the district, which neighbored some large factories.

The Café de la Gare was usually a quiet spot. But one afternoon in August, 1927, at the hour of the apéritif, I found it filled with a large group of factory workers whom I had not seen there before. They seemed excited or angry about something, as if they were out on strike; they should normally have been at work at that time. As I came in they fell silent, glowered at me, and one even shook his fist in my direction. I had never been treated in this way by French working-class people, who are often cheeky but also, as a rule, very genial. As I drew up to the bar they stopped their talk and moved away from me. Then the proprietor leaned over the bar and said to the workers in an authoritative tone: "I tell you he's all right, even though he is an American. I know that he is writing a book on Émile Zola."

At this their angry faces brightened up; one of them, a young worker in rough velveteens, introduced himself politely and shook hands with me. I now learned what had been eating these people. It was the time of the Sacco and Vanzetti affair in Massachusetts, when the two prisoners awaited their execution, all measures of appeal having failed. All France, as well as Italy, was greatly agitated over the case. That very morning, the men told me, there had been a popular protest in Paris by trade-union men who had taken the day off to demonstrate, as many of the Éragny workers had done. Crowds had marched upon the American Embassy in Paris; the police charged them and fighting began, while the rioting people threw up barricades in the streets. The men in the café who had just come back from the street fighting in Paris had been talking about the demonstration; they had recognized me as an American when I entered the café. Perhaps they would have liked to give me a good beating; if so, the *cafetier's* statement about my interest in Zola had spared me that.

The leader of the group exclaimed to me: "Have you Americans no humanity? You say you believe in democracy. How can you do such things to innocent men because they are poor workers and foreigners!"

Though I was not interested in politics prior to this time, I had read the news of popular demonstrations in cities all over the world, where people were registering their protest at the impending execution of Sacco and Vanzetti after their six-years' ordeal, a sentence which most of the world believed unjust. In fact, I myself had been struck, some time ago, by the remarkable parallel between this case and that of Captain Alfred Dreyfus, who was sentenced as a spy to life imprisonment on Devil's Island at a time when public passion, national hysteria, and race prejudice—as in the Sacco-Vanzetti case—had made a fair trial impossible. I had even entered into correspondence with persons in America who were agitating for the reprieve of the prisoners' death sentence; for the first time in years I myself had felt the keenest interest in the outcome of such an affair.

I now explained to the people in the café that there were many people in America who felt exactly as they did, and that among those demonstrating in Boston in behalf of the condemned men were several of my acquaintances. The French workers were greatly cheered at hearing of this and called for a round of drinks to my health and that of Sacco and Vanzetti. Among those who picketed the State House in Boston at this time were Edna St. Vincent Millay, John Dos Passos, and Edmund Wilson. The case of Sacco and Vanzetti made a profound impression on many intellectuals in America.

The next day I was in Paris and found people there in a state of the highest excitement. The poet, Robert Desnos, who was working as a reporter for *Paris-Soir*, told me that he had been in one melee after another, and that he himself had been beaten by the police. Not only the police, but the military were out in force to keep order. As the case had become a burning issue in France, the premier appealed to President Coolidge for the grant of a pardon to the condemned. Over the weekend there was a false rumor that a stay of execution had been allowed at the last hour. But on the Monday following a young engineer who was my neighbor in Éragny brought me definite news, heard over his radio, that Sacco and Vanzetti had been executed. We could not bring ourselves to believe this brief, grim news item. It is a curious thing that the French public, which had been so greatly agitated during the period of tension preceding the execution, took the end of the affair calmly.

While the Sacco-Vanzetti case was approaching its denouement, I had been writing, at great speed, the concluding chapters of my book on Zola, which consisted in a sustained narration of the Dreyfus case, the Zola trial, Zola's flight into exile, and the final vindication of Dreyfus. It was at once a spy drama on the grand scale and a picture of a national political crisis, in fact a revolutionary transition. To France's glory, her people though bitterly divided over the Dreyfus affair—unlike anti-Semitic Germany a generation later in the time of Hitler—brought about the triumph of the liberal and rational party. Dreyfus was eventually exonerated, the real spies were exposed, the movement of racism and obscurantism was defeated.

Emotion over the contemporary Sacco-Vanzetti case in Massachusetts spurred me as I wrote of Zola and Dreyfus. At periods before the execution I had the illusion that, somehow, knowledge of the earlier *cause célèbre* might be of some little help for the victims of what I believed to be a new miscarriage of justice. As the intrigue of the Dreyfus Affair was a perfect labyrinth, and I was trying to carry it all in my head, I decided that the best way of presenting it in a clear sequence would be to write it all down at once; and so I completed the long chapter describing the Affair, about forty pages in length, in a sustained session of writing that lasted from nine one morning through the night to the following noon. I let that chapter stand as it was and retouched it very little afterward.

Zola's life had been the sedentary career of the typical man

of letters, but in the end it had become ennobled and trans-
figured by his act of heroism. He had "set the truth on the
march" by writing the powerful pamphlet *J'Accuse*, denouncing
his own government and forcing them to put him on trial. I
pictured him facing the howling mobs of anti-Dreyfusards at his
court, and was far more moved by his example than I could have
foretold when beginning my work. As he himself said: "He who
suffers for truth and justice becomes at last august and sacred."

SIXTEEN

THE END OF

OUR TWENTIES

Returning to the United States early in 1928 I was much occupied in the final revision of my long book on Zola, which appeared in the autumn of that year. It was favorably received by the press and enjoyed what was considered in those days a successful sale; that is to say a work of nonfiction having two editions amounting to about ten thousand copies was ranked as a "best seller." At any rate, it was for me a wholly novel experience —up to the age of twenty-eight—to write and publish something that did not bring losses to everyone concerned. My friends (who were also beginning to establish themselves in the literary profession) looked upon me for a while as a man of fortune.

Since the age of nineteen I had been writing and publishing things for a diminutive, almost an invisible, literary audience, those whom Stendhal described in self-compensatory terms as "the happy few." I had written poetry, criticism, and general essays designed to interest only those who, like myself, regarded literature as a "religion" and formed a sort of chapel of snobs. Now, having taken up the medium of biography, I found that it provided me with all the range of the extended "family novel" or the historical novel and, as a literary medium, was deeply satisfying to me. I could communicate with my readers on a variety of ideas—on art and life, love and death, on human freedom and justice—and could feel myself in contact with a real public. In short, I addressed myself directly to the "common reader"—instead of a few literary initiates—and found that I greatly enjoyed the act of communication. (Some of the most recondite or "unpopular" of authors, including Henry James, as I have discovered, always secretly pined for a larger audience than they were granted.)

Zola and His Time was much favored by writers as diverse as Sinclair Lewis and F. Scott Fitzgerald. As Van Wyck Brooks said at the time: "No European author has had as much influence on the American novel as Émile Zola."[1] The appendix of my book included Zola's own notes describing how he organized his series of novels. Some years later Scott Fitzgerald wrote me that the account of Zola's method of work had enabled him to pull himself together after a long period of "writer's block" and complete his own novel, *Tender Is the Night,* which otherwise, he believed, "would never have reached the stalls."

I was to follow the calling of the biographer for the next three decades. As the German writer Hermann Kesten said to me: "After all, every biography is really an autobiography."

In 1928, when the first complete "talkie" pictures were appearing, the migration of writers to Hollywood began in earnest. The Macaulay Company's book editor, who was also a novelist, departed for the new literary Eldorado in California, and so in the autumn of 1928 I replaced him on a temporary basis and worked in their office half-time.

For about a year, during which I had a fairly free hand in publishing books of my own selection, I served a useful role for other writers, many of whom beat a path to my door. My employers had experience only of the business side of their affair and little taste for literature as such. They had formerly made large profits by printing the works of that old Victorian war

horse, Elinor Glyn, whose romances of illicit passion, though in
"veiled" or bowdlerized language, had been the delight of millions of chambermaids. Now that the public had turned to writers like Ben Hecht and Ernest Hemingway, the owners of The
Macaulay Company counted on persons like me to find the sort
of literature that was coming into fashion. Their trade book list,
like many others, was a mixed bag of novels about Arab sheiks
complete with harems, seriously documented biographies like
my recent volume, and a notable anthology of contemporary
writers, *The American Caravan*, edited by Alfred Kreymborg,
Lewis Mumford, and Paul Rosenfeld.

Publishing books can be a very amusing game if one is careful to choose only works that are bound to lose money, which
was mainly the service I performed for The Macaulay Company
—until they found me out and returned to their Elinor Glyns.
Meanwhile, with my counsel, they published various modern
French and German authors and the work of some new American
novelists, including Robert M. Coates's *The Eater of Darkness*—
an experiment in literary Dadaism—as well as *Relics and Angels*,
the first novel of Hamilton Basso. I also assigned writing, translating, or editing jobs to William Carlos Williams, Malcolm Cowley, Kenneth Burke, Slater Brown, James Thurber, and E.B.
White.

One day there appeared in our publishing office a young
Southern woman, who had a fine head and very large gray eyes.
She was Katherine Anne Porter, and had been recommended to
us for some routine copy editing to be done at home. Miss Porter, then in her early thirties, had had some education in a con-
vent in New Orleans, but was mainly self-taught. It was her
second visit to New York where, a few years earlier, she had
tried in vain to earn her way by writing. More lately she had
lived in Mexico, where she had been married and then divorced.
A small woman, she bore herself with great poise, was low-voiced,
soft-spoken, and full of old-fashioned airs and graces that made
her seem very different from the New Women one saw in New
York at this time, who habitually wore the "dead-pan" expres-

sion then in vogue. Katherine Anne also had much wit, and soon won many friends among the members of my own circle. Like some of them, she too had experienced an interesting phase of "exile," though in revolutionary Mexico instead of Europe, and the subject was very much on her mind. At first we enjoyed only oral versions of her stories; they were reminiscences of her early life in Texas and Louisiana and of her years in Mexico. Her way of telling them was fairly "mesmerizing," as Edmund Wilson once remarked; we often expressed the wish that she would write them down. She would begin:

Today is the 105th birthday of my name grandmother. She died when I was ten years old. When I remember that indomitable woman . . .

There would follow an unforgettable portrait of a crusty, humorous, and hard-swearing lady of the Old South.

Soon I was shown the fragments or rough drafts of stories Katherine Anne was trying to write, and invited to criticize them unsparingly. She worked over these things and reworked them in a tormented way, as if depending on autohypnosis to call forth language that truly conveyed her emotion. I was astonished at the high quality of her fragmentary sketches or drafts of stories and exhorted her to finish them. When she came to me afterward with the completed version of a story of Mexico in revolutionary days, *Flowering Judas*, I read it with delight and sent it off to be published in *transition*. Here was a person with some knowledge of the world who had come to writing rather late—compared with most of us—had a great deal to say, and said it very well. There was little that I could contribute beyond my positive enthusiasm, though Katherine Anne, at the time, declared that this gave her confidence.

In 1929 I persuaded her to make a collection of her stories, and I sent them to Harcourt, Brace, my new publishers. One of their young editors, Charles A. Pearce, after reading the manuscript, exclaimed that it sounded like something out of the classics; I assured him that her work was her own, but would become a classic in the future. Issued soon afterward in a limited edition, the book, *Flowering Judas,* became a collector's favorite almost at once, and has been reprinted in popular editions ever since.

The accident of finding a person like Katherine Anne Porter, who wrote like an old master, was one of the most rewarding episodes of my term as a book editor. Although I was invited to continue this work on a permanent basis, I resigned my post in 1929, holding that for me it was really a lazy man's life. I pined for the ardors and excitements of writing a book of my own.

In the last season or two of the decade of the twenties one became aware that the literary life, or the highbrow life, in New York, Boston, or Chicago had become much more amusing and civilized than it seemed at the end of World War I or just prior to the war. The change was gradual; in part it derived apparently from the advancing maturity and self-confidence of our generation, as reflected in members of my circle of friends whose progress in life during many years was bound up with my own. Only in retrospect did the slow alterations of time seem clearly evident, as if fixed by certain contrasting images. For example, at some point in time such as 1925 or 1926 the residual figures of old men with long whiskers—like those in the Smith Brothers Cough Drops advertisements—completely disappeared from the literary scene. Instead of waiting in the anterooms of those aged men of letters while they finished their siestas, the young writers of the late twenties found themselves pursued by sleek, youthful publishers in full chase for unknown genius or talent. These people now bowed to the rising sun of an Ernest Hemingway or a Thornton Wilder.

It was in many ways a time of fruition in the fields of the literary, dramatic, and plastic arts in America. Formerly, in order to see the plays of some modern European dramatist such as Strindberg or some new American such as O'Neill one had to go downtown to one of the grubby Little Theaters of Greenwich

Village. Now the Little Theater had become big; it had moved uptown to the heart of the Broadway entertainment district and presented its repertory with the aid of skilled stage professionals.

I remember one episode that marked the corresponding change in the taste for the arts. When somewhat earlier Edward Steichen, the photographer, brought some of the beautiful abstract sculptures of Brancusi to New York, they were seized by the customhouse authorities who ruled they were "not art" and demanded that an import duty be paid on them as so much raw copper or brass. Steichen threatened suit against the United States Treasury, and raised such a scandal over the affair in the newspapers that the Brancusi works were eventually yielded to him without charges. But after my second visit to France, I found on my return to New York in 1928 that occasional pieces by Brancusi were often to be seen in the homes of persons with some taste for the arts, and were being accepted without dispute as the modern masterpieces they were.

New York, seen after an absence abroad, appeared more than ever as the city of white towers, a new Venice rising from the sea, but of monster scale. The graduated setbacks required by the zoning laws had lent the imperial skyline of Manhattan a decidedly Cubist style by 1929. Here was a monumental form of art indigenous to America and created by the demands of industry itself.

The streets of the city and the roads leading out to the country were now solidly blocked by motorcars on holidays and weekends. Little man, I wondered, where are you going now with your automobile, your cigar in mouth, and your hip flask in pocket? You are going, doubtless, to one of those big Roman circuses where the gladiators of the Ivy League colleges play football.

Although I had traveled about Europe a good deal I had really not seen enough of my own country, and was now resolved to do something about it. We talked much in those days of "rediscovering America" or "accepting" her, as if one had much choice. Under similar circumstances Margaret Fuller had once remarked that she was resolved at last to "accept the universe," and Ralph Waldo Emerson, hearing of this, exclaimed: "Well, by George, she had *better!*"

Many voices, native and foreign, clashed in intermittent debate over the country's destiny. We read those Cassandra-like philosophers of history, Henry Adams and Oswald Spengler, who warned us that our barbarous materialism confirmed the declining phase of Western civilization, which they prophesied. Others, such as Irving Babbitt, exhorted us to become classical Humanists or perish. Lewis Mumford recalled the charm of the handicrafts era in the arts and industries of early America and mourned its passing. (Soon afterward, however, he expressed hope in the perfection of a new "functional" epoch in our arts and in the planning of our cities for human welfare.) The French novelist, Georges Duhamel, after a quick visit to New York and Chicago (in his book, *Quarantième Étage*) pictured us as a race of racketeers who fired machine guns at each other or dropped "pineapples" from skyscrapers. A few of our contemporaries, like Allen Tate and John Crowe Ransom, abandoned all hope in the Machine Age and planned to return as Southern Agrarians to the provincial traditions and the "racial myth" of the Old South. In a discussion with my Connecticut neighbor, Charles A. Beard, about the Southern "fugitives" who had gone back to the soil of Tennessee, I reported that they were able to survive as men of letters by living in old houses, buying green bourbon at a dollar a quart, and hiring capable Negro servants at three dollars a week. "Yes, but how do the servants like this economy?" Beard asked.

Still other seers in more optimistic terms predicted that the United States of America would rule the world, and set forth their prophecies, as did Lucien Romier, under such titles as: *America or Russia? Who Will Be Master?* Meanwhile, our own economic experts assured us that our expanding productive system would lift our people to a high plateau of "eternal prosperity." But what were the human goals of this seemingly auto-matized economy? Were we to become *Masse Menschen*, a regi-mented community of Capitalists, technicians, and machine workers, like the robots in Karel Capek's play *R.U.R?* Or would there be some place left in the new society for Homo sapiens and for the artist and poet?

A great eagerness to visit Juggernaut in his native habitat seized me. When the editors of *The Outlook and Independent*, a national weekly that used to ornament the anterooms of doctors and dentists, invited me to write for them, I proposed doing a series of "portraits" of great cities in America. They would be informal surveys of different urban centers as seen by a traveler coming with a fresh perspective gained by long residence in Europe, and trying to discern the new social and cultural phe-nomena sprouting up in different localities. The editors liked the idea and authorized me to begin with the industrial midlands— Chicago, Detroit, Cleveland, Pittsburgh—and then go on perhaps to San Francisco, if the series proved successful.

I was full of enthusiasm for my mission. Our historic expatri-ates, Nathaniel Hawthorne and Henry James, had long con-tended that it was impossible to create a good literature in the United States because there was no aristocracy here; there were no quaint folk customs and no picturesque ruins. Well, I would see the purple slabs of Chicago for myself, and the mechanical monuments Henry Ford had built at River Rouge. If there were no aristocrats in the old style, then I would try to learn some-thing of those new captains of industry and merchant princes described by Charles and Mary Beard in *The Rise of American Civilization*. Were not the Swifts, Armours, Insulls, and Schwabs more powerful in their way than the doges or barons of feudal times? I also proposed to talk with newspaper reporters, minis-ters, labor leaders, college professors, bootleggers, highbrows, and lowbrows. Providing myself with letters of introductions from acquaintances in New York, I proceeded first to Chicago.

Chicago had narrowly missed becoming the "Athens" of America; its natives, whom I described as "overwhelmingly hospitable," called their metropolis an "overgrown village," though it too had an imperial skyline and the widest of boulevards by the shore of Lake Michigan. Just behind the imposing lakeside façade, with its ribbon of parks, were the most hideous and godforsaken slums covering most of the city's interior. With a well-informed architect as my guide I toured the town, examining the already aging steel-cage skyscrapers which men of Chicago had designed in the '80's and '90's. Chicago had created a native American architecture and was justly proud of it. As a piece of engineering construction, the three-level viaducts along the Chicago River seemed as impressive as anything of this order done by the ancient Romans. On the other hand, hideous structures of obsolete design usually stood side by side with the shining edifices of the new order.

Everywhere I found the tempo of human industry being speeded up. At the headquarters of the Sears, Roebuck mail-order empire battalions of errand boys, instead of walking, raced back and forth along the corridors on roller skates with bundles of orders and correspondence. Then, as one of a long queue of hundreds of visitors, I paid my respects to the Swift & Company packing house, where cattle on the hoof in an unending flock moved along conveyor lines to be slaughtered and "processed." Here, we were told, was the original model, dating from about 1870, of the system of quantity production. Henry Ford's assembly lines at Dearborn, Michigan were designed more than thirty years later and were based on Edison's system of electric-power distribution.

In Chicago the local enterprise that appealed to me most because of its dynamic character was that of beer-running, now highly organized under an army of gangsters with the celebrated "Scarface" Al Capone as their chief magistrate. In the company of two experienced crime reporters of the staff of the Chicago *Daily News,* I toured many blind pigs in the Loop and on the South Side, a diverting form of research. These well-appointed and crowded establishments made hardly any effort to conceal their business. (The traffic in liquor was unusually voluminous in Chicago because it served as a center of distribution for a large part of the country.) The liquor racketeers, moreover, controlled a whole chain of brothels as one of their auxiliary enterprises, all of these interests having been "trustified" under Mr. Capone. Finally, the underworld people had formed a close protective alliance with the police and the local politicians, who had become dependent on the underworld's regular and liberal money contributions, so that Capone and his general staff had gradually won the dominant position behind the scenes in the political administration of Chicago and Cook County.

The underworld's dictator and his vassals imposed their own law and order on their republic of thieves, punishing or executing those who violated the rules of the game, and no court dared to act against them. Thus you had, side by side, a pro forma democratic government of Chicago, made up of elected mayor and city councilors, and a de facto government run by Capone and company. In the course of our well-liquored tour, Edward Molloy, one of my guides, pointed out two men whom he knew to be in disfavor with the mob and marked for extinction at some early date. It gave me quite a turn to see a sad-looking fellow drinking at a table near us all alone, who was scheduled to meet his end by machine-gun fire within a week or two. Was there nothing we could do about it? I asked. Nothing, Molloy said; a reporter for the Chicago *Tribune* who happened to publish an advance announcement of such an execution had been rubbed out himself.

At one of the big taverns in the Loop I was standing at the bar with my two guides, discussing this undemocratic situation rather audibly, when a big, hard-faced individual drew up beside us, spoke to the bartender, and received from him a little package of dollar bills. As I had been informed about the pay-off of plain-clothes policemen, I unwisely called the attention of my companions to the incident. The man, hearing this, turned and stared at me; he had mean eyes, the color of a wolf's. Suddenly he moved up behind me, drew a revolver from his hip pocket, and raised it with its butt extended as if to strike me on the head. My two companions, fortunately, seized his arm and grappled with him; Molloy was a powerful man too. With the help of the bartender they calmed the fellow down, then got me out of there quickly.

"Whew, that was a close one," Molloy exclaimed when we were outside. "I know him; he is a plain-clothes man getting his night's pay, and drunk besides. He heard you talk with an Eastern accent and thought you were a Federal man." I might have had my skull fractured, my guides pointed out, and yet would have had no redress—"Because he could have said you threatened an officer, and his word would have been law here." Everything had happened so quickly that I had no time to feel frightened until afterward.

The next night in Chicago offered a striking contrast to the preceding one. I put on a black tie and dinner jacket and went off to a party of literary and musical people at the old brown-stone mansion of Mrs. Kellogg Fairbank on the Gold Coast of Chicago. The scene might have been that of a salon in Paris or Beacon Hill, Boston. My hostess was a writer of light and popular fiction; there were at least two women who contributed regularly to *Poetry: a Magazine of Verse*, which was supported by Chicago philanthropists, some of whom were also on hand. An Italian prima donna from the Chicago Opera sang arias from Verdi in true bel canto style; she was the wife of Louis Swift, one of the heirs of the packing company of that name.

In talking with Mr. Swift I broached the subject of prohibition and asked him if he thought it had been a good thing. We were being served drinks of excellent quality. Mr. Swift, who was on his second or third cocktail before dinner, told me that he strongly favored prohibition—waving his half-filled glass for emphasis—because it was very good for the workers in his meat-packing plant. "Oh yes," he said, "I know they get filled up with bootleg beer occasionally at the weekend. But in the old days they used to show up on a Monday morning so drunk they still had hang-overs on Tuesday, and the place wasn't really running well until Wednesday. Nowadays they come in a bit tired after their Sunday beer, but by Tuesday they are all going strong."

I startled the company at the Fairbanks when I remarked that it was my impression that "the political administration of Chicago is being taken over by the organized party of criminals —they are even moving into your quarter of town—and you are going to be ruled by a Latin-American type republic, a junta of racketeers." Mr. Fairbank, a noted corporation lawyer in this city, said that he knew something of the situation and believed I was painting things rather black. "Anyway, the gangsters just kill off their own kind now and then, but they never bother people like us."[2]

The winter climate of Chicago penetrated one's bones, and the air was thoroughly saturated with smoke rising from the world's biggest railroad yards located in the heart of the city. While present at a dinner gathering in a large club at the top of the Wrigley Chewing Gum Building, I heard discussion of future plans for the development of Chicago and for its approaching world's fair, and was invited to give my own impressions as a visitor. It was my habit then to speak my mind in a way that often invited trouble—though, like a young fool, I believed all the while that I was proceeding with the finesse of a Talleyrand. Why bother about developing Chicago, I put in, when the place was filled with smoke, the air was unbreathable, and no one was doing anything about it. The reports of what followed reached the newspapers of New York, where Harry Hansen, the literary columnist of the *World,* related (December 19, 1928):

. . . a startling tale about the proficiency of Matthew Josephson in the art of self-defense comes from Chicago, where the author of *Zola and His Time* is looking over the terrain with a view of extracting copy from the soil. It seems that Mr. Josephson was one of a party at a famous club which included a number of literary lights and men distinguished in other fields. . . . Mr. Josephson, who had missed the sun for his length of stay in Chicago, declared that the issue in Chicago was . . . the abatement of the smoke nuisance. . .

a large, well-set man, who happened to be the Chicago Smoke Commissioner took this as a personal criticism of himself and began hostilities. . . . from the accounts of witnesses, . . . the Smoke Commissioner landed in the well-known heap, not, however, [without] taking toll of Mr. Josephson's front teeth.

The Smoke Commissioner was a man mountain who had been imbibing freely. When challenged by him to "put up my hands," I had no other recourse but to defend myself. The man was so big that I literally had to climb up on his chest to reach him, but he was so slow that I could hit and run. Ducking one of his lunges, I caused him to land on the floor with a crash. While I stood over him, making a count and cheerfully offering to shake hands, he managed to get to his feet and strike me a glancing blow. Somewhat battle worn, I left Chicago to continue my *tour d'horizon* in Detroit, Cleveland, and Pittsburgh, where I met with no more hostilities.

Some of my friends in New York, judging from the reports in the press, thought I was being a bit of a ruffian myself. But in my own way I was trying to get out of the Ivory Tower in which most American men of letters still confined themselves and learn at first hand what sort of country we were living in.

When I came to write my story of Chicago for *The Outlook and Independent* the editors refused to believe what I had to say about the underworld having won Home Rule. A short time after the article was published, however, there occurred in a garage in the center of Chicago a famous massacre by machine-gun fire of six gangsters belonging to a dissident group, and the press of the whole world buzzed with the story. My article in *The Outlook* was found to be in no sense an exaggerated account of Chicago's underworld and its periodic outbreaks of gang war.

The Ford factories at Dearborn, Michigan, made a deep impression upon me. As artifact, my favorite machine was a giant press, standing about five stories high, that smashed up whole railroad cars and automotive trucks into scrap steel in seconds, while making a monstrous music such as the composer

Edgard Varèse, with all his sirens and noise machines, could not have equalled. The speed of the Ford assembly line in itself was disconcerting. But even more depressing was the fact that the men themselves were made machinelike. Murray L. Godwin, a former plant mechanic who had become a staff writer for Ford's Dearborn *Independent*—but also contributed to *transition*—kindly described to me his own experience of several years in these factories. In his private view the utopia of mass production had little to offer in terms of human happiness. Charles Chaplin said as much in his memorable film, *Modern Times*. In New York my friend George Soule, editor and writer on economic questions for *The New Republic*, assured me, however, that the big idea of modern engineers was to eliminate all routine manual labor by replacing it with automatic machinery.

Would engineers and technicians be the salvation of our society, as Thorstein Veblen had once hoped they would? My own feeling was that America was becoming not only mechanized but *collectivized*—much like Soviet Russia, though under the program of monopoly capitalism instead of Marxist dictatorship. In the end there would perhaps be little to choose between the two systems of standardized production and distribution. The managers and the Capitalists seemed driven by their destiny. "The American captains of industry are also conscripted by the Machine," I wrote in 1928. The historian Charles A. Beard was saying at the same time: "We are entering the Age of Technology."

Meanwhile, I reflected, the human unit participating in our mass life was forced to a more bitter effort to survive:

The very problem of preserving one's human identity assumes a more immediate and absolute character. . . . The creative effort can never be a mechanical or collective one . . . art demands a lonely and personal action. No branch of art or knowledge can be pursued through mass methods. Under pressure the effort to preserve the identity, the *I*, is magnified. The only answer to standardization in America . . . the destiny of creative effort, is the preservation of the human type, the defense of the human self from destruction.[3]

The enigma of America's future civilization continued to haunt me. In a general way I believed in the movement of enlightenment that distinguished the eighteenth century in Europe, and still believe that we need more rather than less light. So far as my own country was concerned I wanted to be *engagé*, for better or worse, in the "progress" or the "evolution" of its society, rather than take flight to some island of Majorca or Capri where one practiced a pleasurable sort of delayed suicide. Even the difficulty of life here was challenging.

There was Ezra Pound, who had followed the trail of Henry James into exile in England, France, and now Italy, still weeping into his wine glass and railing at his fatherland. At this time I had the whim to publish an "Open Letter to Ezra Pound," urging him to return to the United States.[4] "We have learned much from you, and I shall not be one of those who deny it," I began. But his idea of the poet's function was still that of the 1890 decadents. He was striking attitudes, making words play with each other. Yet time was passing, and it seemed vain for the exiles to linger in a Europe still ruled by old doctrines and national hatreds that had brought her to disaster many times before. If war did not destroy the old continent, then the big machines would soon come to Americanize her, too.

In the field of the literary as well as the plastic arts I saw that the logical direction for the men of the future would be to bring about a marriage of art with industry and mass entertainment. Such was the significance of Frank Lloyd Wright's long career. In Germany, the year before, I had been deeply impressed by my visit to the school of the Bauhaus-Dessau where Walter Gropius, Moholy-Nagy, and their confreres carried on a movement for the teaching and propagation of modern industrial design. These people had been frank to tell me that much of their inspiration was derived from an American artist whom Americans scarcely knew: Frank Lloyd Wright.

Wright had struggled to impose his ideas upon the anarchy of construction in this country; could one not conceive of poets and novelists similarly seeking to adapt themselves to the new media, especially the movies and radio? Even the aged Tolstoi, around the turn of the century, on seeing the first motion-picture device of Edison, had become enchanted with its possibilities, and urged his younger Russian confreres to begin writing plays for motion pictures; though these things might be crude at the beginning, the motion pictures, he predicted, would eventually make the old methods of literature obsolete. I expressed some such notions in my "Open Letter to Ezra Pound."

We may become centurions of Soap for a time, pro-consuls of Hydro-electricity; we may sing before the microphone, dance before the television box. A period of discipline will elapse; but in the end the force of mind will leaven this society too . . . The beauty of automobiles, spotless kitchens, and geometrical office buildings will have been organized and will have achieved integrity. . . .

Tolstoi and others after him, including myself, were much too sanguine about the time that would be needed before the machines for mass entertainment could be put to good usage in our commercial society. The cinema achieved effects of great art only sporadically, or near enough to be tantalizing. The flood of hideous or mediocre work, however, drowned everything else. Many a true *Dichter* fell by the wayside. In 1938 I spent two days in Hollywood with Scott Fitzgerald, who was cutting a sad figure there. His understanding of the new medium was penetrating, nevertheless, and his interest in it was genuine. "The individual writer's part in the 'regime' of a motion-picture production," he said to me, "amounts to only ten per cent of the finished job, after the rest of the team have done their part."

At about the same time I saw the young Nathanael West, author of the wonderful, then little-known satirical novel *Miss Lonelyhearts*. He had tried Paris for a while, then had come back to take work in Hollywood, with some such ideas as I had entertained. "I write Grade-C scripts only—dog stories and such things for low pay," he said to me ruefully. "If the director's wife finds them sloppy enough, then they are accepted."

But in 1928 we had high hopes. "Return to America, Mr. Pound!" I wrote. Pound, however, ignored such appeals. He continued to play the Eternal Exile in Rapallo, and to write silly diatribes against his country, calling it "the most collossal monkey-house and prize exhibit the world has ever seen." He clung to "the Old World view that one is foolish to disturb one's leisure by taking thought or action," or joining in any "party program" that promised the artist more satisfaction. Yet not long afterward he violated his own engagements of 1928, and accepted at face value the promises of Mussolini and the Fascist Party of Italy.

In the summer of 1929 there were unusually big, noisy drinking parties in the country every weekend; and in the autumn when we came back to town there were cocktail crushes either at my apartment or at the homes of my friends.

Who could pretend any longer during that "golden Boom," as Scott Fitzgerald named it, that America was still a nation of frontiersmen upholding a puritan code of ethics because of the scarcity of women and the need to grow families. Our middle classes, at any rate, were inordinately prosperous and were becoming, if not Bohemian, definitely sybaritic. Much money flowed to the bootleg liquor industry, whose system of distribution was by now very efficiently organized. In the country one obtained an applejack of fair quality, delivered by car in wooden kegs holding five or ten gallons, at only five dollars a gallon. In the city one called a certain telephone number and, presto, a respectable-looking chap appeared at one's door with a metal can of grain alcohol and a flask of juniper spirits. These were mixed in a basin, or in the proverbial bathtub after being cut with water, and combined with nonalcoholic vermouth to make a martini cocktail that really grated in your esophagus.

Generally, Americans (including myself) drank badly, I was forced to admit; perhaps the stunning effect of our liquors also tended to make us combative. I remember a gathering at Edmund Wilson's, in the course of which several of the guests fell to brawling in various corners of a rambling apartment he had in the "Village." On this or perhaps a later occasion our host himself was engaged in combat with Mr. Burton Rascoe and bit him in the calf.

The gatherings at my own place were no more edifying. At one party held in a barn in Connecticut that I rented in the summer of 1929, Hart Crane turned up from France where he had gone to live for a while on a small inheritance. His hair was now prematurely gray. He had not behaved very well in Paris; he had not worked well—though he had gone as far as he could toward finishing *The Bridge,* soon to be published. Bob Coates had brought his thin, long-legged friend James Thurber of the staff of *The New Yorker,* who under normal circumstances was the most entertaining and lovable of men. But Hart Crane was always likely to be the unruly guest; while Thurber, though well-read and knowledgeable, used to pretend to be a simple middlebrow with no taste for such "obscure" poetry as Crane's. Evidently Hart said something that gave offense to Thurber; there were high words and they began to brawl.

I heard Thurber cry: "Hold me back before I hit him." Crane had drawn himself up in fighting posture, while two persons seized Jim Thurber and held his arms as he had requested. Then Thurber stepped backward, and one of his legs went into a big bucket filled with water and ice just behind him. He howled with surprise at the cold and the wetness, then hopped about on one leg so that all the fight went out of him. He laughed at himself; we all laughed until the tears came. Thurber was enacting the character of Walter Mitty long before that absurd and sorrowful personage appeared in print.

The New Woman seeking her career in New York and appearing at our festivities toward 1929 was decidedly different from her older sisters of the bluestocking type, whom I used to meet in the "Village" ten years earlier. The Dutch bob had given way to a variety of hairdos; instead of being clad in tweed business suits her dress, as a rule, was more feminine and more elegant than that of her predecessors of 1916–1919. Though college-bred, she was not interested in women's political rights (long ago won) nor in any crusades for other freedoms (also largely won). As to her attitude toward sexual freedom, she did not plump for that as a matter of high principle, but frankly admitted to enjoying sex; instead of acting as an overt rebel and talking a lot about free love, she just practiced it with discretion, taking or leaving her male partners at will. This was now called Companionate Marriage. From the Suffragism and Socialism of her older sisters, the New Woman, who was something of a "culture snob," turned to the arts and poetry.

In plain words, some of these women were huntresses—sometimes very attractive huntresses—and no matron's husband was safe from their predations. My literary friends by now had advanced themselves in the world; instead of writing only for the little reviews they contributed regularly to *The New Republic* and *The New Yorker*. At those offices there was usually at least one young career woman who devoted herself to the editorial personnel of her magazine staff, and so we used to call one "Miss New Republic" and the other "Miss New Yorker." At our parties in New York, which kept growing larger, there were likely to be at least two or three huntresses; and there were hunters, too. The wars of sex raged on.

I am moved with admiration, however, when I recall the career of Miss D., a handsome, vivacious, and intellectual person who worked on the editorial staff of one of the Madison Avenue publishers. She had a keen wit, was full of lively sallies, and her distinguished middle-aged employers were entranced with her. One of those old gentlemen would regularly pinch her bottom in the morning when he passed her by, and would not forget to do the same at the end of the day when he left.

One evening I came to her apartment for cocktails, together with some friends, and found not only that her home was decorated in the austere "international" style that was coming into vogue, but contained a remarkable library of rather specialized books. "How did you come upon all this group of charming and obscure Tudor poets?" I asked her in surprise. "Oh that can be explained easily," she answered blandly. "There was that nice English boy friend of mine from Oxford University, who was working in New York three years ago . . . "

"And what of this choice group of Dada and Surrealist volumes?"

"Oh those were given me by that Russian émigré last year who wrote in French."

"And those art books on the great abstract painters and the School of Paris?"

"It was that young architect who presented them to me two years ago," she explained with a laugh. "You see, each of my friends, on going away, has left me his favorite books; and so I have been gathering quite a library and improving my mind."

The moral of Miss D.'s story is that, after having for years "lived in sin" with a series of accomplished young men, she learned enough—for she was a brilliant student—to choose her own vocation and become a celebrity in her field. She ended by marrying a man who was handsome, talented, and rich into the bargain; and she lived happily ever afterward. This is just one of the stories of the twenties that has a happy ending.

Two of the prettiest girls who ever came down from a woman's college in New England to make their careers in New York became huntresses among the circle of my friends. They appeared at parties in the city or in the country, creating a little aura of scandal by their derring-do and the speed with which they passed from one male companion to another. But a year or two later I found these same girls walking about Washington Square Park, each with her pretty hands pushing a pram containing a rosy infant. In short, they were settled into the matronly life—though none could say for how long.

That puritanism was in full rout was also evidenced by the spread of nudist colonies around that time, at beaches as far apart as Cape Cod and San Francisco Bay. At country parties in earlier times the guests, after having become overheated by dancing and gin, sometimes refreshed themselves by moonlight bathing in an adjacent pool or stream. But by 1929 moonlight bathing was consigned to the era of our grandmothers. Groups of like-minded, sun-worshiping men and women were making it a practice to bathe together in mixed groups in full daylight at sheltered ocean beaches or ponds in the interior. The conviction seemed to have come to them all at once that if they cast aside their fig leaves and came out into the sun together they would be the better for it, would rid themselves of their complexes, and perhaps achieve a true inward peace.

My own experience of such gatherings was rather limited; I did not mind them, but expected no great wonders to come of them. People looked both sensible and comfortable, in fact happier, without their wet bathing garments. The sight of athletic young persons playing games, doing calisthenics, or simply turning cartwheels in the sand was also agreeable. These scenes sometimes assumed for me an atmosphere that was antique or Hellenistic.

But as the groups of people became ever larger, and stout grandparents appeared with their grandchildren to read the Sunday newspaper at the beach while taking their sun baths, the nudist congregations assumed a ritualistic character that spoiled one's visual enjoyment and made them seem not only *hygienic,* but downright conventional. One felt disposed thereafter to limit oneself to private nudities.

A rather diverting episode comes back to me as occurring at a very beautiful private beach owned by the wealthy Mrs. T., a matron of the most liberal and intellectual type. At this secluded site all were as God made them and anyone who came wearing a bathing suit was treated as an outcast; no one would even *look* at them. But the members of that charmed circle always behaved with the utmost decorum. Mrs. T. only admitted to her ocean beach those friends who were known to be of good breeding and well acquainted with the rules. I never heard of any scandal whatsover in connection with the place.

One day, however, an habitué brought, by permission, a certain merry old acquaintance of mine whom we shall call Jones, a very intelligent and entertaining companion, but also by disposition a rake and a whisky guzzler. He was enchanted with all he saw; but on his second visit made the mistake of coming to the beach with a pint of whisky which he thought he might, somehow, be able to hide on his person. Just how our exuberant libertine expected to conceal a pint bottle while bathing in the nude heaven only knows! And he had no idea of the regime scrupulously enforced here. Our hostess saw him tippling from his bottle; and, in the presence of twenty guests and friends of his, turned upon poor Jones in majestic wrath, commanding him to leave the place and never show himself there again. Even naked, Mrs. T. was quite a dowager.

Another curious episode is associated in my mind with that same beach, only because it occurred several years after I had ceased to visit it. I was in New York in the winter, attending a rather sedate literary party in an old mansion on Gramercy Park. A tall young woman stepped up to me and greeted me by name. I was puzzled, not remembering at first glance who she was, though there was something vaguely familiar about her prominent teeth and deeply tanned face. She said in surprise: "Don't you remember me? But we used to see each other often at Mrs. T.'s beach—three summers ago."

Then I recalled her and exclaimed apologetically: "Oh, of course I remember you now. You are Mrs. H. But as I have always previously seen you without any clothes on, I had no idea of what you looked like when you were dressed!"

At all events, the vogue for nude bathing in groups declined among my acquaintances with the onset of age or embonpoint.

"Everybody Ought to Be Rich," was the title of an article in one of the popular magazines written in 1929 by John J. Raskob, former vice-president of General Motors. How easy it was to accumulate wealth rapidly was also explained in other popular economic treatises under such titles as "The Road to Plenty." We were told that we were witnessing a revolution in industry, defined as the New Capitalism, and promised an endless economic growth. All that was needed for everyone to participate in the nation's future prosperity was to borrow some money and buy shares in America's leading corporations.

The fever for stock-market speculation was noticeable everywhere in 1928 and 1929. I knew of college boys who threw aside their textbooks to read only the ticker tape. Members of my own family, like millions of others, speculated on margin; indeed one of my relatives babbled about having become a millionaire overnight and dreamed of becoming a power in the New York financial world—before his structure of paper values was swept away in October, 1929, and he suffered a coronary stroke.

I myself had inherited a portion of a small family estate, consisting mainly in bank shares which advanced a great deal. Although I proceeded with the prudence that my own experience in Wall Street had taught me years ago, I too caught a little of the contagion and began to dream of expanding my small capital to provide me with an independent income. Thus I could always feel free to "spit in the editor's eye" and walk out if I disagreed with him—or if any question arose of compromising with my principles of beauty and truth. "To be a free man in America, one should have a *competence*," Justice Louis D. Brandeis had once said.

In October, 1929, the bull market of the twenties collapsed with a crash heard around the world. As in the collapse of other great financial bubbles, capital itself shrank even more rapidly than it had previously expanded. In my own family the losses were unusually severe, owing to the mismanagement of affairs by men who had succeeded my father and to the great money panics that followed 1929. My anticipated competence was just about gone. It was an odd feeling to know oneself poor, after having felt, during a brief season, almost rich; but many others just then were experiencing the same chilling sensation.

Scott Fitzgerald has contributed to history the striking image of a whole people, a generation, given over to frivolities and temptations and dancing its way over the brink of catastrophe in 1929. I believe, however, that Fitzgerald in his stories of the debacle of the Jazz Age was really writing a romantic elegy on the passing of his own gilded youth. In my own cross section of the "generation" there were none of us who might pass for the spoiled darlings of fortune. Most of us, including myself, were accustomed to plain living if not high enough thinking; no one had been overpaying us for our writings; a good many of my friends lived very simply in the country; they were able to subsist on little and were not immediately affected by the Great Slump. Some of our Madison Avenue friends, however, who had been eating high on the hog, were suddenly separated from their comfortable salaries and thrust out on the street. "Better go and dig potatoes!" Alfred Harcourt, grim-mouthed, used to say to some of his young editors. He was a sharp Yankee, able and independent of mind, but no philanthropist.

The beginning of the Great Depression recalled to some men of letters that they had been all too ignorant of political economy. They now began to inquire into the subject and to scrutinize the financial and political news in the morning newspaper. There seemed to be a good deal of truth at the end of 1929 in what John Dos Passos, a fervent Marxist throughout the twenties, had long been saying about "the inevitable decline" of the capitalistic regime in the United States. Almost all the American protagonists of his novels were poor duffers destined to lose out in the race of life. In *The New Republic*, Edmund Wilson called attention to the steadfastness with which Dos Passos—though himself a man of independent means and liking the comforts of life—had clung to his unpopular and apparently pessimistic views, which now suddenly assumed much validity.

For a period, John Dos Passos exercised a certain leadership over many writers and intellectuals. I had always thought him one of the most knowledgeable of the literary men of his epoch, as well as a man of real integrity. Now that he has since the 1940's become the most conservative of Virginia country squires— still sincere in his convictions, I believe—he will doubtless be amused to recall the influence he enjoyed as a sort of heretic among the contented cows and complacent minds of the 1920's.

On November 6, 1929, I read in the newspapers that my old friend of Dadaist-Surrealist days in Paris, Jacques Rigaut, had committed suicide in New York. I was greatly saddened at the extinction of this young life, and felt anger and disgust too, because this tragedy cast a long ugly shadow over the Surrealist movement with which the charming Jacques had always been associated and in which there had been so much wild talk of suicide as a "vocation in life."

Since 1924 Jacques had mainly resided in the United States, though he returned occasionally to France. I had seen him soon after his arrival in New York, where he lived in a small furnished room of an old house on Washington Square. He had traveled light; the most important articles of clothing he brought were his evening suit and a silk hat, which he took out of its traveling case to show me, declaring with his sad little smile that it was his principal weapon for purposes of survival.

I had only the vaguest ideas of how he supported himself. He once told a friend that he had dreamed up an amusing business of getting American women to donate money for the purpose of replacing all the wooden crosses over the graves of American soldiers buried in France with white marble slabs. After a while I heard that he had married a young American woman of fortune; I also heard reports that he both used drugs and tried at times to cure himself of the habit. Meanwhile, Jacques had his fixed idea about suicide.

His friend, Pierre Drieu la Rochelle, once esteemed as a spokesman for France's young soldiers of World War I, had long ago written a story called "The Empty Valise," which everyone who knew Rigaut recognized as a heavily ironic portrait of him. He was represented as a coxcomb and a blower, given to wild talk about his alleged attempts at suicide. It seemed to me quite possible that Drieu's cruel satire affected Jacques and hardened his resolve.

Drieu, formerly a pamphleteer on the liberal side, ended by joining the Nazi camp during the German Occupation, serving as a pro-Nazi dictator of the French press for several years; in 1944, as the Allied armies approached Paris, he too blew out his brains.

In the end Rigaut took his life without any formal good-byes, lightly and casually, but after having made thorough preparations that would not fail.

A few weeks after Rigaut's death, in late November, I attended a party given by Hart Crane in honor of Harry Crosby, who had entertained Hart at his home in France. Crosby, the son of a Morgan partner, was supposed to be very rich, but had spent much and lost a good deal in the market; he was also given to dissipation, and wrote poetry, as a gloomy sort of Surrealist, about his black despair, his opium dreams of "death in the sun," and his will to do violence to mankind—thin stuff, Baudelairean spleen unrelieved by Baudelaire's verbal wit. In person, Crosby seemed just a shy and mild-mannered young man. A week or so after that party, which took place at Hart's rooms in Brooklyn Heights, I read that Crosby had shot himself to death, and also killed a young woman companion, following an opium orgy in a hotel room in New York City. The Crosby tragedy was commemorated in a rather curious elegy written by his fellow Bostonian, John Brooks Wheelwright, who strongly condemned Crosby's action on religious and social grounds. The somber autumn of 1929 was decidedly a season of suicides.

Then, a few weeks later, in the early winter of 1930, my own demise *almost* followed—through no wish of my own, I hasten to add, but through the most hideous accident I had ever suffered.

At the end of January, 1930, my wife and I were preparing for a journey to Europe that was to last several months, during which I was to be engaged in research for a new book. I was telling myself that this third voyage would be a new departure toward new interests. I was also mentally bidding good-bye to Surrealism and all its rebels without a cause. At the same time I looked forward to leaving New York, whose social life and whose Gargantuan gin parties, a feature of that period, had become not only physically exhausting but had recently shown some unpleasant overtones. My wife and I had been much "on the town"; our social life had become crowded, complicated, and finally somewhat wearying. I had, as a consequence, come down with the grippe for a week in January. The people we saw used to think they were all charm and wit after they had had three drinks; but late at night, on occasion, some curtain would go up and something ugly, perhaps one of the current wretched scandals overhanging one or another, would suddenly be exposed to us.

In Europe, however, people drank with moderation; this would surely help introduce some personal reform into my own life which, out of weakness, I had been postponing, but now promised myself I would carry out.

Our home at the time was a spacious apartment on an upper floor of an old brownstone mansion, at 218 East Fifteenth Street, overlooking the green lawns of Stuyvesant Square. We were scheduled to sail on the S.S. *Europa* at noon on February 1st. On the night preceding our departure a great many friends came to our home, making it an impromptu farewell party. Some of them were so affectionate in their boozy way that it was all we could do to send them along and finish packing our luggage. One of them, I remember (for he died young, not long afterward), was Harcourt, Brace and Company's editor, Raymond Everitt, who, in a parting gesture—as agile as Douglas Fairbanks—leaped up to one of the massive old chandeliers in our parlor and hung suspended there for awhile, kicking and waving his legs at everyone. Then I was left alone with our last guest, Jack Wheelwright—my wife having retired—and we sat playing some chamber music on the phonograph and talking in a relaxed mood until two in the morning. When he left, I went to bed rather heavy-headed, reminding myself of last-minute errands to be done in the morning before our sailing.

I was too fatigued to sleep soundly; three or four hours passed during which I dozed and woke intermittently. But I consoled myself with the thought that I would do nothing but rest at sea, and that Geneva, where I was bound, would be quiet itself after New York.

Suddenly in the dark there was our janitor, a colored man, standing over my bed, shaking me violently by the shoulders, crying out hysterically: "*Wake up, hurry*, for God's sake, Mr. Josephson! The house is on fire! Everybody out!"

For a few seconds I could not conceive what this was all about or what this man was crying in a voice of sheer terror—which undoubtedly affected my half-sleeping mind with its suggestion. I struggled to rouse myself, as did my wife; we became aware that the place reeked of foul smoke. How had this horrible thing happened? The lights were out, and we had to grope our way through the house toward the rear of the apartment. The children's room was there; they were awake, as was the maid-nurse, a little Bavarian woman; and all were ready to go to the fire escape by their window overlooking the back yard—by which route that maddened janitor had come and gone.

The five of us went out the window and stepped onto the fire escape: I was holding my infant son, Carl, who was not quite a year old; the elder boy, Eric, managed for himself, holding his mother's hand. As we began our descent I saw a big burst of flame shoot out of the second floor, just below us. We needed only to hurry down past those flames for an instant to be safe. The fire had started in the cellar, caused by a faulty furnace.

The thought that everything I had in the world—papers, books, pictures, clothing—was going up in flames then struck me with great force. Because of my fatigue, or my recent heavy drinking, or my weakness after the siege of grippe, I seemed to go blotto, and was heard to cry out some almost inarticulate words: "The pictures—my papers!" I dropped my infant son into the arms of the maid who was near me, then dashed up a few steps, and plunged back through the window into my apartment. It is clear to me now that I was in a state of hysteria; I had some fixed idea of retrieving a few of my possessions. It seems that I spoke of saving an oil painting by Charles Sheeler that I prized as one of the best examples of his work. I may have taken it up, then dropped it as I blundered through those dark rooms filled with smoke. The others continued down the iron fire escape to safety in the back yard.

By mischance I opened a door in the center of the apartment that led to the main hallway. At once a great tongue of smoke and flame leaped up the stairwell, because of the added draft I had created, and filled the apartment. Unable to endure the smoke I retreated toward the front of the house, for the sudden advance of the flames had cut me off from the rear windows and the fire escape; I then climbed out on the ledge of the parlor window in front and took breath.

Snow had fallen that night; it felt very cold outside, and I was clad only in pajamas. I was calm now and took stock of my position. It was plain that I was entirely boxed in, cornered on an upper floor of a burning house. The inside of the apartment behind me was ablaze, and it was too late to dash through it. On my high ledge, perched against the window frame, about forty feet above the street, I could survive for a while, though this old building was making a quick bonfire. Acrid smoke swirled about me, making me gasp; I leaned out as far as I dared.

It was still dark outside, at about 5:45 A.M.; few were awake in the neighborhood, but I saw two or three figures down below in the street who were pointing at me. About five minutes may have elapsed since I was roused from sleep; no fire wagons

had appeared. Someone called out: "There's a man up there."
I shouted for help with all my lungs.

The flames now swept out of the window and licked at me.
The brick walls I grasped grew heated; I felt the skin of my
hands being scorched and the flames attacking my legs and my
head. With a prodigious effort I managed to pull myself over to
an adjacent window at the right-hand corner of the house—almost losing my footing during this maneuver—and lodged
myself there. The blasts of flame and smoke seemed less powerful at the corner of the building than at the center window. I
groped for a way to climb to the next building, but its windows
were too high and far from me and I could find no purchase. I
had cut my hand on broken glass at the second window ledge
and it bled; the smoke increased in volume and set me coughing.
A few minutes more passed while I waited.

I thought: such things never happen to anyone. How stupid
that it should have happened to me. I realized that I had behaved insanely in returning to the apartment when I was on my
way to safety. Now I tried to think coolly of what I might still
do to save myself, though the chances of escape seemed poor
enough.

It came to me in those moments that I was like a cornered animal, or rather like a bird perched high up on this ledge of a
burning house, a poor weak thing about to die. I recall the
thoughts passing through my mind because they came back to
me clearly in reveries later on. (Afterward, many persons asked
me what it felt like to face death by fire, to be "burned alive." I
remembered, though I have never said much about it before. It is
evidently true enough that in the seconds or minutes of a
supreme crisis, a time of terrible danger, thoughts race through
the mind at great speed and in a confusion of the serious and
the trivial.)

The image of martyrs burned at the stake came to me and
I reflected: "It isn't as bad as it has been made out to be. Fire
doesn't kill you quickly. I may be able to hold out for a while

yet, until help comes. If only it weren't for those horrible fumes that make me feel like vomiting . . . " The fire licked my neck; the outer skin of my hands and legs seemed to be burning off, for I had to stand facing the house. Yet by an effort of will I could shut off the sensation of pain and think of other things.

Some other thoughts ran: "Better men than I, cleverer men, have come to such a pass, as for instance soldiers in battle during the last war." There seemed to be more people down below in the frozen street; some were calling to me. I wondered how long it would be before firemen came and made attempts to rescue me. But what if everything fell in on me before they arrived? I did not think of prayer; though I am susceptible to feelings of religious emotion, I have not the habit of "surrendering myself" in prayer. I shifted about or bent down a little in efforts to dodge the worst of the flame, and kept peering about through the smoke, but hung on firmly.

"Well it looks as if I am done for," I said to myself again, "but I have had a pretty good life for over thirty years; it has been active, and I was always one to enjoy things while I could, and there were some who loved me and whom I loved." I thought of my wife and children, and calculated that they, fortunately, had made their escape and were safe now. But I was winding things up in a rather foolish and undignified way: in my scorched night clothes, trapped on a high window ledge over a cauldron whose smoke and fumes gave me a horrible taste and a pain in the chest. "What a crazy joke!" was a bitter thought that now came to me. "And it's all on me—I played it on myself, when I could have got out of the place in a moment or two if I hadn't lost my head." The fire was now making a roar like the low notes of many great church organs; I would never forget that deep sound, which seems in recollection musical. I hung on, though I was now becoming so scorched that I thought the end would be restful, at least, and therefore pleasing; and I wished for it, yet could not let go.

Now I heard the fire trucks come rolling in; I could distinguish a good deal of activity below me, and heard firemen in a ladder truck near the house calling to each other and yelling encouragement to me. I yelled back with all my strength though the effort almost made me drop off.

Sudden hope now gripped me with incredible force. Could it be true that they were going to take me off my impossible niche on the edge of my furnace after I had given them up? A wave of joyful emotion suffused me, and I laughed aloud.

The ladder truck had been maneuvering slowly into position; the driver turned a winch steadily and a long ladder rose slowly, slanted toward me, and approached my window. A man began to climb up the ladder. But when he reached the top there was still a wide gap of four or five feet between us. I was making ready to spring toward him, when he called out in warning that I must wait and hold on. He swore an oath and cried out to the operators down below that he could not reach me, that they must bring him down and do the job over again. "I'll be back in a few moments—hold on!" he called to me.

I was desperate, feeling I could scarcely endure much longer. Something had gone wrong with the ladder mechanism and the men in the truck spent *ten minutes* more (so I was told later) maneuvering their vehicle and extension ladder closer to the building. My hair was burning, my hands and throat were bleeding, and I felt very nauseated, but I tightened my grip on the hot walls of the window aperture. At this stage, as seen from below, I stood out as a form completely enveloped in flame. But hope gave me a maniac strength.

The winch turned steadily, the ladder neared me again, and came so close that the flames touched its tip. The big red-faced fireman—George Peterson by name—stretched out his arms, grasped me firmly under my shoulders, and drew me backward to that slanting, swaying ladder. I was under him, holding the rungs of the ladder; exultant, I said that I was still able to climb down on my own legs. But he asked me to clamber around him and rest on his back; I managed this. The top of the ladder was now pivoted away from the flames into the clear air. I clung to Peterson's burly shoulders while we slowly made the descent together.

I stepped to the ground, laughing in my excitement. The firemen carried me into the basement of the next building, laid me on the floor, and covered me with an old blanket. The man who had brought me down apologized for the delay in my rescue, which was caused by a mechanical failure in the ladder truck operation. He said the firemen were all surprised at the length of time during which I had hung on. The delay made my injuries more serious. From official reports giving the time when the fire broke out and that of my rescue, I was able to estimate later that I had been closely exposed to fire and fumes (worst of all) at my window ledge for approximately twenty-five to thirty minutes. My night clothes were reduced to burnt rags; my face and limbs showed wide-area burns; I was a bloody-looking thing, but still I felt wildly elated over my escape, answered everybody's questions, and even tried to order some whisky and cigarettes for the firemen as well as myself. An interne, arriving in an ambulance after a good half-hour had passed, quieted me with a heavy injection of morphine and carried me off to Bellevue Hospital.

My wife and children and other residents of the house had meanwhile been penned up in the back yard until the blaze was extinguished at about 7:30 A.M. Thus my wife, during almost two hours, had been unable to find out what had happened to me since we had been separated, and feared that I was dead. The first platoon of firemen had left and another group were cleaning up, but they did not know where I was and whether I was alive or dead. At length, after some of the firemen had searched the smoldering ruins for bodies, she was informed by the policeman in attendance of my whereabouts.

At Bellevue, the great public hospital of New York, I awoke shortly after my arrival, and asked that I be sent on to a private hospital; but, being told that I could not be moved, insisted upon being given a private room "with a view." The nurses actually found such a room for me, though there were only two, reserved for doctors. The wide-area burns on my hands and throat, which were of the first degree, and the second-degree burns elsewhere, plus the effects of heavy smoke poisoning, caused me to be placed on the critical list.

Toward noon of that first day I awoke for a few minutes and, to my surprise, saw Jack Wheelwright, the last man I had seen before the fire. He had been up all night, had learned of my accident in the morning, and though no one was allowed to visit me had bulled his way past the hospital attendants into my room and sat down at my bedside. He was wearing his worn old raccoon coat and bowler hat, looking, as he often did, like a somewhat decayed dandy. Tears were streaming down his face and he was praying for me fervently, with rapid movements of his lips. My poor wife had seen me earlier, while I was unconscious; she had become prostrated with shock and grief, and had been led away.

To Jack and my wife my appearance was rather frightening. One of the experts on the Bellevue staff had ordered that my whole head, and throat and limbs as well, be covered with thick layers of tannic acid, which, as it blackened, made me look like an African mask. (It was the newest treatment for severe burns, and remarkably effective.) Poor Wheelwright was certain that if I survived at all, I would be horribly disfigured for life.

Actually the treatment I underwent restored a perfect new "baby skin" to my face; I was left only with some scars on my throat and hands. The most serious danger was from blood poisoning, which raised my temperature to the maximum for about ten days, so that it needed all the skill and vigilance of the Bellevue medical and nursing staff to bring me around. Six weeks passed before I was allowed to leave the hospital, weighing forty pounds less than my normal weight.

When I was well enough to read the newspapers, I was amused at accounts of my accident, which were not only wildly inac-

curate but illustrated by fake photographs of the rescue operation. One ran:

AUTHOR BRAVES FIRE TO SAVE SCRIPT

Matthew Josephson, author of *Zola and His Time,* plunged into the
flames at No. 218 East 15th Street to rescue a precious manuscript,
after he had conducted two children, his wife and a maid to the
street, and was severely burned. . . . He saved it, but his life may
be the price he'll pay. For when Mr. Josephson was carried down a
ladder . . . he was suffering from many burns.

Nothing of any value had been saved, but no manuscripts of
any consequence were lost, except for a few dozen pages of notes
for a new book. Most of my correspondence had been in a steel
cabinet and survived, though scorched at the edges and partly
discolored by chemicals. It was curious how little the destruction of all our worldly goods affected either my spirits or those
of my wife. We were beginning the 1930's with a clean slate.

The pathetic ragged little Joe Gould, who had nearly engaged
in a "duel" with me seven years ago, came to offer me his
compliments and extend his hand in conciliation. He said he
had put down the story of my "Great Fire" in his manuscript,
History of the Modern World, as "the only known instance of a
writer who was courageous enough to risk his skin for his own
writings!" It was not more exact as history than the inaccurate
reporting of the newspapers, but some sort of myth of my
"purgation by fire" at the end of the twenties attached to me
thereafter.

A tranquil period of convalescence followed. Thanks to the
hospitality of Peter Blume, I was able to spend several weeks
resting in South Carolina and watching the spring make its
early arrival there. Then I came back to my farmhouse in Connecticut and sat in my garden on the knoll above the big brook,
enjoying the renewal of springtime in the North.

I was fortunate to have this brook valley and the old house
which I came to love and managed to hang onto during the worst
Depression Years and still hold. It was also fortunate—indeed

quite a trick—to find myself alive and, after a little while, able to resume writing a paragraph or two on a typewriter each day as a means of hastening the recovery of articulation in my injured hands. My friend Cowley, seeing me working with fingers that still hurt as I typed, declared that I was "incorrigible, like an habitual drunkard."

For my part, working on a new book after an interruption was the most agreeable form of mental distraction. In the thirties both the subject matter and the moral character of the books I would be writing, as in the case of many of my contemporaries, would reflect a marked change of interest.

At the end of 1929 the United States was experiencing probably the most severe depression in its history. The very atmosphere seemed to be transformed during those lean years; at first political unrest assumed a massive form in old Europe—ministries were overthrown one by one; world markets continued to decline; gold hoardings went into "flight" now here, now there—and even the threat of war appeared in the Far East.

Our prospects at home seemed to grow darker; we were working harder for less money; many were suffering real need. Yet it would be far from the truth to say that we were less happy than we had been before in our "fat" years. Surely no epoch in our history seemed more interesting and exciting to be "engaged in" than that which opened for us in 1930. The members of my "generation," who were born toward the year 1900, were growing up with their century; for better or worse they were becoming more like men of reason. For many of them the thirties were to be the years of fruition.

ACKNOWLEDGEMENTS

My recollections of the events and personalities discussed in this book have in many cases been reinforced by consulting that portion of my own correspondence dating from the 1920's which escaped destruction by fire—through being in the possession of friends. I have also tried to refresh my memory through talks with friends and by checking my own recollections against those to be found in a number of autobiographical books written by some of my contemporaries. During two journeys to Europe after World War II, I was also able to meet again with a good many of my old associates who had taken part in the Dadaist and Surrealist movements. I am under special obligation to two of them. Philippe Soupault and Jacques Baron, who have often and patiently replied to my queries about the movements of ideas in the twenties in France.

I am most grateful to the Museum of Modern Art of New York for the opportunity afforded me to read through its excellent collection of Dadaist and Surrealist literature, which contains the private library of my old-time acquaintance Paul Éluard (d. 1952). I also wish to give thanks to Mr. Bernard Karpel, Librarian of the Museum of Modern Art, for his aid in gathering photographs and other memorabilia touching the period covered by this work. Acknowledgments are further due the Columbia University Library, for permission to study and quote from the Hart Crane papers; to the Princeton University Library for the opportunity to read and quote from the Harold A. Loeb papers; and to the Yale University Library's Special Collection, and especially its

387

director, Dr. Donald A. Gallup, for help and advice and the opportunity
to consult the papers of Gertrude Stein.

NOTES: CHAPTER ONE

1. André Masson to author, as noted in my journal for 1941.
2. Malcolm Cowley: *Exile's Return.* New York: W.W. Norton, 1937. Pp. 84–85.
3. Gertrude Stein, in answer to a questionnaire: "Why Do You Live Abroad?" *transition*, September, 1928.
4. Van Wyck Brooks: *Days of the Phoenix.* New York: Dutton, 1957. Pp. 17–18.

NOTES: CHAPTER THREE

1. Sherwood Anderson to Hart Crane: December 17, 1919; Hart Crane papers, Columbia University Library.

NOTES: CHAPTER FOUR

1. Joseph L. Freeman: *An American Testament.* New York: Farrar and Rinehart, 1936. P. 249.
2. *Exile's Return, op. cit.*, p. 59.

NOTES: CHAPTER FIVE

1. Brom Weber (ed.): *The Letters of Hart Crane.* New York: Hermitage House, 1952. Pp. 26–27.

NOTES: CHAPTER SIX

1. Philip Horton: *Hart Crane.* New York: W.W. Norton, 1937. Pp. 102–103. *See also* Richard Blackmur: *The Lion and the Honeycomb.* New York, Harcourt, Brace and Company, 1955. Pp. 61 ff., for the chapter, "The American Writer as Expatriate."
2. *Ibid.*, p. 102.
3. Robert McAlmon: *Being Geniuses Together.* London: Secker and Warburg, 1938. Pp. 77–80.
4. *Der Querschnitt, Autumn,* 1924.
5. *The Letters of Hart Crane, op. cit.*, pp. 64–65.

NOTES: CHAPTER SEVEN

1. Philippe Soupault: *Charlot.* Paris: Plon, 1931.
2. "L'Affair Barrès," *Littérature,* August, 1921.

NOTES: CHAPTER EIGHT

1. George Ribémont-Dessaignes: *Histoire de Dada.* Paris: Gallimard, 1931. *See also* the authentic, though brief memoir by the Surrealist

painter, Georges Hugnet: *L'Aventure de Dada*. Paris: Galérie de l'Institut, 1957.

NOTES: CHAPTER NINE

1. Author to Kenneth Burke: December 15, 1921, Matthew Josephson papers, Yale University Library Special Collection.
2. Malcolm Cowley to Kenneth Burke: January 28, 1922, Montpelier, France, Matthew Josephson papers, Yale University Library.
3. Kenneth Burke to author: December 27, 1921, Matthew Josephson papers, Yale University Library.
4. *The Letters of Hart Crane, op. cit.*, pp. 77–79.
5. G.B. Munson to Hart Crane: February 7, 1922, Hart Crane papers, Columbia University Library.
6. Edith Sitwell: *The New Age*, September 25, 1922.
7. Harold Loeb: *The Way It Was*. New York: Criterion Books, 1959. P. 118.
8. Malcolm Cowley: "Matthew Josephson," *Book-Find Notes*, January, 1947.
9. Harold Loeb to Gertrude Stein: November 29, 1922, Gertrude Stein papers, Yale University Library Special Collection.
10. Author to Kenneth Burke: January 5, 1923, Matthew Josephson papers, Yale University Library.

NOTES: CHAPTER TEN

1. Edmund Wilson: "The Aesthetic Upheaval in France," *Vanity Fair,* February, 1922.
2. *The Way It Was, op. cit.*, p. 122.

NOTES: CHAPTER ELEVEN

1. Matthew Josephson: "Letter to My Friends," *The Little Review*. Spring, 1926.
2. During the German occupation, Desnos was engaged in very hazardous intelligence work in Paris as a member of the Resistance Movement; he was caught, tortured by the Nazis in 1944, and imprisoned in the camp of Auschwitz, where he died of typhus in April, 1945, during the last hours of the war.

   Robert Desnos' dream novel, *La Liberté ou l'amour* (1927), is a superb example of poetic and hallucinatory erotica, and is deeply inspired by the "innocent vision" that the Surrealists sought to recapture. Something of the same "innocent" quality is to be found in the writings of Henry Miller, the American Surrealist.
3. Patrick Waldberg: *Max Ernst*. Paris: J.-J. Pauvert, 1958. p. 185.

NOTES: CHAPTER TWELVE

1. G.B. Munson to Harold Loeb: May 29, 1922, Harold Loeb papers, Princeton.
2. Harold Loeb to Malcolm Cowley: March 10, 1923, Harold Loeb papers, Princeton.
3. G.B. Munson to author: December 11, 1922, Harold Loeb papers, Princeton.
4. G.B. Munson: "The Fledgling Years, 1916–1924," *Sewanee Review*, January–March, 1932. Pp. 24–54.
5. Author to Kenneth Burke: January 5, 1923, Matthew Josephson papers, Yale University Special Collection.
6. Harold Loeb to author: September 13, 1922, Harold Loeb papers, Princeton.

NOTES: CHAPTER THIRTEEN

1. Author to Harold Loeb: May 16, 1923, Harold Loeb papers, Princeton.
2. Burton Rascoe: "A Bookman's Day Book," New York *Tribune*, July 26, 1922.
3. Author to Harold Loeb: October 10, 1922, Harold Loeb papers, Princeton.
4. *Ibid.*
5. Malcolm Cowley to Harold Loeb: August 31, 1923, Harold Loeb papers, Princeton.
6. Author to Harold Loeb: October 25, 1923, Harold Loeb papers, Princeton.
7. "The Fledgling Years," *op. cit.*
8. Harold Loeb to author: October 2, 1923, Harold Loeb papers, Princeton.

NOTES: CHAPTER FOURTEEN

1. Author to Harold Loeb: July 10, 1924, Harold Loeb papers, Princeton.
2. Jane Heap to author: April 8, 1926, Matthew Josephson papers, Yale University Library.
3. One may read Miss Moore's version of the poem in *The Dial*, May, 1926, and compare it with Hart Crane's original and complete version in *White Buildings*, in which he completely rejected her editing.
4. Brom Weber: *Hart Crane:* A Biographical and Critical Study. New York: The Bodley Press, 1948. Pp. 264, 267.
5. Paul Friedman: "The Bridge: A Study in Symbolism," *The Psychoanalytic Quarterly*, January, 1952. Pp. 49–81.

NOTES: CHAPTER FIFTEEN

1. Samuel Putnam: *Paris Was Our Mistress.* New York: The Viking Press, 1947. P. 130.
2. *Ibid.,* p. 129.
3. André Breton: *Entretiens:* 1913–1952. Paris: Gallimard, 1952.
4. Cited in Marice Nadeau: *Histoire du Surréalisme.* Paris: Editions du Seuil, 1945.
5. "Recherches sur la sexualité," *La Revolution Surréaliste,* March 15, 1928, No. 11.
   Among the persons participating in two sessions of questionnaires on sex were André Breton, Louis Aragon, Raymond Queneau, Jacques Prévert, Yves Tanguy, Benjamin Péret, Man Ray, and Jacques Baron.
6. Malcolm Cowley and Hannah Josephson (ed.): *Aragon:* Poet of the Resistance. New York: Duell, Sloane and Pearce, 1944. Introduction, p. xi, quote from Louis Aragon to Hannah and Matthew Josephson.
7. Under the German occupation of France, Deffoux, then an old man, directed the press-wire service of the Havas Agency and helped convert it into a pro-Nazi propaganda instrument; in 1944, however, as the Allied armies entered Paris, he committed suicide by throwing himself into the Seine River.

NOTES: CHAPTER SIXTEEN

1. Matthew Josephson: *Zola and His Time* with an Introduction by Van Wyck Brooks. New York: Book League of America, 1928.
2. Matthew Josephson: "Chicago," *The Outlook and Independent,* January 30, 1929.
3. *transition,* Summer, 1928.
4. Matthew Josephson: "Open Letter to Ezra Pound," *transition,* Summer, 1928.

INDEX

Josephson.

Life among the surrealists.